by ear and eyes

by ear and eyes

The Whitechapel Murders
Jack the Ripper
and
The Murder of Mary Jane Kelly

Karyo Magellan

Longshot Publishing

First Published in 2005

© Karyo Magellan 2005

www.karyom.com

Karyo Magellan is hereby identified as the author of this work
in accordance with the Copyright,
Designs, and Patents Act 1988

A CIP catalogue record for this book
is available from the British Library

ISBN 0-9550240-0-5

Published by
Longshot Publishing
PO Box 6965
Derby
DE1 9JL
United Kingdom

www.longshotpublishing.co.uk

Printed and bound in the United Kingdom by
Antony Rowe Ltd., Chippenham, Wiltshire

For Victoria, Camilla, Lydia, and Alexander

AUTHOR FOREWORD AND ACKNOWLEDGEMENTS

Attempting to solve the mystery of the identity of Jack the Ripper has often been likened to trying to complete a jigsaw puzzle for which most of the pieces are missing. During the course of sifting through the mass of accumulated information I have come to realise the truth of this but would go a step further and suggest that there is more than one incomplete puzzle among the pieces! My efforts here have been something of a solitary task but any theorist is inevitably indebted to an enormous degree to those dedicated researchers whose unceasing and diligent efforts have produced such a wealth of material to work with. As well as my sincere thanks they have my admiration as do those longstanding contributors whose efforts and objectivity have served well the search for Jack the Ripper over many years, producing some excellent books in the process. Acknowledgement is also due to Casebook at www.casebook.org whose database is always a useful reference source and to John Barber at www.johnbarber.com who has researched the murder of Emily Dimmock, known as The Camden Town Murder.

I would also specifically like to thank for their efforts in assisting me: the staff at The National Archives; staff at the Ordnance Survey; and the City of Westminster Archivist.

Material in the National Archives in the copyright of the Metropolitan Police is reproduced by kind permission of the Metropolitan Police Authority. The image of Mary Jane Kelly is reproduced by kind permission of the National Archives Image Library.

My appreciation and thanks are also due to those authors whose work I have referred to and whose groundwork I have tried to build upon.

Derbyshire 2005   KM

CONTENTS

Introduction

Few historical events have attracted so much attention as the series of murders that occurred in the Whitechapel district of London towards the end of the Victorian era. It is hard to imagine that such callous ferocity could have the power to enchant, but events surrounding the vicious slaying of several prostitutes well over a century ago have endured as a source of intrigue. Over a period of three years, eleven women were murdered and mutilated and there is convincing evidence that a serial killer was at work. Although the same man did not murder all eleven victims, he was undoubtedly responsible for more than one, which raises a crucial question; exactly how many victims were murdered by the same man? It is difficult to overestimate the importance of this fundamental question, since without an answer it is impossible to build a reliable case against any named suspect.

Although the identity of the serial killer remains elusive, a debt of gratitude is owed to the individual who invented the sobriquet 'Jack the Ripper' since it has allowed convenient reference to an otherwise unidentified assailant. Jack the Ripper has since become synonymous with heinous murder and 'Ripper' has, on many occasions since, been used to label a serial killer. In spite of attempts by many authors over the years to convince their readership that the mystery is solved, information crucial to revealing the true identity of the serial killer has yet to emerge, or if it is already available then its significance has yet to be realised. It seems impossible that the murderer remains unidentified given the mass of information that already exists in relation to the Whitechapel murders but inevitably not all of it is useful. In keeping with any historical event facts become muddled with fiction with the consequence that it is occasionally difficult to separate the two. Although researchers continue to do an excellent job by unearthing fragments of information their efforts are more than outweighed by those whose objective is to entertain rather than to inform. That is unfortunate since the known circumstances of the murders are sufficiently bizarre to make invention unnecessary.

This book is primarily concerned with identifying what information can be relied upon and what must be dismissed when searching for conclusions. This is a theoretical approach to existing information, for in truth there is probably little remaining that will come to light. Much has already been lost and it could be that researchers are close to reaching the limit of available documentation. An inevitable consequence of this impasse is that increasingly absurd proposals will be made and ever more unlikely suspects dragged into the frame, so there is a good case for looking at the vast amount of information that has already accumulated and assessing its true and accurate value.

Encouragingly, sufficient information may already be available to help to identify the serial killer and it may not be an absence of data that is the limitation but the manner in which it is examined. Crucial details may still lie within the accumulated mass waiting to be teased out by careful examination, whereas the misinterpretation of even a small detail could well have misled researchers and theorists for many years. Reappraisal of information should be a continuing process and one of integration not addition. Researchers also need to be directed in their searches by fresh theories and in this respect there is an opportunity for new documents to surface. Only by looking in the right place can relevant information be discovered and the opportunity for that lies in new directions of investigation. By a meticulous examination of the details of each murder it is possible to open up new directions, to get closer to the truth, and thereby closer to the identity of the murderer who was undoubtedly one of the most insouciant and clinically accomplished serial killers that civilisation has ever experienced.

1: Conclusions are only as good as the data upon which they are based

When Joseph Barnett gave evidence at the inquest into the murder of Mary Jane Kelly, a prostitute murdered in her lodgings at 13 Miller's Court, Whitechapel on the morning of 9 November 1888, he told the coroner that he had seen the body of his former partner and he identified her 'by the ear and eyes'. Such was the extent to which Mary Jane Kelly's body had been mutilated that the man with whom she had lived for twenty months could barely recognise her.

It has been suggested that Barnett did not actually say 'ear and eyes' but 'hair and eyes' and that those reporting his testimony misheard. 'Ear and eyes' was reported in the official inquest notes and in *The Daily Telegraph*, and 'ears and eyes' was reported in *The Star*, so it is unlikely that all three independent sources misheard, assuming of course that the newspaper reporters did not take their wording from the same source, that of the official inquest records.[1, 2, 3] Could Barnett have accurately recognised Kelly by her hair, eyes or ears? Mary Jane Kelly had fair hair and her nickname was Ginger, but from examination of the crime scene photograph of her corpse and of the post mortem report of Dr Thomas Bond it is doubtful that her eyes would have been of significant value in identification and her ears had been mutilated.[4, 5] This confusion over such a relatively trivial point illustrates superbly the almost ubiquitous problem facing students of the Whitechapel murders – the quality of the witness evidence and the accuracy and thoroughness of recording and reporting.

Even where there appears to be an objective approach towards investigation there are clearly gaps in the information and not always because documents are missing. From the undistorted perspective afforded by hindsight it is easy to identify countless questions that should have been asked by the police, doctors, and even by the coroners at the time of the investigations. Such is an inherent frustration in Ripperology. Sadly the majority will remain unanswered so we are left to interpret and re-interpret what we have in the hope of finding a fresh perspective that may provide a hitherto unidentified lead. The police investigation was criticised at the time of the murders and from our present perspective there are definitely indications of mismanagement. But one significant problem with the use of hindsight is an unavoidable tendency to assess nineteenth century events by twenty-first century standards.

At the end of the nineteenth century, forensic science was in its infancy, although a little later in 1910 an important principle and the very foundation of forensic science was established by Edmund Locard who suggested that every contact leaves a trace; a criminal will always carry away with him some trace from the scene of the crime and will leave behind some trace of his presence. Fingerprint classification was first used to secure a successful criminal prosecution in England in 1902; dental records were non-existent; and blood grouping was only developed after the identification of the different types in 1901 with the consequential ability to serologically identify other body fluids. The unique identification of individuals by DNA profiling did not follow until 1985 with the first criminal conviction based on such evidence in 1987. Although Victorian investigators showed some awareness of the potential value of closely examining and recording the details of a crime scene, they had the benefit of no specialist techniques. Even fundamental procedures, such as the identification of bodies, were open to mistakes, being dependent largely upon facial recognition, distinguishing marks, or papers on the corpse. Misidentification of bodies, either by accident or design, especially those subject to decomposition and including the very many corpses pulled from the Thames must have been commonplace. The police did the best that they could, but with next to no science to point them in the right direction or to substantiate their suspicions, apprehending murderers and securing convictions was always an uphill struggle.

1.1 The quantity of information

There is certainly no shortage of information available on the Whitechapel murders and Jack the Ripper but not all of it is necessarily useful. Information generated and accumulated at or about the time of the murders falls into several categories, the most important of which are the original police files and inquest records. However, there is another category of information that has since contributed significantly to the knowledge base and this includes privately held notes and records and unofficial correspondence between individuals. Collectively I regard these categories of information as the raw or original data from which theories are derived, but much of it is known to be missing and there must be much more that has not surfaced and will never come to light. Many of the official files are no longer available, the records having been plundered at various times since the murders.

The official files comprise those compiled by the Metropolitan Police and those by the Home Office – the majority of files originally held by the City Police were destroyed by bombing during the Second World War. What remains of the original official documents are held in the National Archives where they have been microfilmed, but not before a great many were pilfered by souvenir hunters with total disregard for their historical significance and value to researchers. Both the Metropolitan Police and Home Office files have been open to researchers since 1976 and 1986 respectively and some writers and researchers were fortunate to see many of the missing files prior to their misappropriation. With regard to unofficial information held by individuals, much of this has certainly been destroyed upon the death of the individuals, either without being read, without their significance being realised, or at the direct instruction of the person concerned.

In addition to the raw data, there are numerous other sources of information in the form of books, essays, and articles that can be regarded as secondary sources. Beyond vast accumulations of primary and secondary information there is another category of 'information' that has no place in any serious investigation within the realms of Ripperology. The potential to make financial gain from the discovery of documents is understandable and an inevitable consequence of this is a proliferation of hoax documents, produced either at or around the time of the Whitechapel murders, or many years later. Researchers quickly identify such documents and give them short shrift so it is not my intention to become involved with such distractions in the course of this work.

Throughout this investigation I have sourced many original documents but occasionally I have also relied upon the written interpretations of others. In this latter case I have only placed reliance upon the opinion of those authors able to demonstrate objectivity. My interpretations are based primarily upon the crime scene and post mortem details and statements from professional police and medical witnesses since this is the most reliable information available. Information given by other witnesses is also examined, but because this comes by the ears and eyes of those with dubious objectivity, it must be regarded with caution.

1.2 The quality of information and approaches to investigation

Authors often choose to distinguish between primary and secondary sources when supporting the validity of their work; primary sources are original documents and secondary sources refer to or use the primary sources. But even experienced authors appear at times confused as to the relative usefulness of primary and of secondary sources of information, the implication being that primary sources are reliable whereas secondary sources are less so. The originality or otherwise of the source should not be confused with the reliability of what is reported in the document, since originality and reliability in this context relate only to the words on the paper and not to their value. The distinction between primary and secondary sources of information is not always clear cut and when an investigation depends upon the quality of the information it is better to refer to raw data as being otherwise unprocessed information.

Bearing this in mind there is, generally speaking, a relationship between the source of the information and its reliability and I would categorise information according to the following levels:

Reasonably reliable: Witness testimony at inquests and witness statements from professional police officers and police surgeons; officially recorded inquest transcripts.

Less reliable: Interpretations of witness statements by senior police officers; newspaper reports of the inquests.

Unreliable: Witness testimony at inquests and witness statements given by non-professional eyewitnesses such as passers-by and casual observers of events; newspaper reports of the crimes, editorial and 'witness' comments therein.

Aside from these categories are numerous published works, some reputable and some less so, that offer interpretation and theories. Some of these are based upon reliable information and others merely speculate upon speculation; some are well thought through with logical and well constructed arguments and others are more aligned with fiction. Indeed, many books about Jack the Ripper are dependent upon wild speculation but very little proof, in the knowledge that there is also an absence of evidence to the contrary. There is thus an eternal open opportunity for authors, and it is not difficult to construct a case against any plausible suspect and write a book on the strength of it. Once a case is made against a suspect it can often be very difficult to convincingly disprove. The memoirs of some of the officials involved in the investigations are also of dubious value as are some documents compiled after the event and conspicuous in this regard is the Macnaghten Memorandum of 1894 which has come to shape aspects of Ripperology and has been pivotal in defining the number of victims attributed to the same serial killer; Mary Ann Nichols, Annie Chapman, Elizabeth Stride, Catharine Eddowes, and

Mary Jane Kelly are known as the canonical victims on the strength of Macnaghten's report.[6] Macnaghten also suggests a number of suspects, and although his conclusions regarding both victims and suspects are unsubstantiated and flawed, this has not stopped the document from becoming a cornerstone for students and researchers.

When reconstructing the murders I have used the most reliable information, the majority of which comes from police surgeons at the inquest into the death of each victim, with this supplemented by statements from police witnesses. Such information, provided as it is by relatively reliable and independent investigators, is far more dependable than information from any other source in the investigations, especially that provided by other witnesses, and by pre-digested and frequently biased newspaper editorial comment. It is, however, fortunate that the newspapers of the day were so thorough in their reporting since in several cases the original inquest transcripts are missing so that reliance has had to be placed upon newspaper reports of proceedings. Both *The Times* and *The Daily Telegraph* reported proceedings in great detail but there were occasional discrepancies between the two, usually presumed to be transcription errors, but occasionally there were factual inaccuracies, making it important not to rely upon just one source.

While the above categorisation of information is logical enough, readers will not be surprised to learn that it is inevitably over simplistic. Witness information from whatever source is almost always biased, frequently inaccurate, confounds more than it informs, and requires examination in far greater depth than is customary at inquests. Because criminal proceedings were never initiated against any suspect, there is probably a significant amount of information that was available but not made public at the time and is unlikely ever to surface. Unfortunately, there were also contradictions among the expert medical testimony and some indications of rivalry between medical men, which resulted in, and further amplified, differences in interpretation. Such rivalry clouded objectivity and seemed to escalate as more potential Ripper victims were investigated. Personal reputations seemed to be more important than discovering the truth, and just occasionally the medical professionals were inclined to be a little too specific on the basis of not much fact. In some instances speculation has since become fact and an educated guess elevated to detail upon which further interpretation may pivot. There is contradiction, confusion, and unjustified interpretation regarding the origins of discolouration, bruises, and abrasions, the position of the victim when the wounds are inflicted, the time of death, and even the handedness of the killer. I have tried throughout to exclude from the reckoning those interpretations by medical and other witnesses that involved the most conjecture. Incidentally, and to avoid confusion, I have referred to the surgeons as doctor with the abbreviation Dr throughout this text even though Mr is the usual form of address for surgeons.

It will be of no surprise that the statements given by ordinary witnesses were often contradictory. Non-professional witness evidence is notoriously unreliable, even today, and when one also considers the lives of the people involved, a reasonable case could be made to disregard it completely. One day was pretty much the same as any other in certain areas of Whitechapel and witnesses were frequently heavy drinkers. Wrist watches were not commonplace, especially for the poor, and with only the chiming of church clocks by which to observe the passage of time, there is little doubt that stated times could be awry by as much as fifteen minutes or even longer, and there are occasionally suggestions that witnesses were reporting events that took place on another day entirely from the one in question. It is also likely that, given the opportunity of a few moments in the limelight, some witnesses took full advantage by providing overly colourful testimony. Often these people had lives that were otherwise meaningless and the chance to be centre stage was fleeting relief in the midst of the drudgery of a life of poverty. But even where testimony was not deliberately skewed, there remained much contradiction and nowhere is this better illustrated than when witnesses described suspects. Inconsistencies among witnesses were such that on occasion it was difficult to imagine that they were describing the same person if such were indeed the case; a degree of confusion that could only have bolstered the confidence of an already arrogant killer. However, it is tantalising to consider that on at least one occasion the murderer was seen by a witness – but which witness and which description we shall never know until the killer is identified by other means.

Although there is reason to be grateful that the newspapers of the day reported the Whitechapel murders in great detail, in another sense they reported far too much about the killings, which resulted in a disturbing potential for copycat murders and thus a decreasing certainty of correctly ascribing the killings to a series. Newspaper reporting was certainly sensationalistic towards the end of the nineteenth century; the Victorians were fascinated with crime and the middle classes developed an appetite for crime reporting, which was fed by coverage in the daily papers. When *The News of the World* made its debut in 1843, crime coverage was the staple of the paper and by the beginning 1888 *The Daily Telegraph*, established in 1855, had a circulation of over 300,000 copies a day thanks largely to its comprehensive coverage of the Whitechapel murders. Unfortunately, apart from factual reporting of the inquest proceedings, very little of the associated reporting in connection with the Whitechapel murders can be regarded as reliable and thus useful. Journalists did not undertake investigative reporting in the same way that they do now and rather more reporting was founded upon speculation. Sensationalism rather than facts sold newspapers then in much the same way that it does today, although the readership then was perhaps generally a little less discerning.

A common problem with assessing data of any kind is that of bias; sometimes it can be difficult to be neutral, to not have an opinion, or to not work towards an objective. There is already a significant amount of bias inherent in much of the raw data, but when an author fails, either by accident or design, to exhibit objectivity, the investigation will be seriously flawed. The fundamental approach to scientific investigation is to set a hypothesis and then prove it to be either true or false. Unfortunately it is too often the case that authors come up with a theory or a marginally credible suspect and in the belief that they are being objective then set out to prove their assertion to be true without entertaining the possibility that such might not be the case. This approach is highly biased and is widely open to the criticism of being selective about the use of data. There is also the matter of distortion whereby authors make the facts fit the objective, often by ignoring a simple explanation that does not fit the theory in favour of a more complicated explanation that can be made to fit. Pushing a square peg in a round hole is nothing to what authors on Jack the Ripper can achieve! Selecting those facts that fit their theory, stretching the ones that do not quite match, and ignoring those that counter the premise are commonplace in Ripperology and students should be very wary.

There are actually very few facts concerning the Whitechapel murders, and all that one can say with any degree of certainty is that eleven women, most of whom were prostitutes, were murdered in the Whitechapel district of East London between April 1888 and February 1891. From that point onwards the quality of information is only as good as the objectivity used to view it. By far the best approach is to review data in total ignorance of theories and conjecture but alas, with a subject such as the Whitechapel murders such an approach is almost impossible. The intention in the following pages is to sift through the information and identify as far as possible that upon which we can rely and separate it from that which is perhaps unreliable. By using reliable information as a foundation it is then possible to reconstruct each of the murders and identify those that were undertaken by the same killer. This information is then used to assess the already identified suspects to see which individuals, if any, could have been Jack the Ripper and to attempt to unravel the complex events surrounding the death of Mary Jane Kelly.

2: The Whitechapel murders

The Metropolitan Police defined eleven murders that at some stage looked as though they may have been attributable to a serial killer. The list of possible victims is given in the following table:

Date	Victim	Circumstances
3 April 1888	Emma Elizabeth Smith	Assaulted and robbed in Osborn Street, Whitechapel. Died later
7 August 1888	Martha Tabram	Murdered George Yard Buildings, George Yard, Whitechapel
31 August 1888	Mary Ann Nichols	Murdered Buck's Row, Whitechapel
8 September 1888	Annie Chapman	Murdered rear yard 29 Hanbury Street, Spitalfields
30 September 1888	Elizabeth Stride	Murdered yard side of 40 Berner Street St Georges-in-the-East
30 September 1888	Catharine Eddowes	Murdered Mitre Square, Aldgate, City of London
9 November 1888	Mary Jane Kelly	Murdered 13 Miller's Court, off Dorset Street, Spitalfields
20 December 1888	Rose Mylett	Murdered Clarke's Yard, High Street, Poplar
17 July 1889	Alice McKenzie	Murdered Castle Alley, Whitechapel
10 September 1889	Unidentified Female	Torso found under railway arch Pinchin Street Whitechapel
13 February 1891	Frances Coles	Murdered under railway arch Swallow Gardens, Whitechapel

In addition to the above listed cases, on 3 September 1888 the headless torso of a woman was found to have been recently deposited in the newly built cellar of the New Scotland Yard building under construction on the Embankment. The woman's arms were found in the Thames. This case was never regarded by the police in connection with the Ripper murders although there is a remote possibility of the case being linked to the torso found in Pinchin Street on 10 September a year later.

All of the Whitechapel murders remained unsolved but that alone is no reason to assume that they were all conducted by the same person, for almost certainly they were not. Over the years and largely as a result of the Macnaghten Memorandum of 1894 in which the Chief Constable Sir Melville Macnaghten made know his beliefs, the list has been reduced to five likely Ripper victims, known as the canonical victims, and comprising Mary Nichols, Annie Chapman, Elizabeth Stride, Catharine Eddowes, and Mary Jane Kelly.[1] Macnaghten's report has come to be generally accepted and authoritative even though the collective grouping of these five women as victims of the Ripper is based, not upon any detailed analysis, but only upon subjective and largely arbitrary grounds.

It is of course quite possible that each of the Whitechapel murders was conducted by a different killer or that more than one serial killer was in operation in Whitechapel at the end of the nineteenth century. Realistically, however, it seems that just one serial killer was at large and that he was responsible for some of the murders. Several suspects have been identified and some clearly could have assumed the role of serial killer but other suspects seem to be proposed with complete disregard for their ability to kill. It takes a very special type of person to coldly cut the throat of another human being, especially while the victim is conscious. Mental illness aside, an individual does not suddenly take on the role of serial killer without earlier indications of abnormal psychology and other forms of violence would almost certainly have been prevalent in the killer's early life.

Crucial in establishing the activity and identity of a serial killer is the need to determine exactly how many murders were committed by the same person. If, as seems likely, a serial killer was in operation from 1888 to 1891, then the erroneous inclusion of just one victim could throw an investigation completely off course from several perspectives, not least of which being those of alibi and motive. There is thus strong justification for a meticulous examination of each murder in order to assign victims to one or more killer and thereby establish multiplicity. As a starting point for this exercise the circumstances of the murder of each of the five canonical victims were analysed in detail and the aspects tabulated to allow direct comparison. Wherever possible only the facts reported at inquest have been used, although some additional medical opinions are also included, and throughout the exercise those medical interpretations that involve the most conjecture have been excluded. With regard to localisations and orientations given in the text, 'left' and 'right' are relative to the victim and not to the victim as viewed, such that a wound to the left side of the neck refers to the victim's left. It is assumed in all cases that original reporting used the same convention but this may not always have been the case other than when surgeons and experienced police officers provided descriptions.

After a particularisation of the murders of Mary Ann Nichols, Annie Chapman, Elizabeth Stride, Catharine Eddowes, and Mary Jane Kelly, certain components of the killer's 'signature' were identified and these were then used to evaluate the deaths of the remaining Whitechapel victims. Having established shared components, the Whitechapel murder victims could then be more reliably placed into two categories – those not attributable to the same serial killer, and those who more than likely died by the same hand. On the basis of this fundamental division, the circumstances of each murder were then considered in detail and attempts made to clarify events. Traditionally, authors have tended to examine the murders either in chronological order or merely concern themselves with the canonical victims, but the categorisation used here allows the likely victims of Jack the Ripper to be considered as a group with continuity and without the distraction of those who were the victims of other killers.

It is not the purpose of this investigation to look specifically at the lives of the victims; this is more than adequately undertaken elsewhere and I do not think that clues to the identity of the killer lie in the personal history of any of the women he murdered.

2.1 Analysing the data

A tabulated breakdown of the details of the murder of each of the canonical victims is given in Table 1. Components of the serial killer's *modus operandi* are then used to examine the remaining Whitechapel murder victims and the findings are reported in Table 2.

2.1.1 Comments on the tabulated details of the murders

Serial killers who undertake complex murders are very likely to leave behind a 'signature' among the components of their actions, or *modus operandi*. The signature is rarely a single component and often occurs subconsciously through habitual actions. The simple act of killing a victim by cutting the throat would not in itself be a signature; this was a relatively common means of killing at the end of the nineteenth century. The more bizarre the component the more clearly identifiable is the work of the same killer, but the easier it would be to perform a copycat crime if the details were widely available, which was unfortunately the case since the newspapers of the day were rather too specific in the way that details of murders were reported and almost every detail mentioned at the inquest would be in print for public consumption.

When undertaking an evaluation of this type, caution is necessary because not every component of the killer's *modus operandi* need necessarily be present at each crime scene and anomalies will be inevitable given that the circumstances of every crime are different and dependent to a large extent upon individual responses and reactions that are infinitely variable. This section examines the components without elaborating further. The killer's *modus operandi* will be fully discussed later, but from an examination of the tabulated details of the circumstances of death of each of the five canonical victims recorded in Table 1, a number of signature components appear and these are as follows:

- Each victim was a prostitute
- Each victim was probably murdered at the first opportunity
- Each victim was murdered at the scene and not transported
- Four out of five murders were carried out under cover of darkness
- Four out of five victims were killed outdoors in the street or in a yard
- Each victim was killed by one or two cuts to the neck which led to fatal haemorrhage from the carotid arteries
- Four out of five victims received a fatal cut to the left side of the neck
- The trachea was severed in all cases
- Each victim bled to death at the place at which the neck wounds were inflicted and, with the exception of one victim, there was minimal distribution of blood
- With the exception of one recorded external stab wound to one victim all knife wounds were cuts, and stabbing was not a feature of the Ripper murders
- There was no evidence of strangulation or suffocation with the exception of one victim

- There was mutilation or attempted mutilation occasionally involving the removal of organs from the body in four out of five cases and in the one in which there was no mutilation it seems that the killer was disturbed before he had the opportunity to progress
- Organs were removed from the scene in three out of five cases
- Four out of five victims were fully clothed when attacked and in only one instance was there evidence of the clothing being torn by the killer. In no case was the clothing cut and usually it was lifted or otherwise disturbed to allow access for mutilation
- There were no indications that any of the five victims struggled sufficiently to sustain defensive wounds
- In four out of five cases the assailant was probably right-handed
- In no instance was there any attempt to conceal the body
- In each case the killer used a very sharp knife, probably with a pointed blade of six inches or so in length
- In each case the killer had sufficient anatomical knowledge to target the carotid arteries and in two cases there was evidence of greater anatomical knowledge and dissecting skills

In addition, there were three other elements that may also be components:

- Each murder was carried out at or around the weekend
- Four out of five victims were aged in their forties
- Four of the five victims were 5ft 5in or less in height

The many similarities between the murders of Nichols, Chapman, Stride, and Eddowes convincingly suggest that they were perpetrated by the same killer and the common components of these murders contribute greatly to a picture of the killer's signature that can thus be used to evaluate the remaining Whitechapel murder victims. Several components of the Ripper's *modus operandi* establish his signature and it is clear that several facets of Mary Jane Kelly's murder do not fit well with the other four murders strongly suggesting that she was killed by someone else.

Features of the death of Mary Jane Kelly as detailed in Table 1 that do not fit with the killer's signature are as follows:

- Kelly was killed in her room
- Kelly undressed, folded her clothes and placed them on a chair – the killer thus did not strike immediately he was alone with his victim and she was probably not attacked at the first opportunity
- Kelly lay on the bed and wore only a chemise at the time of the attack – it is possible that her killer may have at some point engaged with her in a sexual act

- Kelly's carotid artery was severed on the right side of the neck and she bled considerably against the wall on that side.
- There are strong indications that the killer may have been left-handed
- At 25 years, Kelly was much younger than the other victims but this may not be significant
- At 5ft 7in Kelly was the tallest of the six victims and she was appreciably taller than three of them
- Kelly's breasts were removed – this was not undertaken for any other Ripper victim although there would have been opportunity in at least two other cases
- Kelly's heart was removed from the scene, but the thorax was not opened in the case of any other victim
- Neither Kelly's uterus nor kidneys were removed from the scene
- The killer did not demonstrate the same level of skill as that apparent for the other mutilated victims

2.1.2 How many women were victims of the same serial killer?

Having established the components of the serial killer's *modus operandi* these can be reliably used to evaluate the remaining Whitechapel murders, those of Smith, Tabram, Mylett, McKenzie, and Coles, and the results are presented in Table 2. In addition, the details of the murder of Emily Dimmock – The Camden Town Murder victim – have also been included to see whether or not the circumstances of her death fit with those of the other victims. Dimmock has been included here because of recent assertions that she was another victim of Jack the Ripper.[2]

The remaining Whitechapel murder, that of the unknown female whose torso was discovered in September 1889, must be excluded without further consideration because so little information is available on the victim and the circumstances of her death. There were reported abdominal mutilations but this alone is insufficient to justify the inclusion of this victim in the series. There may have been other murders and incidents occurring in the area during the same period but one imagines that, had the police considered any of these to have Ripper associations, they would have received a rather higher profile than was actually the case.

From an overview of Table 2 it is immediately apparent that the murders of Emma Smith, Martha Tabram, and Rose Mylett share very few components with those of the serial killer responsible for the other murders; significantly, the mode of death was different in each of these cases. Important components are absent and there are several contra indications. On balance it seems that the Ripper committed none of these three murders. The murder of Emily Dimmock is similarly dismissed on the grounds that there is insufficient overlap with the techniques employed in the serial killings. Significantly in this instance the killer apparently had plenty of time yet there were no mutilations to Dimmock's body. If the killer had time to wash his hands after the murder then he had time to mutilate; an opportunity that Jack the Ripper would not have missed. In some respects, the murder of Dimmock is similar to that of Mary Jane Kelly, but even excluding the absence of mutilation to Dimmock there is no firm evidence to indicate that the same man murdered both women.

The murders of Alice McKenzie and Frances Coles do, however, share many components with the Ripper murders. If one also considers that the killer may have been disturbed on both occasions, and before he could perform extensive mutilation, then the circumstances of both murders are little different from those of Elizabeth Stride. In other words, if the murders of McKenzie and Coles are excluded from the series then so too must the murder of Stride. There are several aspects of the deaths of McKenzie and Coles that do not fit although the significance of these is uncertain. From examination of medical testimony it is apparent that in both instances the lethal cuts to the neck were somewhat more lateral than for other victims but this may be fortuitous rather than a matter of technique.

There can be little doubt that had the killer opened the abdomen of McKenzie and Coles then both women would have been regarded as victims of the Ripper. That they did not suffer such mutilation could have been because the killer was disturbed before he could proceed to that stage. It is of course very difficult to positively identify these two women as Ripper victims because of what did *not* happen, but certainly, neither can be reliably excluded as victims of the same serial killer. There is also the matter of timing; the murder of McKenzie occurred ten months after Eddowes was found dead and Coles was killed nineteen months after McKenzie. Serial killers can be unpredictable in the frequency of their crimes which can fluctuate with impulse or can be governed by external factors such as being incarcerated in hospital or prison, being abroad, or being otherwise unavailable. There is characteristically a 'cooling off' period between murders which can be a matter of days, weeks, months, or even years.

Based purely on an objective particularisation and evaluation of the data provided from expert witness testimony relating to the crime scene and post mortem findings, it appears that six of the eleven Whitechapel murders had sufficient characteristics in common to indicate that they may have been undertaken by the same man. The likely victims of the same killer are:

Name	Date murdered
Mary Ann Nichols	31.08.1988
Annie Chapman	08.09.1988
Elizabeth Stride	30.09.1988
Catharine Eddowes	30.09.1988
Alice McKenzie	17.07.1889
Frances Coles	13.02.1891

Most significantly it would appear that the murder of Mary Jane Kelly, the most publicised of all the Whitechapel, and Ripper murders, was probably the work of an imitator. Emily Dimmock was never seriously considered as being a Ripper victim and this examination of the data supports the general impression that she was killed by someone else.

2.2 The Whitechapel murder victims not killed by Jack the Ripper

Because these murders were considered to be not the work of Jack the Ripper, they did not receive as much attention or comment in the press or in official documentation. Nonetheless, the circumstances of each death are of interest, if only to detail the reasons for their exclusion from the series.

2.2.1 Emma Elizabeth Smith

There is relatively little information available concerning the death of Emma Elizabeth Smith. The official file seems to have disappeared prior to 1983, although some of the original police reports survived.[3] Walter Dew made comments in his memoirs but his recollections are largely inaccurate.[4] What little information is available demonstrates quite clearly that Smith was not a victim of the Whitechapel serial killer, although she can be regarded as the first victim in the Whitechapel murder series.

Inspector Edmund Reid prepared a report on the murder in which he describes Smith as, 'aged 45 years, 5ft 2in high, complexion fair, hair light brown, scar on right temple'. Smith was a prostitute who worked the streets and lived in a common lodging house at 18 George Street, Spitalfields. According to Reid she regularly went out at between 6.00pm and 7.00pm and returned at all hours, usually drunk. The only other surviving official document is a report by Inspector West in which he stated that; 'According to the deceased's statements' the motive was robbery', although the evidence suggests that it may have been somewhat more than that.

The inquest took place on Saturday 7 April and it was reported in the newspapers. Wynn Baxter was the coroner. The inquest testimony of George Haslip the House Surgeon who attended to Smith was reported in *The Times* on 9 April 1888:

When the deceased was admitted to the hospital she had been drinking but was not intoxicated. She was bleeding from the head and ear, and had other injuries of a revolting nature. Witness found that she was suffering from rupture of the peritoneum, which had been perforated by some blunt instrument used with great force. The deceased told him that at half past 1 that morning she was passing near Whitechapel Church when she noticed some men coming towards her. She crossed the road to avoid them, but they followed, assaulted her, took all the money she had, and then committed the outrage. She was unable to say what kind of instrument was used, nor could she describe her assailants, except that she said that one was a youth of 19. Death ensued on Wednesday morning through peritonitis set up by the injuries.

Smith went out on the evening of Easter Monday and was attacked the following morning at about 1.30am on the 3 April 1888, in the street at the southern end of Brick Lane opposite number 10 and outside Taylor's Chocolate and Mustard Mill. Smith reported that while walking along Whitechapel Road she reached Whitechapel Church and saw three men ahead of her. She clearly felt threatened by their presence so she crossed the road to avoid them, but they followed her when she turned off into Osborn Street, which is a continuation of Brick Lane at the southern junction with Whitechapel Road. Smith was not killed during the attack, but died in hospital the following day from her injuries. She was able to give an account to witnesses, although not directly to the police. According to her account she walked back to her lodgings after the attack, a distance of some 300yds that took her three hours to complete thus indicating the extent to which her injuries caused her pain. Then, in the company of Mary Russell, the deputy lodging house attendant, and Annie Lee, another lodger, she walked to the London Hospital in Whitechapel Road. Smith spoke about the assault to Russell and to the House Surgeon Haslip, but it was not until the inquest that any of this information came to the attention of the police. Smith died on Wednesday 4 April at around 9.00am.

Reid described Smith's injuries thus; 'The peritoneum had been penetrated by a blunt instrument thrust up the woman's passage, and peritonitis set in which caused death'. Additional minor injuries included a bruised head and torn right ear. By 'passage' Reid meant vagina, which was obviously torn by such a violent assault, the weapon entering the abdominal cavity. Infection of the abdomen inevitably followed as an immediate consequence of such an excruciating injury. Before the discovery of antibiotics, peritonitis was as good as a death sentence and such was the case for Emma Smith. To inflict such an injury was totally unnecessary in the course of robbery and it is almost as though the assault was by way of a warning that was not intended to end in death.

The locality in which Smith was attacked was rough by any standards and there has been much speculation that her attackers were members of local gang who were perhaps intent upon taking protection money from prostitutes. Such need not detain us here, however, since Smith was not a victim of Jack the Ripper. Apart from the fact that there were apparently three assailants who were intent upon robbing the victim, every significant aspect of the Ripper's established *modus operandi* is absent from this attack and there are circumstances present in the assault and death of Emma Smith that are not part of the Ripper's *modus operandi*.

2.2.2 Martha Tabram

On the evening of Bank Holiday Monday 6 August 1888, Martha Tabram, also known as Emma Turner, went out with her fellow prostitute Mary Ann Connolly alias 'Pearly Poll'. The following morning Tabram was found dead at 4.45am on the first floor landing of the George Yard Buildings by waterside labourer John Reeves. Tabram was aged 39, about 5ft 3in tall, with dark complexion and hair, and lived in a common lodging house at 19 George Street.

The police file on the murder contains reports and correspondence but it is necessary to rely upon newspaper reports for details of the inquest, which opened on 9 August 1888 without the victim being positively identified.[5] Reeves' inquest testimony was reported in *The Times* on 10 August 1888 and he commented that Tabram was, 'lying on her back in a pool of blood' and her 'clothes were disarranged, as though she had had a struggle with someone'. It wasn't until several days later that Tabram was identified by her husband, Henry Tabram, who had left her some thirteen years earlier due to her 'drinking habits'. Police Constable Thomas Barrett called Dr Timothy Killeen to the scene and he examined the body. Killeen also gave his evidence to the inquest on the opening day and the following day *The Times* reported:

Dr. T. R. Killeen, of 68, Brick-lane, said that he was called to the deceased, and found her dead. She had 39 stabs on the body. She had been dead some three hours. Her age was about 36, and the body was very well nourished. Witness had since made a post-mortem examination of the body. The left lung was penetrated in five places, and the right lung was penetrated in two places. The heart, which was rather fatty, was penetrated in one place, and that would be sufficient to cause death. The liver was healthy, but was penetrated in five places, the spleen was penetrated in two places, and the stomach, which was perfectly healthy, was penetrated in six places. The witness did not think all the wounds were inflicted with the same instrument. The wounds generally might have been inflicted by a knife, but such an instrument could not have inflicted one of the wounds, which went through the chest-bone. His opinion was that one of the wounds was inflicted by some kind of dagger, and that all of them were caused during life.

Killeen's estimate would place Tabram's death at round 2.00am. The statements of other witnesses assisted in establishing the time of death. Elizabeth Mahoney gave a statement to the police to the effect that there was not a body at that point on the landing at 2.00am when she and her husband passed by the spot. Alfred Crow, a cab driver, gave testimony to the inquest and said that at around 3.30am he saw a body lying on the landing at that spot but took no notice because he 'was accustomed to seeing people lying about there', and went to bed. Tabram clearly died at between 2.00am and 3.30am and probably nearer to 2.00am.

Connolly's testimony was given on the second day of the inquest on 23 August, and was reported the following day in *The Times*:

Mary Ann Connolly ("Pearly Poll"), who at the suggestion of Inspector Reid was cautioned in the usual manner before being sworn, stated she had been for the last two nights living at a lodging house in Dorset-street, Spitalfields. Witness was a single woman. She had known the woman Tabram for about four or five months. She knew her by the name of Emma. She last saw her alive on Bank Holiday night, when witness was with her about three-quarters of an hour, and they separated at a quarter to 12. Witness was with Tabram and two soldiers - one private and one corporal. She did not know what regiment they belonged to, but they had white bands round their caps. After they separated, Tabram went away with the private, and witness accompanied the corporal up Angel-alley. There was no quarrelling between any of them. Witness had been to the barracks to identify the soldiers, and the two men she picked out were, to the best of her belief, the men she and Tabram were with. The men at the Wellington Barracks were paraded before witness. One of the men picked out by witness turned out not to be a corporal, but he had stripes on his arm.

Witness heard of the murder on the Tuesday. Since the occurrence witness had threatened to drown herself, but she only said it for a lark. She stayed away two days and two nights, and she only said that when asked where she was going. She knew the police were looking after her, but she did not let them know her whereabouts. The woman Tabram was not drunk. They were, however, drinking at different houses for about an hour and three-quarters. They had ale and rum.

Connolly's evidence strongly implicated a soldier as a likely suspect in the murder of Tabram but her evidence was unreliable and to some extent the victim's contact with the soldier at 11.45pm was rather too early in proceedings if her death was some time after 2.00am the following morning. Detective Inspector Reid made a statement at the inquest on the attempts of the police to identify the soldiers who had been with Tabram and Connolly that evening. *The Times* on 23 August 1888 reported Reid's statement:

Several persons had stated that they saw the deceased woman on the previous Sunday with a corporal, but when all the corporals and privates at the Tower and Wellington Barracks were paraded before them they failed to identify the man. The military authorities afforded every facility to the police. "Pearly Poll" picked out two men belonging to the Coldstream Guards at the Wellington Barracks. One of those men had three good conduct stripes, and he was proved beyond doubt to have been with his wife from 8 o'clock on the Monday night until 6 o'clock the following morning. The other man was also proved to have been in barracks at five minutes past 10 on Bank Holiday night. The police would be pleased if anyone would give them information of having seen anyone with the deceased on the night of Bank Holiday.

Further information was not forthcoming, not that it would likely have been especially important for the purposes of this evaluation. It is quite clear from the medical testimony that Martha Tabram died as a result of multiple stab wounds, in what appeared to be a frenzied attack. There are significant differences between killing by stabbing and by cutting wounds which will be examined later, but essentially, the different types of wound are frequently inflicted by entirely different types of perpetrator. The Whitechapel serial killer was a cutter and Tabram was killed by a stabber. Martha Tabram was the second victim in the Whitechapel murder series, but she was not a victim of Jack the Ripper and the evidence is conclusive. She probably also was not a victim of the soldier with whom she left earlier in the evening but I suspect that she met with her killer after parting company with the soldier. Interestingly, much has been made of the suggestion that two different instruments may have been used in this murder – this coming from Dr Killeen who gave evidence to the effect that most of the wounds had been inflicted by a knife, but one wound that which penetrated the sternum must have resulted from a stronger implement and in his opinion 'some kind of dagger'. This being the case, it is possible that two assailants attacked Tabram.

2.2.3 Rose Mylett

The death of Rose Mylett occurred on 20 December 1888, more than a month after the murder of Mary Jane Kelly, so it is not surprising that there was rather more police interest, and press coverage of this death than with early victims in the Whitechapel murder series. Mylett was reportedly the eighth Whitechapel murder victim although there are doubts that she was actually killed by an assailant.

Rose Mylett, real name probably Catherine Mylett, was a 26-year-old prostitute who resided at a common lodging house at 18 George Street, Spitalfields.[6] Police Sergeant Robert Goulding discovered Mylett dead in Clarke's Yard, High Street, Poplar at 4.15am – the last sighting of the woman had been at 1.45am.

Police and Home Office reports on the death of Mylett are to be found on file, but there are no inquest details so reliance must again be placed upon newspaper reporting.[7] Evidence was taken at the inquest on 21 December 1888, 2 January and 9 January 1889 with details reported in *The Times* on 22 December 1888, 3 January and 10 January 1889. Robert Goulding, the police officer who discovered the body was the first to give evidence:

Police-sergeant Robert Golding [*sic*], 26 K, deposed that he was patrolling High-street, Poplar, on Thursday morning about 4:15. He was in company with Police-constable Thomas Costella. While passing Mr. Clarke's yard he saw something lying under the wall, and on going close found it to be the body of a woman. She was lying on her left side, her left arm underneath her. The right leg was at full length, and her left leg slightly drawn up. The body was quite warm. Her clothes were not disarranged, nor could he detect any mutilation of the body. She was lying under the wall, with her head away from the street. The witness left the constable in charge of the body while he went for the divisional surgeon. Dr. Harris, the assistant, returned with him and examined the body before it was moved. He at once pronounced life to be extinct. The witness then sent for the ambulance, and the body was taken to the mortuary. He searched it and made an examination of the clothing. Round the neck the deceased was wearing a blue-spotted handkerchief, tied loosely. There was no string round the neck. In the pocket of the dress he found 1s in silver and 3½d in bronze, together with a small empty bottle or phial. The woman was about 5ft. 2in. high, had light hair, hazel eyes, and hair frizzed close to the head. She was wearing a black alpaca dress, brown stuff skirt, and red flannel petticoat. She also had on a dark tweed jacket, double-breasted, a lilac print apron, blue and red striped stockings, and side-spring boots. She had no hat on, nor was any found near the spot. The witness said he believed he had seen the woman before, and that she was of loose character. After leaving the mortuary he carefully searched the yard where the body was found, but could not discover any traces of a struggle having taken place.

Sergeant Golding, recalled at the request of the jury, stated that when he found the body there was a spotted handkerchief round the throat, which he now produced, It was not tightly round the throat, and was not tied at all. It did not appear to have been tied or pulled tightly round the throat.

There was no sign on the handkerchief of there having been a struggle. When witness found the body it was lying parallel with the wall, and the head was about a foot from the wall. Witness's first impression was that deceased had been leaning against some posts near the wall and had fallen down. The yard was not paved, but was composed of earth, and would show signs of a struggle had one taken place.

George Harris, surgeon and assistant to K Division Police Surgeon, Matthew Brownfield, attended the scene on behalf of his employer and gave evidence to the inquest. Harris' testimony was reported in *The Times* on 3 January 1889:

On Thursday, December 20, witness was called by the police at 4:30 a.m., and was taken to Clarke's-yard. He there saw deceased, who was dead, and was lying with her left cheek on the ground. There was a little blood-stained mucus issuing from the nostrils. The head was lying over the jacket, but he did not think it was in such a position as to cause strangulation. The collar of the jacket was quite loose. Her lips were livid, the mouth closed, and the eyes were normal. The left arm and leg were stiff.

Witness assisted Dr. Brownfield to make the post-mortem examination, and with regard to the internal examination he agreed with Dr. Brownfield's evidence.

With regard to the cause of death, witness noticed a mark which commenced at the spine and passed round the neck to the ear. There was a space of two or three inches at the back of the neck which was not marked. That mark might be produced with a piece of string. He did not see any other way by which the mark could be produced. In his opinion it was not possible for the collar of the jacket to have produced it. It was a much finer mark than he thought the collar could have produced. There were five superficial abrasions on the left side of the neck and three on the right side. Witness was of opinion that they were caused by finger nails, resulting from an endeavour to remove something from the neck. On the left side of the jaw there was a small bruise. In his opinion the cause of death was asphyxia, from strangulation.

Witness believed the string was crossed over, and used in a way similar to the way used when soap was cut. The marks on the neck could not have been caused by a man's hand.

Witness examined the windpipe and found no foreign matter in it.

The mark on the neck was above the necktie.

When witness first saw the body he did not notice the mark and did not then suspect foul play. He then thought deceased had died from asphyxia, from drunkenness or natural causes. Death would be brought about very quickly if the string was used in the way he described. The deceased's tongue was not protruding, nor were the eyeballs.

He should have expected that the face would have been more disturbed had the strangulation been slow.

Brownfield undertook the post mortem examination of Mylett's body and reported his findings to the inquest. Once again they were detailed in *The Times* on 22 December 1888:

Mr. Matthew Brownfield, of 170, East India-road, Poplar, deposed that he was divisional surgeon of police. At 4:25 on Thursday morning he was sent for, but his assistant went instead and found the body of a woman lying in Clarke's yard. She was dead. Yesterday morning the witness saw the body in the mortuary and subsequently made a post-mortem examination. He found the body to be that of a woman about 30 years of age and well nourished. He noticed marks of mud on the front of the left leg. The eyes were normal and the tongue did not protrude. There were slight marks of blood having escaped from the nostrils, and the right side of the nose showed a slight abrasion, while on the left cheek was an old scar. The mark on the nose might have been caused by any slight violence. On the neck there was the mark apparently of a cord extending from the right side of the spine round the throat to the lobe of the left ear. He had, by experiment, found that a piece of four-fold cord would cause such a mark. On the neck he also found marks as of the thumbs and middle and index fingers. He had tried his thumb and fingers and found that they could cause such abrasions. The marks ran perpendicularly to the line round the neck before described. There were no injuries to the arms or legs as if any violent struggle had taken place. On opening the head he found the brain engorged with blood of a very dark colour. The lungs were normal. In the stomach was some food which had only very recently been eaten. There was no sign of any poison or alcohol in the stomach. From his examination he was of opinion that the cause of death was suffocation by strangulation. The strangulation could not possibly have been done by the woman herself, but must have been caused by a person standing behind and slightly to the left of her. The witness said the person must have wrapped the ends of the cord round his hands and then, from behind, thrown the noose over the deceased's head and pulled tight, crossing both hands. This would account for the mark round the neck not completing the circle. The cord was held round the throat till after death had taken place.

There was no reported estimation of time of death from the medical evidence to the inquest as reported by the newspapers, although in an interview with a reporter from *The Star* on 24 December 1888, Brownfield indicated that when the body was discovered 'death had not taken place more than three quarters of an hour', so it can only be assumed that death occurred between 1.45am and 4.15am and probably around 3.30am. Police Sergeant Goulding reported that the body was warm when he discovered it but if the stiffness of the left arm and leg reported by Harris is to be interpreted as rigor mortis, then this would tend to suggest that death occurred nearer to the earlier limit of 1.45am. The conclusion of the two medical examiners was that Mylett had died from strangulation and that such was a consequence of her being murdered. However, this conclusion was not entirely in keeping with the evidence of Goulding who reported that there was no indication whatsoever of a struggle. Both Harris and Brownfield reported that there was the mark of a cord across the neck of the victim but her features were not consistent with prolonged throttling in that the tongue was not swollen and discoloured and the eyes did not protrude. There were in effect no facial changes to indicate asphyxiation at the neck. However, both surgeons were detailed in their description of the manner in which Mylett could have been strangled by the use of a length of four-fold cord. Brownfield spoke to the newspapers and in *The Star* on 24 December 1888 he confirmed his assertion that a cord had been pulled around Mylett's neck until she was dead and that the mark of strangulation was a white mark with no evidence of sloughing of the skin or inflammation that would have been apparent had death not been simultaneous with tightening of the ligature. The only discrepancy seems to have been the absence of any evidence of a struggle and presumably this was the reason why the Police Surgeon to Westminster Division, Thomas Bond, was called in by Assistant Commissioner Robert Anderson to give his expert opinion – a move that did not go down especially well with the coroner, Wynn Baxter. Bond's opinion was given at the inquest and reported by *The Times* on 3 January 1889:

Dr. Thomas Bond, 7, Sanctuary, Westminster Abbey, F.R.C.S., stated that he was asked to examine the body by Mr. Anderson, Assistant Commissioner of Police. Witness examined the body on the 24th of December. Mr. Hibbard [*sic* probably Hibbert], Demonstrator of Anatomy at Westminster Hospital, had examined the body on the Saturday with Drs. Brownfield and Harris, and he supplied witness with his notes. On the Monday witness had the body reopened, and compared his notes with his (witness's) observations. He and the other doctors agreed, with the exception of the mark on the throat. At the date of his examination the mark, which had been described as the mark of a cord, had disappeared. The other marks, which were described as finger marks, witness saw. He also saw in front of the larynx three extravasations of blood, where incisions had been made, and found blood effused around the larynx and deep congestion of the mucous membrane of the larynx. Witness took possession of the contents of the stomach and had what remained analysed. Witness could find no injury to the skin where the mark had been. He agreed with the deductions of Drs. Brownfield, Hibbard, and Harris that the deceased died from strangulation, but his opinion was that it was not murder. The amount of violence which would be required to rapidly strangle an able-bodied woman would leave such a mark on the neck that it would not disappear even during the five days that had elapsed. Witness should have expected to find injuries to the skin and tissues under the skin. The woman's skin was of such a nature that it would take a mark like wax, and from previous experience witness knew that strangulation might occur through a tight dress or a collar and leave deep marks. His opinion was that the woman, in a state of drunkenness, fell down and the larynx was compressed against the neck of the jacket, and that the mark described as the mark of a cord must have been produced by the rim of the collar, either while she was dying or while she was dead in the interval between the finding of the body and its being undressed.

The injury to the larynx must have been caused before death, but the mark above that might be caused before or after death.

The collar of deceased's jacket measured 14 in. Witness did not think the collar of deceased's jacket was stiff enough to strangle her. He thought it was possible that the woman made the finger marks herself. Had it been a case of quick strangulation he should have expected to find more contortion of the face.

Brownfield was recalled to give comment on what Bond concluded but he merely reiterated his opinion that Mylett had been murdered and stated that another medical man, the Chief Surgeon to the Metropolitan Police, had also seen the body. Brownfield was of the opinion that the mark on the neck was 'too straight and too even' to have been caused by the dress or collar of the jacket. By the time of Mylett's inquest, Bond had already been called in by Anderson to give an opinion on the death of Mary Jane Kelly and he would be involved with other deaths in the series after that of Mylett. More often than not he either passed judgement on the notes of the other surgeons or saw the body either days after death or after it had been dissected by others. On this occasion in particular, Bond's opinions were not altogether consistent with the findings. The coroner had clearly been irritated by the procession of doctors that viewed the body of Rose Mylett, and their wrangling in support of personal reputations assumed an importance beyond the objective of the inquest. Baxter's summary comments were reported in *The Times* on 10 January 1889:

After Dr. Brownfield and his assistant, duly qualified men, came to the conclusion that this was a case of homicidal strangulation, some one had a suspicion that that evidence was not satisfactory. At all events, they heard that doctor after doctor went down to view the body without his knowledge or sanction as coroner. He did not wish to make that a personal matter, but he had never received such treatment before. Of the five doctors who saw the body, Dr. Bond was the only one who considered the case was not one of murder. Dr. Bond did not see the body until five days after death, and he was, therefore, at a disadvantage.

Baxter appeared convinced that Mylett had been murdered and the jury agreed when they returned their verdict but the police remained sceptical and to such an extent that the death was not subsequently investigated with any enthusiasm. There was much correspondence about Brownfield's conduct in not immediately informing the police that he thought Mylett had been murdered and in his readiness to talk to the press. The Chief Surgeon Alexander MacKellar wrote to Assistant Metropolitan Police Commissioner James Monro on the matter but there is no evidence that Brownfield was directly rebuked.[8] On the basis of the evidence it is difficult to agree with Bond's interpretation and it does not always follow that a victim of homicidal strangulation must demonstrate facial consequences of a prolonged assault. Death in such circumstances can occasionally result from 'vagal inhibition' or reflex cardiac arrest in which sudden pressure on the neck can precipitate rapid death before any congestive signs have time to appear, so that the victim dies without a discoloured face or swollen tongue.[9] This cause of death was not documented in 1888, but could easily have accounted for the appearance of Mylett assuming that a cord was applied sufficiently tightly around her neck. The fact that the ligature mark described by Brownfield had disappeared by the time Bond examined the corpse five days later does not entirely agree with a ligature applied sufficiently tightly that it cut into the skin. Unfortunately, Bond did not offer an especially convincing alternative means by which Mylett died.

Monro reported on 23 December 1888, that; 'The police believed from the appearance of the body that the case was one of suicide or sudden death from natural causes', and that the findings of Brownfield were, 'certainly a matter of surprise to the police'.[10] One can thus imagine that Bond was sent to examine the case and as good as instructed to return an opinion that Mylett's demise was not at the hands of a murderer. In his memoirs, Anderson, wrote that; 'the Poplar case of December, 1888, was death from natural causes, and but for the 'Jack the Ripper' scare, no one would have thought of suggesting that it was a homicide'.[11]

If Rose Mylett was murdered then she was not a victim of Jack the Ripper. Although there were indications that one of his victims did suffer partial throttling, strangulation was not part of his usual technique. The newspapers, however, were convinced that strangulation was part of the serial killer's routine and they espoused the theory that the victims were all rendered at least helpless by partial strangulation prior to having their throats cut, offering much speculation, but nothing by way of proof.[12]

2.2.4 The unidentified female torso

On 10 September 1889, between the murders of Alice McKenzie and Frances Coles, the dismembered body of a woman was found at 5.15am beneath a railway arch in Pinchin Street, St George's in the East. The torso, headless but with arms still attached, was discovered just inside the first railway arch in Pinchin Street from the junction with Back Church Lane. Home Office and Metropolitan Police files detail events to some extent.[13] A report by Chief Inspector Donald Swanson dated 10 September 1889 gives much of the detail of the circumstances surrounding the discovery.[14] On the spot at which the body was found there was no sign of blood. There were no footmarks, nor anything in which the torso could have been carried. The place of disposal according to Swanson must have been selected in advance because it was secluded from view and disposal was easy. The appearance of the torso was also reported although Swanson's description must have been taken from a medical examination of the corpse:

The head which had been cut off by clean right handed cuts, the vertebra being 'jointed' left the neck with blood oozing from it while both legs had also been 'jointed', by right handed cuts, but the dismemberment had taken place at an earlier period than the head for the raw flesh had from continued exposure dried on the surface which presented a blackened appearance in consequence. The wound beginning at the lower point of the sternum, cutting through the skin, fatty substance, and penetrating the bowels, and uterus slightly, extended to the left side of the labia major. The trunk presented the undoubted appearance of having decomposition begun. Upon the chemise which was cut at the arms and down the front, I understand from Inspr Reid who examined it, there was not a single mark of any kind and the article itself of common manufacture and fabric. Beyond a small semi-circular cut on the index finger of right hand, and bruises on both arms, which the surgeons say they will be better able to describe after the post mortem examination there is absolutely nothing by which the trunk could be identified.

Swanson concluded that death had not taken place at the spot where the body was found and had occurred twenty-four hours earlier according to Dr Charles Hibbert, Curator of the Museum of the Westminster Hospital, who was present at the post mortem examination, or two days prior to discovery according to Percy Clark, assistant to George Bagster Phillips Police Surgeon to Whitechapel Division. Swanson suggested that the surgeons considered that the body was so full of blood that death did not result from massive haemorrhage and the Chief Inspector thought that death must have been caused by injury to the head since there were no stab wounds to the torso.

The next task was to discover the missing parts of the body so that the identity of the victim could be established. The best endeavours of the police were not to prove fruitful. All that they could say of the victim was that she was perhaps aged about 40 years, height probably around 5ft 3in, and with dark brown hair. Both of the victim's elbows were discoloured as if from habitually leaning on them. The inquest opened on 11 September and medical evidence was taken on day two of the proceedings on 24 September and reported in *The Times* the following day. Percy Clark gave his evidence:

I was called by the police to Pinchin-street. Under a railway arch there, about 8 ft. from the road and about 1 ft. from the right wall of the arch, I saw the trunk of a woman, minus the head and legs. It was lying on its anterior surface, with the right arm doubled under the abdomen. The left arm was lying under the left side. The arms were not severed from the body. There was no pool of blood, and there were no signs of any struggle having taken place there. On moving the body I found that there was a little blood underneath where the neck had lain. It was small in quantity and not clotted. The blood had oozed from the cut surface of the neck. Over the surface of the neck and the right shoulder were the remnants of what had been a chemise. It was of common length and such a size as would be worn by a woman of similar build to the trunk found. It had been torn down the front, and had been cut from the front of the armholes on each side. The cuts had apparently been made with a knife. The chemise was bloodstained nearly all over, from being wrapped over the back surface of the neck. There was no clotted blood on it. I could find no distinguishing mark on the chemise. Rigor mortis was not present. Decomposition was just commencing. The body was lifted, in my presence, on to the ambulance and taken to the St. George's mortuary by constables. On re-examining it there I found the body appeared to be that of a woman of stoutish build, dark complexion, about 5ft. 3in. in height, and between 30 and 40 years of age. I should think the body had been dead at least 24 hours. Besides the wounds caused by the severance of the head and legs, there was a wound 15ins. long through the external coat of the abdomen. The body was not bloodstained, except where the chemise had rested upon it. The body had not the appearance of having been recently washed. On the back there were four bruises, all caused before death. There was one over the spine, on a level with the lower part of the shoulder blade. It was about the size of a shilling. An inch lower down there was a similar bruise, about the middle of the back, also on the spine, and that was a bruise about the size of a half-a-crown. On the level of the top of the hip bone was a bruise 2½ins. in diameter. It was such a bruise as would be caused by a fall or a kick. None of the bruises were of old standing. Round the waist was a pale mark and indentation, such as would be caused by clothing during life. On the right arm there were eight distinct bruises and seven on the left, all of them caused before death and of recent date. The back of both forearms and hands were much bruised. On the outer side of the left forearm, about 3in. above the wrist, was a cut about 2in. in length, and half an inch lower down was another cut. These were caused after death. The bruises on the right arm were such as would be caused by the arms having been tightly grasped. The hands and nails were pallid. The hands did not exhibit any particular kind of work.

Phillips also gave evidence, which largely substantiated the findings of his assistant and also those of Charles Hibbert who reported his findings and commented but did not give evidence to the inquest.[15] Phillips' testimony was reported in *The Times* on 25 September 1889:

I first examined the body at 6 o'clock on the day the remains were found. I confirm, so far as I have observed, the evidence given by my colleague, Mr. Clarke [sic], who was present when I first examined the body. The next morning at 10 o'clock, in the presence of Dr. Gordon Brown and Mr. Hibberd [sic], I further examined the body. Having described the nature of the cuts by which the head and limbs had been separated, witness continued: The marks on the fingers had fairly healed, and had evidently been in a process of healing for some time previous to death. The pallor of the hands and nails is an important element in enabling me to draw a conclusion as to the cause of death. I agree with the remarks of Mr. Clarke as regards the marks on the arms. I found the length of the trunk to be 2ft. 2in., and the measurement round the nipple 34in., and below the breast 31¾in. The length of hand was 6½in. The weight of the body, taken with a balance which was not exactly accurate, was 67lb. There was throughout the body an absence of blood in the vessels. The right lung was adherent, except at the base; the left lung free, and, taking them both together, fairly competent. All the other organs, except the spleen and the liver, were fairly healthy. The liver weighed 50oz. In my opinion it was diseased and fatty before death.

I believe that death arose from loss of blood. I believe the mutilation to have been subsequent to death, that the mutilations were effected by some one accustomed to cut up animals or to see them cut up, and that the incisions were effected by a strong knife 8in. or more long.

The supposition that presents itself to my mind is that there was a former incision of the neck, which had disappeared with the subsequent separation of the head.

The loss of blood could not have come from the stomach, and I could not trace any sign of its coming from the lungs. I have a strong opinion that it did not. There was no tubercle, but the top part of the lung was diseased. The draining of the blood from the body was such that it must have been a main artery that was severed and was almost as thorough as it could be although not so great as I have seen in some cases of cut throats. I have no reason for thinking that the person who cut up the body had any anatomical knowledge.

The medical examiners were unanimous in their conclusion that the Pinchin Street victim had died following extensive blood loss; contrary to initial impressions reported by Swanson. There was every possibility that this blood loss occurred as a consequence of a deep cut to the throat that severed the major vessels and since the killer was well on the way to removing the victim's head he continued with the cut and separated the head from the body through an intervertebral joint. This act would make identification of the body next to impossible and by removing the legs by skilfully cutting through the hip joints the corpse was not only unidentifiable but also more easily transportable. The fact that the victim had apparently been wearing a chemise that was cut from her body suggests that she was not killed fully clothed or at a type of location favoured by the Ripper, but that she was murdered indoors. The victim was also possibly kicked and punched at some time prior to her death during which she sustained defensive wounds to her arms. That the killer had to remove the body to elsewhere suggests that had he not done so, discovery of the corpse at the murder site would have strongly implicated him as the killer. In other words the victim was probably related to or in a relationship with her killer and she was murdered at home. Moving dead bodies around is a risky business for a killer and would not be undertaken other than out of absolute necessity. Having removed the body there would also be a considerable amount of blood to clear away as well as the matter of disposing of the victim's head and legs. What may have been a simple, if impulsive killing, had immediate and complex consequences. The cut to the abdomen does not appear to have been a Ripper type mutilation and may have been an abandoned attempt to further lighten the considerable weight of the body by removing the internal organs or it may have been a deliberate attempt to make the murder resemble a Ripper killing. The victim may or may not have been killed by a single cut to the neck and she was undoubtedly dismembered with some limited skill, but that is where any similarity with the Ripper murders ends.

On 5 October 1889 the remains of the victim were interred in grave number 16185 at the East London Cemetery. Spirit was added to the container and the lid soldered down to preserve the remains in case future identification was necessary in the event that a trial before judge and jury followed at sometime in the future.[16] The body remained unidentified and the services of the judiciary were not called upon.

2.3 The Whitechapel murder victims of Jack the Ripper

Having dealt with those Whitechapel murders that were in all probability not perpetrated by Jack the Ripper those likely to have been collectively a series can now be considered at length. The circumstances of each murder are given below together with a critical appraisal of the evidence and an indication of a likely course of events in each case. The details are supplemented by location maps taken from the 1894-6 Ordnance Survey Series and diagrams of the wounds as reported or deduced from post mortem findings.[17]

2.3.1 Mary Ann Nichols (1845-88)

Mary Ann 'Polly' Nichols was born on 26 August 1845 in Dawes Court off Shoe Lane.[18] In 1864 Mary Ann married William Nichols, a printer from Oxford, and the couple had five children, the last of which was born in 1879. Nichols was 5ft 2in tall with greying hair and grey eyes. She had small delicate features with high cheekbones and a youthful appearance. She reportedly had a small scar on her forehead and five of her front teeth were missing. At the time of her death Nichols wore a black straw bonnet trimmed with black velvet, a reddish brown ulster with large brass buttons, a brown linsey frock, white flannel chest cloth, black ribbed wool stockings, two petticoats (one grey wool, one flannel and both stencilled on bands 'Lambeth Workhouse'), brown stays (short), flannel drawers, and men's elastic (spring) sided boots with the uppers cut and steel tips on the heels. Nichol's possessions when her body was discovered were; a comb, a white pocket-handkerchief, and a broken piece of mirror. The wounds to Nichols are detailed in Diagram 1 and the location of the murder is illustrated in Map 1 and a complete tabulation of relevant findings is given in Table 1. Several Home Office and Metropolitan Police files relate to the murder of Mary Ann Nichols.[19]

Nichols was murdered in the early hours of 31 August 1888, and the following day, *The Times* carried details:

Another murder of the foulest kind was committed in the neighbourhood of Whitechapel in the early hours of yesterday morning, but by whom and with what motive is at present a complete mystery. At a quarter to 4 o'clock Police-constable Neill [*sic*], 97J, when in Buck's-row, Whitechapel, came upon the body of a woman lying on a part of the footway, and on stooping to raise her up in the belief that she was drunk he discovered that her throat was cut almost from ear to ear. She was dead but still warm. He procured assistance and at once sent to the station and for a doctor. Dr. Llewellyn, of Whitechapel-road, whose surgery is not above 300 yards from the spot where the woman lay, was aroused, and, at the solicitation of a constable, dressed and went at once to the scene. He inspected the body at the place where it was found and pronounced the woman dead. He made a hasty examination and then discovered that, besides the gash across the throat, the woman had terrible wounds in the abdomen. The police ambulance from the Bethnal-green Station having arrived, the body was removed there. A further examination showed the horrible nature of the crime, there being other fearful cuts and gashes, and one of which was sufficient to cause death apart from the wounds across the throat.

Because the official inquest papers into the death of Mary Ann Nichols have not been discovered, it is necessary to rely upon the details reported in the newspapers. Both *The Times* and *The Daily Telegraph* covered the inquest but they do occasionally differ in detail. The inquest into the death of Mary Ann Nichols was opened on Saturday 1 September 1888 and reporting in the newspapers commenced on Monday, 3 September 1888.[20]

Nichols' body was identified by her father and by her husband. Nichols was 43 years old and inclined to drink rather heavily – her husband left her eight years previously on account of her drinking. William Nichols had not seen or heard from his wife during the previous three years during which time she had evidently formed 'irregular connexions', as the coroner Wynne Baxter put it. Since separating from her husband, Nichols lived at various locations, including a period with her father and several stays at Lambeth Workhouse. However, it was pretty clear that she had been living an 'intemperate, irregular, and vicious life', mostly in common lodging houses, for several years. According to the coroner there was nothing in the evidence as to Nichols' movements on the day before her death, except a statement made to her friend Emma Holland with whom she had previously lodged at 18 Thrawl Street, to the effect that she had spent the last week living in a common lodging house called the White House at 56 Flower and Dean Street, Spitalfields.[21] Men and women were allowed to sleep together at this particular doss house, but her movements had been traced by the police and were considered not to have any connection with her death.

Early on Friday morning, the 31st of August, at around 2.30am Nichols was seen by Holland at the corner of Osborn Street and Whitechapel Road, nearly opposite the parish church. According to Holland, Nichols was alone and drunk against a wall. Holland tried to persuade her to go home, but she declined because she could not pay for her room, and she was last seen attempting to walk eastward down Whitechapel Road and clearly not in the direction of her lodgings in Flower and Dean Street. Nichols told Holland that she had earned her lodging money three times that day but that she had spent it, that she was going to get some money to pay her lodgings, and she would soon be back. No other witnesses saw Nichols after this time and at 3.40am she was found dead less then three-quarters of mile away in Buck's Row. According to a report in *The Times* on 1 September 1888, Buck's Row was 'a street tenanted all down one side by a respectable class of people, superior to many of the surrounding streets, the other side having a blank wall bounding a warehouse'.[22]

Police Constable John Neil was not in fact the first to encounter Nichols' body; she was first discovered by Charles Cross on his way to work as a carman. As Cross walked down Buck's Row he noticed, on the opposite side of the road, a dark object lying across a gateway to stables. He at first thought the object was a tarpaulin sheet, but when he realised it to be the body of a woman he called to another man approaching down the street. The other man was Robert Paul who was also on his way to work. Although it was dark they could see that her clothing was raised almost to her stomach and they initially thought that she had been attacked and fainted but they noticed her hands to be cold and limp. Paul said that he felt a slight movement of her breast, and thought she was breathing. Because of the darkness of the location, neither of the men appeared to have realised the extent of Nichols' injuries and saw no blood. The men decided not to move her, but instead went off to find a constable and at the corner of Hanbury Street, some 300yds away, they found Constable Jonas Mizen. Although Mizen started without delay, he found that another constable was already with Nichols when he arrived. Constable Neil had independently found her body shortly after Cross and Paul had left. According to Neil's inquest testimony reported in *The Daily Telegraph* on 3 September 1888:

I was on the right-hand side of the street, when I noticed a figure lying in the street. It was dark at the time, though there was a street lamp shining at the end of the row. I went across and found deceased lying outside a gateway, her head towards the east. The gateway was closed. It was about nine or ten feet high, and led to some stables. There were houses from the gateway eastward, and the School Board school occupies the westward. On the opposite side of the road is Essex Wharf. Deceased was lying lengthways along the street, her left hand touching the gate. I examined the body by the aid of my lamp, and noticed blood oozing from a wound in the throat. She was lying on her back, with her clothes disarranged. I felt her arm, which was quite warm from the joints upwards. Her eyes were wide open. Her bonnet was off and lying at her side, close to the left hand. I heard a constable passing Brady-street [John Thain], so I called him. I did not whistle. I said to him, "Run at once for Dr. Llewellyn," and, seeing another constable [Mizen] in Baker's-row, I sent him for the ambulance. The doctor arrived in a very short time. The doctor looked at the woman and then said, "Move her to the mortuary. She is dead, and I will make a further examination of her." We placed her on the ambulance, and moved her there. Inspector Spratley [*sic*] came to the mortuary, and while taking a description of the deceased turned up her clothes, and found that she was disembowelled. This had not been noticed by any of them before. On the body was found a piece of comb and a bit of looking-glass. No money was found, but an unmarked white handkerchief was found in her pocket. There was a pool of blood just where her neck was lying. It was running from the wound in her neck.

At 4.00am on Friday 31 August Dr Rees Llewellyn was called to Buck's Row to examine the body of Nichols and gave an opinion that she had been killed within half an hour of his examination. In inquest testimony reported in *The Daily Telegraph* on 3 September 1888 Llewellyn said:

On reaching Buck's-row I found the deceased woman lying flat on her back in the pathway, her legs extended. I found she was dead, and that she had severe injuries to her throat. Her hands and wrists were cold, but the body and lower extremities were warm. I examined her chest and felt the heart. It was dark at the time. I believe she had not been dead more than half-an-hour. I am quite certain that the injuries to her neck were not self-inflicted. There was very little blood round the neck. There were no marks of any struggle or of blood, as if the body had been dragged. I told the police to take her to the mortuary, and I would make another examination. About an hour later I was sent for by the Inspector to see the injuries he had discovered on the body. I went, and saw that the abdomen was cut very extensively. I have this morning made a post-mortem examination of the body. I found it to be that of a female about forty or forty-five years. Five of the teeth are missing, and there is a slight laceration of the tongue. On the right side of the face there is a bruise running along the lower part of the jaw. It might have been caused by a blow with the fist or pressure by the thumb. On the left side of the face there was a circular bruise, which also might have been done by the pressure of the fingers. On the left side of the neck, about an inch below the jaw, there was an incision about four inches long and running from a point immediately below the ear. An inch below on the same side, and commencing about an inch in front of it, was a circular incision terminating at a point about three inches below the right jaw. This incision completely severs all the tissues down to the vertebrae. The large vessels of the neck on both sides were severed. The incision is about eight inches long. These cuts must have been caused with a long-bladed knife, moderately sharp, and used with great violence. No blood at all was found on the breast either of the body or clothes. There were no injuries about the body till just about the lower part of the abdomen. Two or three inches from the left side was a wound running in a jagged manner. It was a very deep wound, and the tissues were cut through. There were several incisions running across the abdomen. On the right side there were also three or four similar cuts running downwards. All these had been caused by a knife, which had been used violently and been used downwards. The wounds were from left to right, and might have been done by a left-handed person. All the injuries had been done by the same instrument.

The Times on 1 September 1888 carried a report on Llewellyn's initial impressions:

Dr Llewellyn has called the attention of the police to the smallness of the quantity of blood on the spot where he saw the body, and yet the gashes in the abdomen laid the body right open. The weapon used would scarcely have been a sailor's jack knife, but a pointed weapon with a stout back – such as a cork-cutter's or shoemaker's knife. In his opinion [Llewellyn's] it was not an exceptionally long-bladed weapon. He does not believe that the woman was seized from behind and her throat cut, but thinks that a hand was held across her mouth and the knife then used, possibly by a left-handed man, as the bruising on the face of the deceased is such as would result from the mouth being covered with the right hand. He made a second examination of the body at the mortuary, and on that based his conclusion, but will make no actual post mortem until he receives the Corner's orders.

This is curious because in all newspaper accounts of the inquest there is no mention that Llewellyn actually forwarded this opinion at the inquest, although it does seem that some portions of his testimony have been overlooked by the newspapers because another version of the inquest report given in *The Woodford Times* on 7 September 1888 reported slightly different details and an additional response to a question by a juryman:

Questioned by jurymen, the witness [Llewellyn] said the deceased was a strong woman. The murderer must have had some rough anatomical knowledge, for he seemed to have attacked all the vital parts. It was impossible to say whether the wounds were inflicted with a clasp-knife or a butcher's knife, but the instrument must have been a strong one. When he first saw the body life had not been out of it more than half-an-hour. The murder might have occupied four or five minutes. It could have been committed by one man so far as the wounds were concerned.

Llewellyn was recalled to the inquest on 17 September according to the report in *The Daily Telegraph* and said he had re-examined the body and confirmed there was no part of the viscera missing. The need for this further examination was initiated by the discovery of another murder victim, Annie Chapman, a little over a week after the murder of Nichols. The inquests on the two women overlapped and not only had the second victim been mutilated, but organs had been removed from her abdomen. In the course of his summing up on the final day of the inquest, and as reported in both *The Times* and *The Daily Telegraph*, the coroner Wynne Baxter stated:

Dr Llewellyn seemed to incline to the opinion that the abdominal injuries were inflicted first, and caused instantaneous death; but, if so, it seemed difficult to understand the object of such desperate injuries to the throat. Or how it came about that there was so little bleeding from the several [sic] arteries that the clothing on the upper surface was not stained and the legs not soiled, and there was very much less bleeding from the abdomen than from the neck. Surely it may well be that, as in the case of Chapman, the dreadful wounds to the throat were inflicted first and the others afterwards. This is a matter of some importance when we come to consider what possible motive there can be for all this ferocity.

The coroner suggested that Llewellyn formed the opinion that the abdominal wounds preceded the cuts to the throat, in which case the surgeon immediately vaporised his credibility. It is also difficult to understand how Llewellyn managed to reach the conclusion that the killer was left-handed and attacked his victim from the front when the all the evidence indicates the exact opposite. Unfortunately once a professional judgement was made by the medical examiners, as will be seen again in relation to other investigations, it seems that they were rather disinclined to change their opinion regardless of the evidence. Of course it can be argued that they had the evidence in front of them and Llewellyn obviously didn't have the benefit of subsequent murders against which to make a comparison, but even so it is apparent that the practical aspects of what was suggested in respect of the mode of the attack on the victim were never actually taken into serious consideration or questioned.

The Times by way of a barely veiled criticism mentioned that Llewellyn, 'made a hasty examination' of the dead woman at the scene having pronounced her dead; in fact, his cursory examination of the corpse was almost contemptuous. With clear evidence that the clothing had been disturbed it is astounding that Llewellyn did not look more closely at the lower part of Nichols' body when he first attended the scene. It was undoubtedly dark in Buck's Row, but the police carried lamps and that can not be an excuse. Llewellyn then had the embarrassment of being called to the mortuary in Old Montague Street an hour later by Inspector John Spratling, to observe the extensive abdominal wounds that were subsequently discovered. The divisional surgeon spent a further ten minutes examining the body, which at this point was still clothed. Fortunately, at least Spratling had the good sense to record some details of the body as it lay on an ambulance in the mortuary yard while someone went for the keys to the building.[23] Spratling continued his note taking inside the mortuary, which is when he discovered that Nichols' abdomen had been mutilated.

Later that morning and without instruction from anyone in authority, in fact quite to the contrary of instruction, the mortuary attendants, two paupers from the workhouse, stripped and washed Nichols' body. Much to the consternation of the coroner, clothing was cut from her corpse and dumped outside in the mortuary yard. But by account of Spratling the clothes were fastened when he first saw the body, although the stays did not fit very tightly for he was able to see the abdominal wounds without unfastening them.

Nichols suffered two cuts to her throat. One, probably the first cut, was shorter (four inches long) than the other and just affected the left side of her neck whereas the second cut was much longer (eight inches long) and went almost from ear to ear. This longer cut had severed all tissues of the neck down to the vertebrae; the carotid arteries as well as other vessels on both sides were cut through, as was the windpipe, and Nichols bled to death quickly and in silence. A right-handed assailant would almost certainly make a cut to the left side of the neck regardless as to whether he was positioned at the front of the victim or behind the victim when the attack was made. That there were two cuts in this instance does not detract from that, but the presence of an extended cut across the throat increases the probability that the cut was delivered from behind so that the killer would be able to draw the knife across the full width of the throat without awkwardness. Llewellyn described various marks on the face, which further supports the theory that Nichols was attacked from behind. To reiterate Llewellyn's testimony as reported in *The Daily Telegraph*:

There is a slight laceration of the tongue. On the right side of the face there is a bruise running along the lower part of the jaw. It might have been caused either by a blow from a fist or by pressure of the thumb. On the left side of the face was a circular bruise, which also might have been done by the pressure of the fingers.

According to further detail reported in *The Woodford Times* on 7 September 1888, the bruise on the right side of the face was, 'a recent and strongly marked bruise, which was scarcely perceptible when he first saw the body'. It is not unusual for bruises inflicted just prior to or at the death of a victim to appear more strongly with the passage of time post mortem, and this is something that will be encountered again and discussed more fully for later murders. It can be assumed that Nichols suffered the bruises reported by Llewellyn around the time of the assault. Of the reported lesions, the circular bruise to the left cheek is suggestive of pressure applied by the thumb of an assailant standing behind his victim and with his left hand across her mouth, with the marks on the right jaw corresponding to fingers gripping tightly. That Nichols' tongue would suffer a minor laceration in the process would be quite possible. Contrary to Llewellyn's conclusions, the injuries to Nichols suggest that her attacker approached from behind and placed his left hand across her mouth to silence and immobilise her while he made the cuts to her neck as she stood or while he was in the process of pulling her backwards and to the ground. It is interesting to note that Nichols' bonnet was found on the ground close to her body; a bonnet would easily become detached in the course of such an assault from behind. The shorter cut was probably the first to be made but apparently it did not sever the carotid vessels, thus forcing the killer to make a second cut while still grasping his victim. He would have known whether or not his knife had cut deep enough – even in the darkness of Buck's Row – and clearly did not need a third attempt. In any event the first cut would have surprised the victim to such an extent that she would have been unable to respond in the moments before the second wound was inflicted. Nichols would have been immediately in shock as the vessels were severed, and her legs would have collapsed beneath her.

Looking at the alternative suggested by Llewellyn, we have to believe that Nichols' attacker approached his victim from the front and somehow held her across the face with his right hand while cutting the left side of her neck or drawing the knife around and across the width of her neck with a long knife held in his left hand. If Nichols is not standing at this time then we also have to work out how her assailant managed to get her to the ground, which would require the use of both hands, before then holding her with one hand and inflicting the cuts to her throat after producing the knife. Any combination of manoeuvres associated with an attack from the front leads to protracted complexity that invites the victim to put up a noisy defensive struggle and there are no signs that such happened in this instance even though, as Llewellyn told the inquest, 'the deceased was a strong woman'. Nichols died without a struggle and without making a sound. The spot where she was killed was almost under the window of Emma Green, who was by her own account, 'a light sleeper, and had a scream been given she would have heard it'. The attack took place opposite the house of Walter Purkiss whose wife was awake at the time and heard nothing, and there were also various watchmen within very short distances of the murder and not a sound was heard by any. The coroner indicated that the fact that Nichols died without a struggle could have arisen from her intoxication, or from being stunned by a blow. There was no evidence of a debilitating blow and although Holland reported seeing Nichols in a state of intoxication some seventy-five minutes earlier, Llewellyn did not detect alcohol in her stomach, although that may not have been a very reliable indicator as to the extent of her inebriation.

There were suggestions that because of an apparent absence of blood at the scene Nichols had been killed elsewhere and her body dumped in Buck's Row. This seems to have been initiated by a statement from Llewellyn who remarked at the inquest that, 'there was very little blood round the neck', and *The Times* on 1 September 1888 reported that Llewellyn, 'has called the attention of the police to the smallness of the quantity of blood on the spot where he saw the body'. The testimony of Inspector Joseph Helson was reported in *The Times* on 4 September 1888 as follows:

Inspector Helston [*sic*], J Division, deposed that it was a quarter to 7 on Friday morning when he received information of the murder. Having learnt full particulars, he proceeded to the mortuary, where he saw deceased, who had her clothing on. He saw the things removed. The bodice of the dress was buttoned down to the middle and the stays were fastened. There were no bruises on the arms to indicate that a struggle had taken place. The wounds on the abdomen were visible with the stays on, and that proved they could have been inflicted while the stays were on the deceased. He did not examine the spot where the body was found until after the blood had been washed away. Witness was of opinion that the murder was committed at the spot where the body was found. The clothes were very little disarranged, thus showing that the body could not have been carried far.

Additional reporting in *The Daily Telegraph* on 4 September 1888 suggests that Helson 'noticed blood on the hair and on the collars of the dress and Ulster, but not on the back of the skirts. Constables Neil and Thain told the inquest that there was a pool of congealed blood about six inches in diameter, some of which had run towards the gutter and which appeared to Thain to be 'a large quantity of blood'. Most significant was the likelihood that much of the victim's blood had been absorbed into her clothes. Constable Thain helped to lift the corpse onto the ambulance and reported Nichols' back to be 'covered with blood, which, he thought, had run from the neck as far as the waist'. Taken into consideration with Helson's observation at the mortuary it seems likely that the throat wounds had bled mostly into Nichols' clothing rather than onto the ground, or blood had been absorbed from the ground into the clothing.

Not being one to follow logic Llewellyn accounted for his observation of a lack of blood at the scene by a rather confusing assertion at the inquest that, 'nearly all the blood had drained out of the arteries and veins, and collected to a large extent in the loose tissues'. This is not entirely convincing given that there isn't anywhere for such a quantity of blood to collect among the tissues of the neck – unless of course blood had run into the trachea or oesophagus and there is no mention of that. The abdominal wound also has to be considered with regard to blood loss, but in spite of the enormity of the laceration it is doubtful if other than relatively small vessels would have been severed and thus there would be little haemorrhage into the abdominal cavity from wounds to the skin and muscle. It is more likely that Llewellyn simply did not do his job properly at the murder scene or on his first visit to the mortuary, and it was left to the recollections and notes of others to provide a more reliable record of circumstances.

Fortunately, the police were not confused by their surgeon and were quite convinced that Nichols had been murdered where she was found and the evidence for this is strong. Apart from anything else, the timing of Nichols' death would not have allowed her to be transported from elsewhere. She was almost certainly in the final stages of dying when Cross and Paul discovered her and even when Neil came across her body moments later, blood was still 'oozing from a wound in the throat', which really does suggest that she was killed probably within a few minutes of that moment. Llewellyn was of the opinion that; 'the deceased's wounds were sufficient to cause instantaneous death'. This being so, there is a strong likelihood that Cross disturbed the killer – it is also worth recording that both Cross and Paul were eliminated as suspects as were several slaughtermen and the much mentioned 'leather apron' or John Pizer around whom a certain amount of myth has accumulated.

With regard to the abdominal wounds, there was one very deep and jagged cut located four inches in from Nichols' left side, several cuts running across the abdomen, and three or four similar cuts running downwards on the right side. Apparently all wounds had been made by the same knife used 'violently and downwards'. It would have been more useful if the surgeon had mentioned the position of the cuts relative to surface body anatomy or even to the midline, so we cannot be entirely sure as to the location and dimensions of the wounds. Indeed, further confusion is provided by a report by Inspector Spratling written on the same day of the murder, in which he describes the wounds as, one imagines, Llewellyn described them as he examined the body in the mortuary.[24] According to Spratling's description, the abdomen had been cut open from a point just below the centre of the ribcage and along the right side to the left of the stomach to a point under the pelvis. The wound was jagged and cut into the omentum, the large fatty membrane attached to and beneath the stomach. However, there must have been some confusion of understanding when Spratling made his notes, later reiterated in a report by Swanson, since a cut to the left of the stomach could not run down the right side of the body, whereas a cut to the right side of the stomach from the base of the sternum could indeed travel down the left side of the abdominal midline towards the pubis.[25] There could have been some confusion of terminology between 'stomach' and 'abdomen' in the course of Spratling's note taking. In any event, it appears from this description that the wound was much larger than might have been imagined from the information given at the inquest. Whether or not Llewellyn kept better records that he detailed at the inquest we shall probably never know.

Some of the wording used by Llewellyn is also ambiguous. In the process of inflicting the abdominal cuts, Llewellyn suggests that the knife was used 'downwards' and from this one is entitled to infer that he meant either that the knife was held vertically in the killer's hand with the tip of the blade downwards so that it was almost perpendicular to the victim's skin when the cuts were made, or that the direction of the cuts was downwards with reference to the orientation of the body. A knife held vertically would likely result in jagged cuts of the type described by the surgeon and a deep cut with a vertically held knife would be expected to lacerate the intestines. Llewellyn makes no mention of damage to any internal organs at the inquest, although Spratling's report confirms the presence of such damage. Llewellyn had already qualified the direction of the cuts by reference to 'downwards' so it is probable that this was his intention in all cases. In fact, given the limited space in which the killer was attempting to operate a vertically held blade would be a distinct disadvantage as well as being not entirely natural under such circumstances. Llewellyn also made it quite clear that the smaller abdominal cuts were made from left to right and this was the basis upon which he concluded that the assailant was left-handed. However, it is fairly likely that Nichols was lying on the ground when the killer commenced the abdominal mutilation after lifting her skirts so unless it could be determined where he was positioned at the time the cuts were made it is impossible to determine the handedness of the assailant. In all probability the killer stood to one side of his victim, but which side? An assailant positioned to Nichols' right would naturally draw the knife towards him from left to right across her abdomen, and if he knelt on the other side of his victim then the cuts would run from right to left, but in either case he could be right or left-handed. In a report by Swanson dated 19 October 1888 the Chief Inspector noted that; 'At first [Llewellyn] was of the opinion that the wounds were caused by a left-handed person but he is now doubtful'.

Llewellyn suggested that the murderer would have been occupied for four or five minutes, and that one man could have inflicted the wounds. All injuries were made by the same instrument using a long bladed stout knife and that the killer must have had 'some rough anatomical knowledge' in that he knew where to attack the 'vital parts'. These comments seem reasonable enough, but all things considered Llewellyn did not make a very good job of his investigation into the circumstances of Mary Ann Nichols' death and it is probably fortunate that she was the only Ripper victim that he examined otherwise matters might have become even more confused.

Because the mutilations to Nichols were not as extensive as those inflicted upon some subsequent victims, it has often been suggested that the Ripper gained in confidence and motivation with each murder so that he progressively went from simply killing his victims to extensively mutilating them. This is superficially plausible, but it is flawed by virtue of the locations at which this and subsequent murders took place. By electing to kill and mutilate in public places there was every chance that the perpetrator would be disturbed in the course of his actions. Thus, in instances where there is no mutilation or only partial mutilation of a victim, there is no certainty as to whether it was not his intention to mutilate, or whether he was merely disturbed before being able to progress. If the deep abdominal wound to Nichols was of the dimensions described in Spratling's report then the probability exists that the killer was in the process of gaining access to the abdominal organs when he was disturbed.

We know from evidence given at the inquest by Constable Neil that the victim was 'lying on her back with her clothes disarranged', thus it seems that the killer lifted Nichols' clothing and held it up to expose as much of her abdomen as possible in order to make the cuts. The jagged cut started at a point beneath the sternum, but because of the nature of Nichols' clothing, and even though her stays were loose, merely throwing her skirts up and over her body would not have given him sufficient access and he would need to hold them aloft to allow as much room as possible to work. The superficial cuts to the abdomen may have resulted from attempts by the killer to insert the knife beneath her clothing. There is no evidence to suggest that any of the victim's clothing was cut during an attack. It is also worth mentioning that the Ripper was not a man to conceal his activities as we shall later see, thus I think he would not have pulled down skirts that he had previously thrown up merely to cover up what he had done. The Ripper was disturbed in this matter and immediately dropped the skirts that he was holding aloft. That the killer's approach was imperfect can also be to some extent attributed to the darkness in Buck's Row at the time of the murder.

As far as the events leading up to the death of Mary Ann Nichols are concerned there is very little around which to speculate. There were no witnesses to her whereabouts after Holland saw her at 2.30am and no one saw or heard anything in connection with the attack. According to the coroner in his summing up as reported in *The Times* on 24 September 1888:

The condition in which the body was found appeared to prove conclusively that the deceased was killed on the exact spot in which she was found. There was not a trace of blood anywhere, except at the spot where her neck was lying, this circumstance being sufficient to justify the assumption that the injuries to the throat were inflicted when the woman was on the ground, while the state of her clothing and the absence of any blood about her legs equally proved that the abdominal injuries were inflicted while she was still in the same position. Again, the deceased could not have been killed long before she was found. Constable Neil was positive that he was at the spot half an hour before, and then neither the body was there nor was any one about. Even if Paul were mistaken in the movement of the chest, Neil found her right arm still warm, and even Dr. Llewellyn, who saw the body about a quarter of an hour afterwards, found the body and lower extremities still warm, notwithstanding the loss of blood and abdominal injuries and that those extremities had been uncovered. It seemed astonishing, at first thought, that the culprit should escape detection, for there must surely have been marks of blood about his person. If, however, blood was principally on his hands, the presence of so many slaughter-houses in the neighbourhood would make the frequenters of that spot familiar with blood-stained clothes and hands, and his appearance might in that way have failed to attract attention while he passed from Buck's-row in the twilight into Whitechapel-road and was lost sight of in the morning's market traffic.

After a short consultation the jury returned a verdict of wilful murder against some person or persons unknown. There is every indication from the circumstances of this murder that Mary Ann Nichols was a victim of Jack the Ripper and in my opinion she was his first victim in what was to become a series. In spite of the apparent absence of significant findings at the scene of Nichols' murder, the central elements of the Ripper's subsequently established *modus operandi* are clearly present and they can be outlined at this early stage to be considered when examining the details of other murders. The Ripper selected Nichols at random, engaged with her by negotiating for sex, and, at an opportune moment on route to a suitable location, he attacked her from behind with precisely delivered wounds from a very sharp knife that severed the major blood vessels on the left side of the neck, and at the second attempt sliced through the windpipe. The attack was so clinically accomplished and the victim so much taken by surprise that she was unable to struggle or utter a sound before the fatal wounds were delivered and she slumped to the floor. With his victim lying on the ground he undertook mutilations to the abdomen that probably commenced before she was even unconscious, but with a severed larynx and shock from fast haemorrhaging blood vessels there was nothing she could do by way of defence. On this occasion the Ripper was disturbed before he could complete his work but he managed to slip away effortlessly, unseen and unheard, into the miasmic maze of Whitechapel. He was skilled enough to avoid being covered in the blood of his victim, but if by chance his activities left him contaminated, perhaps his left arm might be bloody, then he knew how to conceal the fact. Even from the first murder in the series there is every indication that the Ripper knew his business well; he was a man with the knowledge of how to kill with precision and to such an extent that he needed little light and could almost murder by touch. The Ripper was a cutter not a stabber; a cool operator and by no means a lunatic. There can be little doubt that he was a killer before Mary Ann Nichols had the misfortune to encounter him, but she was the first of the Whitechapel murder victims to die by his blade.

2.3.2 Annie Chapman (1841-88)

Jack the Ripper's murder of Mary Nichols without detection on the streets of Whitechapel was either an amazing feat or an incredible stroke of good luck. Probability suggests that luck eventually runs out and the Ripper's next act of butchery undoubtedly brought him even closer to being caught in the act. Early on the morning of Saturday 8 September 1888 the mutilated body of Annie Chapman was found in the back yard of number 29 Hanbury Street Whitechapel.

Annie Chapman was born Eliza Anne Smith in 1841 in Paddington. She married John Chapman in 1869 and had three children. The marriage broke up circa 1982, allegedly as a consequence of her alcoholism and immoral behaviour. John Chapman died in 1886. Annie Chapman was only 5ft tall; she was stout with dark brown wavy hair, blue eyes, and a thick nose. At the time of her death she wore a long black figured coat that came down to her knees, a black skirt, a brown bodice, another bodice, 2 petticoats, a large pocket worn under the skirt and tied about the waist with strings (empty when found), lace-up boots, red and white striped woollen stockings, and a neckerchief (white with red border – folded tri-corner and knotted at the front of her neck). Chapman's possessions were; three brass rings (missing after the murder), a scrap of muslin, one small toothcomb, one comb in a paper case, and a scrap of envelope containing two pills.[26]

The wounds to Chapman are detailed in Diagram 2 and the location of the murder is illustrated in Map 2 with a complete tabulation of relevant findings in Table 1. Files are archived that relate to the murder of Annie Chapman and to the inquest and police enquiries.[27]

Hanbury Street ran from Commercial Street in the west to Baker's Row in the east. It was a perfect example of the very worst that Whitechapel had to offer and, according to *The Daily Telegraph* on 10 September 1888, 'respectable people are accustomed to avoid it'. Hanbury Street was inhabited by 'dock labourers, market porters, the tenants of common lodging houses, and a certain number of cabinet makers' who supplied the furniture establishments of Curtain Road. By accounts, knives were numerous, violence commonplace, and flesh wounds frequent in 'these squalid parts of the metropolis' in which there were also 'many scenes of degradation and immorality'. The block in which number 29 was located was towards the west end of Hanbury Street and enclosed by Wilkes Street and Brick Lane to the west and east respectively. To the north of and behind the block was the Black Eagle Brewery. The inquest into Chapman's death opened on Monday 10 September with newspaper reporting commencing the following day.

At the inquest the coroner Wynne Baxter, eloquent as ever, gave a description of Hanbury Street in his summary of events:

This place is a fair sample of a large number of houses in the neighbourhood. It was built, like hundreds of others, for the Spitalfields weavers, and when hand-looms were driven out by steam and power, these were converted into dwellings for the poor. Its size is about such as a superior artisan would occupy in the country, but its condition is such as would to a certainty leave it without a tenant.

Number 29, in common with other houses along Hanbury Street, was a four-storeyed dilapidation with a cellar, a ground floor and three more above and there were suggestions that it was originally occupied by silk weavers.[28] Hanbury Street is marked on the 1894-6 Ordnance Survey Town Plan and on the 1873-80 map and the exact location of number 29 can be established.[29] At each level above ground there was a front and a rear room, each with windows either overlooking Hanbury Street or the yard to the rear. To the left of the house as viewed from the street there was a single entrance door from the street leading into an enclosed corridor with a bare and rough floor that ran the length of the house and to the yard at the rear, and there was a single front window at this level. To the rear of the corridor there was another door that opened into the yard and three steps down into the yard. At the far end of the yard there was a shed and beside that a privy. On the 1873-80 maps a building is recorded at the northern end of the yard and extending across the yard from fence to fence.

The external width of 29 Hanbury Street is estimated from scaled maps as being some 17ft and the depth of the building from street to yard some 35ft. Internal stairs and landings would have significantly reduced the internal dimensions of the rooms, and 10ft by 15ft may be a generous estimate. The yard measured some 17ft wide by 30ft excluding the shed and WC, which combined were probably in the region of 17ft wide by 10ft deep.[30] The yard was separated from the neighbour's yards on either side by close wooden fencing, about 5ft 6in high. There was no means of exit from the yard other than by the passageway to Hanbury Street. The floor of the yard was paved roughly with stones in some places, the remainder being earth. The door to the yard from the corridor opened outwards into the yard and swung against the paling fence. The stone steps from the passageway projected into the yard and were some three feet from the fencing to the left side of the yard; that forming the boundary with number 27 Hanbury Street. It was in the vicinity of this 3ft gap between the steps and the fence that Chapman's body was discovered.

The official transcript of inquest proceedings is not available among the records and it has been necessary to construct events on the basis of reports of the inquest given in daily newspapers supplemented from other sources. These are not always accurate and there is some degree of selective reporting and editing so wherever possible, more than one source has been checked and a composite account given.

Mrs Amelia Richardson rented half of 29 Hanbury Street and by her testimony at the inquest this included the cellar, the ground floor, and the first floor. Richardson carried on a packaging business from the premises, using the cellar as a workshop, and the shed in the yard was used to store wood for the packing cases. Richardson almost certainly sublet the rooms that she rented and at the time of the murder no fewer than seventeen persons occupied 29 Hanbury Street. No one lived in the cellar, but Mrs Harriet Hardiman and her sixteen-year-old son occupied the ground floor. Hardiman used the front room as a 'cats' meat shop' and the rear ground floor room as living accommodation. The front room of the first floor housed Richardson and her grandson Thomas, who was fourteen, and the rear of the first floor was occupied by the elderly Mr Walker and his twenty-seven year old 'weak minded but inoffensive' son. Walker was a 'maker of lawn tennis boots'. In the front room of the second floor lived Mr Thompson and his wife and their adopted little girl. Thompson was a carman, or cart driver, at the market. Two unmarried sisters, named Cooksley, occupied the rear of the second floor and they worked in a cigar factory.[31] An old woman, Mrs Sarah Cox, occupied the rear room of the third floor at the charity of Richardson, although one is given to wonder about this arrangement since Richardson only rented the lower half of the house. In the last room of the house, the third floor front room, there lived John Davis, his wife, and their three sons. Davis was also a carman employed at Leadenhall Market and it was he who discovered Chapman's body. Davis had only lived at 29 Hanbury Street for two weeks.

By her own account, Amelia Richardson had occupied the house for 15 years and some of her lodgers had been there for 12 years. She said that most of her lodgers worked at the fish market or in the Spitalfields Market; some carmen left home as early as 1.00am while others went to work at 4.00am and 5.00am to work at the markets. She confirmed that 'the place is open all night and anyone can get in', an admission confirmed by Davis who said that, 'neither of the doors' at either end of the corridor from street to yard 'was able to be locked', and he had 'never seen them locked'. When questioned by the coroner at the inquest, Richardson was emphatic in her denial that she had any knowledge that a part of the house or yard was used at any time for immoral purposes. She said that she 'never missed anything, and had such confidence in her neighbours that she had left the doors of some rooms unlocked', an action that had resulted in the theft of a saw and a hammer from the cellar some time previously.

Davis discovered Chapman's body after having a cup of tea and going downstairs to the back yard. He found the door to the yard shut, but that to the street was wide open and thrown against the wall, which was apparently not unusual. He opened the back door at some time shortly before 6.00am and stood in the entrance. According to his testimony reported in *The Daily Telegraph* on 11 September 1888:

Directly I opened the door I saw a woman lying down in the lefthand recess, between the stone steps and the fence. She was on her back, with her legs towards the wood shed. The clothes were up to her groins. I did not go into the yard, but left the house by the front door, and called the attention of two men to the circumstances.

Davis went to Commercial Street police station to report what he had seen and then returned to 29 Hanbury Street. Excluding the victim and her killer, Davis was not the first to enter the yard that morning; Amelia Richardson's son, John, arrived at between 4.45am and 4.50am. John Richardson assisted his mother in her packaging business and went to see if the cellar was secure; he routinely checked the cellar on market mornings after the recent theft. When John Richardson arrived, the door from the street was closed and he lifted the latch to enter. The door to the yard was also closed and he opened it and sat on the middle step with his feet on the flags of the yard and cut from his boot a piece of leather that caused him some discomfort. He did not enter the yard but could see that the padlock to the cellar was secure from where he was on the steps. After cutting off the leather he tied up his boot and went out of the house and to the market. He did not close the back door, it closed itself, and he shut the front door as he left. Richardson was there for no more than three minutes and although it was only just getting light, he 'could see all over the place'. To some extent this is confirmed by the fact that Richardson was able to cut a piece of leather from his boot and see the padlock in place on the cellar door without moving from the steps. Richardson was asked if he saw anything outside to which he replied that; 'I could not have failed to notice the deceased had she been lying there then'. John Richardson later saw the body from an adjoining yard, two or three minutes before the doctor came, having been told about the murder by someone at the market. He would have been seated on the steps very close to where the body was found and it is almost certain that Chapman's body was not there at 4.50am. According to meteorological records, dawn broke at 4.51am and the sun rose at 5.25am on the morning of 8 September 1888.[32]

John Richardson rather contradicted his mother's general account of activity in the yard by suggesting that he had been to the house and in the passage at all hours of the night and had seen lots of strangers there, both men and women, but had turned them out. This suggests that his mother was rather more concerned about being rebuked by the coroner and in the newspapers for allowing such activities than she was about telling the truth about immoral activities in her own back yard. John Richardson was sent by the coroner to get the knife that he used to trim his boot in order that the court could assess its candidacy as the murder weapon. In fact, the knife was 'a much-worn dessert knife'. It was handed to the police on the instruction of the coroner, although it did not feature any further in the investigation.

Albert Cadosch, a carpenter, lived next door to the murder scene at number 27 and gave testimony to the inquest. At 5.15am on the morning of 8 September he got up and at about 5.20am went into the yard. 'Going into the yard' was a euphemism for visiting the outside privy, which most houses had at that time. His testimony to the inquest as reported in *The Daily Telegraph* on 20 September 1888 is as follows:

As I returned towards the back door I heard a voice say "No" just as I was going through the door. It was not in our yard, but I should think it came from the yard of number 29. I, however, cannot say on which side it came from. I went indoors, but returned to the yard about three or four minutes afterwards. While coming back I heard a sort of fall against the fence which divides my yard from that of 29. It seemed as if something touched the fence suddenly.

The coroner asked Cadosch whether he had looked over the fence to see what had made the sound, but he had not, nor had he heard any noise while he was at the end of the yard and specifically no rustling of clothes. Cadosch then went back into the house and from there to work, and as he passed by Spitalfields Church Clock the time was 5.32am. Spitalfields Church was around 175yds from 29 Hanbury Street. In answer to a question from the foreman, Cadosch said that the fence dividing the yards was around 5ft 6in to 6ft high. He again confirmed that he did not have the curiosity to look over then fence and added that it was not unusual to hear thumps against the palings since packing cases were made next door. Additional inquest testimony reported in *The Times* on 20 September 1888 suggests that Cadosch needed to return to the yard because he 'had been under an operation at the hospital'.

Before considering Cadosch's testimony in detail it is necessary to examine it in relation to that of another witness who may have actually seen Chapman in the company of her killer. Mrs Elizabeth Long gave evidence shortly before Cadosch on the fourth day of the inquest. Long supposedly left her home at about 5.00am bound for Spitalfields Market. According to her testimony reported in *The Daily Telegraph* on 20 September 1888, on route to the market she passed along Hanbury Street and saw a man and a woman standing outside number 29:

On the right hand side, the same side as the house, I saw a man and a woman standing on the pavement talking. The man's back was turned towards Brick Lane and the woman's was towards the market. They were standing only a few yards nearer Brick Lane from 29 Hanbury Street. I saw the woman's face. Have seen the deceased in the mortuary, and am sure the woman that I saw in Hanbury Street was the deceased. I did not see the man's face, but I noticed that he was dark. He was wearing a brown low-crowned felt hat. I think he had on a dark coat, though I am not certain. By the look of him he seemed to me a man over forty years of age. He appeared to me to be a little taller than the deceased.[33]

In answer to questions from the coroner Long said that she thought the man looked like a foreigner, of shabby appearance.[34] Long did not think the pair were drunk, nor did she think it unusual to see a man and a woman standing there talking to each other at that hour of the day. Long overheard the man say to the woman;

'Will you?' to which she replied; 'Yes'. Long was specific as to the timing of this encounter because the Black Eagle Brewery clock in Brick Lane struck 5.30am just before she got to Hanbury Street, implying that her approach was along Brick Lane. Long reached the Spitalfields Market 'a few minutes after half past'.[35]

The light would have been good by the time Long passed the couple on the pavement on the northern side of the street and, as she approached from east to west along Hanbury Street, the woman would have her face towards Long and the man would have his back towards the witness. Although Long recognised Chapman's corpse at the mortuary as being that of the woman that she had seen in the street, she did not actually know Chapman and had not seen her before, so such an identification can not be entirely reliable. The post mortem details also revealed that Chapman's face was swollen, after she had been partially strangulated, this potentially further confounding identification.

Nonetheless, this is the first possible sighting of Jack the Ripper, which is why it is tempting to place emphasis on Long's testimony. However, her description of the man she saw was not in itself too useful, her only contribution being to suggest that he was below average height and that he may have been a foreigner, but in reality this latter deduction was based on very little of substance; his dark complexion and hair perhaps. Importantly, Long only had a rear view of the man and she admitted that she would not be able to recognise him if she saw him again – she couldn't even say whether or not he had whiskers. If it was the Ripper then her description tells us that he was dark and slightly taller than Chapman's diminutive height of 5ft 0in, placing her killer probably at around 5ft 2in. His brown, low crowned felt hat and dark coat were hardly of descriptive value. Long estimated the age of the man to be over forty but it is difficult to see how she arrived at this conclusion based upon what little she could see. In a sense her description would only be confirmed if there was another witness to some future Ripper murder. We must also bear in mind that witnesses were unlikely to say that they had seen the killer's face even if they had done so, and would certainly be reluctant to suggest that they would recognise him again for fear of placing their own life in danger.

Much has been speculated and written about the testimony of Long and Cadosch because both may have witnessed events involving Chapman, but there is appreciable variance between reported timings even though both witnesses made reference to clocks. It is quite possible that one or both of these witnesses saw or heard events that were nothing to do with Chapman but it is always tempting to interpret such evidence with some degree of subjectivity and even to distort matters to force the reconciliation of details. Various writers have sought to isolate movements to the last minute, but this is generally pointless without accurate reference points and even if an event happened dead on the stroke of the hour by one church clock there is no saying that it told exactly the same time as another clock by which another witness made a further crucial observation. Little reliance can be placed on timings down to the exact minute reported by any witnesses, especially when given well after the event. A possible exception might be the timings given by police officers and police surgeons who were aware of the importance of times and recorded such but even so there can be discrepancies since the accuracy of timepieces was not what it is today. Realistically, five-minute interval timing is probably the best attainable accuracy when assessing witness reports where reliance is placed upon different time sources, but relative timing is probably more reliable than absolute timing.

The coroner in his summing up seemed to prefer Long's timing as opposed to Cadosch's recollections, but for no good reason. Perhaps he thought that because Long had seen Chapman and her killer he should place more credence on her version. By her own account, Long left her home in Church Row at 5.00am and passed the couple in Hanbury Street over half an hour later.[36] Long's most likely route to Spitalfields Market from Church Row would have taken her south into Hare Street then west into Brick Lane and south past the Black Eagle Brewery and into Hanbury Street. This would have been the quickest and most direct route for her to take to work and the journey would total some 940yds, which she would cover within 10mins at average walking speed.[37] To complete the journey in 15mins would necessitate Long dawdling or stopping off on route, although there is no mention of this, and the implication that she may have taken half an hour suggests that there is an error in reporting, since it would have been far more reasonable to assume that she left home sometime shortly after 5.15am. Chisholm and others have used Long's estimate of when she left home to calculate the time at which she reached Hanbury Street and suggested that she arrived there at 5.15am and mistook the brewery clock striking 5.15am for 5.30am, but I think it is highly unlikely that she would have been fifteen minutes out.[38] It is perhaps better to back-calculate timing from Long's arrival at Spitalfields market which she suggested was 'a few minutes after half-past five' – in all probability she aimed to start work at 5.30am as indeed, did Cadosch. The distance from Spitalfields Market entrance to the corner of Hanbury Street and Brick Lane is some 270yds, which at an average walking speed can be covered in a little less than three minutes assuming no stops on route.[39] This would place Long exactly where she said she was at 5.30am when the brewery clock struck and her sighting of the woman and the man between 29 Hanbury Street and Brick Lane is thus corroborated by two timings – one when Long heard the brewery clock and another when she arrived at the market. The Spitalfields Christ Church clock would have been visible to Long if she entered the market from Commercial Street although she was not obliged to have used that entrance. There were other routes that Long could have taken from Church Row to Spitalfields Market that would have brought her into Hanbury Street at a more easterly point meaning that she would walk a greater distance along Hanbury Street. Such routes are more convoluted and would undoubtedly take a little longer to walk but it is difficult to see why anyone on route to work would deliberately take anything other than the most direct and quickest route.

I see no reason to reconcile the testimony and timing of Long and Cadosch, nor do I think that we have to believe the timing of one witness at the expense of the other. It is far more likely that the testimony of one witness is irrelevant, although such could actually apply to both witnesses. Cadosch saw nothing but heard something, and Long identified the body of a dead woman, whom she did not know, as the woman she had seen standing in the vicinity of 29 Hanbury Street the same morning as Chapman was killed. Although Long was 'sure the woman [she] saw in Hanbury Street was the deceased' we shall see time and again that there is no such thing as certainly regarding witness observations.

The timing of the murder according to the Police Surgeon Dr George Bagster Phillips further confuses matters since he estimated that Chapman died at least two hours prior to his initial examination of the body at 6.30am thus suggesting that what witnesses saw or heard was nothing connected with the murder. If the surgeon was correct then Chapman was dead in the yard at Hanbury Street well before Cadosch visited the privy and before Long entered Hanbury Street, and Davis must have overlooked the corpse when sitting beside it on the steps at 4.45am. However, there are reasons why Phillips may have got his estimate of the time of Chapman's death significantly incorrect.

On balance I am inclined to the opinion that what Cadosch heard was nothing to do with the murder. There is a tendency to think that the backyards of these houses were wide and long but they were not. The distance from back door to privy was probably no more than twenty feet and each yard was a little less than that in width. It would be quite possible to hear sounds from other than the yard next door and in addition there was a packing case manufacturer's yard over the fence at the end of the yard of number 27. Bearing in mind that number 29 Hanbury Street was also a house filled with humanity, and, as Amelia Richardson told the newspapers, some of the residents at the rear of the house slept with their windows open, it becomes quite easy to appreciate that Cadosch may have heard a woman speak from within the house and not necessarily from outside in the yard.[40] It could also be the case that another couple were active in the yard of number 29 at 5.20am and Chapman could even have taken another man into the yard before meeting her killer when she emerged at 5.30am. This is all speculation too far, but serves to illustrate how many alternative scenarios may exist to explain what Cadosch heard in the yard of number 29, and without any corroborative sighting, the source of what he heard can be no more than conjecture. We should also not forget that witnesses frequently give their accounts in the knowledge of what happened thus their observations and recollections are invariably tainted by what they *thought* might have taken place.

There thus exists a strong possibility that what Cadosch witnessed was unconnected with the murder of Annie Chapman, but that the timing of both witnesses is in fact correct and this is one instance when a detailed examination of the timing might prove useful because the timings are relative and not absolute. Although we still have no guarantee of accuracy of timekeeping or estimates, it must be said that the workers of the day were probably slightly better at being aware of the time than we are today even though most of them would not have had wristwatches. There was no shortage of church and other public clocks by which they could estimate whether they were going to be late for work and Long clearly had an established daily routine because in testimony to the inquest she confirmed that it was not unusual to see 'lots of [men and women] standing [in Hanbury Street] in the morning', even at that hour of the day, and she was quite certain as to the time. So, if we ignore the testimony relating to Cadosch's experiences in the back yard then we can concentrate on timing and all the indicators suggest that Cadosch left 27 Hanbury Street before Chapman and her killer and Elizabeth Long appeared in Hanbury Street, which is why he saw no one else when he set off for work. It would take Cadosch three minutes to walk the 265yds from 27 Hanbury Street to Christ Church and by his testimony he looked at the clock and saw that it was 5.32am. By back estimation he must have left his home at very close to 5.29am. Long said the brewery clock struck 5.30am just *before* she reached Hanbury Street as she approached from Brick Lane, so she would have arrived in Hanbury Street shortly after Cadosch had left for work and disappeared from view at something like 5.31am. When Long turned the corner from Brick Lane into Hanbury Street she saw a man and a woman who were most likely Chapman and her killer a short distance away from Brick Lane. She continued to walk to work without turning around to look at the couple and it would have taken her around three minutes to walk from the corner of Hanbury Street and Brick Lane to Spitalfields Market which would be consistent with her estimate of arriving at work a few minutes after half-past five and shortly after Cadosch. As soon as Long passed them by, for they had clearly completed negotiations, the man and woman could have entered 29 Hanbury Street.

I doubt that they would have been in the yard for more than a few seconds before Chapman was attacked. The Ripper was not inclined to delay his purpose once he was alone with the victim and from the killer's point of view that is logical enough and of course he no longer had the protection of darkness. Chapman's throat would have been cut by 5.35am and his work completed by 5.45am at which time he left the scene. The only slight reservation that I have with this scenario is the suddenness of the appearance of Chapman with a man within a minute or so of Cadosch leaving number 27. People do not suddenly appear although it could be that Cadosch simply did not notice them or maybe they were in the vicinity – in Brick Lane for instance and not visible to Cadosch – or not together and engaged in conversation when he left for work.

Speculation aside, there is little doubt that Chapman died between 4.45am when John Richardson sat on the step inches from where the body would have been and 5.45am, some fifteen minutes before 6.00am when Davis discovered the corpse. If we take account of testimony from Long, then it seems likely that Chapman met her end between 5.30am and 5.45am and more likely closer to 5.35am. That Davis heard nothing while he drank his cup of tea after waking up at 5.45am is thus of no surprise; the business was probably complete by the time he heard Spitalfields Church clock strike a quarter to the hour.

When asked how long it would have taken the killer to carry out the injuries to the body, Dr Phillips replied, as reported in *The Daily Telegraph* on 15 September 1888, that:

I think I can guide you by saying that I myself could not have performed all the injuries I saw on that woman, and effect them, even without a struggle, under a quarter of an hour. If I had done it in a deliberate way, such as would fall to the duties of a surgeon, it would probably have taken me the best part of an hour.

Phillips was perhaps being a little over generous in his estimate. The Ripper certainly did not wait until life was extinct in his victim's before he commenced mutilation so after cutting Chapman's throat he would have immediately turned his attention to her abdomen. With a sharp knife and some basic knowledge, the mutilations undertaken to Chapman could probably have been completed within ten minutes from when her throat was cut leaving the killer ample time to calmly exit the scene. There is no evidence to suggest that he was disturbed during his activities although he must have been aware of the threat of being interrupted which must have made the completion of his work more urgent. The Ripper was indeed a calm and focussed operator, who seemed to have no fear of being interrupted – fairly characteristic of the psychopathic personality. There can be little doubt that had he been interrupted during his activities, or had anyone made an attempt to apprehend him, then he would not have hesitated to kill them as well.

Thus, we have an indication that Annie Chapman was killed in the yard at the back of 29 Hanbury Street up to half an hour before her body was discovered at 6.00am, even though Dr Phillips suggested the time of Chapman's death to be at least an hour earlier than that, a point we shall examine later. Detective Inspector Joseph Chandler arrived at the scene at 6.10am and according to the report of the third session of the inquest published the following day in *The Daily Telegraph* on 14 September 1888 he described what he found:

I was on duty in Commercial Street. At the corner of Hanbury Street I saw several men running. I beckoned to them. One of them said, "Another woman has been murdered." I at once went with him to 29, Hanbury Street, and through the passage to the yard. There was no one in the yard. I saw the body of a woman lying on the ground on her back. Her head was towards the back wall of the house, nearly two feet from the wall, at the bottom of the steps, but six or nine inches away from them. The face was turned to the right side, and the left arm was resting on the left breast. The right hand was lying down the right side. Deceased's legs were drawn up, and the clothing was above the knees. A portion of the intestines, still connected with the body, were lying above the right shoulder, with some pieces of skin. There were also some pieces of skin on the left shoulder. The body was lying parallel with the fencing dividing the two yards. I remained there and sent for the divisional surgeon, Mr Phillips, and to the police station for the ambulance and for further assistance. When the constables arrived I cleared the passage of people, and saw that no one touched the body until the doctor arrived. I obtained some sacking to cover it before the arrival of the surgeon who came at half-past six o'clock, and directed that it should be removed to the mortuary.

In answer to queries raised by the coroner, Chandler confirmed that there were no signs of a struggle and that there was no evidence to suggest that anyone had climbed over the rather insubstantial paling fence that may have just about supported the weight of a man. He confirmed that there were some bloodstains on the palings near to the body and a few spots on the back wall near the head of the deceased 2ft from the ground; the largest spot being the size of a sixpence and all were close together. There were no bloodstains elsewhere and specifically none in any of the other yards. Having searched the clothing at the mortuary Chandler confirmed that there were bloodstains around the neck, inside and outside of Chapman's black jacket and two or three spots on the left sleeve. There was also a little blood on the outside of her black skirt, but little on her petticoats, and both bodices were bloodstained around the neck. There was no blood on her stockings.

Chandler gave his opinion that there were no signs from the clothing that a struggle had taken place. None of the clothing was torn or cut in any way.

Chapman's body was removed by ambulance to the mortuary of the Whitechapel Union Infirmary and was received by Robert Mann, the mortuary attendant at 7.00am. Mann, an inmate pauper of the workhouse, remained at the mortuary until Dr Phillips arrived, and the mortuary remained locked apart from when two nurses, resident nurse Mary Elizabeth Simonds and senior nurse Frances Wright, from the infirmary arrived to undress the body.[41] The coroner did not lose an opportunity to comment on such inappropriate arrangements and his remarks were reported in *The Daily Telegraph* on 14 September 1888:

The fact is that Whitechapel does not posses a mortuary. The place is not a mortuary at all. We have no right to take a body there. It is simply a shed belonging to the workhouse officials. Juries have over and over again reported the matter to the District Board of Works. The East End, which requires mortuaries more than anywhere else, is most deficient. Bodies drawn out of the river have to be put in boxes, and very often they are brought to this workhouse arrangement all the way from Wapping. A workhouse inmate is not the proper man to take care of such an important matter.

The body of Mary Ann Nichols had also been taken to the dead house of the Whitechapel Union Infirmary just over a week previously and the Nichols and Chapman inquests overlapped. Although Nichols was the first to be murdered, Baxter's castigation of Mann for allowing Chapman to be undressed in the absence of a medical witness came first, and three days later the hapless mortuary attendant was in the firing line again for allowing Nichols' body to be similarly stripped. In fairness to Mann, both bodies had been stripped before his testimony was dealt with on the third day of the Chapman inquest on 13 September. On day three of the Nichols inquest on 17 September Baxter said of Mann; 'It appears the mortuary keeper is subject to fits, and neither his memory nor statements are reliable'. Simonds testified that Inspector Chandler had instructed the body to be stripped and washed, which he denied, but in fact, the instruction came from the Clerk of the Parish Guardians.

Dr Phillips then gave his evidence and I have cited the details of his testimony according to that reported on 14 and 20 September in *The Times* with reference to that reported in *The Daily Telegraph* on the same dates in order to give as accurate an account as possible of the medical evidence on days three and four of the inquest. At the third session of the inquest on 13 September 1888, Phillips proceeded as follows:

On Saturday last I was called by the police at 6.20 a.m. to 29, Hanbury-street, and arrived at half-past six. I found the body of the deceased lying in the yard on her back, on the left hand of the steps that lead from the passage. The head was about 6in in front of the level of the bottom step, and the feet were towards a shed at the end of the yard. The left arm was across the left breast, and the legs were drawn up, the feet resting on the ground, and the knees turned outwards. The face was swollen and turned on the right side, and the tongue protruded between the front teeth, but not beyond the lips; it was much swollen. The small intestines and other portions were lying on the right side of the body on the ground above the right shoulder, but attached. There was a large quantity of blood, with a part of the stomach above the left shoulder. I searched the yard and found a small piece of coarse muslin, a small-tooth comb, and a pocket-comb, in a paper case, near the railing. They had apparently been arranged there. I also discovered various other articles, which I handed to the police. The body was cold, except that there was a certain remaining heat, under the intestines, in the body. Stiffness of the limbs was not marked, but it was commencing. The throat was dissevered deeply. I noticed that the incision of the skin was jagged, and reached right round the neck. On the back wall of the house, between the steps and the palings, on the left side, about 18in from the ground, there were about six patches of blood, varying in size from a sixpenny piece to a small point, and on the wooden fence there were smears of blood, corresponding to where the head of the deceased laid, and immediately above the part where the blood had mainly flowed from the neck, which was well clotted. Having received instructions soon after two o'clock on Saturday afternoon, I went to the labour-yard of the Whitechapel Union for the purpose of further examining the body and making the usual post-mortem investigation. I was surprised to find that the body had been stripped and was laying ready on the table. It was under great disadvantage I made my examination.

There then followed further criticism of the mortuary facilities before medical evidence continued:

The body had been attended to since its removal to the mortuary, and probably partially washed. I noticed a bruise over the right temple. There was a bruise under the clavicle, and there were two distinct bruises, each the size of a man's thumb, on the fore part of the chest. The stiffness of the limbs was then well-marked. The finger nails were turgid. There was an old scar of long standing on the left of the frontal bone. On the left side the stiffness was more noticeable, and especially in the fingers, which were partly closed. There was an abrasion over the bend of the first joint of the ring finger, and there were distinct markings of a ring or rings - probably the latter. There were small sores on the fingers. The head being opened showed that the membranes of the brain were opaque and the veins loaded with blood of a dark character. There was a large quantity of fluid between the membranes and the substance of the brain. The brain substance was unusually firm, and its cavities also contained a large amount of fluid. The throat had been severed. The incisions of the skin indicated that they had been made from the left side of the neck on a line with the angle of the jaw, carried entirely round and again in front of the neck, and ending at a point about midway between the jaw and the sternum or breast bone on the right hand. There were two distinct clean cuts on the body of the vertebrae on the left side of the spine. They were parallel to each other, and separated by about half an inch. The muscular structures between the side processes of bone of the vertebrae had an appearance as if an attempt had been made to separate the bones of the neck. There are various other mutilations of the body, but I am of opinion that they occurred subsequently to the death of the woman and to the large escape of blood from the neck.

Phillips then expressed reluctance to describe the extent of the abdominal mutilations in open court. His reasoning being that he was quite able to give the cause if death and the mutilations having been inflicted after death were of no consequence in this regard. This was an extraordinary suggestion and the coroner, Wynne Baxter, did not accept his logic saying:

The object of the inquiry is not only to ascertain the cause of death, but the means by which it occurred. Any mutilation which took place afterwards may suggest the character of the man who did it. Possibly you can give us the conclusions to which you have come respecting the instrument used.

After a further exchange the coroner agreed to postpone detailing the injuries and Phillips gave his opinion that 'breathing was interfered with previous to death, and that death arose from syncope, or failure of the heart's action, in consequence of the loss of blood caused by the severance of the throat'. In answer to questions from the coroner Phillips confirmed that a single knife was used by the killer to inflict all of the injuries and that the instrument used was at least six to eight inches in length, perhaps longer, and very sharp. He did not think that any instrument used by a military man, such as a bayonet, would have inflicted such injuries but agreed that; 'They could have been done by such an instrument as a medical man used for post mortem purposes, but the ordinary surgical case might not contain such an instrument'.[42] A slaughterer's knife was also a possible candidate, but those used by cobblers and others in the leather trade would be unlikely to have a long enough blade. Importantly, Phillips was of the opinion that the injuries were probably inflicted by someone who had knowledge of anatomy, saying that; 'anatomical knowledge was only less displayed or indicated in consequence of haste. The person evidently was hindered from making a more complete dissection in consequence of the haste'. The coroner then asked Phillips if the whole of the body was present to which he replied that it was not and that 'portions' were absent from the abdomen. He once again confirmed that some anatomical knowledge was indicated from 'the mode in which they were extracted'. Testimony then moved on to the matter of the time of death and the coroner asked Phillips how long he thought the deceased had been dead when he saw her at 6.30am. Phillips replied that he thought she must have been dead for at least two hours, and probably more; 'but it is right to say that it was a fairly cold morning, and that the body would be more apt to cool rapidly from its having lost the greater portion of its blood'.

Phillips also confirmed the absence about the body of any signs of a struggle and he was positive that Chapman had entered the yard alive and had died at the spot where she was found. He was also of the opinion that she had not taken much alcohol for at least 'some hours before death'. As to her general condition, there was little food in her stomach and there were signs of 'great privation'. Chapman had chronic lung disease and meningeal pathology. Regarding the bruising Phillips suggested that; 'the bruise upon the temple and the bruises in front of the chest were of longer standing, probably of days', but 'the marks on the face were recent, especially about the chin and sides of the jaw'. These bruises of longer standing correlate with the testimony of Amelia Palmer who had earlier seen the injuries and told the inquest that Chapman had been in a fight a week earlier. This contretemps over a bar of soap was confirmed by Chapman's adversary, one Eliza Cooper, who also gave evidence to the inquest.

Phillips was of the opinion that; 'the person who cut the deceased's throat took hold of her by the chin, and then commenced the incision from left to right'. By this action it was further suggested that the victim would be unable to cry out and would be subjected to at least partial suffocation if pressure were to be applied for long enough. Thickening of the victim's tongue was a sign of suffocation and Phillips confirmed his opinion that Chapman was partially strangled.

When the inquest resumed for the fourth session of the inquest on 19 September 1888, with newspaper reports the following day, Phillips was recalled but before asking him to give evidence, the coroner said:

Whatever may be your opinion and objections, it appears to me necessary that all the evidence that you ascertained from the post-mortem examination should be on the records of the Court for various reasons, which I need not enumerate. However painful it may be, it is necessary in the interests of justice.

Phillips was unconvinced and continued to protest that the details of his testimony were 'disgusting' and not relevant and suggested that by making the details public the coroner would be 'thwarting the ends of justice'. The coroner, supported by the Forman of the jury and members of the jury, became increasingly impatient and in the end forced Phillips to detail the abdominal wounds, but only after two women and a number of newspaper messenger boys left the courtroom after being invited to retire by the coroner. Baxter's impatience was palpable:

We have delayed taking this evidence as long as possible, because you said the interests of justice might be served by keeping it back; but it is now a fortnight since this occurred, and I do not see why it should be kept back from the jury any longer.

Phillips capitulated and continued with his testimony, but neither *The Times*, nor *The Daily Telegraph*, nor any other major newspaper printed the details. Both Phillips and the press would be rather less reticent as more of the Whitechapel murders came to inquest. We are indebted to an article in *The Lancet* for providing details of the mutilations to Chapman:

It appears that the abdomen had been entirely laid open; that the intestines, severed from their mesenteric attachments, had been lifted out of the body and placed on the shoulder of the corpse; whilst from the pelvis, the uterus and its appendages, with the upper portion of the vagina and the posterior two thirds of the bladder, had been entirely removed. No trace of these parts could be found and the incisions were cleanly cut, avoiding the rectum, and dividing the vagina low enough to avoid injury to the cervix uteri. Obviously the work was that of an expert - of one, at least, who had such knowledge of anatomical or pathological examinations as to be enabled to secure the pelvic organs with one sweep of the knife, which must therefore, as Mr Phillips pointed out, have been at least 5 inches long.
Certainly the murderer must have done his work quickly; this, again, points to the improbability of anyone but an expert performing the mutilations described in so apparently skilful a manner.[43]

Swanson's report on Chapman's murder of 19 October adds little but confirms the mutilations thus:

Removed from but attached to the body, & placed above right shoulder were a flap of the wall of the belly & "Pubes" were placed above the left shoulder in a large quantity of blood. The following parts were missing - part of belly wall including naval; the womb, the upper part of the vagina & greater part of bladder. The Dr gives it as his opinion that the murderer was possessed of anatomical knowledge from the manner of removal of viscera, & that the knife used was not an ordinary knife, but such as a small amputating knife, or a well ground slaughterman's knife, narrow & thin, sharp & blade of up to six to eight inches in length.[44]

The first issue to be examined in connection with Phillips' testimony is the matter of the time of death and the rather large discrepancy between his suggested time of death and that deduced from witness statements. If Phillips' estimate was correct then it meant that Chapman's body would have been in the yard when John Richardson was on the steps at 4.45am, a discrepancy that caused the police to question Richardson's story and thus examine his clothes and search his house; but, according to Swanson, 'there was not a shred of evidence' and 'suspicion could not rest upon him'. Acceptance of Richardson's testimony is not helped by the fact that we must believe, not what he saw, but what he did not see. However, there is a further fragment to support the possibility that Chapman and her killer entered the yard to number 29 after Richardson had left and that is by virtue of the open street door. Richardson was clear that he closed the door to the street when he left but it was wide open when Davis entered the passage an hour later. There is of course the possibility that another occupant of number 29, and there were plenty of them, left between 5.00am and 6.00am, but there is no testimony to support this. The door to the yard apparently closed by itself so that can be no indicator of activity. The likelihood is that Chapman was not there when Richardson went into the yard with the obvious consequence that Phillips' estimate of the time of her death was out by at least an hour. It would be unfair to be too critical of Phillips, since relying on the combination of reduced body temperature and the progress of rigor mortis for estimating the time of death is, even today, fragile at best, especially in the hour or so immediately after death when the body core temperature changes little. In 1888 the business was even more heavily dependent on guesswork although it is fair to say that Phillips was not inexperienced and he had encountered enough dead bodies under all manner of circumstances to gain an instinctive *feel* for time of death which was then unaided, even by the use of thermometers.[45]

The situation regarding Chapman's body was undoubtedly complicated by the fact that her partially clothed corpse had effectively exsanguinated, thus taking heat from the core and effectively reducing body mass, and the abdominal organs had been removed and spread out which significantly accelerated heat loss. Phillips qualified his estimation by referring to the blood loss and the fact that it was a 'fairly cold morning', but even so his estimation was significantly wide of the mark assuming that he was indeed incorrect. In actual fact, it was not an especially cold morning in spite of Phillips' impression.[46] Phillips said that, 'stiffness of the limbs was not marked, but was commencing'. As a general guide, and in an average environment, rigor may be first detectable in the smaller muscle groups around the eyes and mouth, in the jaw, and in the fingers at around one to four hours after death. Rigor would not be expected in the limbs until after four to six hours.[47] But using the extent and severity of rigor mortis as an indicator of time of death is about as unreliable as body temperature. Dead bodies become stiff at a variable time after death, but this gradually passes off with time to allow secondary flaccidity. The process is complex, highly variable, and, because it is the consequence of a chemical process, temperature dependent. Rigor mortis tends to become established more quickly if the body remains warm and is delayed when the body is cold, which is contrary to the circumstances surrounding Chapman's death[48]. Rigor may be absent or hardly detectable in the old or feeble and may be enhanced in someone who died during or soon after physical exertion or exhaustion, but none of these factors would have pertained significantly to Annie Chapman. It is thus quite easy to understand why the surgeon reached the conclusion that he did and to all intents and purposes his estimation was reasonable based upon the condition of Chapman's corpse. Phillips received an endorsement through an article in *The Lancet*:

If the evidence of Mrs. Long is to be credited, the victim was seen alive at half-past five in Hanbury-street, and about six o'clock her mangled corpse was discovered in the yard of the lodging-house. We confess to sharing Mr. Phillips' view that the coldness of the body and commencing rigidity pointed to a far longer interval between death and discovery than this; but, as he remarked the almost total draining away of the blood, added to the exposure in the cold morning air, may have hastened the cooling down of the body.[49]

The only material value in establishing the accuracy of the timing of events in the yard of 29 Hanbury Street may be to lead us to an early, if vague description of Jack the Ripper by Elizabeth Long. Since there were no other sightings, even at an earlier hour, and no one reliably heard anything untoward then a frustratingly inconclusive collection of observations sits before us. It is also worth noting at this point that, assuming Chapman was killed at between 5.30am and 5.45am, then this was the only one of the Whitechapel murders attributable to Jack the Ripper that took place in daylight. All of the other victims were killed much earlier in the night and well under the concealment of darkness.

With each murder the Ripper accepted that he would have to work in darkness and this did not appear to be a deterrent – he did not take his victims to illuminated areas, in fact, he did not *take* his victims anywhere, he more likely allowed them to take him to the place of their choosing. Wynne Baxter made an astute observation during summing up at Chapman's inquest, as reported in *The Daily Telegraph* on 27 September 1888:

There is little doubt that the deceased knew the place, for it was only 300 or 400 yards from where she lodged. If so, it is quite unnecessary to assume that her companion had any knowledge – in fact, it is easier to believe that he was ignorant both of the nest of living beings by whom he was surrounded, and of their occupations and habits. Some were on the move late at night; some were up long before the sun.

Although at this point there are only two victims of Jack the Ripper to compare there are undoubted similarities between the murders of Mary Ann Nichols and Annie Chapman – there are also differences. Both were victims of the same murderer and my earlier assertion that Jack the Ripper was no stranger to killing is reinforced by this second death. He already had an established *modus operandi* before he attacked Nichols and he tried to use exactly the same method with Chapman, but I believe that on this occasion all did not go entirely to plan.

Phillips opined that Chapman was probably partially strangled during the assault, but he offered no useful opinion as to the mechanics of this. With regard to the partial strangulation of Chapman, *The Lancet* again gives Phillips support:

There could be little doubt that he first strangled or suffocated his victim, for not only were no cries heard, but the face, lips and hands were livid as in asphyxia, and not blanched as they would be from loss of blood. Then, with one long and deep incision he must have severed the poor woman's throat, so that almost all the blood from her body drained out of the divided vessels, accounting for the almost bloodless effect of the subsequent incisions in the abdomen and pelvis.[50]

During summing up, the coroner made the assumption that the couple were standing when the attack took place and that when he had 'produced suffocation and insensibility' the killer lowered Chapman to the ground and cut her throat. But there are significant practical difficulties with this that were not addressed. It is not possible to suffocate or strangle a standing victim from the front with one hand unless they are against a wall, thus two hands must be employed. The victim must then be rendered unconscious before a knife can be produced and used. In spite of frequent misinterpretation to the contrary, Annie Chapman is the *only* victim for whom there are any post mortem signs of prior suffocation or strangulation. By his normal methodology, the Ripper would have no need for such. With strangulation there is an almost inevitable consequence that the victim will struggle and make enough noise to attract attention, so wrestling a victim to the ground was not a method employed by the Ripper and it seems that in no other instance did do so. So why were the circumstances of Chapman's murder different from those of Mary Nichols and subsequent victims?

For some reason the Ripper was not able attack Chapman from behind and thus employ his preferred and highly effective technique. The most likely reason for this, and regardless of when she was killed, was that Chapman ended up facing the Ripper within the confines of the corner of the yard at number 29 and he was unable to gain the advantage of being behind her. As an alternative ploy, Chapman was probably persuaded to lie down – the back yard of 29 Hanbury Street was perhaps marginally more acceptable for such than a public street. With his victim prostrate he could then partially suffocate or throttle her before cutting her throat. Had he not rendered her insensible before using his knife there would have been sufficient opportunity for her to struggle and bring her hands up in defensive manoeuvres once she realised his intention. When Chapman ceased to struggle, though still alive, precise cuts were inflicted to her neck and thereafter the abdominal mutilation commenced. Albert Cadosch may have made his visits to the yard during this process, walking four times past the focus of activity, on one occasion hearing a woman say, 'no' and on another occasion he heard something hit the fence, but with respect to timing this seems unlikely.

Blood splashes close to the ground were noted on the wall behind where Chapman lay and there were smears of blood on the palings, adjacent to the position of her head. These bloodstains are probably of little significance and were just as likely to have occurred as a consequence of the killer's activities in the mutilation and removal of organs, as they were a result of inflicting the lethal neck wounds.

With regard to the dissecting skills of Jack the Ripper, Phillips was quite sure that the killer had at least some anatomical knowledge and also implied that he knew how to undertake the dissection and removal of organs. Anyone with an anatomy book can learn about the approximate appearance and location of organs in the body but it is not quite so easy to actually dissect them out – that requires experience. It is already apparent that the Ripper knew the location of major blood vessels in the throat and how fatal wounds could be efficiently inflicted by precise cuts to the neck. But the mutilations to Chapman take this a stage further and his ability to locate and tidily remove the uterus would be beyond that of a layperson, especially in the late Victorian era. This was not merely a matter of luck; the Ripper had anatomical knowledge and the skill to remove organs quickly and precisely under adverse conditions, but this skill need not have been gained through the practice of human medicine.

On each occasion that the Ripper set out with the intention to kill there were no guarantees. He did not know who the victim would be, or even if he would find a victim and it is almost certain that the occasions on which he actually succeeded were not the only times that he was on the streets in search of a victim. When out to kill he would seek victims during a period of several hours; the early hours of the morning until just before dawn. But his compulsion to kill led him to take risks one of which may have been to murder Annie Chapman in daylight, and this was perhaps a risk too far since he confined his subsequent activities to the relative protection of darkness. After the murder of Chapman, the killer would almost certainly have been contaminated with blood, so he took a huge risk by walking the streets in daylight with bloodstained clothing and excised human organs about his person and it is beyond belief that no one saw him or if they did see him, did not realise the significance of what they witnessed.

A side-issue, and to some extent a distraction, concerning the death of Annie Chapman became apparent during the coroner's summing up. After Phillips' testimony on the fourth day of the inquest, a few newspapers detailed that the uterus had been removed from Chapman's body and that the killer had retained the organ. As a consequence to these reports, Baxter received notification that a medical school, and another similar establishment, had been approached some months previously by an American who wished to 'procure a number of specimens of the organ that was missing in the deceased'. The American was prepared to pay £20 for each uterus and had the intention of issuing 'an actual specimen with each copy of a publication on which he was then engaged'. He was apparently informed that his request was impossible to comply with, but he still urged his appeal suggesting that the organs should be 'preserved, not in spirits of wine, the usual medium, but in glycerine, in order to preserve them in a flaccid condition'. Spirits of wine would contain a high proportion of ethanol, which dehydrates tissues and makes them hard whereas glycerine does not have the same effect. In response, an article appeared in *The Lancet*, which was dismissive and took something of a swipe at Baxter in the process:

Although this statement seems to afford a satisfactory explanation of the motive for the deed and mutilation of the corpse, it is impossible to read it without being struck with certain improbabilities and absurdities that go far to upset the theory altogether. We do not for a moment question the possibility of an application being made to museum curators for specimens of uteri. This is not an unnatural or unreasonable request to be preferred by a medical man engaged in the study of disease of that organ. But does it not exceed the bounds of credibility to imagine that he would pay the sum of £20 for every specimen? - whilst the statement that he wished for a large number, because "*his object was to issue an actual specimen with each copy of a publication on which he was engaged,*" is too grotesque and horrible to be for a moment entertained. Nor, indeed, can we imagine that an author of a medical work to be published in America should need have uteri specially procured for him in England and sent across the Atlantic. The whole tale is almost past belief; and if, as we think, it can be shown to have grown in transmission, it will not only shatter the theory that cupidity was the motive of the crime, but will bring into question the discretion of the officer of the law who could accept such and statement and give it such wide publicity.[51]

There are suggestions that the request was an entirely proper one, as Begg discusses, with some authenticity regarding the request for uteri, and subsequent misunderstanding and misreporting.[52] There is no doubt, however, that the matter initiated something of an associated furore and is examined further when considering Francis Tumblety's candidature as Jack the Ripper. It is unlikely that collecting organs for cash was a motive for any of the Ripper murders and presented no more than an unfortunately timed coincidence. The fact that the request for organs was made 'some months ago' makes one immediately question why there was any delay if there was money to be made and the passage of time demonstrated that just two uteri from six murders was an extraordinarily risky way to earn forty pounds. Jack the Ripper had his own reasons for mutilating his victims and for retaining organs and his motives were far more complex than cupidity. The inquest into the death of Annie Chapman was closed after the jury returned a verdict of wilful murder against some person or persons unknown.

2.3.3 Elizabeth Stride (1843-88)

In the early hours of 30 September 1888 two more prostitutes died within an hour of each other on the streets of Whitechapel. The victims were killed three quarters of a mile apart and the first to die was Elizabeth Stride who was found in a yard off Berner Street. The manner of Stride's death strongly suggested that Jack the Ripper had been at work and a tale of confused sightings of victim and suspects began to unfold. The wounds to Stride are detailed in Diagram 3 and the location of the murder is illustrated in Map 3 with a complete tabulation of relevant findings in Table 1. Metropolitan Police and Home Office files relating to the murder are held in the National Archives.[53] Although little of the original documentation survives, we can once again be grateful that much was recorded by the newspapers, including the inquest details. However, considerable care must again be exercised because in this instance some factual details differ depending upon which newspaper report is consulted. For the purpose of this evaluation inquest details are taken from both *The Times* and from *The Daily Telegraph* with accounts often being a composite and significant differences between the two reports noted.

Elizabeth Stride was born Elizabeth Gustafsdotter in the village of Stora Tumlehed, Torslanda, Sweden in 1843. She moved to London in 1866 and married John Stride in 1869. Her husband died in 1884; she told acquaintances that he drowned when the *Princess Alice* sank in the river Thames at Woolwich in 1878, but this was untrue. Elizabeth Stride was 5ft 5in tall with black curly hair and spoke English without a discernable accent. She had lost all of the teeth from her lower left jaw. When her body was discovered she was wearing a long black cloth jacket (fur-trimmed around the bottom with red rose and white maiden hair fern pinned to it), black skirt, black crape bonnet, checked neck scarf knotted on the left side, dark brown velveteen bodice, two light serge petticoats, white chemise, white stockings, and spring-sided boots. Her possessions were; two handkerchiefs, a thimble, a piece of wool around a card, and in the pocket of her underskirt were a key (as of a padlock), a small piece of lead pencil, six large and one small buttons, a comb, a broken piece of comb, a metal spoon, a hook (as from a dress), a piece of muslin, and one or two small pieces of paper. Stride died clutching a packet of cachous in her hand.

Several witnesses at the inquest into the death of Elizabeth Stride provided some insight into the location and arrangement of Dutfield's Yard, as do other sources.[54] In 1888 Berner Street ran from Commercial Road in the north as far as Ellen Street in the south. At around the mid point Berner Street was bisected by Fairclough Street and various smaller roads led off Berner Street to the west. House numbers started at the northern junction with Commercial Road and were even on the west of the street and odd on the east side. Just north of the Berner Street junction with Fairclough Street and on the west side of the road opposite the London Board School was the International Working Men's Educational Club at number 40 Berner Street. To the south of that was number 42 and between the two buildings there was a passageway from the road to a yard at the rear of the buildings. The passageway measured some 9ft 2in wide and there were two wooden gates where the passageway joined the road. In the northern gate there was a small door through which people could enter or exit if the main gates were closed. The passage led to Dutfield's Yard, so named because of a business that was located there several years previously, although it had since relocated. The passageway ran for some eighteen feet before opening slightly into the yard and on either side of the passageway were featureless walls and no illumination. In the yard there was a row of cottages and a couple of privies to the south and opposite the Club, a store and a workshop at the western end of the yard belonging to Messrs Hindley's sack manufacturer, and a disused stable. The kitchen door of the Club opened into the yard but beyond the passageway and out of sight of the gates. Dutfield's Yard was also home to the editorial and printing offices for the radical socialist newspaper *Arbeter Fraint*, which were situated behind the Club but accessed through a separate doorway.

The local site for street prostitutes in that vicinity would have been Commercial Road but there is no doubt that they were also active in the side streets including Berner Street and also, one imagines, at any location at which men appeared late at night after an evening's camaraderie. Inquest testimony from some Club members suggested that Dutfield's Yard was not a place that was frequented by prostitutes, and even a police constable suggested that there were few prostitutes to be seen even in Berner Street. However, there were also suggestions to the contrary and William West, a club member and overseer of the printing office of *Arbeter Fraint*, told the inquest that on some occasions he had noticed low women and men together in Fairclough Street and on one occasion he did go into the yard and heard a conversation between a man and a woman at the gates. Berner Street residents were less reticent; Barnett Kentorrich who resided at number 38 next door to the Club said in a newspaper report that he did 'not think the yard bears a very good character at night, but I do not interfere with any of the people about here. I know that the gate is not kept fastened'.[55]

Again there is a reluctance to acknowledge prostitution as occurring anywhere other than elsewhere and it seems to be very much the case that everyone knows what goes on but no one wishes to admit that it happens in their own back yard.

The inquest opened on Monday 1 October and newspaper reporting commenced on the following day. At 1.00am on the Sunday morning Louis Diemschutz who was steward of the Club and lived on the premises at 40 Berner Street, discovered Elizabeth Stride's body. His testimony to the inquest was reported in *The Daily Telegraph* on 2 October 1888:

I reside at No. 40 Berner-street, and am steward of the International Workmen's Club. I am married, and my wife lives at the club too, and assists in the management. On Saturday I left home about half-past eleven in the morning, and returned exactly at one o'clock on Sunday morning. I noticed the time at the baker's shop at the corner of Berner-street. I had been to the market near the Crystal Palace, and had a barrow like a costermonger's, drawn by a pony, which I keep in George-yard Cable-street. I drove home to leave my goods. I drove into the yard, both gates being wide open. It was rather dark there. All at once my pony shied at some object on the right. I looked to see what the object was, and observed that there was something unusual, but could not tell what. It was a dark object. I put my whip handle to it, and tried to lift it up, but as I did not succeed I jumped down from my barrow and struck a match. It was rather windy, and I could only get sufficient light to see that there was some figure there. I could tell from the dress that it was the figure of a woman.

The fact that the gates to the yard were already open when Diemschutz arrived was not unusual; according to the testimony of West, 'the gates were sometimes closed, and at other times left open all night', but in any event 'they were seldom closed until late at night when all the tenants had retired'. Without touching the body, Diemschutz went into the Club to tell the others and then for the police. He returned without finding a constable, but was accompanied by a young man who lifted the woman's head and for the first time they saw that her throat had been cut. Shortly thereafter the police arrived and ten minutes after that a doctor attended.

Berner Street was poorly illuminated. The coroner after studying the parish plan confirmed that there were just four streetlamps within the 350ft distance from Commercial Road to Fairclough Street, and Dutfield's Yard was by all accounts a very dark yard. It was an overcast night and there was no lighting in the yard and from the comments of West at the inquest, 'none of the streetlamps light it, so that the yard is only lit by lights through the windows at the side of the Club and of the tenements opposite'. West also observed that; 'As to the tenements, I only observed lights in two first floor windows. There was light in the printing office, the editor being in his room reading'. Morris Eagle, a member of the Club, later suggested that; 'There was a light from the upper part of the club, but that would not throw any illumination upon the ground. It was dark near the gates'. Several witnesses commented upon how dark the yard was and especially the passageway from Berner Street. The only source of any illumination in the yard at ground level would have been from the printing office at the far end or from the door into the yard from the kitchen of the Club.

Stride's body according to medical testimony lay some nine feet in from the gateway and close to the wall on the right hand side as viewed from the street, and there must have been just enough room for Diemschutz's pony and cart to move down the passage without touching the corpse.

Constable Henry Lamb, the first policeman on the scene, said, according to *The Daily Telegraph* on 2 October 1888, that:

Last Sunday morning, shortly before one o'clock, I was on duty in Commercial-road, between Christian-street and Batty-street, when two men came running towards me and shouting. I went to meet them, and they called out, "Come on, there has been another murder." I asked where, and as they got to the corner of Berner-street they pointed down and said, "There." I saw people moving some distance down the street. I ran, followed by another constable - 426 H. Arriving at the gateway of No. 40 I observed something dark lying on the ground on the right-hand side. I turned my light on, when I found that the object was a woman, with her throat cut and apparently dead. I sent the other constable for the nearest doctor, and a young man who was standing by I despatched to the police station to inform the inspector what had occurred. On my arrival there were about thirty people in the yard, and others followed me in. No one was nearer than a yard to the body. As I was examining the deceased the crowd gathered round, but I begged them to keep back, otherwise they might have their clothes soiled with blood, and thus get into trouble.

Lamb further explained that; 'The feet of the deceased extended just to the swing of the gate, so that the barrier could be closed without disturbing the body'. Stride's feet were towards the gates and her head was just six inches from the wall with her legs drawn up with knees close to the wall. She was murdered close to the gates and had there been sufficient light the body would doubtless have been visible from the street. But because there were no lights in the yard and no street light in the immediate vicinity to illuminate the area, even with the gates wide open, the body was hardly visible to someone standing right next to it. Testimony suggests that the only way a body would have been discovered in such a location close to the wall was if a light were to have been shone upon it or if someone had tripped over it. It is thus quite possible for Stride's body to have been lying within the gates for up to half an hour before Diemschutz's pony took fright as the Steward entered the yard, even though other witnesses claim to have entered the yard during that period. Constable Lamb closed the gates to secure the scene shortly after the arrival of Edward Johnston, assistant to Dr William Blackwell who had been called in by the police, at 1.05am.

Elizabeth Stride was quite distinctive earlier that night because at some point she acquired a red rose and white maidenhair fern pinned to the front right side of her jacket. There is no indication that she had this with her when she left her lodgings in Flower and Dean Street at 7.00pm but she was almost certainly wearing a red rose at least half an hour before her body was discovered. When Stride left her lodgings she was dressed respectably to go out, but there was no sighting of anyone resembling Stride until later that evening at around 11.00pm. From that time onward there are several possible sightings interspersed with Berner Street residents and members of the Club variously appearing and disappearing in the hours before Stride was found murdered.

At 11.00pm a woman resembling Stride was seen with a man in *The Bricklayer's Arms* in Settles Street by three men.[56] However, these reports were made to a journalist for *The Evening News* and the witnesses did not give evidence at the inquest. Although they reportedly identified the body at the mortuary as being that of the woman they saw, even making mention of a flower pinned to her jacket, their accounts have to be regarded as unreliable and the men were more likely publicity seekers than useful witnesses.

Forty-five minutes later, a more reliable sighting of Stride was made by a labourer by the name of William Marshall when he went to the front door of his lodging house at 64 Berner Street and saw Stride further along the road, three doors away on the opposite side from number 58 Berner Street, between Fairclough Street and Boyd Street, with a man who kissed her and said; 'You would say anything but your prayers', before they walked off down the street. Marshall recognised Stride by her face and her dress but she was not wearing a flower at that time.[57] According to Marshall, there was 'no lamp near', the closest being that over number 70 at the corner of Boyd Street, but Marshall managed to describe the man with the woman he identified as Stride as being about 5ft 6in tall, middle aged, stout, clean shaven, and dressed in a small black coat, dark trousers and a round cap with a peak of the kind worn by sailors. 'He was decently dressed' and in the opinion of the witness, 'worked at some light business and had more the appearance of a clerk than anything else'. Marshall suggested him to be 'mild speaking', and appeared to be an educated man, and although he did not see clearly the man's face, he thought that he did not have whiskers. The man 'was not wearing gloves, and had no stick or anything in his hands'. Neither Stride nor the man were apparently the worse for drink and they stood for about ten minutes between Marshall's lodgings and the Club. They passed Marshall once but he could not see the man's face because it was turned towards the woman. They then walked away down the street, towards Ellen Street; they had already walked past the Club at number 40, which was in the opposite direction. Marshall was quite sure that the woman he saw was Stride. It should be noted that this sighting took place in the next block south along Berner Street, between Fairclough Street and Boyd Street.

At between 12.30am and 12.35am probably the most reliable sighting of Stride that evening came from Constable William Smith who, while on his beat, saw a woman fitting the description of Elizabeth Stride standing with a man in Berner Street a few yards from where the body was found, but on the opposite side of the street.[58] Smith recognised Stride at once when he saw her body at the mortuary and remarked upon the fact that she was wearing a flower pinned to her jacket breast. He had clearly seen her face when she was standing in Berner Street and he also recognised her body in Dutfield's Yard when he attended the murder scene. Unfortunately the constable was unable to give a comprehensive description of the man she was with because he 'did not notice him much'. Smith described the man as about 5ft 7in and wearing a dark overcoat, dark trousers, and a hard felt deerstalker hat of dark colour and he carried a newspaper parcel, 18in by 6in or 8in, in his hand. Smith thought the man to be aged about 28 years and he noticed that he did not have whiskers. He was of respectable appearance. The constable left the couple and continued along his beat into Commercial Road. They were not acting suspiciously, the constable overheard no conversation between them, and neither appeared the worse for drink.

Although both Marshall and Smith report seeing Stride with a clean-shaven man, of 5ft 6in to 5ft 7in in height and wearing dark clothes, there are differences as to the description of exactly what he wore. Their observations were three quarters of an hour apart so it is quite feasible that Stride had found the company of another man by the time Smith encountered her. If the two sightings were of Stride with the same man then he had gained a newspaper parcel by the time Smith saw him and she had gained a flower pinned to her jacket. The origin of the flower remains a mystery, but it was most likely purchased for her, but probably not by her killer.

In inquest testimony Morris Eagle reported that after taking a lady friend home he returned to Berner Street at about 12.40am with the intention of having supper.[59] Finding the front door closed he went into the yard and entered the Club by the kitchen door. Eagle reported that as he passed through the yard he did not notice anything on the ground by the gates and he believed that he passed along about the middle of the gateway. When questioned specifically as to whether or not he would have seen the deceased had she been lying there Eagle replied that it was 'rather dark' and he could not 'say for certain if there was anything there or not'. The witness also did not recall whether he saw anyone else in Berner Street or in the yard at that time, but was sure that had he seen a woman and a man standing there then he would have remembered. He had often seen men and women outside the beershop, although a juryman remarked that it closed at 9.00pm. The location of beershops, public houses, and chandlers shops in Berner Street will be considered later.

Both *The Times* and *The Woodford Times* reported that another member of the club, a Russian named Joseph Lave, went down into the court at 12.40am, about twenty minutes before the body was discovered.[60] Lave was feeling oppressed by the smoke in the clubroom and walked about in the open air for about five minutes or more. He strolled into the street, which was very quiet at the time, and returned indoors without having encountered anything unusual. He would thus have been outside until about 12.45am. This witness did not give evidence to the inquest but there is no reason to doubt his account, which merely reinforces that of Eagle rather than makes any fresh contribution. It is further reported that Lave had to grope his way around in the yard because it was so dark.[61]

The Daily Telegraph on 1 October 1888 carries a report by a witness, Fanny Mortimer, who was at her door at 36 Berner Street and looking into the street for 'nearly the whole time' between 12.30am and 1.00am. She saw nothing untoward apart from a young man with a bag who hurried along Berner Street. The man, one Leon Goldstein, subsequently contacted the police and was eliminated from the inquiry. Mortimer was not called to testify at the inquest, but her account is to some extent verified, as we shall see later. A report in *The Evening News* on 1 October 1888, however, suggests that Mortimer's statement in *The Daily Telegraph* regarding the duration for which she stood at her door was not quite accurate and by this further account she reportedly heard, 'the measured, heavy tramp of a policeman passing the house on his beat' at shortly before 12.45am while indoors. This estimate of timing could quite acceptably have placed her looking out onto the street at 12.40am or even earlier.

The next sighting of a woman resembling Elizabeth Stride was made by Israel Schwartz as he turned from Commercial Road into Berner Street in the early hours, on route to his former lodgings, which he intended to visit to ensure that his wife had completed their move to Ellen Street from Berner Street. In his apparently voluntary account to the police, and according to a report by Chief Inspector Donald Swanson on 19 October 1888, Schwartz entered Berner Street from Commercial Road at around 12.45am and as he reached the gateway to Dutfield's Yard he saw a man stop and speak to a woman who was standing in the gateway.[62] Schwarz then suggested that the man attacked the woman whereupon another man appeared and chased Schwarz along Berner Street and beyond. This account will be considered in more detail later. Schwartz identified the body at the mortuary as that of the woman he had seen and described the first man who attacked the woman as aged about 30, height 5ft 5in, fair complexion, hair dark, small brown moustache, full face, broad shoulders, dressed in dark jacket and trousers with a black cap with a peak. The man had nothing in his hands. The second man was described by Schwartz as aged about 35, height 5ft 11in, fresh complexion, light brown hair, brown moustache, dressed in a dark overcoat with an old hard felt hat with a wide brim. He had a clay pipe in his hand. This man has since been referred to as the 'pipeman'.

At about the same time as Schwartz supposedly witnessed the fracas outside the Club, James Brown was walking along Fairclough Street. Brown, a dock labourer, lived at 35 Fairclough Street and saw a man with a woman that he identified as Stride. Brown gave evidence to the inquest and reports in *The Times* and *The Daily Telegraph* on 6 October 1888 cover his testimony. Brown said that he saw the deceased at about 12.45am on Sunday morning when he went to the chandlers shop on the corner of Berner Street and Fairclough Street, and that she was at that time with a man standing by the Board School in Fairclough Street. They were against the wall and as Brown passed them he heard the woman say; 'Not tonight, some other night'. Brown turned to look at them and although he did not notice any flowers on Stride's breast, he was certain that the woman was the deceased. It was rather dark where they stood, but Brown thought that the man was wearing a long overcoat down to his heels, and that he was 5ft 7in and of stoutish build.[63] Brown could give no details as to the man's hat if indeed he was wearing one and both the man and the woman appeared to be sober. Brown did not know Stride, but he did view her body in the mortuary and was convinced it was the woman he had seen on the night of the murder.

There were additional sightings of men and women together that could have been Stride and her killer, but the details are vague. 'A young man and his sweetheart' were seen by Fanny Mortimer either side of the murder.[64] They apparently told Mortimer that they did not hear a sound and another report detailed that a young girl had been standing at a bisecting thoroughfare not 50yds from the murder scene and talked with her sweetheart for twenty minutes without hearing any unusual noises.[65] It is of course possible that this was the couple seen by

Brown so it is a pity that they were not identified to give evidence at the inquest and certainly there is no reference to them in police reports. It is also possible that their liaison may not have been entirely innocent which would explain why they did not come forward. The couple do however cause a problem because if they were the couple that Brown saw then they were not Stride and her killer and would, one imagines, have seen some of the activity described by Schwartz as well as witnessing Brown's visit to the grocery store. Even if Brown escaped their notice it is doubtful that they would have failed to notice Schwartz running for his life down Berner Street closely followed by a man with a pipe!

One other witness, Matthew Packer, deserves brief, albeit dismissive, mention and only because of the myth relating to poisoned grapes that seems so prevalent, even in supposedly factual accounts of the Ripper murders. Any suggestion that the Ripper drugged his victims before killing them is as erroneous as the suggestion that he carried a black bag on his murderous outings. This latter myth stemmed from the sighting of the bag-carrying Leon Goldstein in Berner Street by Fanny Mortimer even though Goldstein was quickly eliminated from the matter. Packer did not give evidence to the inquest, but he did tell a newspaper reporter that he sold grapes to a man and a woman shortly before Stride's murder from his shop at 44 Berner Street. Packer's story drifted significantly from what he originally told the police and one cannot help but draw the inference that the offer of reward money may have influenced his thinking.[66] Fortunately there is no need to examine the story further since the post mortem examination of Stride's stomach contents revealed 'that the deceased had not swallowed either skin or seed of grape within many hours of her death'. Furthermore, there was no sign that she had consumed alcohol or narcotic drugs.

There was thus no shortage of activity in Berner Street before, after and around about the time that Elizabeth Stride was murdered but the end product is a tangle of observations that do not form a chronological sequence. Unfortunately, we have only two reliable reference points; the sighting of Stride at 12.35am by Constable William Smith and the discovery of her body at 1.00am. What reportedly happened in between is as much of a muddle as any other of the murders committed by the Ripper. There are significant contradictions and shortfalls and in particular there is a crucial ten minutes period, five minutes either side of 1.00am, when it is likely that Stride was murdered and her killer escaped.

The surgeon Dr Blackwell arrived at the scene at 1.16am from his home in Commercial Street after being called by the police. Blackwell arrived some eleven minutes after his assistant Edward Johnston and described what he found on reaching Dutfield's Yard. According to Blackwell's testimony in *The Times* on 3 October 1888:

The deceased was lying on her left side obliquely across the yard, her face looking towards the right wall. Her legs were drawn up with her feet close against the wall of the right side of the yard passage. Her head was resting beyond the carriage-wheel rut, the neck lying over the rut. Her feet were three yards from the gateway. Her dress was unfastened at the neck. The neck and chest were quite warm, as were also the legs, and the face was slightly warm. Her feet almost touched the wall and the face was completely towards the wall. The neck and chest were quit warm; also the legs and face were slightly warm. The hands were cold. The right hand was open and on the chest, and was smeared inside and out with blood. The left hand, lying on the ground, was partially closed, and contained a small packet of cachous wrapped in tissue paper. There were no rings, nor marks of rings, on the fingers. The appearance of the face was quite placid and the mouth was slightly open. The deceased had round her neck a check silk scarf, the bow of which was turned to the left side and pulled very tight. In the neck there was a long incision, which exactly corresponded with the lower border of the scarf. The border was slightly frayed, as if by a sharp knife. The incision in the neck commenced on the left side, two and one half inches below the angle of the jaw, and almost in a direct line with it, nearly severing the vessels on that side, cutting the windpipe completely in two, and terminating on the opposite side one and one half inches below the angle of the right jaw, but without severing the vessels on that side.

In answer to questions from the coroner Blackwell confirmed that he was unable to say whether the bloody hand had been moved and that the blood was running down the gutter into the drain in the opposite direction from the feet. There was about 1lb of clotted blood close by the body, and a stream all the way from there to the back door of the club. There were no spots of blood on the side of the house or splashes on the wall. Nor was there any blood on the victim's clothing. The victim's bonnet lay upon the ground a few inches from her head and the dress was undone at the top, although this was almost certainly due to Edward Johnston placing a hand on Stride's chest to assess the warmth of her body. Blackwell remarked that the victim would have bled to death comparatively slowly on account of the vessels on one side only being severed, and the artery not being completely severed. The deceased could not have cried out after the injuries were inflicted as the windpipe was severed. Blackwell formed the opinion that the murderer probably caught hold of the silk scarf, which was tight and knotted, and pulled the deceased backwards, cutting her throat in that way. He could not say whether the scarf would have been tightened sufficiently to stop her calling out, but the throat might have been cut as she was falling, or when she was on the ground otherwise the blood would have spurted about if the act had been committed while she was standing up. He also thought it possible that a hand might have been put on her nose and mouth and the cut on the throat was probably instantaneous. Blackwell thought that the deceased would have taken a minute or a minute and a half to bleed to death.

The Police Surgeon for Whitechapel Division Dr George Bagster Phillips also attended Dutfield's Yard and arrived some ten minutes after Blackwell according to Constable Lamb. Phillips had nothing to add to Blackwell's description of the murder scene except to say that he picked up the cachous from Stride's hand and gave them to Blackwell. The following day, Monday 1 October, Phillips conducted a post mortem examination of Elizabeth Stride in the presence of Blackwell and others. The details of his examination as reported in *The Times* on 4 October 1888 are as follows:

At three o'clock p.m. on Monday at St. George's Mortuary, Dr. Blackwell and I made a post mortem examination. Rigor mortis was still thoroughly marked. There was mud on the left side of the face and it was matted in the head. We then removed the clothes. The body was fairly nourished. Over both shoulders, especially the right, and under the collarbone and in front of the chest there was a bluish discolouration, which I have watched and have seen on two occasions since. There was a clear-cut incision on the neck. It was six inches in length and commenced two and a half inches in a straight line below the angle of the jaw, three quarter inches over an undivided muscle, and then, becoming deeper, dividing the sheath. The cut was very clean and deviated a little downwards. The arteries and other vessels contained in the sheath were all cut through. The cut through the tissues on the right side was more superficial, and tailed off to about two inches below the right angle of the jaw. The deep vessels on that side were uninjured. From this it was evident that the haemorrhage was caused through the partial severance of the left carotid artery. Decomposition had commenced in the skin. Dark brown spots were on the anterior surface of the left chin. There was a deformity in the bones of the right leg, which was not straight, but bowed forwards. There was no recent external injury save to the neck. The body being washed more thoroughly I could see some healing sores. The lobe of the left ear was torn as if from the removal or wearing through of an earring, but it was thoroughly healed. On removing the scalp there was no sign of bruising or extravasation of blood. The skull was about one sixth of an inch in thickness, and the brain was fairly normal. The left lung had old adhesions to the chest wall, the right slightly. Both lungs were unusually pale. There was no fluid in the pericardium. The heart was small, the left ventricle firmly contracted, and the right slightly so. There was no clot in the pulmonary artery, but the right ventricle was full of dark clot. The left was firmly contracted as to be absolutely empty. The stomach was large and the mucous membrane only congested. It contained partly digested food, apparently consisting of cheese, potato, and farinaceous powder. All the teeth on the lower left jaw were absent. On Tuesday I again went to the mortuary to observe the marks on the shoulder.

It was known that in 1865 Stride had treatment for venereal disease but evidence of syphilitic lesions was either not present or not reported at post mortem examination, unless the reported 'healing sores' related to this.[67]

Elizabeth Stride was murdered between 12.35am when Constable Smith positively identified her by the flower on her the breast of her jacket and 1.00am when Diemschutz found her body. Blackwell suggested that Stride had been killed within thirty minutes prior to his arrival on the scene at 1.16am and probably within twenty minutes, which would place her death and the killer in the yard at between 12.45am and 12.55am. This fits well with what else is known, and it is significant that Blackwell would not have known further details at the time and in that sense his assessment is objective enough. However, even though the investigators of the day had little choice other than to base the time of death on surface body temperature, this is a hopelessly inaccurate way to estimate time of death, especially during the first hour or so after the event, as we have already seen in the case of Annie Chapman. That Blackwell was able to estimate Stride's death to an accuracy of twenty minutes seems incredible if solely based on surface temperature, so it is likely that he took other factors into account.

The situation was complicated to some extent by the fact that Stride's corpse had exsanguinated, but it was a mild evening and the body was fully clothed with just the soles of her boots visible according to Constable Lamb. The ground was probably damp and the body lay on the stone floor of the yard. Lamb viewed the scene with the aid of his lamp. He felt Stride's face, which was slightly warm, then her wrist for a pulse, which was absent. Lamb further remarked that some blood was in a liquid state and some had congealed but he could not say whether it was still flowing. Edward Spooner, a horse keeper employed by Messrs Meredith biscuit bakers, arrived at Dutfield's Yard in response to the commotion after discovery of the body and suggested that blood was still flowing from the body and that it was running down the gutter. However there had been heavy rain earlier that evening and although it had stopped by midnight, residual water would still be on the ground in quantity, so testimony as to the fluidity of blood on the ground is dubious. Indeed, Dr Edward Johnston, Dr Blackwell's assistant, testified that by the time of his arrival at a few minutes after 1.00am, the wound had stopped bleeding and the body was warm apart from the hands, which were quite cold. He undid her dress in order to see whether the chest was warm. He said that there was a stream of clotted blood reaching down to the gutter and that there was very little blood near the neck, as nearly all of it had run away. There was also no evidence of rigor.

When Phillips arrived he estimated the time of death to be within an hour of his arrival. There is, however, some doubt as to the time of Phillips' arrival at the scene, which makes his estimate of the time of death a little vague. According to Blackwell's testimony as reported in both *The Times* and *The Daily Telegraph* on 3 October 1888, Phillips arrived twenty to thirty minutes after Blackwell who arrived at 1.16am according to his own watch. This would suggest that Phillips arrived at between 1.35am and 1.45am meaning that Stride's death would have occurred no earlier than 12.35am. But according to Constable Lamb, as reported in *The Daily Telegraph* on 3 October 1888, Phillips arrived just ten minutes after Blackwell, at 1.25am, placing Stride's death no earlier than 12.25am. *The Times* reported Lamb's estimate of Phillips' arrival to be twenty minutes after Blackwell thus placing Stride's death no earlier than 12.35am.

In fairness to Phillips, an estimate of within an hour was probably the best that he could realistically muster by the time he arrived and Blackwell's rather more specific estimate may have taken into consideration the state of the blood on the ground and around and within the wound, as well as the touch temperature of her torso and extremities. We already know that Stride was killed between 12.30am and 1.00am but Blackwell's opinion reduced the time of death to within fifteen minutes before 1.00am and possibly no sooner than 12.55am.

At the inquest there were some interesting observations resulting from the post mortem examination of Stride's body and authors have relied upon these to speculate as to the events that led to her death. However, apart from the cut to Stride's neck, there were no significant injuries to her body. Unfortunately, as is increasingly the case in the course of the Ripper murders, the doctors, especially Phillips, were inclined to speculate a little beyond what could be justified from what they actually observed. It must of course have been difficult because the murder series was escalating in frequency and apparently in ferocity and pressure to provide answers that may help to apprehend the murderer would undoubtedly have been implicit both at the inquest and during the course of any discussions between the doctors and the police. One major problem was that all doctors involved in the Ripper series knew about the other cases and thus most likely formed opinions as to what happened before autopsies were performed and thus their objectivity was impaired.

There was no disagreement concerning the cut to Stride's neck. It was precisely delivered to the left side, the knife being drawn around the neck from left to right, and tapering away on the right side. The six inch long single cut was almost perfect in that it severed the left carotid artery, although incompletely, and the victim bled to death, albeit relatively slowly. Stride would have been immediately immobilised by the shock of the wound and would have been unable to make any sound since the trachea was divided. From the post mortem description of the injuries it seems that the right carotid artery was uninjured. Stride would probably have been unconscious after thirty seconds or so with death following shortly thereafter. In the opinion of Dr Phillips the cut to the neck was delivered in a few seconds. Stride would have been alive for long enough to bring her right hand up to her neck by way of a spontaneous, almost reflex, response to her injury and at that point the back of her hand and wrist could have become contaminated with blood.

With regard to other injuries the situation is less clear. At the inquest on the first occasion that he gave evidence, Phillips reported 'an abrasion of the skin about an inch and a quarter in diameter under the right clavicle' on Stride's body. He further reported that; 'Over both shoulders, especially the right, from the front aspect under the collar bones and in front of the chest there is a bluish discolouration which I have watched and seen on two occasions since', otherwise there was; 'No recent external injury save to the neck'. Additionally, Phillips noted that; 'The lower lobe of the ear was torn as if by the forcible removing or wearing through of an earring, but it was thoroughly healed' and this requires no further comment. Phillips statement that; 'On removing the scalp there was no sign of bruising or extravasation of blood between it and the skull-cap', clearly suggests that Stride was not hit over the head nor did she fall backwards onto the ground. Specifically, there was no mention by Phillips of any injuries that were consistent with strangulation, partial strangulation, or assault prior to delivery of the fatal cut, and none to indicate that she had been thrown to the ground.

Phillips returned to the mortuary the following day to observe the marks on the shoulders. He commented that; 'The abrasion which I spoke of on the right side of the neck was only apparently an abrasion, for on washing it the staining was removed and the skin was found to be uninjured'. We can assume that this comment refers to the one and one quarter inch abrasion that he reported on the first occasion that he gave evidence so this comment does no more than confirm the presence of this abrasion, although his further comment that the skin was uninjured is a little confusing. An abrasion is the most superficial type of injury that damages only the very surface layer of skin and does not penetrate to the deeper tissues, although there can sometimes be slight bleeding. Redness or haemorrhage on the edges of abrasions or wounds is a good indicator that the injury was sustained while the victim was alive, such a vital reaction may be absent in injuries inflicted at or immediately before death. Abrasions occasionally retain the pattern of the causative object but in this case there is no mention of any detail of the abrasion. Such an injury could have occurred at any time within hours of Stride's death and Phillips' comment that there was no bleeding or 'staining' associated with it suggests that it was probably of no relevance to the assault on Stride. It is not certain whether or not Phillips had in mind this abrasion in concluding the means by which Stride was killed, but we can be fairly sure that the areas of bluish discolouration over the victim's upper body were prominent in his deliberations. 'I have come to the conclusion that the deceased was seized by the shoulders, placed on the ground, and that the perpetrator of the deed was on her right side when he inflicted the cut', he told the inquest. Thus, it seems that Phillips placed much reliance on the areas of bluish discolouration that he described over the shoulders and down as far at the collarbones on Stride's corpse and in earlier testimony had indicated that he had observed the marks on two occasions since in order to follow their progress, although Phillips made no comment as to whether or not bruising had developed. Immediately after Phillips had been recalled and suggested the means by which Stride had been forced to the ground, Blackwell was also recalled and rather contradicted Phillips' remarks about the discolouration on the shoulders. In response to a question from the foreman regarding the areas of discolouration, Blackwell, on being recalled replied, according to the inquest report in *The Daily Telegraph* on 6 October 1888, that; 'They were what we call pressure marks. At first they were very obscure, but subsequently they became very evident. They were not what are ordinarily called bruises; neither is there any abrasion. Each shoulder was about equally marked'. There is then some disparity between reports regarding the next question asked by a juror although it could be that both questions and answers are relevant. According to *The Times*, the juror asked how these marks were likely to have been caused to which Blackwell's reported response was to suggest that they were caused by; 'Two hands pressing on the shoulders'. According to *The Daily Telegraph* report the juror asked how recently these marks might have been caused to which Blackwell replied that he thought that 'rather difficult to say'. But there is a wider issue here.

Elizabeth Stride was killed at between 12.35am and 1.00am on the morning of Sunday 30 October and yet her body was not subjected to a comprehensive post mortem examination until 3.00pm on the following day – some thirty-eight hours after she died. In such temperate conditions and without the benefit of refrigeration it is hardly surprising that when Phillips came to undertake the necropsy of the corpse he reported that decomposition had commenced. Clothing was not removed from the corpse until this time and the discolouration or any associated injuries would not have been observed until the body was stripped. The fact that these areas were only observed over one and a half days after the victim died makes their origin and relevance to the case highly dubious. Much would depended on how the body was manhandled, transported and stored in the time since the victim was killed, and pink or bluish zones of post mortem hypostasis, whereby blood cells effectively settle in the lowest areas under gravity, are common and often unpredictable.[68]

Pressure marks in the post mortem context should be distinguished from pressure marks of a different interpretation. Post mortem pressure marks are pale areas on the body in the midst of hypostasis. These areas have been subjected to maintained pressure after death and thus, because the capillaries are restricted, the development of hypostasis is prevented – such marks are often caused by clothing or the pressure of a body against a hard surface. Bruising occurs when small arteries and veins are damaged and blood leaks into the surrounding tissue. Bruises are commonly seen in the subcutaneous tissues and they readily change with time both in terms of colour and spread, although they can also move in location.

Frequently a bruise may be absent at the moment of injury but appear after hours or even days later in some instances. Curiously, this process can also continue after death which why is can be important to return to a body some time after the original examination to see if any bruises have subsequently developed.

One imagines that this was the intention of Phillips when he took another look at the Stride's corpse to assess the areas of discolouration, but his inquest testimony does not indicate whether or not there were any changes to the affected areas so it is fair to assume that such was not the case. These findings must also be interpreted in the knowledge that Stride bled to death and thus her body would have been virtually exsanguinated. Hypostasis would obviously be significantly reduced where there is no blood, but against that is the fact that an absence of blood would allow the vessels, including capillaries, to collapse and any residual blood may not necessarily be able to gravitate to the lowest portion of the corpse, thus leaving patchy areas of discolouration on the upper surfaces.

The fact that the initial observation of these areas was so long after death makes their value limited and in any event their apparent diffuse nature is not altogether suggestive of someone applying significant pressure to the shoulders in order to force another human being to the ground. Regardless as to whether the assailant was in front of, or behind the victim, one might reasonably have expected to see a pattern of bruising that vaguely matched the spread of the killer's fingers on the victim's shoulders – even through the clothing worn by Stride. There is no indication that this was the case and Phillips would surely have provided such evidence in support of his assertion as to the means by which Stride's killer attacked. Of course, it is impossible to convincingly dismiss Phillips' suggestion any more than it can be reliably embraced, but on balance it should not be assumed that Stride was killed in the manner suggested by the Whitechapel district Police Surgeon. In fact, the method suggested by Blackwell was more probable given the circumstances and the evidence.

There has been some speculation that the murder of Elizabeth Stride was not the work of Jack the Ripper. However, the trademark clinical efficiency is clearly apparent even though on this occasion the killer was unable to progress to mutilate his victim. The odds were always in favour of the Ripper being disturbed in his activities on at least one occasion so that he would not be able to mutilate in every instance. That his work would be interrupted at various stages has proved to be the case. Phillips' assertion that Stride had been forced to the ground by her shoulders is specious but made with a total disregard to the practicalities of such action. Forcing someone to the ground by pressing or pulling down on their shoulders is a completely unnecessary assault given the alternatives when the assailant is in any event carrying a knife. It is a complex manoeuvre that would be highly susceptible to failure, especially if performed from the front, so that the victim is able to put up a defence. As already discussed to some extent, such an attack would require the use of both hands of the assailant but with both hands occupied and his victim presumably by this time on the ground, he is disadvantaged when continuing the attack with a knife. It is impossible for this manoeuvre to proceed without the victim struggling, making the chances of success much reduced and the end result would likely be a tangle of arms and a very sharp knife, which would almost certainly result in bruising and defensive injuries to, and much struggling and noise from, the victim. This was not the manner by which Elizabeth Stride was murdered, and there is further support for the suddenness with which she was killed from inquest testimony. On the fourth day of the inquest the coroner asked a very pertinent question just after Phillips had given his opinion as to how Elizabeth Stride had been killed. The coroner asked; 'Does the presence of the cachous in the left hand indicate that the murder was committed very suddenly and without any struggle?'

Phillips replied that; 'Some of the cachous were scattered about the yard'.

The Foreman then asked; 'Do you not think that the woman would have dropped the packet of cachous altogether if she had been thrown to the ground before the injuries were inflicted?'

Phillips responded; 'That is an inference, which the jury would be perfectly entitled to draw'.

Here we see a hint of arrogance from Phillips at the very idea that his suggestion should be challenged, but unfortunately, moments later he was undermined when Blackwell was also recalled and commented on the cachous, as reported in *The Daily Telegraph* on 6 October 1888:

I may add that I removed the cachous from the left hand of the deceased, which was nearly open. The packet was lodged between the thumb and the first finger, and was partially hidden from view. It was I who spilled them in removing them from the hand. My impression is that the hand had gradually relaxed while the woman was dying, she dying in a fainting condition from the loss of blood.

Blackwell, when he originally gave evidence on day two of the inquest and before Phillips gave testimony, was of the opinion that Stride had been attacked from behind, that the killer had grabbed the silk scarf around her neck and pulled it tight, cutting her throat as he pulled her backwards and to the ground. The scarf was definitely cut when the wound to Stride's neck was inflicted. According to Blackwell, and as reported in *The Times* on 3 October 1888:

There was a check silk scarf round the neck, the bow of which was turned to the left and pulled tightly. There was a long incision in the neck, which exactly corresponded with the lower boarder of the scarf. The lower border of the scarf was slightly frayed, as if by a sharp knife.

According to *The Times* report, Blackwell formed the opinion that:

The murderer first took hold of the silk scarf, at the back of it, and pulled the deceased backwards, but I cannot say whether the throat was cut while the woman was standing or after she was pulled backwards. Deceased would take about a minute and a half to bleed to death. I cannot say whether the scarf would be tightened sufficiently to prevent deceased calling out.

The same testimony reported in *The Daily Telegraph* is slightly different in that Blackwell is reported as saying;

I formed the opinion that the murderer probably caught hold of the silk scarf, which was tight and knotted, and pulled the deceased backwards, cutting her throat in that way. The throat might have been cut as she was falling or when she was on the ground.

Blackwell could not say that the silk scarf was tight enough to prevent Stride from calling out, but he did agree with a suggestion by the coroner that a hand might have been put on her nose and mouth, further suggesting that; 'the cut on the throat was probably instantaneous'. In testimony relating to the post mortem examination, however, there was no mention that the scarf had been pulled tightly and no mention of any corresponding marks on the neck – in spite of the fatal cut these may have been visible. Given the relatively detailed post mortem examination I am inclined to think that had the scarf been tight enough around the neck to restrict breathing then it would have left marks and these would have been mentioned by Phillips. The fact that this was not the case indicates that Blackwell's initial interpretation of what he saw was probably incorrect.

Both at the time of the murders and subsequently by authors on the Ripper murders, much emphasis has been placed on the fact that a cut to the side of the neck that severed the carotid artery would result in significant distribution of blood had the victim been upright at the time of the attack. Upon the absence of any significant spurting or spraying of blood is based the assertion that the throat of each of the Ripper victims must have been cut while they were on the ground because so little blood was found any distance from the victim. But such is not necessarily the case, and the mechanics of blood distribution from such a lesion will be considered when looking in detail at the Ripper's *modus operandi*.

The coroner asked Phillips whether he had 'formed any opinion as to the manner in which the deceased's right hand became stained with blood?', to which the surgeon replied that; 'It is a mystery. There were small oblong clots on the back of the hand. I may say that I am taking it as a fact that after death the hand always remained in the position in which I found it – across the body'. As already mentioned, it would be quite conceivable that at the moment the killer struck Stride brought her hand up towards her neck as an almost reflex response at which point the back of her hand became contaminated with blood. Once again, this is more likely to happen with an attack from behind than responding to an assailant who attacked from the front.

Phillips attempted to suggest that there were differences between the murder of Stride and that of Annie Chapman. In fact, he asserted that; 'There is very great dissimilarity between the two. In Chapman's case the neck was severed down to the vertebral column, the vertebral bones being marked with two sharp cuts, and there had been an evident attempt to separate the bones'. But this is more a matter of degree and not a basis upon which to suggest that Stride and Chapman were murdered by different men, not that such an assertion was directly made.

Twenty-four hours after the murder Thomas Coram, who was an employee at a cocoanut warehouse, found a knife in Whitechapel Road. The knife was produced at the inquest giving Phillips a further opportunity to speculate. Phillips was of the opinion that 'the cut was made from the left to the right side of the deceased, and taking into account the position of the incision it is unlikely that such a long knife inflicted the wound in the neck'. Phillips confirmed that the knife was 'rounded at the tip, which was about an inch across. The blade was wider at the base', but that there was nothing to indicate that the cut on the neck of Stride was made with a pointed knife. Blackwell thought that, 'although the knife might possibly have inflicted the injury, it is an extremely unlikely instrument to have been used. It appears to me that the murderer, in using a round-pointed instrument, would seriously handicap himself, as he would be only able to use it in one particular way'.

Having examined the crime scene and post mortem details it is now worth investigating the statements of other witnesses to see if it is possible to construct the course of events that led to the murder of Elizabeth Stride, and the identification of a suspect. Significant in any such evaluation is the account given by Israel Schwartz, the Hungarian immigrant who supposedly witnessed events in Berner Street and informed the police of what he saw. Schwartz's account is curious in that it does not appear in the inquest records although clearly his testimony is significant and was known to police later on 30 September, the same day that Stride was murdered. The inquest spanned the first three weeks of October so there was plenty of opportunity for Schwartz to appear but evidently he did not, and his input through any means is not mentioned by the coroner, Wynne Baxter, during his summing up on the fifth and final day of the inquest on Tuesday 23 October.[69] Schwartz did make a statement to the police because Abberline refers to it in his report of 1 November 1888 and it is known that Schwartz visited the police on 30 September because a report in *The Star* on the 1 October makes reference to; 'Information which may be important' being 'given to the Leman Street police *yesterday* [italics added] by an Hungarian concerning this murder'.[70] It is interesting to note that *The Star* very obligingly gave an approximation of Schwartz's new address as being in Back Church Lane and although he actually lived in Ellen Street which was off Back Church Lane, the Hungarian may not have been too difficult to find by Stride's killer if he considered Schwartz to be a threat. *The Star* had rather irresponsibly placed Schwartz in considerable danger although there is no indication that he met a premature end.

The statement given by Schwartz to the police is not among the surviving case files. There are two sources relating to Schwartz's account; one is in a report by Chief Inspector Donald Swanson prepared on 19 October 1888 and the other is by way of the newspaper report in *The Star*.[71] The report by Swanson is not in the form of a witness statement but more by way of an overview and there are significant differences between this and the newspaper report. In Swanson's version of Schwartz's statement the witness turned into Berner Street from Commercial Road and got as far as the gateway where the murder was committed when he saw a man stop and speak to a woman who was standing in the gateway. According to Schwartz, the man tried to pull the woman into the street, but he turned her round and threw her down on the footway and the woman screamed three times, but not very loudly. While crossing to the opposite side of the street, Schwartz saw a second man standing lighting his pipe. The man who threw the woman down called out 'Lipski', apparently to the man on the opposite side of the road, and as Schwartz walked away he was followed by the second man and ran as far as the railway arch but the man did not follow so far.[72] Apparently Schwartz could not say whether the two men were together or known to each other.

In the account in *The Star*, Schwartz suggested that there was a man walking before him as if partially intoxicated when he turned from Commercial Road into Berner Street. Schwartz walked behind him and noticed a woman standing in the entrance to the 'alleyway' where the body was found. The 'half-tipsy' man halted and spoke to the woman. *The Star* report then mentioned that Schwartz saw the man put a hand on her shoulder and push her back into the passage, but not wishing to get involved in the incident Schwartz crossed to the other side of the street. Before he had gone many yards, however, he heard the sound of a quarrel and turned back to see what was happening, but just as he stepped from the kerb a second man came out of the doorway of the public house a few yards further on and shouted out some sort of warning to the man who was with the woman and rushed forward to attack the intruder, but to whom this refers is uncertain. *The Star* reported that Schwartz stated that he positively saw a knife in the second man's hand and at that point he went quickly to his new lodgings.

Schwartz did not speak any English so his accounts had to be given through an interpreter and anyone who is familiar with that process will be well aware of how the finer points of any discussion can be misinterpreted or completely lost. For instance, Swanson's account of Schwartz's observations mentions that the man tried to 'pull the woman into the street', whereas *The Star* suggests that the man made to 'push her into the passage'. The discrepant use of 'push' and 'pull', and 'street' and 'passage' are highly likely to have arisen from differences in the interpretation from Hungarian to English. But even allowing for difficulties with interpretation there remain significant problems with Schwartz's account.

In *The Star* interview, Schwartz made no mention of the woman being thrown to the ground by the man, and no mention that he was followed by the man with the knife; and in the Swanson report there is no mention that the man who attacked the woman was 'half-tipsy' or that the pipeman emerged from a public house. There was a public house in Berner Street, the *George IV*, but it was at the end of the next block south at number 68 Berner Street. It has been suggested that the man did not emerge from a public house but from a beershop known as *The Nelson* at 46 Berner Street on the north western corner of the junction with Fairclough Street and three doors south of Dutfield's Yard.[73] *The Nelson* was a beer retailer thus did not sell spirits; it is probably the same beershop mentioned in testimony by Morris Eagle as being on the same side of the street as the Club. A juryman remarked that the beershop is always closed at 9.00pm as opposed to the public houses that closed at midnight, so in either case the pipeman could not have been inside but merely standing in the doorway.

Perhaps the most significant discrepancy between the versions of Schwarz's tale is the absence of any mention of a knife in Swanson's report. This would be a crucial observation by way of indicating intent and it is highly unlikely that Swanson would have omitted such a detail from his report. By the time Swanson wrote his report he would have had plenty of opportunity to discuss further with Schwartz the account in *The Star*, and for Schwartz to have the opportunity to amend his statement. The details of Schwartz's observations as reported by Swanson are probably the more accurate of the two versions even though it is a reworking of the statement of Schwartz by Swanson so again there is room for errors and misunderstanding. Nonetheless, I am inclined to follow Swanson's report. It is worth noting that the details of the murder were well known by the time of Schwartz's interview with *The Star* and this would not be the first occasion on which a journalist had coaxed the required, as opposed to the true, story during the course of an interview. It is quite likely that *The Star* reporter, or maybe even Schwartz, added a little more colour to the account for the benefit of the paper's readership. But discrepancies between reported details are not the only difficulties with Schwartz's account, regardless as to which version we follow.

There is no indication of how Schwartz managed to fix his timing. It could of course be that further details were given in his original statement to the police but all that we have is an indication that he turned from Commercial Road into Berner Street at 12.45am. The police would no doubt have looked into this but clearly if the incident that Schwartz described happened just fifteen minutes earlier than he thought then his account is negated and Schwartz loses credibility at a witness. It has already been noted that Fanny Mortimer who lived with her husband at 36 Berner Street told a reporter for *The Evening News* that 'shortly before a quarter to one she heard the measured heavy tramp of a policeman passing the house on his beat. Immediately afterwards she went to the street door with the intention of shooting the bolts, though she remained standing there for ten minutes before she did so'. The only man she saw in Berner Street was; 'a young man [Goldstein] carrying a black shiny bag who walked down the street very fast from the Commercial Road. He looked up at the club, and then went round the corner by the boarding school'. Mortimer then went back inside her house and five or six minutes later heard Diemschutz's pony and cart pass by and then the commotion as Stride's body was discovered. When Leon Goldstein contacted the police to clear himself from the investigation, he effectively confirmed that Mortimer was standing in her door at some time before the discovery of Stride's corpse, although there is almost inevitably something of a problem with timing and allowances have to be made such that five minutes either way can easily be the margin of error.

If the 'measured heavy tramp of a policeman' was indeed a policeman then it can only have been Constable Smith passing Mortimer's door just two houses north of the entrance to Dutfield's Yard. It should be said that Mortimer did not specify that it definitely was a policeman she heard in which case it could have been anyone and this point has never been clarified. However, because there are two points of reference it may not be important. We know from Constable Smith's testimony that he was in Berner Street at between 12.30am and 12.35am and we are entitled to take the constable's timings as perhaps being the more reliable, so we can assume that Mortimer was adrift by way of a few minutes in her reckoning, in which case she probably went to her doorway sometime between 12.35am to 12.40am. The other end of her period of observation from the door is set by the passage of Diemschutz's pony and cart, which she heard in the street some five minutes after she went back inside and closed the door. Diemschutz reckoned that he arrived at the Club at exactly 1.00am so we can assume that Mortimer closed her door at around 12.50am to 12.55am. She estimated that she had been standing at her door for around ten minutes, which would generally fit with the reference points of Constable Smith and Diemschutz's pony and cart. Mortimer was thus probably at her door and looking out onto Berner Street for a ten minute period within the greater period from 12.35am to 12.55am; or more precisely from 12.40am until 12.50am. Whichever timing one takes it is almost impossible to see how the events that Schwartz described took place at the times mentioned by him given that Mortimer would have been at her door. Also, Mortimer was able to hear the policeman's footsteps and Diemschutz's pony and cart when her door was closed, but heard no commotion as described by Schwartz and neither cry of 'Lipski' nor cries of 'murder'.

None of the other witnesses around at that time saw Schwartz or the events that he described. Morris Eagle arrived at the Club at around 12.40am and Joseph Lave was in Dutfield's Yard from about 12.40am for five minutes or so and he also ventured into the street. Lave probably would not have seen Mortimer at her door unless she was standing on the pavement or unless Lave ventured into the road, because Mortimer lived on the same side as the International Working Men's Educational Club. However, Charles Letchford who lived at number 30 Berner Street walked up the road at about 12.30am and commented to *The Illustrated Police News* that; 'Everything seemed to me to be going on as usual, and my sister was standing at the door at ten minutes to one, but did not see anyone pass by'. Fanny Mortimer was probably Letchford's sister but his remark about her presence should not be taken to imply that he actually saw her, because he may simply have repeated what she had told him.[74]

The testimony of James Brown who saw a couple standing outside the Board School in Fairclough Street at 12.45am is also of interest in relation to Schwartz and would be of greater significance were it not for the fact that it suffers greatly from an absence of definitive identification of Stride. There is also some doubt as to the accuracy of his timing other than retrospectively from when he reached his home in Fairclough Street after the sighting. It is unclear as to whether the couple were there when Brown went into the shop, whether they were there when he came out of the shop three or four minutes later, or on both occasions. Brown said that about a quarter of an hour after he arrived home he heard the commotion surrounding the discovery of the body. Allowing an extra five minutes for Diemschutz to inspect the body in the passageway to the Yard and then for him to enter the Club, tell the members and for them to break out onto the streets it is probable that this occurred at something like 1.05am. This would then place Brown at the corner of Berner Street and Fairclough Street at around 12.45am to 12.50am much in line with his suggestion.

We do not know the perspective that Brown had when he viewed the couple but he does state that he passed them and was probably returning home along Fairclough Street after visiting the shop. The chandlers shop was most likely located at number 48 Berner Street on the south western corner of the junction with Fairclough Street, and on the opposite corner to *The Nelson*. In any event, because Brown lived at number 35 Fairclough Street, near the corner with Christian Street he would inevitably walk past anyone standing against the Board School wall in

Fairclough Street on route to or from a shop on a western corner of the Berner Street junction.

Brown could see enough to know that the woman was inclined with her back against the wall and the man stood in front of her with his arm, presumably outstretched, against the wall and to one side of her head. According to Brown they were standing by the Board School in Fairclough Street, and assuming they were at least a short way into Fairclough Street they would be out of sight of Fanny Mortimer standing in the doorway of number 36 Berner Street, or of anyone coming in or out of the Club. The best view that Brown would have of the man would thus be his profile and the best view that he would have of the woman would be her front, but that would most likely be partially obscured by the man. Unfortunately, Brown did not see a flower on the woman's breast but had she worn one it would probably have been obscured by the man standing in front of her – we know that Stride would have had a flower by this time through testimony from Constable Smith. Brown passed close enough to hear their conversation, but given the darkness of the location it is easy to see why his descriptions lack detail.

There are reasons to dismiss Brown's observations as irrelevant; his timing is vague, his testimony does not correlate with the account given by Schwartz, and his description of the man seen with her does not fit with that of any other witness. However, Brown's testimony is no less credible than that of Schwartz, and even if the couple seen by him were other than Stride and her killer, Brown's presence at that time and in that place still has relevance, because apart from the account by Schwartz, Brown's observations do not conflict with those of anyone else; his testimony must be regarded seriously and it may even be more significant than that of Schwartz. The fact that the woman said; 'Not tonight, some other night', may have many an innocent explanation but it does rather sound like a prostitute attempting to increase the price for her services. We already know fairly accurately as to the timing of Stride's death and the description of the man that Brown gave is next to useless assuming that he was Stride's killer, but the account, if accurate, may throw a little light on Stride's whereabouts at a critical time and place her in a position to move into Dutfield's Yard and to her death. Importantly however, and regardless as to the identities of the man and woman, Brown's account places him in view of Berner Street at a time when Schwartz should have been passing an incident outside the Club, or even running across Fairclough Street.

Brown is not just one witness whose testimony does not correlate with that of Schwartz, but he is *another* witness who did not see Schwartz or anything described by Schwartz. Not one single aspect of Schwartz's account correlates with any other observation, presence, or evidence from the corpse or murder scene, and one could almost imagine that he described an incident that occurred at a completely different time or in another place. It is thus rather difficult to accommodate Schwartz's story. Although Schwartz was supposedly familiar with the area he could have been mistaken about his route.[75] The only other possibility for error relates to timing in which case he would need to be at least fifteen minutes adrift and estimated the timing as being later than it actually was. I doubt very much that Schwartz would have bothered to check the timing of the incident that he witnessed at the time that it happened – there would be no need for him to do so. And since he then made his way home he may not have heard about the murder until later that day at which time he would have to retrospectively estimate his timings relative to other events late on Saturday. This could another example of a witness interpreting what he saw in the light of what he subsequently learned.

Swanson's report gives Schwartz's address as 22 Ellen Street, Back Church Lane, which would have been his current address after he had moved lodgings. The report in *The Star* suggested that Schwartz had previously lodged in Berner Street but that he was uncertain as to whether or not his wife had actually moved house that day during his absence. In any event, Schwartz was on route to lodgings in Berner Street or Ellen Street so it is a little difficult to understand why, when chased, he ran all the way to the railway arch instead of to the safety of his home? Berner Street did not continue directly to the arches, above which ran the London and Blackwall Railway, and in order to travel to a point similar to that described by Schwartz it would be necessary to turn either east or west into Ellen Street and then south into Back Church Lane, Philip Street, Stutfield Street, or Christian Street in order to reach Pinchen Street and the railway arches. The distance covered by Schwartz in his panic to escape was significant and it is curious as to why he had to run quite so far before realising that he had not been followed. In a moment of panic such as that experienced by Schwartz one would imagine that he would instinctively head for the safety of home rather than running aimlessly about the streets. And regardless as to whether or not he had moved that day he would have been close to his new or previous lodgings and may even have passed the door of 22 Ellen Street. It is reasonable to assume that he was worried because he thought he was being followed, but whichever way one views this, Schwartz would have had the opportunity to get home without running as far as the railway arch. This is totally baffling and at some point he must have returned to his new or old lodgings that same evening.

Given the much mentioned darkness of Berner Street, let alone Dutfield's Yard, it is amazing that Schwartz managed to give such detailed accounts of the suspects and victim. By his own account, Schwartz crossed the road and so did not walk close to the man and the woman and he would have been more inclined to glance in their direction rather than stare directly for fear of attracting too much attention. He would have hurried through the gloom. Unfortunately we do not know whether he was able to positively identify Stride by the flower on her jacket and that would have been extremely useful.

In the report by Swanson, Schwartz apparently suggested that the man threw the woman to the floor and that she then screamed three times but not very loudly. The fact that she was not screaming 'murder' with the full force of her lungs suggests that she did not feel that her life was under any particular threat of coming to a premature end, which is hardy surprising since street scuffles of this kind – usually involving a woman and two men – were commonplace on the streets of Whitechapel, especially after a Saturday night's drinking. It is more likely that the woman's screams would be those of pain as she hit the ground and at the indignity of being so treated. In any event anyone being thrown to the ground, or even falling to the ground would almost inevitably suffer at least minor injuries by way of abrasions to the palms or knees or elsewhere depending upon how they fell and how they tried to cushion their landing. There were no injuries to Stride, according to the detailed post mortem examination by Phillips, that could be regarded as being consistent with her being thrown to the ground and although there was mud on Stride's clothing, face, and hair, this soiling was not associated with injuries and was more likely a consequence of events in the yard, rather than on the street even though both were probably equally muddy.

With regard to the cachous, Schwartz's account does illustrate a useful point. If Elizabeth Stride was the woman observed by Schwartz being assaulted then we have to assume that she was standing outside the gates to the Club soliciting for business, in which case it would be of no surprise for her to have taken a cachou in order to sweeten her breath a little, and that would certainly explain why she had a packet of cachous in her hand when she was killed. But would she have held onto them while being thrown to the ground in the gateway before being pushed into the yard and murdered, according to Schwartz's account, and without spilling any? A thorough search would have been made of the gateway and street outside and it is unlikely that any spilled cachous would have been missed. Taken into consideration with the fact that Stride had no injuries consistent with being thrown to the ground, there are strong indicators that the woman allegedly seen by Schwartz was not Elizabeth Stride.

If one does accept the account of Schwartz then there are two other suspects, a drunkard, and a man with a pipe (or knife). However the drunkard who allegedly assaulted Stride would have been unable, through intoxication, to conduct himself in the clinically precise manner that was necessary to kill Stride, which leaves the second man referred to as the pipeman, regardless as to whether or not he actually had a pipe, and the fact that he was lurking alone in the vicinity suggests that he may have been watching Stride when the drunkard went into action. Perhaps it was the pipeman who yelled 'Lipski'?[76] If a knife, and not a pipe, were produced during the process, as suggested by Schwartz in his interview with *The Star*, then this would hardly be surprising and whatever happened caused one of the two men to flee the scene in addition to Schwartz. Whether the second man carried a pipe or a knife we shall probably never know, but a knife would certainly be a more threatening weapon than a pipe and a better reason to flee the scene. I do not think that Schwartz became a target to be chased from Berner Street and whichever of the two men 'chased' Schwartz was running away in the interest of self-preservation, following Schwartz for part of the same route before taking another street to safety. It would make sense for the pipeman to challenge a drunk he saw assaulting a woman in the street. He yelled 'Lipski' at the man because he was assaulting a woman and not because he thought him to be a Jew, then he produced a knife at which point the drunk ran off in the same direction as Schwartz. This left the woman alone with the pipeman, so was the woman Stride and was she murdered by the pipeman? Was the pipeman Jack the Ripper? I suspect that the woman as not Stride but that she was another prostitute and that the pipeman was her minder.

There is also another possibility, albeit rather unlikely; did Schwartz kill Stride and concoct a story about the assault? It certainly would not be the only time that a killer had placed himself in the role of good citizen to dupe the police. Killers often masquerade as witnesses in order to avert suspicion and to find out how the police are progressing with their investigations. Israel Schwartz is someone about whom very little is known; he appears quite by chance and did not give evidence at the inquest. We do not even have a description of him apart from the fact that he allegedly spoke no English and according to *The Star* reporter was well dressed and had the appearance of being in the theatrical line, or according to Abberline had a 'strong Jewish appearance'. There is, however, no justification for assuming that he was a murderer and certainly nothing to indicate even the possibility. I do not think that Schwartz killed Elizabeth Stride and he was not Jack the Ripper.

Schwartz's account is so out of step with the circumstances and testimony of other witnesses that it is almost impossible to accommodate as detailed and there is clearly something amiss. It appears that the police regarded Schwartz's account of what he saw as significant to the investigation, but on balance I am inclined to the opinion that Schwartz is probably more unreliable than any other witness in the Stride murder, and to dismiss the episode as irrelevant, which is a pity since Schwartz has come to be regarded by many as pivotal in identifying a suspect and in determining what could have happened to Elizabeth Stride. In any event, Schwartz's account did not really add much to the story except to throw two more rather vague suspect descriptions into the arena, and his story does not affect the timing of Stride's death and only marginally detracts from the fact that she was another victim of Jack the Ripper. I think that Schwartz made an appreciable mistake as to his whereabouts in space or time. Whether or not the woman was Stride then becomes irrelevant, as do the 'half-tipsy' man and the pipeman as suspects. It is more likely that the incident witnessed by Schwartz was a simple street brawl involving two men and a woman and that the event either preceded Mortimer's scrutiny of the street or happened in another street completely. In his testimony to the inquest Constable Lamb admits that he, 'saw lots of squabbles and rows such as one sees on Saturday nights', on the night of Stride's death, and Charles Letchford told the press that; 'disturbances are very frequent at the club', a suggestion supported by Fanny Mortimer who referred to 'another row at the Socialist's Club'.[77] One either accepts Schwartz's story to the exclusion of most other witness accounts, or one excludes Schwartz to be guided by the remaining witnesses, and in this respect they are mutually exclusive.

So what actually happened in Dutfield's Yard? The witnesses, William Smith, Joseph Lave, Morris Eagle, Fanny Mortimer, and possibly also James Brown form a loose continuity that runs from 12.30am until 12.50am and although they do not appear to overlap, they leave a very small window of opportunity for Stride and her killer to go into Dutfield's Yard without being observed. The medical testimony from Blackwell suggests that Stride was killed between 12.45am and 12.55am. The method by which Stride was killed strongly indicates that she was another victim of Jack the Ripper and that in all probability he was disturbed by Louis Diemschutz as he turned his pony and cart through the gates of Dutfield's Yard. The fatal wound to Stride was inflicted in a matter of seconds and she was probably dead in less than two minutes. Elizabeth Stride was thus murdered shortly before her body was discovered and probably around 12.55am, which is the very time at which witness continuity comes to an end.

Stride was on the streets that night looking to earn money by the only means that was open to her, and she would quite likely be in the company of several men until she found one who wanted to pay her for sex. There was nothing unusual in this and she would be disinclined to spend too much time in the company of any man if there was ultimately to be no financial reward from the association. Stride knew that men met at the Club, they were always there on a Saturday night, with some staying later than others. Such would be a good and probably safe place for her to loiter and she had probably been there on other weekends. But her evening had been unsuccessful, or at least it had been since the pubic houses closed at 12.00pm, because she was penniless when her body was discovered and, reasonably assuming that her assailant did not rob her, she had presumably spent on drink the small amount of money with which she had started the evening. It was thus unlikely that she had engaged in a sexual encounter since midnight at the latest, in spite of being allegedly seen in the company of at least one man during that time. The matter of the cachous is important because it tells us that Stride was probably no longer with any of the suspects with whom witnesses had placed her earlier in the evening and that she was looking for business in the vicinity of the Club when she met her killer. The cachous clutched by Stride as she died indicate that she was probably between potential clients or was anticipating close contact when she took the sweets from her jacket pocket.

There is an impressive collection of witnesses who were out and about but did not see Stride. An absence of sightings of Stride in Berner Street between 12.35am and 12.50am is significant because she would probably have been seen by Eagle, Lave or Mortimer had she been in the street during that time. Brown's sighting of a woman that he thought to be Stride with a man outside the Board School in Fairclough Street would place her within a few steps of Dutfield's Yard at precisely the right time.

Excluding the evidence of Schwartz, and apart from the possible sighting of Stride by Brown, the last occasion on which Stride was seen in the company of a man was at between 12.30am and 12.35am when Constable Smith saw her across the road from the Club. The description of the man given by Smith is broadly similar in terms of height, dark clothing, and the absence of whiskers to that furnished by Marshall when he witnessed a woman he identified as Stride with a man some forty-five minutes earlier. But the descriptions are far too general to be uniquely identifying and there is a possibility that Stride was in the company of two different men for the sightings by Marshall and Smith. The Club was a source of potential clients and Dutfield's Yard an ideal place for a prostitute to earn her money, being close to the street and in darkness and with the noise from the singers in the room above. Stride would have been familiar with the arrangements. Of course there would be possibility that they might be disturbed but that was always a risk with street sex and of little concern. The man with the newspaper package could have been Stride's killer, but if so they probably did not enter Dutfield's Yard until close to 12.55am so where were they for twenty minutes or so after the sighting by Constable Smith and why did they not go into the yard as soon as Smith was out of sight? I do not think that Stride stayed with the man with the newspaper parcel and I do not think he was her killer. But if Stride was alone for a while then where was she? She did not loiter in Berner Street, or outside the Club, at least up until 12.50am otherwise witnesses would in all probability have seen her.

Jack the Ripper was not a man to lurk in the shadows so I do not think that it was part of his technique to wait in a given location on the chance that a victim would pass by. He was not waiting in Dutfield's Yard in the hope that a prostitute would pass unaccompanied by the gate. The Ripper almost certainly engaged with his victims before they took him to a location for sex where they were murdered. He was highly efficient in the execution of his victims and his technique also ensured that he would not be covered in blood; at least not to such and extent that anyone would have noticed.

The ten minutes after Fanny Mortimer closed her door to Berner Street provided ample time for Stride and her killer to appear in Berner Street and to enter Dutfield's Yard unseen. But while there was sufficient time for the killer to strike there was not sufficient time for him to lift her skirts to commence the remainder of his work before he heard the sound of an approaching pony and cart. That was enough to check his progress and when he saw the vague silhouette of the pony's head appear in the gateway he retreated beyond the passageway and into the darkness of the yard. Not for the first or the last time good fortune was with the Ripper and while Diemschutz was in the Club telling the members what he had discovered, the Ripper escaped unseen into Berner Street and by the time the alarm was raised and the police arrived he was gone from the immediate area. In all probability and in spite of many suggestions to the contrary, it is likely that no one saw Stride with her killer and she engaged with him after the last confirmed sighting by Constable Smith at between 12.30am and 12.35am.

By way of an interesting additional observation, *The Star* on 1 October 1888 carried a report that a man was observed at about 1.30am sitting in a doorway in Church Lane, between Whitechapel Road and Commercial Road and on route to Mitre Square, apparently wiping his hands. The man attempted to conceal his face but was described as wearing a short jacket and a sailor's hat. Although hardly unique, this description is broadly similar to that of a suspect reported near to the scene of the murder of Catharine Eddowes later that night. The timing is awry and there must be some doubt as to whether the murderer would stop and wipe his hands in a doorway – much more likely that he would keep on the move given that police officers would be searching the streets. I think that he would have moved on very quickly from Berner Street and well away from the vicinity avoiding the main roads and any direct routes to the police station in Leman Street. He could of course have discarded a bloodstained overcoat in the process.

There is also an interesting possibility that Stride's killer may have been a member of the International Working Men's Educational Club who had left some moments before meeting Stride outside the gates. After killing her did he then make his way across Whitechapel to the Imperial Club in Duke Street where he met Catharine Eddowes? Prostitutes would regularly hang around outside such men's clubs in the hope of picking up late night business, but the Ripper need not have been a member of any club to realise that. After listening to all of the evidence presented in connection with the death of Elizabeth Stride, the inquest jury, after a short deliberation, returned a verdict of wilful murder against some person or persons unknown.

2.3.4 Catharine Eddowes (1842-88)

Well within an hour after the murder of Elizabeth Stride, the body of another murdered prostitute was discovered on the streets of Whitechapel and on this occasion her body had been extensively mutilated. The murders on 30 September became collectively known as the 'double event', a phrase taken from the *saucy Jacky* postcard. The second victim was Catharine Eddowes.

Catharine Eddowes was born in Wolverhampton in 1842, the daughter of a tinplate varnisher. In the early 1860s Eddowes left home in the company of an army pensioner by the name of Thomas Conway who was formerly of the 18th Royal Irish Regiment. Although Eddowes claimed to friends that she had married Conway there is no evidence in support of this. The couple had three children, a girl and two boys. In 1880 Eddowes and Conway separated, Eddowes having custody of the girl, Annie, and the boys went with their father. Annie said that her mother's habitual drinking and periodic absences caused the breakdown, whereas Catharine's sister, Elizabeth attributed the separation to Conway's drinking and violence. In 1881, Eddowes entered a relationship with an Irish porter by the name of John Kelly with whom she lived at his lodgings in Flower and Dean Street until her death.

When murdered, Eddowes wore a straw bonnet in green and black velvet with black beads and black strings worn tied to the head, a black cloth jacket trimmed around the collar and cuffs with imitation fur, an old white apron with repair, a dark green chintz skirt with three flounces, a man's white vest, a brown linsey bodice, a grey stuff petticoat, a very old alpaca skirt (worn as undergarment), a very old ragged blue skirt with red flounces (worn as undergarment), a white calico chemise, no drawers or stays, a piece of red gauze silk worn as a neckerchief, a large white pocket handkerchief, a large white cotton handkerchief, two unbleached calico pockets with tape strings, a blue stripe bed ticking pocket, brown ribbed knee stockings (darned with white cotton) and a pair of men's lace-up boots (right boot repaired with red thread). Eddowes' possessions were; two small blue bags, two short clay pipes, a tin box containing tea, a tin box containing sugar, an empty tin matchbox, 12 pieces of white rag, a piece of white coarse linen a piece of white shirting, a piece of red flannel with pins and needles, six pieces of soap, a small toothcomb, a white handled table knife, a metal spoon, a red leather cigarette case, a ball of hemp, several buttons and a thimble, two pawn tickets with false addresses, a printed handbill, portion of a pair of spectacles and one red mitten

The wounds to Eddowes are detailed in Diagram 4 and the location of the murder is illustrated in Map 4 with a complete tabulation of relevant findings in Table 1. Files relating to the murder of Catharine Eddowes are held in the National Archives and in this instance the official inquest papers have survived. [78, 79] Witness statements were prepared during the inquest and are not necessarily verbatim, but a précised account that reflects questioning by coroner, jury, or lawyers. Each statement was nonetheless signed by each witness as being a true summary of what was said and many of the extracts included below are taken from the official transcript. In addition, the inquest was comprehensively covered in *The Times* and in *The Daily Telegraph* on 5 and 12 October 1888, and both newspapers are quoted as appropriate. The coroner Samuel Langham conducted the Eddowes inquest.

Catharine Eddowes was murdered in Mitre Square, close to Aldgate High Street and just within the jurisdiction of the City Police force. Mitre Square measured some 72ft by 75ft at the widest points and was situated between Duke Street to the north east and Mitre Street to the south west. Both of these streets connected with Aldgate High Street to the south east. There were three routes of access to Mitre Square; a short roadway from Mitre Street, a narrow unnamed passageway to the north west connecting with St James's Place, and the Church Passage connection with Duke Street. Mitre Square was quiet, being bordered by warehouses and private houses. Only two houses were occupied, and one of these by a police constable. Even though the Square would have been a shortcut from Duke Street to Mitre Street it was not the only route between the two and was probably little used. Fredrick William Foster, the City Surveyor, provided a plan of Mitre Square to the inquest showing pavements, lighting and other details. Foster also provided a more general map of the location, a sketch of the murder site and diagrams of Eddowes' corpse to illustrate the mutilations, and all have survived in public records.

According to inquest testimony by Foster, the distance from Berner Street, where Elizabeth Stride had been murdered some fifty minutes earlier, to Mitre Street is three quarters of a mile and a man could walk it in twelve minutes.[80] Thus Stride's killer would have had ample time to flee the scene of her murder and compose himself in readiness for the next slaughter. It is worth noting that, assuming the same man killed both women, he can not have been covered with blood to any extent by the time he mingled in the vicinity of Mitre Square or engaged with Eddowes since he would have been more than usually conspicuous at that time. The implication is thus that he either managed to murder Stride without any bloody contamination whatsoever or he discarded any contaminated clothing, such as an overcoat, on route from Dutfield's Yard to Mitre Square. It should not be assumed that anyone finding such a garment after the murders would have informed the police; an overcoat, especially if it was a quality garment, would have had greater value, either to sell or to keep against the cold of an approaching winter. Gloves, had he worn them, could have been similarly disposed of.

Some details are known about Eddowes' movements that evening and at 8.30pm on Saturday 29 September she was discovered 'lying drunk on the footway' of Aldgate High Street by Police Constable Louis Robinson. The woman, subsequently identified by Robinson as Eddowes, was unable to stand up by herself and the constable needed assistance to get her back to Bishopsgate Police Station where she was put into a cell. Eddowes was detained in the cell until early the following morning when Station Sergeant James Byfield judged her sober enough to be released. At this time she gave her name and address as Mary Ann Kelly of 6 Fashion Street, Spitalfields, both of which were false. Another policeman, Constable George Henry Hutt, saw Eddowes out of the police station at 1.00am and noted that she turned left along the street. Hutt estimated that it would have taken her just eight minutes 'ordinary walking' to reach Mitre Square. Eddowes was concerned that she might get 'a Damned fine hiding' when she reached home. However, she did not reach home and in all probability didn't even intend to return to her lodgings in Flower and Dean Street.

When Eddowes stepped out of Bishopsgate police station at 1.00am she set off along Bishopsgate Street in a direction that would not take her by the shortest route back to her lodgings where she lived with John Kelly, whom she had known for seven years and with whom, according to Kelly, she had been living with for all that time. Earlier in the month Eddowes and Kelly were 'hopping', or hop picking in Kent, but their venture was not very successful so they returned to London on foot at the end of the month. On 27 September Eddowes and Kelly reached London and spent a night in the casual ward at Shoe Lane Workhouse and the following night they separated. Eddowes went to the casual ward at Mile End Workhouse and Kelly slept in lodgings at 52 Flower and Dean Street – their usual lodging house was 55 Flower and Dean Street. Eddowes was well known at Shoe Lane and she reportedly told the superintendent that she intended to earn the reward money offered for the apprehension of the Whitechapel murderer because she thought she knew him. The superintendent warned her to take care that she was not murdered to which she replied; 'Oh, no fear of that'.[81]

In spite of her drunken evening in the police cells Eddowes clearly intended to spend further time on the streets with the objective of earning a little more money. After leaving the police station and walking a short way along Bishopsgate Street, Eddowes almost certainly turned into Houndsditch, or possibly even Camomile Street, in the direction of Aldgate, both of which would take her to Duke Street. Eddowes likely knew that she would connect with a client or two if she stood outside the Imperial Club in Duke Street, but she was not positively seen again until her mutilated corpse was discovered.

Two police beats are of significance; that of Constable Edward Watkins, and that of Constable James Harvey. The details that Watkins gave of his beat and of the discovery of the body are recorded in the official inquest papers. Watkins testified that:

I have been in Police for 17 years. On Saturday 29th September, I went on duty [at] a quarter to ten. My beat returns from Duke Street/Aldgate, through Heneage Lane, a portion of Bury Street, through

Cree Church Lane, into Leadenhall Street, along Leadenhall Street into Mitre Street, then into Mitre Square, round the Square into Mitre Street, then into King Street, along King Street to St James Place, round St James Place thence into Duke Street. It takes about 12 or 14 minutes. I had been continuously patrolling that beat from 10 in the evening until 1.30 o'clock. Nothing excited my attention during those hours. I passed through Mitre Square about 1.30 on Sunday morning, I had my lantern freed in my belt and on. I looked into the different passages. At half past one nothing excited my attention, I saw no one about. No one could have been in any portion of the Square without my seeing. I next came in [from Mitre Street] at 1.44. I turned to the right. I saw the body of the woman lying there on her back with her feet facing the Square, her clothes up above her waist. I saw her throat was cut and her bowels protruding. The stomach was ripped up, she was lying in a pool of blood. I ran across the road to Messrs. Kearley and Tonge, the door was ajar, I pushed it open and called to the Watchman who was inside. He came out. I sent him for assistance. I remained by the body until the arrival of Police Constable Holland. Dr. Sequira [*sic*] followed. Inspector Collard arrived about 2, and Dr. Gordon Brown, the surgeon to the Police Force. I did not hear the sound of any footsteps, at the time I entered no one was in the Square. The watchman at Messrs. Kearley and Tonge's was at work inside cleaning the offices. The watchman blew his whistle as he was going up the Street.

Watkins recounted his statement at the inquest and in answer to questions confirmed that he was continually patrolling his beat from 10.00pm up to 1.30am and noticed nothing unusual until he saw the body at 1.44am. He also said that he did not sound an alarm when he discovered Eddowes' body because; 'We do not carry whistles'. Watkins confirmed that his was not a double but a single beat and that no other policeman entered Mitre Street in the course of their beat. James Harvey's beat and involvement are detailed in the official transcript as follows:

I went on my beat at a quarter to 10 on the 29th ulto. My beat is from Bevis Marks, to Duke Street, into Little Duke Street, to Houndsditch. From Houndsditch back to Duke Street, along Duke Street to Church passage, back again into Duke Street to Aldgate. From there to Mitre Street, back again to Houndsditch. Up Houndsditch to Little Duke Street, again back to Houndsditch to Goring Street, up Goring Street to Bevis Marks, to where I started. At 20 to 2 on Sunday morning I went down Duke Street and down Church Passage as far as Mitre Square. I saw no one. I heard no cry or noise. When I got to Aldgate returning to Duke Street I heard a whistle blown and saw the Witness Morris [the watchman] with a lamp. I went to him and asked what was the matter. He said, 'A woman has been ripped up in Mitre Square.' I saw a Constable on the other side of the street. I said, 'Come with me.' We went into Mitre Square and saw Watkins there and the Deceased. Constable Holland who followed me went for Dr. Sequeira. Private individuals were sent for other Constables, arriving almost immediately. I waited there with Watkins and information was at once sent for the Inspector. I passed the post office clock between 1 and 2 minutes to the half hour.

In response to questions Harvey confirmed that he went only as far as to the end of Church Passage and that he was at the end of Church Passage at about 1.41am or 1.42am, his certainty as to timing being with reference to the post office clock which was in Aldgate High Street almost on the eastern corner with Duke Street. Thus, Harvey looked into Mitre Square when he reached the end of Church Passage at 1.41am at the earliest, and Watkins entered Mitre Square at 1.30am and again at 1.44am when he discovered the body. Assuming the constables to be vigilant that leaves a maximum of just three minutes for Eddowes to be murdered and mutilated. Realistically the time keeping of the individuals was unlikely to be synchronised thus there could be a margin of error of probably one or two minutes.

Eddowes would have reasonably arrived at Duke Street at around 1.10am to 1.15am and at some time on route or after her arrival in Duke Street she met her killer. Although there was no positive sighting of Eddowes between the time she left the police station in Bishopsgate Street and the discovery of her body in Mitre Square, there were witnesses who saw someone resembling Eddowes shortly before her death. Joseph Lawende, a commercial traveller who had spent the evening at the Imperial Club in Duke Street gave his statement as recorded in official inquest records:

On the night of the 29th I was at the Imperial Club. Mr. Joseph Levy and Mr. Harry Harris were with me. It was raining. We left there to go out at half past one and we left the house about 5 minutes later. I walked a little further from the others. Standing in the corner of Church Passage in Duke Street, which leads into Mitre square, I saw a woman. She was standing with her face towards a man. I only saw her back. She had her hand on his chest. The man was taller than she was. She had a black jacket and a black bonnet. I have seen the articles which it was stated belonged to her at the police station. My belief is that they were the same clothes which I had seen upon the Deceased. She appeared to me short. The man had a cloth cap on with a cloth peak. I have given a description of the man to the police. I doubt whether I should know him again.

The number of the Club is 16 & 17 Duke Street. It is 15 or 16 feet from the Club to the passage where they were standing. I fix the time by the Club clock and my own watch at half past one. I did not hear a word said. They did not either of them appear to be quarrelling. They appeared conversing very quietly. I did not look back to see where they went.[82]

Lawende confirmed that it would have been 1.35am when he passed the couple.[83] At the inquest Lawende was prevented from giving a more detailed description of the man, but a description did appear in *The Times* on 2 October 1888. Lawende described the man as aged 30, of shabby appearance, height 5ft 9in, of fair complexion, with a small fair moustache and a cap with a peak. In the *Police Gazette* dated 19 October 1888, the suspect's height was reported as 5ft 7in or 5ft 8in, being of medium build with the appearance of a sailor and dressed in a pepper and salt colour loose jacket, grey cloth cap with a peak of the same material, and a reddish neckerchief tied in a knot. Of the two individuals who were with Lawende only Joseph Hyam Levy gave evidence at the inquest. His testimony is reported in the official inquest papers:

I was with the last Witness and Harris at the Imperial Club in Duke Street. We got up to go home at half past one. We came out about 3 or 4 minutes after the half hour. I saw a man and woman standing at the corner of Church Passage. I passed on taking no further notice of them. The man I should say was about 3 inches taller than the woman. I cannot give any description of either of them. We went down Duke Street into Aldgate leaving the man and woman still talking behind. I fix the time by the Club clock. I said when I came out to Mr. Harris, "Look there, I don't like going home by myself when I see those characters about".

This latter comment by Levy was a little strange but in answer to a question he confirmed that there was nothing that he saw about the man and woman that caused him to fear them. He also confirmed that the point at which the man and woman stood was poorly lit, but Levy was not entirely forthcoming and a newspaper report suggested that he might know more than he was ever likely to tell.[84] This has led to speculation that Levy may have recognised the man accompanying the woman believed to be Eddowes.[85] Harry Harris also saw the couple witnessed by Lawende and Levy but paid little attention to them and said that he would be unable to identify either which is probably the reason why he did not give evidence at the inquest. He did however tell a newspaper reporter that neither Lawende nor Levy saw any more than he did, thus no more than the back of the man who was the suspect.[86] Levy's estimate of the height of the man was significantly shorter than that given by Lawende. There were no other sightings of anyone resembling Eddowes or her killer.

There is little problem in ascertaining the time of death in this instance so there is no need to scrutinise the medical evidence in that regard. However, medical testimony will be useful in determining whether or not Eddowes was a victim of the serial killer who had already murdered Nichols, Chapman, and Stride. The first surgeon on the scene was Dr George William Sequeira who arrived in Mitre Square at 1.55am and formally pronounced Eddowes to be dead but he did not conduct a further examination while awaiting the police surgeon. Dr Frederick Gordon Brown, surgeon to the City of London Police Force who was called by the police on Sunday morning at shortly after 2.00am arrived at the scene at about 2.18am. Brown's inquest statement, recorded as an official transcript was as follows:

The body was on its back - the head turned to left shoulder - the arms by the side of the body as if they had fallen there, both palms upwards - the fingers slightly bent, a thimble was lying off the finger on the right side. The clothes drawn up above the abdomen, the thighs were naked, left leg extended in a line with the body, the abdomen was exposed, right leg bent at the thigh and knee. The bonnet was at the back of the head - great disfigurement of face, the throat cut across, below the cut was a neckerchief. The upper part of the dress was pulled open a little way. The abdomen was all exposed. The intestines were drawn out to a large extent and placed over the right shoulder - they were smeared over with some feculent matter. A piece of about 2 feet was quite detached from the body and placed between the body and the left arm, apparently by design. The lobe and auricle of the right ear was cut obliquely through. There was a quantity of clotted blood on the pavement on the left side of the neck, round the shoulder and upper part of arm, and fluid blood coloured serum which had flowed under the neck to the right shoulder - the pavement sloping in that direction. Body was quite warm - no death stiffening had taken place. She must have been dead most likely within the half hour. We looked for superficial bruises and saw none - no blood on the skin of the abdomen or secretion of any kind on the thighs - no spurting of blood on the bricks or pavement around. No marks of blood below the middle of the body - several buttons were found in the clotted blood after the body was removed. There was no blood on the front of the clothes. There were no traces of recent connection. When the body arrived at Golden Lane some of the blood was dispersed through the removal of the body to the mortuary. The clothes were taken off carefully from the body, a piece of deceased's ear dropped from the clothing.

Dr Brown conducted the post mortem examination of Eddowes' corpse in the mortuary at 2.30pm the same afternoon and in the presence of George Bagster Phillips, Police Surgeon to the Whitechapel division. Brown's thorough and gruesome description was given at the inquest and the official record of his testimony is more comprehensive than newspaper reports:

Rigor mortis was well marked, body not quite cold - green discolouration over the abdomen. After washing the left hand carefully a bruise the size of a sixpence, recent and red, was discovered on the back of the left hand between the thumb and first finger. A few small bruises on right shin of older date. The hands and arms were bronzed - no bruises on the scalp, the back of the body, or the elbows. The face was very much mutilated. There was a cut about one quarter of an inch through the lower left eyelid dividing the structures completely through the upper eyelid on that side, there was a scratch through the skin on the left upper eyelid - near to the angle of the nose the right eyelid was cut through to about on half an inch. There was a deep cut over the bridge of the nose extending from the left border of the nasal bone down near to the angle of the jaw on the right side, across the cheek - this cut went into the bone and divided all the structures of the cheek except the mucous membrane of the mouth. The tip of the nose was quite detached from the nose by an oblique cut from the bottom of the nasal bone to where the wings of the nose join on to the face. A cut from this divided the upper lip and extended through the substance of the gum over the right upper lateral incisor tooth. About half an inch from the top of the nose was another oblique cut. There was a cut on the right angle of the mouth as if by the cut of a point of a knife the cut extended an inch and a half parallel with lower lip. There was on each side of cheek a cut which peeled up the skin forming a triangular flap about an inch and a half. On the left cheek there were 2 abrasions of the epithelium. There was a little mud on the left cheek - 2 slight abrasions of the epithelium under the left ear. The throat was cut across to the extent of about 6 or 7 inches. A superficial cut commenced about an inch and a half below the lobe and about 2 and a half inches behind the left ear and extended across the throat to about 3 inches below the lobe of the right ear. The big muscle across the throat was divided through on the left side - the large vessels on the left side of the neck were severed - the larynx was severed below the vocal chords. All the deep structures were severed to the bone the knife marking intervertebral cartilages - the sheath of the vessels on the right side was just opened, the carotid artery had a fine hole opening. The internal jugular vein was opened an inch and a half not divided. The blood vessels contained clot. All these injuries were performed by a sharp instrument like a knife and pointed. The cause of death was haemorrhage from the left common carotid artery. The death was immediate and the mutilations were inflicted after death. We examined the abdomen, the front walls were laid open from the breast bone to the pubes. The cut commenced opposite the ensiform cartilage. The incision went upwards not penetrating the skin that was over the sternum. It then divided the ensiform cartilage. The knife must have cut obliquely at the expense of the front surface of that cartilage. Behind this the liver was stabbed as if by the point of a sharp instrument. Below this was another incision into the liver of about 2 and a half inches and below this the left lobe of the liver was slit through by a vertical cut. 2 cuts were shewn by a jagging of the skin on the left side. The abdominal walls were divided in the middle line to within 1 of an inch of the navel, the cut then took a horizontal course for two inches and a half towards right side. It then divided round the navel on the left side and made a parallel incision to the former horizontal incision leaving the navel on a tongue of skin. Attached to the navel was 2 and a half inches of the lower part of the rectus muscle on the left side of the abdomen the incision then took an oblique direction to the right and was shelving. The incision went down the right side of the vagina and rectum for half an inch behind the rectum - There was a stab of about an inch on the left groin, this was done by a pointed instrument, below this was a cut of three inches going through all tissues making a wound of the peritoneum about the same extent. An inch below the crease of the thigh was a cut extending from the anterior spine of the ilium obliquely down the inner side of the left thigh and separating the left labium forming a flap of skin up to the groin. The left rectus muscle was not detached. There was a flap of skin formed from the right thigh attaching the right labium and extending up to the spine of the ilium. The muscles on the right side inserted into the poupart's ligament were cut through. The skin was retracted through the whole of the cut in the abdomen but vessels were not clotted – nor had there been any appreciable bleeding from the vessel. I draw the conclusion that the cut was made after death and there would not be much blood on the murderer. The cut was made by some one on right side of body kneeling below the middle of the body – I removed the contents of the stomach and placed it in a jar for further examination. There seemed very little in it in the way of food or fluid but from the cut end partly digested farinaceous food escaped - The intestines had been detached to a large extent from the mesentery. About 2 feet of the colon was cut away – The sigmoid flexure was invaginated into the rectum very tightly – right kidney pale bloodless with slight congestion of the base of the pyramids. There was a cut from the upper part of the slit on the under surface of the liver to the left side and another cut at right angles to this which were about an inch and a half deep and 2 and a half inches long. Liver itself was healthy - the gall bladder contained bile, the pancreas was cut but not through on the left side of the spinal column 3 and a half inches of the lower border of the spleen by half an inch was attached only to the peritoneum. The peritoneal lining was cut through on the left side and the left kidney carefully taken out and removed - the left renal artery was cut through - I should say that some one who knew the position of the kidney must have done it. The lining membrane over the uterus was cut through. The womb was cut through horizontally leaving a stump three-quarters of an inch, the rest of the womb had been taken away with some of the ligaments. The vagina and cervix of the womb was uninjured. The bladder was healthy and uninjured and contained 3 or 4 ounces of water. There was a tongue like cut through the anterior wall of the abdominal aorta. The other organs were healthy - There were no indications of connexion - I believe the wound in the throat was first inflicted - I believe she must have been lying on the ground - They [*sic*] wounds on the face and abdomen prove that they were inflicted by a sharp pointed knife and that in the abdomen by one six inches long. I believe the perpetrator of the act must have had considerable knowledge of the position of the organs in the abdominal cavity and the way of removing them. The part removed would be of no use for any professional purpose. It required a great deal of ['medical' – deleted] knowledge to have removed the kidney and to know where it was placed, such a knowledge might be possessed by some one in the habit of cutting up animals - I think the perpetrator of this act had sufficient time or he would not have nicked the lower eyelids. It would take at least 5 minutes - I cannot assign any reason for these parts being taken away. I feel sure there was no struggle – I believe it was the act of one person - the throat had been so instantly severed that no noise could have been emitted. I should not expect much blood to have been found on the person who had inflicted these wounds. The wounds could not have been self inflicted. I believe the wounds on the face to have been done to disfigure the corpse.

Dr Sequeira also gave evidence at the inquest and confirmed that he heard the whole of the evidence of Dr Gordon Brown and agreed with it 'in every particular'. However, when questioned by Henry Crawford, the City of London solicitor acting for the police, Sequeira said that he had 'formed the opinion that the perpetrator of the deed had no particular design on any particular organ', and that he did 'not think he was possessed of any great anatomical skill'. This was something of a strange deduction since Sequeira only saw Eddowes' corpse in the dark and by his own admission did not make a detailed examination of it. Sequeira further suggested that he knew the locality and that although the body lay in the darkest portion of the Square, 'There would have been sufficient light to enable the perpetrator of the deed to have committed the deed without the addition of any extra light', and he would not have expected that the killer would necessarily be spattered with blood.

Contrary to Dr Sequeira's assertions about illumination in the Square, Constable Watkins had to turn his lantern upon the 'darkest corner of Mitre Square' in order to clearly see Eddowes' body, and moments later George Morris the watchman at Kearley & Tonge also found it necessary to a shine light on the corpse. A report in *The Illustrated Police News* on 6 October 1888 suggested that; 'In the south east corner, and near to the entrance to Mitre Street, is the back yard of some premises in Aldgate, but the railings are closely hoarded. It was just under these that the woman was found quite hidden from sight by the shadow cast by the corner of the adjoining house'. It seems that the corner of the Square in which Eddowes was attacked was not quite as well illuminated as Dr Sequeira suggested and for some reason, he seemed to have adopted a contradictory stance. The darkness of the location is important when considering the precision and accuracy of the attack and subsequent mutilations and has significant bearing upon the knowledge and skill of the killer.

Catharine Eddowes was killed by a single cut to her neck. The wound measured some six to seven inches in length, divided the sternocleidomastoid muscle and the windpipe through the cricoid cartilage just below the level of the vocal cords, and completely severed the blood vessels including the carotid artery on the left side. The cut was deep enough to go down to the vertebral column on the left side and even marked the cartilaginous disk between the vertebrae. The wound also cut into the blood vessels on the right side of the neck making a pinhole opening in the left carotid artery and a larger cut in the internal jugular vein on that side. This was a powerful cut that started on the left side of the neck and tapered off to some extent on the right side of the neck. Eddowes died as a result of haemorrhage from the left common carotid artery. A very sharp knife was thus drawn across almost the full extent of the neck from left to right of the victim, the greatest depth being on the left side where the attacker could comfortably apply the most pressure. It is virtually impossible to deliver such a cut from the front or from the side of a victim whereas an approach from behind would almost certainly result in such injuries. The importance of surprise in the Ripper's method can not be overstressed and there is absolutely no way that he could fell his victims so quickly if forced to engage in any kind of a struggle. There was no time for attempted strangulation or time to engage in complex manoeuvres, and the murder of Eddowes largely proves the theory. She was taken completely by surprise with a cut to her neck that was delivered accurately, with force, and in virtual darkness, and the only way that this could possibly have been achieved was through an attack from behind. She immediately slumped to the ground supported by her attacker, but death was not instantaneous. Although she would quickly have been unconscious with death following shortly thereafter, such was the speed with which the Ripper worked it seems probable that she was still sentient as he commenced mutilation. However, her blood volume and pressure quickly diminished to the extent that there was relatively little bleeding from subsequent wounds.

Access to the upper portion of the uterus would have been possible with little difficulty after opening the abdomen, but in order to locate and remove the kidney the attacker would need to displace the intestines. Eddowes' killer cut through the colon and according to Dr Brown's testimony the intestines had been 'detached to a large extent from the mesentery' and were removed and placed over the right shoulder, with a 2ft length of colon being cut away. This detached length of large bowel lay beside Eddowes at the murder scene. Such an arrangement of the intestines does not quite fit with the sketch made of Eddowes' body by the City Surveyor Fredrick Foster, which clearly shows only a portion of the intestinal tract lying along the victim's right side with the cut end of the colon over the victim's right shoulder. In all other respects the sketch is accurate and it also shows the detached length of intestine lying between Eddowes' body and her left arm. There is no indication as to what time Foster attended the scene so the arrangement of the body could have changed slightly between when he drew the victim and Brown's examination. It seems likely that the victim's intestines were displaced to the right side of her abdomen and partially removed outside the body, with the cut end of the large intestine lying close to her head. Constable Watkins noted that the woman's bowels were 'protruding' but made no mention of them being over her shoulder.

The sole objective in removing or displacing the victim's intestines was to gain access to the left kidney but sorting out the tangle of intestines in the dark with some degree of urgency can not have been easy. It seems likely that the killer made a cut through the intestines so that their bulk could be easily displaced but his cut through the colon was too high and his access to the kidneys was partially obscured by a residual length of lower intestine. This being the case he then severed the remaining 2ft length of colon and discarded it to the left of the victim. According to the available testimony, the intestines were still connected to the victim by the stomach and were thus not completely excised. Dr Brown's description of the sigmoid flexure becoming tightly invaginated into the rectum is a likely consequence of muscular contraction of the bowel at level of the colorectal boundary following severance. This further suggests that the colon was cut at the junction with the rectum.

Brown testified that the intestines had been 'placed' in their dislocations, and when asked whether the intestines about the victims shoulder and to the side of the victim were put there by 'design' Brown replied that he thought they were. This form of words has been seized upon by some investigators to suggest a ritualistic element to the killings, but 'by design' does not necessarily suggest that the intestines were ritualistically arranged. There is no evidence for this and the intestines ended up where they were for no reason other than expediency.

With the intestines out of the way the killer was then able to access the kidneys, which are covered by a peritoneal membrane as well as being partially enclosed in renal fat. There is no indication that Eddowes carried an excess of body fat, which would have hampered dissection if present. By accounts the killer cut the membrane and removed the left kidney, which would have necessitated severing the organ's attachments to blood vessels and ureter. The kidneys are well defined but relatively concealed organs and some anatomical knowledge would be necessary for excision in the apparently tidy manner that Eddowes' killer was able to display, although he did catch the abdominal aorta with his knife at some point which resulted in a tongue-like cut through the anterior wall of the vessel.

While the kidneys are not easily discovered by chance, the uterus is rather more visible but it would need anatomical knowledge to be recognised as such. The uterus lies behind the urinary bladder, which in Eddowes' case contained a small amount, some 100mls or so, of urine and in front of the rectum. The killer severed the organ just above the cervix and cut it free from attaching ligaments without damage to the bladder. Presumably, the ovaries and fallopian tubes remained in the body together with the lower three quarters of an inch of uterus, the cervix, and vagina. The removal of the uterus could have sexual significance but the removal of a single kidney has no immediate significance and is rather more puzzling. Why not remove other, more accessible, discrete organs such as the spleen or, more particularly, the heart? By a cut through the diaphragm the killer would have quickly gained access to the heart instead of which he was apparently focussed on the more intricate procedure of removing a kidney. It is of course possible that he intended to remove both kidneys and other organs, and that his progress was unavoidably halted. More obvious sexual mutilation would have involved the external genitalia and although there were cuts to the labia these were incidental to longer cuts to the upper thigh on either side of the victim just below a line from the anterior iliac spine to the inner thigh. There were two additional wounds above this on the left side but no stab or cut wounds to or into the genitalia. In the case of Eddowes the breasts were not mutilated.

By 'connection' Brown meant sexual intercourse and there was no evidence from the murder scene or later from the post mortem examination that Eddowes had recently engaged in sexual activity. Specifically Brown mentioned that there was 'no evidence of secretion of any kind on the thighs'. Brown also made no mention of any disease affecting the right kidney apart from suggesting it to be congested at the base of the pyramids, which is not necessarily indicative of any underlying pathology. This absence of renal pathology is of significance when considering the portion of kidney sent, supposedly from Eddowes' killer, to the Chairman of the Vigilance Committee, which will be discussed later.

The process of mutilation and excision of organs would have been extremely difficult to undertake efficiently for anyone without anatomical knowledge and operating with urgency and in such dimly lit conditions. In inquest testimony Dr Brown said; 'I think the perpetrator of the act had sufficient time or he would not have nicked the lower eye lids'. This is rather misleading and suggests that the killer, having done the essence of his work, turned his attention to mutilating Eddowes' features, and assumes that the facial mutilations were carried out after the other mutilations, which of course may not be the case, and there is nothing to substantiate this either way. It is just as likely that the facial mutilations were carried out first, possibly as Eddowes continued to blink and breathe.

Brown sent the contents of Eddowes' stomach for analysis. William Sedgwick Saunders, the medical officer of health for the City, gave testimony at the inquest and his statement is documented in the official records:

I received the stomach of the deceased from Dr. Gordon Brown, carefully sealed, and I made an analysis of the contents, which had not been interfered with in any way. I looked more particularly for poisons of the narcotic class, but with negative results, there being not the faintest trace of any of those or any other poisons.

Frederick Brown reported that Eddowes' abdomen was opened 'from the breast bone to the pubes' and the skin retracted. The midline cut through Eddowes' abdominal skin 'stabbed' into the liver as the knife cut through her flesh indicating that the killer held the instrument as though cutting off a slice of bread with a back and forth action with downwards pressure. Brown suggested that Eddowes' killer crouched to the right of her body while cutting her abdomen. His position would be crucial since he would not wish to cast a shadow over the corpse in what little light reached the scene from the streetlight situated outside Kearley & Tonge's warehouse across the Square. From an entirely practical perspective it would have been far better for the killer to position himself on the left of Eddowes thus he would not obstruct light from the lamp and would be able to keep an eye on each of the three passageways into the Square. With his back to the Square, he would risk being surprised by someone approaching unheard from the passage leading to St James's Place, from along Church Passage, or even from Mitre Street. Whether or not the Ripper had completed his work on Eddowes, it is quite possible that he was interrupted and was forced to hurry from the scene as either Harvey approached from Church Passage or footsteps in Mitre Street heralded the nearby presence of Constable Watkins.

There was a streetlamp situated at the opposite end of Church Passage near the junction with Duke Street – this lamp would probably not have directly illuminated the spot in Duke Street where witnesses saw the man and woman standing together just prior to the murder, but it would have clearly illuminated the Duke Street entrance to Church Passage and this point is significant. From the location of the murder, Eddowes' killer would have a direct line of vision along the full length of Church Passage and given that he would be very alert to the sight or sound of anyone approaching he could have seen Constable Harvey as he entered Church Passage, well before the constable had an opportunity to see him.

The corner of the Square in which Eddowes was killed was also in a direct line of vision along Church passage. But there was another streetlamp situated in the passage at the junction with the Square, and if Constable Harvey stood beneath it as he viewed the Square it is entirely possible that he would not have seen the body of Eddowes lying on the floor in the darkest corner some 70ft away. The body was partially concealed by her dark clothing with very little intact flesh exposed; Eddowes had dark stockings on her lower legs and the torso would have been something of a bloody tangle of organs. This lamp, situated at the edge of the Square, would also likely prevent anyone approaching from along Church Passage from seeing anything beyond the immediately illuminated area.

The Ripper was either totally uninformed as to the beats and the direction in which they patrolled, and thus was extremely lucky, or he was exquisitely familiar with the constables' progress down to the last minute. By taking any exit from Mitre Square he ran the risk of colliding with a constable either in Mitre Street, in Duke Street, or in St James's Place and it seems on balance more likely that the Ripper was lucky rather than calculating in this respect. Any location suitable for sex would also be a suitable place for murder, and this fact the Ripper relied upon. Women who worked the streets would be well acquainted with the regular beats patrolled by the constables although given the heightened police activity in Whitechapel they could not be sure whether additional beats, especially by non-uniformed police, had been established. There were few streets and locations that were not patrolled, so prostitutes would need to be aware of their movements, perhaps to the extent that they would know how much time they had in which to earn their money before being interrupted. However, it is rather more likely that they knew of plenty of suitable locations to which they could take their clients and trusted to luck and the sound of approaching footsteps to warn of the presence of beat constables. The darkest corner of Mitre Square would be as good a place as any for sex, and although it is possible that Eddowes was attacked on route to somewhere else this seems unlikely.

With regard to the killer's exit from the Square, it is improbable that he left via Church Passage and into Duke Street. Even if Constable Watkins did not disturb him, the timing is so tight that Constable Harvey, approaching Church passage along Duke Street, would surely have seen the killer had he entered Duke Street.

And if the killer was prompted into leaving the scene by the appearance of Harvey as he started along Church Passage, then he could clearly only leave via the passage to St James's Place or out into Mitre Street. To leave via the passage to St James's Place would mean that he would have to cross the Square diagonally although he would be quickly out of the line of vision from Church Passage and this would probably have been the safer option assuming that he knew the vicinity. Instinctively, and if he was less familiar with his surroundings, he would move in the opposite direction from the approaching danger and this would take him out into Mitre Street. Since Watkins did not encounter anyone as he turned from Aldgate High Street and into Mitre Street along his beat, there is every possibility that the killer left the scene via the passage to St James's Place. He would probably have heard the sound of the watchman's whistle as he made his retreat from the vicinity and would have been very aware that officers would soon invade the area and many would come from Bishopsgate police station; the very direction in which he was moving. At this time his safest option would have been to travel north or north west and deeper into Whitechapel. Such a move was expedient and need not necessarily indicate that his home lay in that direction.

At 2.55am, a little over an hour after the murder of Catharine Eddowes, Police Constable Alfred Long found a portion of bloodstained white apron lying in a passage during the course of patrolling his beat in Goulston Street, Whitechapel. The cloth was discovered in the passage leading to numbers 106 to 119 of the Wentworth Model Dwellings. Goulston Street runs roughly north to south between Wentworth Street in the north and Whitechapel High Street in the south and is parallel with Castle Alley where the body of Alice McKenzie was found less than a year later. Above the apron on the wall was written in chalk, *The Juwes are the men That Will not be Blamed for nothing*, wording that has come to be known as the Goulston Street graffito.[87] Long searched the staircase and the building but did not find anything else. He then took the piece of apron back to the station in Commercial Street and reported to the inspector on duty. Detective Constable Daniel Halse had also walked along Goulston Street at 2.20am and did not see the portion of apron, although he admitted that he would not necessarily have noticed it had it been there. It was the first time on duty in Goulston Street for Constable Long thus it is likely that he would have been extra diligent in his duties. Long's assertion that the portion of apron was not in the passageway when he past by earlier probably means that it was not there, and not that he missed seeing it. There is every indication that the piece of apron had been deposited in Goulston Street between 2.20am when the constable walked his beat and observed nothing in the street and 2.55am when he returned to Goulston Street. Long was adamant that the apron was not there when he passed along Goulston Street at 2.20am even though he could not say whether the writing was there then or not. He only noticed the writing after seeing the portion of apron so it is quite possible that the writing had been done earlier. The message, written in white chalk on a fascia of black bricks edging the doorway, was on the right of the stairwell and Constable Long noticed it, 'while trying to discover whether there were any marks about'. Long was only able to see the writing with the aid of his lantern thus it would not have been easy for someone to have written the message in almost complete darkness. Much has been made of this message and authors and researchers have pondered at length over its relevance. I am of the opinion that it has no relevance and was not the work of Jack the Ripper. The portion of apron was identified as matching the piece missing from the garment worn by Eddowes and its presence in Goulston Street is worthy of consideration.

Why did Eddowes' killer remove a piece of her apron and how did it end up in Goulston Street? If the piece of apron had been taken simply to use to clean hands or knife then it would have likely been discarded at or close to the scene. And in any case there would be no need to cut away a piece of apron simply to clean knife or hands; the killer could have used Eddowes' apron *in situ* for that purpose, and even if it had been used is such a way then why retain it? The fact that it was found within fifteen minutes walking distance from the scene at least forty-five minutes after the murder is also puzzling. It is possible that Eddowes' killer used the cloth to wrap and safely conceal his knife although one imagines that he would already have arrangements to conceal the weapon in the first place. There is a more likely possibility that he removed a piece of her apron in order to wrap up and conceal the excised organs as he fled from the scene.

There is little doubt that the portion of apron found in Goulston Street was that missing from Eddowes' apron. Dr Brown's testimony recorded in the official transcript confirms:

My attention was called to the apron – it was the corner of an apron with a string attached. The blood spots were of recent origin – I have seen a portion of an apron produced by Dr Phillips and stated to have been found in Goulston Street. It is impossible to say it is human blood. I fitted the piece of apron which has a new piece of material on it which was evidently sewn on to the piece I have. The seams of the borders of the two actually corresponding – some blood and apparently faecal matter was found on the portion found in Goulston Street.

Removed organs would not necessarily bleed to any great extent especially since the victim had already been exsanguinated via the neck wound by the time the organs were excised. Contrary to what may be imagined, a cloth used to wrap such organs would not necessarily be heavily bloodstained but the blood would be more patchy and smeared than concentrated in one location. Dr Brown also suggests that the piece of apron had 'smears of blood on one side as if a hand or knife had been wiped on it'. Unfortunately his assertion may not be wholly objective and could have been influenced by what he surmised about the killer's actions. In any event the blood pattern from wiping a bloody knife and that from wiping bloody hands on cloth would be quite different, the former providing a much more distinct pattern than the latter. It would seem that the blood stains on the portion of apron were rather diffuse.

If the piece of apron had been used by the Ripper to conceal the organs removed from Eddowes' body then the fact that the cloth had been subsequently discarded may also indicate that the organs had been disposed of. If the Ripper intended to remove the organs and not necessarily to retain them then disposing of them quickly would make sense. Having done this he would then have no further need for the piece of apron. That any discarded human organs were not found would be of no great surprise. Fresh offal, human or otherwise, would be quickly consumed in an environment rife with rats and feral cats and dogs, or simply remain hidden amid rubbish that littered the streets. It is highly possible that in the course of roaming the streets and avoiding the substantial police presence Eddowes' killer decided that carrying around a couple of human organs was not a good idea, wrapped as they were as a small bundle in a portion of the victim's apron. Carrying such incriminating evidence would provide a direct route to the gallows and he would certainly be aware of intense police activity on the streets.

There was clearly an inherent danger in using a very sharp knife in the dark. During the process of mutilating Eddowes' body the killer would need to use both hands; the right to hold the knife and the left to hold his victim or parts of his victim while he cut through the tissues. There is thus a possibility that the killer actually cut himself in the process of mutilating Eddowes' body and such being the case he would need to wrap the bleeding wound in a makeshift bandage. A piece of apron would be perfect for such a purpose and the injury sustained would probably have been to his left hand or wrist. The exact size of the piece of apron removed and the pattern or extent of blood stains upon on it would certainly have helped to suggest why the killer needed the cloth.

Fredrick Foster, architect and surveyor, testified at the inquest that there were two routes to Goulston Street from Mitre Square; one from Church Passage through Duke Street crossing Houndsditch, through Gravel Lane, Stoney Lane crossing Middlesex Street (Petticoat Lane), and through Goulston Street.[88] The surveyor suggested that; 'A person going from Mitre Square to Flower and Dean Street would go as the most direct route across Goulston Street – it would take within one quarter of an hour to get there'. The reference to Flower and Dean Street resulted from a suggestion from Crawford that the Eddowes' killer may have been on route to a lodging house after his escape from the murder scene. However this was not an entirely justified leap in logic. In any event, the timing is curious.

Eddowes was murdered in Mitre Square some time between 1.30am and 1.44am and her killer had fled the scene by the time Police Constable Edward Watkins found her body at around 1.44am. If the killer left the Square into St James's Place or via Church Passage to Duke Street then across Houndsditch, along Gravel Lane, and across Middlesex Street then he would have been in Goulston Street in a matter of minutes; five at the most. But the earliest time at which the piece of apron was actually deposited in Goulston Street, if we assume that Constable Long was diligent, would have been just after 2.20am, say 2.25am or a minimum of forty-five minutes after the killer had left Mitre Square. In reality however, the delay was probably much longer than this and up to seventy minutes after the murder. So if the Ripper did deposit the piece of apron at this point why was there such a delay? Having committed such horrendous murder and mutilation, Eddowes' killer would hardly have dawdled his way around the streets of Whitechapel carrying a knife, a bloodstained piece of white cloth, a human uterus and kidney. It is of course quite possible that the apron was discarded, with or without the organs, by the killer immediately after leaving the scene and that the bloody apron was removed to the site of discovery by a dog! Indeed, there are far too many alternative scenarios for the discovery of the portion of apron to be anything other than of peripheral interest.

Using the most lenient interpretation of witness timings then the following breakdown would just about allow the Ripper sufficient time to kill and mutilate his victim before fleeing the scene. Debates as to the precise timing of Eddowes' death are of academic value only, although the murder of Eddowes does yet again illustrate that even when there are reliable witnesses there is no guarantee that their presence will add any useful contribution to determining exactly what happened.

Whether or not the couple seen by witnesses at the corner of Church Passage and Duke Street were Catharine Eddowes and her killer is of importance from the point of view of identifying a possible suspect, but of little consequence as far as timing the murder is concerned. Even if the woman seen with the man in a peaked cap was not Eddowes the facts remain that there was not a body in Mitre Square at 1.30am but there was at 1.44am according to the same witness using the same time reference point. The situation is somewhat complicated by the appearance of Constable Harvey who briefly cast an eye over the Square at 1.40am and saw nothing, which suggests that Eddowes was killed and mutilated in an incredibly short window of opportunity. If the couple standing at the entrance to Church Passage and witnessed by Joseph Lawende and Joseph Levy were indeed Eddowes and her killer then they must have moved immediately into Mitre Square via Church Passage after being seen by the witnesses and then across the Square to the southern most corner where Eddowes was murdered the instant the Ripper realised that they were alone. The distance from Duke Street to the point where Eddowes was murdered is around 160ft, or a casual walking time of no more than one minute.

There exists a period from 1.36am to 1.44am during which Eddowes was murdered and mutilated but this period was interrupted by the arrival of Constable Harvey on the periphery of the scene at around five minutes before Watkins patrolled the Square or three minutes after Eddowes and her killer likely moved into the Square. Realistically, neither of these short periods allows sufficient time for Eddowes and her killer to move into the Square, for her to be murdered and mutilated, and for the killer to leave the scene. There is little doubt that Eddowes was not murdered prior to Watkins' visit to the Square at 1.30am, but there must be some doubt as to whether or not Harvey was able to see sufficiently well into the dark corner of the Square distant from his vantage point at 1.38am to 1.39am. Harvey did not mention seeing the couple witnessed by others standing in Duke Street at the entrance to Church Passage thus by 1.37am or 1.38am they must have moved on and can not reasonably have been anywhere other than in Mitre Square by that time – unless of course, the couple seen by Lawende and others were not Eddowes with her killer.

On balance I am inclined to the opinion that the couple probably were Eddowes and her killer and that after they were seen by Lawende and friends at 1.35am they moved into Church Passage, placing their arrival there at 1.36am to 1.37am. Harvey may not have been too thorough in his examination of Mitre

Square since he knew that Watkins would patrol the whole of the Square a few minutes later. If Harvey had not been as thorough as he might have been in the conduct of his duties then he would be unlikely to admit as much during the inquest or at any other time. Seventy feet is a sizeable distance in badly lit conditions, especially when the viewer is standing beneath a lamp and Harvey can not have been certain that there was no one in the Square when he supposedly looked. It must be remembered that the streets were dimly lit by gaslights that punched holes in the darkness rather than illuminated it and the contrast between light and shadow were accentuated. It is my belief that Eddowes and the Ripper were in Mitre Square when Harvey reached the limit of his beat along Church Passage and that he did not see them as they hid in the shadows at the opposite end of the Square. The constable would have been clearly visible to anyone in the Square as he stood beneath the gas lamp on the wall just inside Church Passage. Harvey saw no one and nothing stirred in the gloom so he turned away and set off back towards Duke Street. It is possible that Eddowes may even have been lying on ground dead but not mutilated when Harvey surveyed the darkness but I doubt that her killer would have loitered when he saw the approaching constable at the far end of Church Passage. It is far more likely that they stood together in the darkness of the corner in which she died until the policeman turned back along Church passage. A man with a very sharp knife can do a considerable amount of damage in five minutes and I believe that there was then sufficient time for him to complete his objective then flee along the passage to St James's Place when he heard the approaching footsteps of Constable Watkins. It would be of no surprise that Watkins heard no sound of a man leaving the scene, since one would imagine that a killer of the ilk of the Ripper would be wearing soft-soled boots – unlike those worn by the constables. In an article in The *Illustrated Police News* on 6 October 1888, George Morris, the night watchman at Kearley and Tonge stated that as a rule he could 'hear the footsteps of the policeman as he passed on his beat every quarter of an hour'. If Morris could hear Watkins' footsteps from inside the warehouse then it is likely that the Ripper would also have heard them as the constable approached Mitre Square from Mitre Street, and likely that Morris would have heard the Ripper had his boots been other than silent.

As the Ripper made his escape he would be aware of the police stations in Bishopsgate Street and Seething Lane (City of London Police) and Leman Street (Metropolitan Police) and would have avoided the major routes, preferring the relative safety of side streets. In *The Times* on 1 October 1888 a reporter observed that by 'leaving the square by either of the courts [the killer] would be able to pass quickly away through the many narrow thoroughfares without exciting observation. Many people would be in the immediate neighbourhood, even at this early hour, making preparations for the market which takes place every Sunday in Middlesex Street and the adjacent thoroughfares'. If the Ripper was present at some point in Goulston Street such does not necessarily imply that this was the direction in which his 'home' was located. He may have needed to avoid constables on patrol since many more had been drafted into the area by the time of Eddowes murder and as soon as they were alerted to the latest murder the area would quickly have become the centre of attention. Additional police officers would have moved into the area from Bishopsgate station via Houndsditch and Middlesex Street to the north and from Lemen Street police station from the south via Leman Street and Whitechapel High Street. The Metropolitan Police would already be heavily engaged in Berner Street after the murder of Elizabeth Stride earlier that evening and the nearest station to that location would be Lemen Street. In other words the City and Metropolitan Police would have converged in numbers upon the very route that the Ripper would have taken had he gone directly to Goulston Street from Mitre Square. However, if the Ripper was not directly involved in depositing the portion of apron in Goulston Street then he could have been anywhere by the time the area was saturated with police officers.

By 2.00am orders had been given for the neighbourhood to be searched in all directions and for every man to be stopped and examined. Can it be pure good fortune that the Ripper continually avoided being apprehended? It is reasonable to assume that he fitted in well with the surroundings, at least when out with murderous intent. He would dress and behave accordingly, even if such was not his normal style or manner. To do otherwise would be absurd and the Ripper was not a man to draw attention to himself. If Eddowes and her killer were witnessed at the Duke Street entrance to Church Passage just before the murder then the description of the suspect given by Lawende fits well with what one may expect – an inconspicuous individual whose manner of clothing was completely in keeping with those around him.

The jury at the inquest into the death of Catharine Eddowes needed just a few moments to return a verdict of wilful murder against some person or persons unknown.

On 16 October 1888, sixteen days after the murder of Catharine Eddowes, George Lusk, president of the Whitechapel Vigilance Committee, received half a kidney through the post. The tissue was packed into a three-inch square cardboard box and wrapped in brown paper, and accompanied by a letter known subsequently as *The Lusk Letter* and sent *From hell*. The postmark on the package was unclear. Lusk immediately considered the kidney to be a hoax but nonetheless presented it for medical opinion and confusion ensued not least of all because of the interpretation of the pathological condition of Eddowes' remaining kidney and that of the portion received by Lusk. As a general observation, conditions that affect the kidneys, other than localised lesions, manifest equally in both kidneys thus the appearance of one such organ of the pair in respect of generalised renal disease is a fair indicator of what the second of the pair will look like. Had Eddowes suffered from renal disease and had the portion of kidney received by Lusk presented the same picture then the possibility that they came from the same individual could not be excluded. However, if the two kidneys were dissimilar in terms of generalised pathology then the chances are strong that they would not be from the same individual. The first medical opinion came from Dr Thomas Openshaw, curator of the Pathology Museum at London Hospital. Openshaw reportedly described the organ to be the 'ginny' kidney of a 45-year-old woman afflicted by Bright's disease, and removed from the body during the previous three weeks. The following day Openshaw denied that he had made such an astounding deduction and suggested that he had merely described the kidney as being of human origin and preserved in spirits of wine. This version had clearly been embellished before appearing in the press, since any reference to 'ginny', implying excessive drinking of gin, the sex and age of the individual could hardly be assessed without the accompanying corpse. Dr Sedgwick Saunders, the City pathologist, passed further comment although there is no evidence that he actually examined the kidney. Saunders said that if the organ had been preserved in spirits of wine then this indicated that it was from a hospital or dissecting theatre and that in all probability it was a student hoax. Twenty-two years later, the memoirs of Major Henry Smith, Acting Commissioner, City of London Police, September 1888, added further to the debate. According to Smith, he had shown the kidney to Henry Sutton, Senior Surgeon at the London Hospital, who was of the opinion that the kidney showed symptoms of Bright's disease and that the length of renal artery attached to the portion of kidney was what would have been expected considering what remained of the left renal artery in Eddowes' corpse.[89]

Dr Frederick Brown reported the condition of the kidney that remained in Eddowes' body as 'pale, bloodless, with slight congestion at the base of the pyramid'. Given that Bright's disease would almost certainly affect both kidneys to more or less the same extent in an individual then we can reasonably assume that Eddowes' left kidney, the one removed from her body by the Ripper, had a similar appearance to the one remaining. Some have taken Brown's description to indicate that Eddowes' suffered from Bright's disease but there is no evidence of this. The fact that the kidney remaining in her body was generally pale is of little surprise given that most of her blood had drained from her tissues and although congestion can be indicative of disease it can also represent no more than retained blood and in an organ that had largely exsanguinated the difference would be pronounced indeed. Moreover, the area described as being congested by Brown was 'at the base of the pyramid', or towards the middle of the kidney, and in a different location from that in which Bright's disease would be apparent. Thus, it seems that Catharine Eddowes did not suffer from Bright's disease and Sedgwick Saunders indeed gives his opinion that Eddowes' remaining kidney was healthy. This being the case and if the portion of kidney received by George Lusk was affected by Bright's disease then it is unlikely to have originated from the body of the Ripper victim.

Brown also examined the portion of kidney sent to Lusk and conveyed his impressions to a reporter from *The Sunday Times*. According to the newspaper Brown commented as follows:

So far as I can form an opinion, I do not see any substantial reason why this portion of the kidney should not be the portion of the one taken from the murdered woman. I cannot say that it is the left kidney. It must have been cut previously to its being immersed in the spirit which exercised a hardening process. It certainly had not been in spirit for more than a week. As has been stated, there is no portion of the renal artery adhering to it, it having been trimmed up, so, consequently, there could be no correspondence established between the portion of the body from which it was cut. As it exhibits no trace of decomposition, when we consider the length of time that had elapsed since the commission of the murder, we come to the conclusion that the probability is slight of its being a portion of the murdered woman of Mitre Square.[90]

Even allowing for the ambiguous double negative in the opening sentence, this report has to be viewed with caution since it appears in a newspaper and thus may have been edited to some extent but assuming the essence is reported accurately, then there are points of interest. First of all Brown makes no mention of Bright's disease, either in Eddowes' kidney, or in the portion of kidney received by Lusk; furthermore, he states quite clearly that there is no attached renal artery which seems to contradict the recollections of Smith in his memoirs, and that the portion of kidney showed no signs of decomposition but had been in spirit for no longer than a week. The 'spirit' used was alcohol and Brown could probably determine from the degree of hardening and the absence of any obvious decomposition that the tissue must have been immediately placed in preservative but to have not been immersed in such for longer than a week, although he could not have been entirely objective about this since he clearly had in mind the death of Catharine Eddowes. Eddowes was murdered sixteen days earlier and had the kidney not been placed into preservative until over a week after death then signs of decomposition prior to immersion in alcohol would have been apparent to Brown's experienced eye.[91] The letter that accompanied the package sent to George Lusk was not signed by 'Jack the Ripper' and the handwriting differed from that on the contemporaneous *Dear Boss* letter and the *saucy Jacky* postcard.

On balance there is no evidence to support the suggestion that the portion of kidney was from that removed from the mutilated body of Catharine Eddowes and the episode was a hoax that served as yet another distraction for the police and, no doubt, a huge source of amusement for the Ripper.

2.3.5 Alice McKenzie (c1849-89)
It was almost ten months before Whitechapel saw another murder that bore the characteristic touch of Jack the Ripper. In the early hours of Wednesday 17 July 1889 Constable Walter Andrews discovered the body of prostitute Alice McKenzie lying on the pavement close to a lamppost in Castle Alley. Her throat had been cut. The wounds to McKenzie are detailed in Diagram 5 and the location of the murder is illustrated in Map 5 and a complete tabulation of relevant findings is given in Table 2. Metropolitan Police and Home Office files relating to the murder of Alice McKenzie are held in the National Archives.[92]

Said to have been born in Peterborough in 1849, McKenzie was also known as Alice Bryant and went under the nickname 'Clay Pipe' on account of her smoking habit. A clay pipe and a farthing were found under her body. When discovered, McKenzie was wearing old clothing amounting to a dress, red stuff bodice patched under the arms and sleeves, odd coloured stockings (one maroon and one black), a brown stuff kilted skirt, a brown linsey petticoat, white apron, white chemise, paisley shawl, and button boots. McKenzie was known to drink excessively. From 1883 onwards, she cohabited irregularly over six years with a porter by the name of John McCormack and the couple lived in various common lodging houses most recently 54 Gun Street, Spitalfields. According to McCormack who was the only source of information about McKenzie, she did not have any children so far as he knew, and she worked as a washerwoman and charwoman for East End Jewish residents. There has been some speculation as to whether or not she worked as a street prostitute but she almost certainly did, and her 'honest' employment may not have been quite so regular as she led others to believe. McKenzie crushed the top of her left thumb following a machine accident, which left just half the nail. She allegedly never wore a hat but she often wore a shawl.

Until the murder of Mary Jane Kelly the police had been reliant upon the opinion of the Whitechapel district Police Surgeon George Bagster Phillips, but after Kelly's death the police became so desperate to make progress that Assistant Commissioner Anderson of the Metropolitan CID sought a second opinion to determine how many of the Whitechapel murders were the work of one killer. Clearly by this time they realised the overriding importance of this fundamental piece of information. Thomas Bond, Police Surgeon to Westminster A Division of the Metropolitan Police was requested to be present at the post mortem examination of Mary Jane Kelly and from that point onwards he had practical involvement and wrote reports on the deaths of Alice McKenzie, and Rose Mylett, as well as giving an overview of the murder series and a rather speculative profile of the killer based upon the accumulated information. Because this latter report was addressed specifically to Anderson we are entitled to assume that the Assistant Commissioner involved Bond in the process from, and including, the murder of Kelly. However, if Anderson thought that Bond's involvement would provide the police with a clearer understanding then he was wrong and it was almost inevitable that the police surgeons would be at variance, especially since Bond's appraisal of the murders prior to Kelly was based upon an examination of the case notes and not consequential to any practical involvement. The exercise turned into something of a competition between Bond and Phillips with the entirely predictable outcome that neither would win.[93]

After the murder of Mary Jane Kelly, seen by many as the culmination of the Ripper's malignancy, the frenzy of interest and demands for the killer to be apprehended subsided to some extent. But with the murder of Alice McKenzie there came a renewed urgency and it was of paramount importance to determine whether or not Jack the Ripper was back at work again after an absence of so many months. After their deliberations Phillips concluded that the murder of Alice McKenzie was not, on 'purely anatomical and professional grounds', the work of the Whitechapel serial killer, but Bond was of the opinion that the murder was performed by 'the same person who committed the former series of Whitechapel murders'.

Wynne Baxter presided over the inquest into the death of Alice McKenzie, which opened on 17 July. Official transcripts of the inquest are not available but proceedings were reported in the newspapers and *The Times* commenced reporting on 18 July 1889. Police Constable Joseph Allen gave evidence to the inquest:

Last night I was in Castle-alley. It was then 20 minutes past 12 when I passed through. I was through the alley several times. I remained there for five minutes. I entered the alley through the archway in Whitechapel-road. I had something to eat under the lamp where the deceased was found. Having

Alice McKenzie

remained in the alley for five minutes, I went into Wentworth-street. There was neither man nor woman there. There were wagons in the alley - two right underneath the lamp.

I would not swear that there was no one in the wagons, as I did not look into them; one of the wagons was an open one. Everything was very quiet at the time. The backs of some of the houses in Newcastle-street faced the alley, and in some of the upper windows were lights. That was not an unusual thing at that time. I cannot say if any of the windows were open. No sounds came from those houses. On leaving the alley I met Constable Walter Andrews, 272 H, in Wentworth-street. It was about 100 yards from the alley where I met Andrews. I spoke to Andrews, who then went towards Goldston-street [sic].

I looked at my watch. It was 12:30 when I left the alley. At the end is a publichouse - the Three Crowns - and as I passed the landlord was shutting up the house. After leaving Andrews I went towards Commercial-street and met Sergeant Badlam, [sic] 31 H, who told me a woman had been found murdered in Castle-alley, and he directed me to go to the station. When the sergeant spoke to me it was [between] five minutes to 1, and 1 o'clock when I got to the station.

Police Constable Walter Andrews who discovered the body told the inquest that:

About ten minutes to 1 this morning I saw Sergeant Badlam [sic] at the corner of Old Castle-street, leading into Castle-alley. That was on the opposite corner of the publichouse. The sergeant said, "All right," and I said the same. I then proceeded up Castle-alley, and tried the doors on the west side of the alley. While doing so I noticed a woman lying on the pavement. Her head was lying eastward, and was on the edge of the kerbstone, with her feet towards the building, which was a wheelwright's shop and warehouse.

McKenzie's body lay across the pavement between the wheelwright's shop and warehouse and two wagons, a scavenger's wagon and a brewer's dray, that were parked in the road and chained together. She was underneath the lamp, about 2ft from the lamppost. Her head was over the kerb and almost beneath the scavenger's wagon. According to Andrews, her clothing was raised to her neck such that her legs and body were exposed and he noticed blood running from the left side of her neck and into the gutter. Andrews touched her abdomen and 'it was quite warm'. He raised the alarm by blowing his whistle and after two or three minutes Sergeant Edward Badham arrived and gave him orders to stay with the body until the doctor appeared. Dr Phillips arrived at about 1.10am.

Andrews was of the opinion that McKenzie had been standing up against the lamppost, and then pulled or dragged down and killed. McKenzie's body was not visible from cottages on the opposite side of the road and Andrews said that there was no trail of blood away from the body, and no splashes of blood. The coroner asked Andrews if people came there to sleep in the vans and the constable, who had been on that beat for a fortnight, replied that people often came to sleep in the vans, but that they were turned out when found. Andrews added that he had not seen the alley used for immoral purposes, nor had he seen any women there at all.

Constable George Neve gave information to the inquest as reported in *The Times* on 18 July 1889. When asked by the coroner whether he knew the deceased and whether he had seen her about at night Neve said:

I have known her about the place for 12 months, and have seen her the worse for drink. [I have seen her at night] Between 10 and 11 o'clock. It was my opinion she was a prostitute. I have seen her talking to men. I have seen her in Gun-street, Brick-lane, and Dorset-street. I did not know where she lived.

I had not seen her before that evening. In fact, I had not seen her for about a fortnight.

Neve rushed to the scene at 12.55am after meeting sergeant Badham in Commercial Street. He searched the vicinity, looking over the hoarding and in the wagons but saw no movement and heard no sound.

In testimony reported in *The Times* on 18 July 1888, Detective Inspector Edmund Reid commented on the locality where the murder took place:

I do not think any stranger would go down there unless he was taken there. I did not go into the High-street, Whitechapel, within a few minutes of my arrival in the alley. There are people in High-street, Whitechapel, all night. Two constables are continually passing through the alley all night. It is hardly ever left alone for more than five minutes. Although it is called an alley it is really a broad turning, with two narrow entrances. Any person standing at the Wentworth-street end would look upon it as a blind street. No stranger would think he could pass through it, and none but foot passengers can. No person, unless he went along the pathway, could have seen the body on account of the shadow of the lamp and the vans which screened the body. Any person going along the road would have seen it. If I wanted to watch any one I would stand under the lamp. The darkness was so great that it was necessary to use the constable's lamp to see that the throat was cut, although it was just under the lamp. I think the alley is sufficiently lighted; there are five lamps here.

Castle Alley was the southerly portion of a thoroughfare from Wentworth Street in the north to Whitechapel High Street in the south. The northerly portion of the thoroughfare was known as Old Castle Street, the change to Castle Alley being a right angle bend in the road at the rear of the Public Baths and Wash Houses that opened onto Goulston Square part way along Goulston Street which featured in the murder of Catharine Eddowes. Access to Castle Alley from the north was wide enough for carts, but from the south the alley narrowed to a passageway before opening onto the High Street. Sarah Smith lived at the Wash Houses and gave the following testimony at the inquest, reported in *The Times* on 18 July 1889:

I live at the Whitechapel Baths and Washhouses. My husband is a retired police-officer, and is superintendent of the baths. I am money-taker there. The baths back on to Castle-alley, and the window of my room looks into Castle-alley, close to where the body was found. I went to bed this morning between 12:15 and 12:30. I did not go to sleep, and had no idea that anything had happened, until I heard a knock at the door, and also a whistle blown. If there had been any call for help in the alley I would certainly have heard it. My bedstead is up against the wall, next to Castle-alley.

Several cottages backed onto the alley on the north side and directly opposite the rear of the Wash Houses and it seems likely that McKenzie was murdered just south of the rear of the Wash Houses and on the same side of the road at the widest part of Castle Alley, around two-thirds of the way along the alley from the entrance to Whitechapel High Street.

It is highly likely, judging from Inspector Reid's testimony, that McKenzie's killer would not have been in Castle Alley unless he was familiar with the area and if that were the case then he would be aware that the Alley was patrolled by two constables and that it was 'hardly left alone for more than five minutes'. It would thus have been a risky choice as a place to commit murder and mutilation, and it seems rather more likely that the killer engaged with McKenzie and that she proposed to take him to a place that she knew where they could have sex. It is possible that she intended to use one of the wagons for the purpose but it really matters not. As soon as they were alone the killer cut her throat and set about the objective of mutilation before being disturbed by the sound of footsteps as Constable Andrews approached from Old Castle Street. The only route of escape was to the south and via the passageway onto the High Street where the killer was able to mingle easily enough and could not have been sufficiently bloodstained to attract attention, although it must also be said that people would not have been as vigilant as they had been after the murder of Mary Jane Kelly nine months earlier. There is no way of knowing whether the couple were travelling north or south along Castle Alley when the attack took place but it is generally assumed that they had entered Castle Alley from the High Street and travelled north towards Old Castle Street and Wentworth Street.

Phillips gave rather brief evidence at the inquest, but behind his testimony was a very detailed post mortem examination. *The Times* on 18 July 1888 reported Phillips' testimony as follows:

Dr. George Baxter Phillips, divisional surgeon of the H Division, said that he was called, and arrived at Castle-alley at 1:10 a.m. on Wednesday, when it was raining very hard. On his arrival in Castle-alley, at the back premises of the washhouses he found the body lying on the pavement in the position already described, as to which the witness gave full details. Having inspected the body, he had it removed to the shed used as a mortuary in the Pavilion-yard, Whitechapel. There he re-examined the body and left it in charge of the police. Yesterday he made a post-mortem examination at the same shed - a most inconvenient and altogether ill-appointed place for such a purpose. It tended greatly to the thwarting of justice having such a place to perform such examinations in. With several colleagues he made the examination at 2 o'clock, when rigor mortis was well marked. The witness then described the wounds, of which there were several, and these were most of them superficial cuts on the lower part of the body. There were several old scars and there was the loss of the top of the right thumb, apparently caused by some former injury. The wound in the neck was 4 in. long, reaching from the back part of the muscles, which were almost entirely divided. It reached to the fore part of the neck to a point 4 in. below the chin. There was a second incision, which must have commenced from behind and immediately below the first. The cause of death was syncope, arising from the loss of blood through the divided carotid vessels, and such death probably was almost instantaneous.

Dr Thomas Bond was not among the 'several colleagues' although he did later inspect the corpse and he did provide a lengthy assessment of the post mortem findings and his own opinion on them in a report that I shall consider later. On the third day of the inquest, reported in *The Times* on 15 August, Phillips gave further medical testimony:

On the occasion of my making the post-mortem examination, the attendants of the mortuary, on taking off the clothing of the deceased woman removed a short clay pipe, which one of them threw upon the ground, by which means it was broken. I had the broken pieces placed upon a ledge at the end of the post-mortem table; but it has disappeared, and although inquiry has been made about it, up to the present time it has not been forthcoming. The pipe had been used. It came from the woman's clothing. The attendants, whom I have often seen there before, are old workhouse men.

There were five marks on the abdomen, and, with the exception of one, were on the left side of the abdomen. The largest one was the lowest, and the smallest one was the exceptional one mentioned, and was typical of a finger-nail mark. They were coloured, and in my opinion were caused by the finger-nails and thumb nail of a hand. I have on a subsequent examination assured myself of the correctness of this conclusion.

[She had been dead for] Not more than half an hour, and very possibly a much shorter time. It was a wet and cold night. The deceased met her death, in my opinion, while lying on the ground on her back. The injuries to the abdomen were caused after death. The great probability is that he was on the right side of the body at the time he killed her, and that he cut her throat with a sharp instrument. I should think the latter had a shortish blade and was pointed. I cannot tell whether it was the first or second cut that terminated the woman's life. The first cut, whether it was the important one or not, would probably prevent the woman from crying out on account of the shock. The whole of the air passages were uninjured, so that if she was first forced on to the ground she might have called out. The bruises over the collar-bone may have been caused by finger pressure. There were no marks suggestive of pressure against the windpipe.

The coroner asked whether Phillips thought that there was any skill involved in inflicting the injuries and whether they were similar to those 'seen in other cases'. Phillips responded that the killer must have had some knowledge of, 'how effectually to deprive a person of life, and that speedily', but that the injuries to the throat are not similar to those in the other cases'. Phillips also forwarded his opinion that; 'The knife that was used could not have been so large as the ordinary butcher's slaughter knife' and that the fingernail marks on the body were not caused by McKenzie but by another hand and after the throat was cut.

John McCormack viewed McKenzie's corpse in the mortuary and recognised her instantly by her thumb, which had half the nail missing. McCormack also noted the scars on her forehead and recognised the clothes that she wore, and confirmed that she was aged about 40. McCormack had last seen McKenzie alive at between 3.00pm and 4.00pm on the afternoon before her death at which time he gave her one shilling and eight pennies in order that she could pay their rent for the following night of eight pennies and she could 'do what she liked with the remainder'. McCormack did not see her alive again, and when he woke up at between 10.00pm and 11.00pm he discovered that she had gone out. When questioned by the coroner McCormack denied any knowledge that McKenzie worked as a prostitute but that is hardly surprising, since McCormack would hardly wish to be accused of living off immoral earnings. Alice McKenzie had secondary syphilis.

Elizabeth Ryder the deputy of the common lodging house in Gun Street, Spitalfields, where McKenzie and McCormack resided also suggested that McKenzie earned her money honestly, that she did not get money on the streets, and that she was generally in bed by 10.00pm. However, Ryder also stated that McKenzie was in the habit of staying out all night if she had no money to pay for her lodgings; not of course that she would have much choice to do otherwise. Ryder last saw McKenzie when she left the lodging house at about 8.30pm on the evening of 16 July. It was originally thought that a friend of McKenzie, the delightfully named Mog Cheeks, had also been killed because she also did not come home that night. Cheeks turned up the following day having spent the night at her sister's house.[94]

Two women, Margaret Franklin and Catherine Hughes, saw McKenzie in Flower and Dean Street at between 11.00pm and midnight on Tuesday. Franklin knew McKenzie and spoke to her. At that time McKenzie was heading in the direction of Brick Lane. By account of Hughes it started raining at 12.45am on

Wednesday, but she was certain that it was not raining at 12.30am. Detective Inspector Edmund Reid testified that; 'It was raining when the body was removed. It was raining when I arrived, but a very little. The spot under which the deceased was lying was dry except where there was blood'. Which rather suggests that McKenzie was killed between 12.45am, when it started to rain, and when Constable Andrews discovered the body at 12.50am. Give or take a couple of minutes either way we have another example of an extremely tight window of opportunity at the end of which the killer is able to escape from the scene unseen and unheard.

During his summary to the jury on the final day of the inquest on 14 August 1889, reported in *The Times* the following day, the coroner Wynne Baxter commented that:

There is an interval of nearly five hours from when M'Cormack saw the deceased until she is seen between half-past 11 and 12 by some women in Flower and Dean-street. This is the last that was seen of her. At a quarter past 12 a constable had his supper under the very lamp under which the deceased was afterwards found, and at that time no one was near. Another constable was there at 25 minutes past 12, and the place was then all right. The officer next entered the alley at 12:50 and it was between those times that the murder must have been done. When the body was discovered there was no one about, and nothing suspicious had been seen. Had there been any noise, there were plenty of opportunities for it to have been heard. There is great similarity between this and the other class of cases which have happened in this neighbourhood, and if this crime has not been committed by the same person, it is clearly an imitation of the other cases. We have another similarity in the absence of motive. None of the evidence shows that the deceased was at enmity with any one. There is nothing to show why the woman is murdered or by whom. I think you will agree with me that so far as the police are concerned every care was taken after the death to discover and capture the assailant. All the ability and discretion the police have shown in their investigations have been unavailing, as in the other cases.

Some indication as to why Phillips thought that the murder of McKenzie was not attributable to the Ripper comes from a report by Superintendent Arnold dated 17 July who suggests that Phillips though the 'injuries in this case are not so severe and the cut on the stomach is not so direct'.[95] A report on the post mortem findings for Alice McKenzie written by Dr Bond and sent to Robert Anderson is also in the records, but for a comprehensive record of the post mortem findings we need to look at Dr Phillips' report of 22 July 1889.[96, 97] The report is in the form of notes and in spite of the detail, the structure is somewhat haphazard. It is also worth mentioning that although Phillips describes the abdominal wounds, he does not do so with sufficient detail to allow accurate visualisation of the lesions.

The most significant abdominal wound was some seven inches long running longitudinally but not quite straight from seven inches below the right nipple and cutting through the skin and subcutaneous tissue but without dissecting the musculature or opening the abdominal cavity. Apart from this wound, Phillips described multiple abrasions and small cuts to the abdomen and pubis. With regard to the neck wounds, the surgeon described two jagged wounds that commenced behind the left sternocleidomastoid muscle leaving a triangular piece of skin attached at its base to the remaining skin of the neck. The deepest of these incisions divided the sternocleidomastoid muscle except for a few posterior fibres and severed the common carotid artery above the omohyoid muscle, cutting right down to the transverse processes of a cervical vertebra, but without severing the windpipe.

Rather than further detail the whole of Phillips' report I have included just the conclusions with further reference to the details as necessary. For ease of reading and interpretation of this I have edited the text without changing the factual content, so this is not a verbatim transcript.

Phillips came to the following conclusions after his post mortem examination of Alice McKenzie's body:

Death was caused through syncope arising from the division of the vessels of the left side of the neck. The wounds were caused by a sharp cutting instrument with at least two strokes and were not suicidal. The wounds were made from left to right while the body was on the ground and effected by someone who knew the position of the vessels or at any rate knew where to cut with reference to causing speedy death.

There was no sign of a violent struggle but there were signs that the victim had been held down by hand as evidenced by bruises on the upper chest and collarbone. There was more pressure on the right side.

There was no physiological reason why the woman should not have uttered a cry because her larynx/trachea was not severed. The wound to the throat tending to confirm the conclusion submitted as to the wounds of the abdominal wall in that death almost immediately followed from incision of the neck, the woman did not move after the incision, and all other wounds were made after death.

The superficial marks on the left side of the abdomen were characteristic of pressure with a thumb and fingers suggesting that the right hand of the assailant had pinched a fold of abdominal skin for at least three inches. Smearing of blood on the abdominal skin occurred as a consequence of this

The scoring and cuts on the pubis were caused through the endeavour to pass the obstruction caused by the clothing.

The long wound to the right side of the abdomen was inflicted by a sharp pointed instrument from above downwards and there is evidence of two thrusts of the instrument before withdrawal. The instrument turned laterally while making the undermining portion of wound which was made from right to left.

The appearance of the lesions on the left side of the abdomen suggested they were caused by the pressure of a right hand (possibly to facilitate the introduction of and instrument under the clothing. Wounds to the right side were produced by a left-handed cut.

The instrument used was smaller than the one used in most of the other Whitechapel murder victims.

By way of final comment, Phillips wrote the following:

After careful and long deliberation I cannot satisfy myself on purely anatomical and professional grounds that the perpetrator of all the Whitechapel murders is one man.

I am on the contrary impelled to the contrary conclusion. This noting the mode of procedure and the character of the mutilations and judging of motive in connection with the latter.

I do not here enter into the comparison of the cases neither do I take into account what I admit may be almost conclusive evidence in favour of the one man theory if all surrounding circumstances and other evidence are considered.

Holding it as my duty to report on the PM appearances and express an opinion solely on Professional Grounds, based upon my own observations. For this purpose I have ignored all evidence not coming under my own observation.

Dr Frederick Brown the City Police Surgeon concurred with Phillips on his conclusions so they were at least not reached in complete isolation and the day after the post mortem examination, Thursday 18 July, Phillips accompanied Dr

Thomas Bond to view the body of Alice McKenzie in order that the Westminster Divisional Police Surgeon could make his own assessment. By this time McKenzie's corpse showed signs of decomposition and Phillips had difficulty in describing his findings because the body was no longer open and had since been washed. Bond produced his report on the same day that he examined McKenzie's body whereas Phillips did not produce his until four days later, and he even took another look at the corpse in the presence of Brown two days after Bond, and presumably after he had seen Bond's report or at least been made aware of differences in opinion. Phillips was very proper in the means by which he reached his conclusions but in some respects he was too rigid and his appraisal of McKenzie's death may have been flawed.

Of significance when examining the circumstances of this murder and in relation to others in the series is the tightness of McKenzie's clothing. The type of victim targeted by the Ripper greatly facilitated his objectives; prostitutes had no need for restrictive clothing and only Nichols wore any 'drawers' so he readily gained access for mutilation by lifting the skirts of his victims and their clothing was loose enough to present no obstruction. But this was not the case for McKenzie and the tightness of her clothing, provided an obstruction causing the Ripper to modify his attack. Although Constable Andrews mentioned at the inquest that, 'her clothing was almost level to the chin' and, 'Her legs and body were exposed', we must interpret this slightly differently in view of Phillips' report and I suspect that what Andrews meant was that the hem of her skirt was up to her chin. In his notes Phillips specifically mentions that the clothing was 'fastened round the body somewhat tightly and could only be raised so as to expose about one third of the abdomen'. Thus her skirts could probably be lifted no higher than the iliac crests or just below the naval without removing any clothing, which is consistent with Phillips' impression when he first arrived at the murder scene that her clothes were turned up and exposing her genitals. Phillips suggested that, 'the scoring and cuts of skin on the pubis were caused through the endeavour to pass the obstruction of the clothing', and Bond suggested that the killer might have had to hold up her clothing with his left hand in order to inflict wounds with the knife held in his right hand. Phillips impression was rather different suggesting that instead of the clothes being held up with the left hand the killer pushed down on McKenzie's abdomen with his right hand in order to push the knife held with his left hand under the clothing. The neck wounds were clearly delivered by a right-handed assailant so why Phillips should then suggest that the abdominal wounds were inflicted by a knife held in the left hand does not make sense and in any case there is no real evidence to support this.

Exposing just one third of the victim's abdomen was not enough for the Ripper who enjoyed working with a somewhat more extensive canvas. He could certainly have gained access to the uterus by cutting into the lower abdomen but I suspect that so tightly was he focussed that the slightest deviation from his anticipated progress would give him a problem. The logical solution to such a predicament would be to cut through the victim's clothing and a knife sharp enough to cut through skin and muscle would make short work of tight clothing. But in no instance did the Ripper ever cut the clothing of any of his victims and this establishes a fascinating aspect to his *modus operandi*. McKenzie's attacker was clearly intent upon mutilation and had he been an imitator he would, without hesitation, have cut through her clothes at the waist to expose the total of her abdomen in order inflict deep wounds. The fact that McKenzie's killer did not do this is, in my opinion, a very strong indicator that the Ripper was involved. Cutting the clothing would have been an immediate and instinctive response as soon as McKenzie's killer realised there was an obstruction and if there was sufficient time to wriggle the knife around beneath her clothing then there was sufficient to make at least an attempt at cutting through the restriction. Even though the killer was disturbed in a matter of minutes by the approach of Constable Andrews, time was not a factor. Clearly the Ripper had a problem with cutting or tearing clothing. I suspect that this was rather more than just concern about dulling the blade of his knife and most likely a significant psychological issue. In a sense, the very argument used by Phillips to support the suggestion that McKenzie was not a victim of the Ripper is a very significant reason why she most probably was a victim of the same man who had previously killed four other prostitutes. In any event, an absence of mutilations was no evidence of an absence of intent to mutilate.

Bond was of the opinion that Alice McKenzie was murdered by the same person responsible for other Whitechapel murders and submitted his report in the form of a letter to Robert Anderson on 18 July 1889:

Dear Sir,

I beg to report that in accordance with your instructions I this day inspected the dead body of a woman, who has been identified as Alice McKenzie, at Whitechapel. Before I went to the mortuary I called on Dr Phillips & he kindly accompanied me. He informed me that the post mortem was completed yesterday & that the wounds on the throat of the woman had been so disturbed that any examination I might make, unassisted would convey no definite information as to the nature of the injuries. He pointed out to me the original wounds, their character and direction & I was able to form an opinion that there could be no doubt that the cuts were made from left to right & as far as I was able to make out, the knife appears to have been plunged into the neck on the left side of the victim below the sterno mastoid muscle & brought out by a tailed incision just above the larynx on the same side. There appeared to have been two stabs, & the knife then carried forward in the same skin wound, except that a small tongue of skin remained between the two stabs. The incisions appeared to me to be in a direction from above downwards and forwards with several small superficial cuts extending upwards & tailing off into mere scratches. The two main cuts appeared to be about 3 inches long but Dr Phillips stated that before the parts were distributed the cuts which I saw extending downwards, really were in a direction upwards.

The cuts appeared to have been inflicted with a sharp strong knife. I could form no opinion as to the width of the blade or the length of the knife, but undoubtedly the cuts might have been done with a short knife; it must in my opinion have had a sharp point. I believe the cuts were made from the front while the woman's head was thrown back on the ground. There were two bruises high up on the chest which looked as if the murderer had made the cuts with his right hand while he held the woman down with his left. There were no bruises on the woman's face or lips.

On the right side of the abdomen extending from the chest to below the level of the umbilicus there was a jagged incision made up of several cuts which extended through the skin & subcutaneous fat & at the bottom of this cut there were 7 or 8 superficial scratches about 2 inches long parallel to each other in a longitudinal direction. There was also a small cut eighth of an inch deep, quarter inch long on the mons veneris. I think that in order to inflict the wound which I saw on the abdomen the murderer must have raised the clothes with his left hand & inflicted the injuries with his right.

Dr Phillips showed me a small bruise on the left side of the stomach which he suggested might have been caused by the murderer pressing his right hand on the stomach while he used the knife with his left hand, but I saw no sufficient reason to entertain this opinion. The wounds could not have been self inflicted, & no doubt the wound to the throat would cause almost immediate death & I do not think the woman could call out if held down in the position she appears to have been in when the wounds were inflicted. The wounds on the abdomen could have nothing to do with the cause of death & were in my opinion inflicted after death. I see in this murder evidence of similar design to the former Whitechapel murders viz. sudden onslaught on the prostrate woman, the throat skilfully & resolutely cut with subsequent mutilation, each mutilation indicating sexual thoughts & a desire to mutilate the abdomen & sexual organs.

I am of opinion that the murder was performed by the same person who committed the former series of Whitechapel murders.

I am dear Sir,
Yours faithfully,
Thos. Bond.

R. Anderson esq.[98]

Bond's suggestion that the wounds to McKenzie's neck were by nature stab wounds rather than cuts is an unnecessary confusion. The exact means by which a knife enters the flesh will undoubtedly vary from one victim to the next and may depend on circumstances such as movement at the point of wounding. In any event, the wounds described by Phillips were not stabs but well-defined cuts into the neck and it should be noted that Bond did not see the wounds as they first presented, but after further dissection and then stitch closure by Phillips. The important aspect is that the wounds were delivered to the left side of the neck and the victim bled to death though a severed carotid artery. In common with each other Ripper murder, there are no indications that McKenzie struggled or that she had the opportunity to make a sound. There is no convincing evidence that McKenzie was attacked while already lying on the ground – she would hardly have positioned herself voluntarily beneath a lamp with her head over the kerb if the killer invited her to lie down for sex. Once again the Ripper took his victim by surprise while on route to a supposed sexual engagement. In an instant he attacked from behind and cut into her neck. The shock of the attack silenced her and she immediately sank to the floor without any opportunity for spurting of arterial blood.

Having requested Bond's involvement and opinion on the murder of McKenzie, Anderson clearly disagreed with his conclusions in favour of the opinion of Phillips that the murder was not one of the series. In his memoirs published over twenty year later Anderson recalled:

I am here assuming that the murder of Alice M'Kenzie on the 17th of July 1889, was by another hand. I was absent from London when it occurred, but the Chief Commissioner investigated the case on the spot and decided it was an ordinary murder, and not the work of a sexual maniac.[99]

In spite of Anderson's assertion, James Monro, Chief Commissioner of the Metropolitan Police force who directed the investigation during the absence of

Anderson on leave, disagreed. In a report to the Under Secretary of State dated 17 July 1889, Monro wrote:

I need not say that every effort will be made by the Police to discover the murderer, who, I am inclined to believe is identical with the notorious "Jack the Ripper" of last year.[100]

In keeping with his belief, Monro ordered 3 sergeants and 39 constables to be 'employed in plain clothes on special patrol duty in connection with the Whitechapel Murder'. This increase in covert manpower is revealed in a request dated 26 July from Monro to The Under Secretary of State for an additional plain clothes allowance.[101] Anderson's recollection may not necessarily have been what he thought at the time, and may also be less than objective since he maintained that the police knew well enough at the time who the Ripper was but never had enough evidence with which to charge him.

The Ripper's technique was unique and for an imitator to replicate his activities would not only require a carefully study of his methods, but would also necessitate putting the results into practice. To imitate the Rippers *modus operandi* successfully and without prior practice would not be possible. One also has to be very careful when excluding victims because a particular characteristic of the Ripper's *modus operandi* is absent from that murder, and absence should not be taken as lack of intent. Throughout Ripperology there are instances in which authors have built a case against the inclusion of one victim or another merely because it is convenient for their thesis to do so and the problem with such a course is that by excluding one victim the same argument may well exclude another. I am of the opinion that McKenzie was another victim of the serial killer. The fact that she was not extensively mutilated was a consequence of opportunity rather than intent and there are sufficient other indicators from the circumstances of her death and from the manner in which she was killed to implicate Jack the Ripper and to exclude her death as the work of an imitator. It is unfortunate that there was some dispute as to the relevance of McKenzie's death to the murder series since it seems as though the police response was rather half hearted; certainly the newspapers no longer had such a thirst for the Ripper murders and the frenzy of press activity that accompanied the death of Mary Jane Kelly did not return.

The inquest jury considered the evidence relating to the death of Alice McKenzie and after a short deliberation returned a verdict of wilful murder against some person or persons unknown.

2.3.6 Frances Coles (1865-91)
In the early hours of the morning of February 13 1891, Frances Coles was found lying in the roadway to Swallow Gardens. She was bleeding to death from wounds to her neck and the nature of her demise suggested that she was another victim of Jack the Ripper who had struck again, nineteen months after the murder of Alice McKenzie.

Frances Coles was born in 1865, the daughter of a respectable boot maker named James William Coles. Frances, nicknamed 'Carrotty Nell', seemed quite promising during her early years. Her sister, Mary Ann Coles, lived a respectable life as a single woman and Frances had every opportunity to do the same. She worked for some time 'stoppering bottles' at a Hora's wholesale chemist in Minories, which would earn her up to seven shillings per week. But she often complained to her sister that the work was painful to her knuckles and she apparently quit the job after some time. How Frances became involved in prostitution is unknown but she likely did so sometime around 1883, when she was about eighteen years of age. This suggestion comes from one of her clients, James Murray, who in 1891 informed police that she had been working the areas of Whitechapel, Shoreditch, and Bow for eight years. She also became a heavy drinker.

Frances Coles kept her situation a secret from her family and when her sister had her over for tea on Boxing Day, 1890, Frances claimed she was living with an elderly woman in Richard Street, Commercial Road, and still working at the chemist in Minories. Mary Ann sensed that all was not well, and noticed that her sister 'was very poor, and looked very dirty', and thought she could detect the faint odour of alcohol on her breath on many occasions. In 1891, Frances' father James was an inmate of the Bermondsey Workhouse, Tanner Street and in spite of her circumstances, Frances made every attempt to visit him and even attended church services with him on Sundays and as far as he was aware she still worked at the chemist. The last time he saw her alive was on Friday, 6 February, only a week before her death after which he was called to identify the body of his youngest daughter in the Whitechapel Mortuary. Both Frances' sister and her father gave evidence at the inquest. Frances Coles is often regarded as the prettiest of the Whitechapel murder victims.

The wounds to Coles are detailed in Diagram 6 and the location of the murder is illustrated in Map 6 and a complete tabulation of relevant findings is given in Table 2. Files relating to the murder of Frances Coles are held in the National Archives.[102] The only reported possessions of Frances Coles were a black crape hat that she had purchased the night before that lay beside her, her old hat pinned beneath her dress, and in the pocket of her dress were a few pieces of black lace or crape, a vulcanite earring, an old striped stocking and a comb, but no money. Eighteen yards from where the body was found Inspector Flanagan discovered two shillings wrapped in two pieces of old newspaper, but there was nothing to connect this finding with the murder.

The original inquest papers have not survived so researchers are dependent upon details reported in the newspapers. *The Eastern Post* on Saturday 14 February 1891 gives one of the first newspaper reports of the murder:

Swallow-gardens and Orman-street are two thoroughfares, narrow, boldly-lighted, and at the early hour of the morning rarely traversed. The buildings are partly dwelling houses, partly warehouses or storerooms. The arch, which was the actual theatre of the crime, is about fifty yards in length, and while fairly lighted at each end by lamps, the centre remains in deep shade. It was in the centre, where the shadow lies deepest, that the deed was committed. One side of the archway is walled up by a hoarding, the space enclosed being used as a builder's store. The place is notorious as a resort of women of the unfortunate class, despite the efforts of the police to keep them away. In fact, two women were arrested for loitering at this spot earlier in the night by one of the constables who assisted to remove the body.

The deceased was known to the local police as an 'unfortunate,' who was in the habit of frequenting the locality, and had been seen about Leman-street early in the evening. It is surmised that she could not have been long in the company of her murderer, at least in the vicinity of the place where the deed was committed, as one of the Great Northern Railway men employed as a shunter passed through the archway at a few minutes past two o'clock, and saw no one about then. A City detective also passed some minutes later without perceiving anything amiss. The theory of the police is that the deceased was lured into the archway and at once murdered, and that the perpetrator of the crime was prevented from committing further outrages on the body by some one approaching.

Immediately to the west of Leman Street Railway station an elevated section of tracks passes between Chamber Street to the north and Royal Mint Street to the south. Towards the western end of Chamber Street, the road passes beneath the railway before running into Mansell Street. At around this point and opposite the Roman Catholic School there is a narrow passageway between one of three arches beneath the elevated railway. The passageway runs for a distance of around 73yds from Chamber Street to Royal Mint Street. After emerging from the arches, the passageway widened to form Swallow Gardens, before narrowing again and emerging into Royal Mint Street.[103]

The first day of the inquest was Saturday 14 February and *The Times* commenced inquest reporting on Monday 16 February 1891. According to the inquest testimony of Constable Earnest Thompson, the roadway under the arch was reduced by being boarded up from the crown of the arch to the ground so that what remained was a roadway that was wide enough to allow one cart to pass at a time. Thompson estimated the length of road beneath the archway to be 40yds, and he described there to be 'two ordinary street gas lamps to light this arch, and they throw a light down the archway'. Thompson could not tell the exact position of the light at the Royal Mint Street entrance, but he suggested that if he stood at the Chamber Street entrance to the archway then he should be able to see anyone in the centre of the arch. In effect, he could see right through it and could also do the same at night, although the centre of the passageway beneath the arch was not very light during the day. Thompson confirmed that the archway was 'much used by carts and horses belonging to the Great Northern Railway Company' who had stables about 30yds away from the arch in Chamber Street. Between Chamber Street and Royal Mint Street and on either side of Swallow Gardens there was a Goods Depot.

At 2.15am on 13 February 1891 Constable Thompson was patrolling his beat along Chamber Street, approaching from Leman Street. He had been in the police force for less than two months and this was his first night alone on that beat which included Prescot Street and Chamber Street with short portions of Mansell Street and Leman Street and took him about fifteen to twenty minutes to complete. When about 80yds from the railway arches, Thompson looked at the clock on the tower of the Co-operative stores in Leman Street and saw that the time was very nearly 2.15am, he continued along Chamber Street and turned into the arch with the intention of walking along the passageway through Swallow Gardens as far as Royal Mint Street. At the time, Thompson was not aware that the place was known as Swallow Gardens. On the first day of the inquest he testified that:

While proceeding from Leman-street to the arch I did not see any one. When I turned into the passage I could see the woman lying under the arch on the roadway, about midway under the arch. I turned my lamp on as soon as I got there. I could not see it was a woman until I turned my lamp on. I noticed some blood. I saw her open and shut one eye. I blew my whistle three times. Constables 161 H and 275 H came to me in three or four minutes. They both came from Royal Mint-street; 161 H came first. I heard footsteps when I was going up Chamber-street and before I reached the arch. The sound was in the direction of Mansell-street, but I did not see any one. They sounded like a person walking at an ordinary rate.

Thompson was unable to follow whoever walked away from the scene because police policy dictated that he should stay with the victim. Having blown his whistle constables Frederick Hart and George Elliott were on the scene within a matter of minutes from their respective beats. Hart arrived first and described what he found:

I was then [at 2.15am] in Royal Mint-street, and heard a whistle. I was then about 250 yards from the arch. I went in the direction of the sound, which turned out to be in Swallow-gardens. There I found Police-constable 240 H, and alongside was the body of a woman. She was lying in the centre of the roadway. I turned my light on and examined the woman. I then saw that her throat was cut. I ran for Dr. Oxley, of Dock-street, and he came as soon as possible. He was in bed when I called him. I then searched the vicinity, but could not find any trace of any person that was likely to have done the deed.

Hart said that he could see Thompson immediately that he turned into Swallow Gardens. He could see Thompson by the constable's lamp, but could also have seen him without it, because there was an ordinary streetlamp at the Royal Mint Street end of the arch and according to Hart, 'the place is lighter at night than in the daytime in the centre of the arch'. Hart confirmed that he had seen no one in the vicinity within half an hour of the discovery of the body and suggested that the place was pretty well deserted after 1.00am, a statement somewhat at variance with that of Thompson who suggested that railway men from the Great Northern Railway Company were about all night and often went through the arch with the horses that were engaged in shunting. However he had not seen anyone on his previous passage along Chamber Street and confirmed that there was no one around when he discovered the body. At the time there were some men working in the stables 30yds away from the arch in Chamber Street and some men with horses arrived at the scene after the other officers arrived. Hart heard no cries for assistance during the previous half hour and he described the position of the body when he arrived at the scene as lying with the feet towards Royal Mint Street and the head towards Chamber Street, partly on its left side. He did not feel for a pulse and as soon as he saw the gash on the throat he ran for the doctor. According to Hart it was around ten minutes before Dr Frederick John Oxley arrived at the scene. Detective Constable George Elliott also gave evidence on the first day of the inquest but had little to add:

I was on duty in front of Baron Rothschild's refinery in Royal Mint-street until 2:15 a.m., when I heard a whistle blowing. I went in the direction of the sound, and when I got to the entrance of Swallow-gardens I saw the constable's lamp turned on and heard his whistle again. I went to him. He was standing under the arch, close to the body of a woman. I looked round and then went off to Leman-street Police-station. I had not been far from this spot since 10 o'clock the previous night, and nothing unusual attracted my attention. Plenty of men and women passed through Swallow-gardens up to 12:30 a.m. I do not recollect seeing any man or woman pass after that time.

Elliott confirmed that he was about 250yds from Swallow Gardens when the whistle blew, that he was wearing 'ordinary boots', and that he would have heard a cry for help from the archway because it was so quiet.

Solomon Gutteridge, a shunter in the employ of the Great Northern Railway, told the inquest that on the morning of Friday 13 February he left home at 1.55am and went to the stables to get his horse out. He then went along Chamber Street and through Swallow Gardens to the depot. Gutteridge went through the arch at between 2.10am and 2.12am but was certain that there was not a body lying in the road at that time.

The inquest then became involved with testimony surrounding the arrest of Thomas Sadler, a ship's fireman, who was remanded from the Thames Police Court, charged with causing the death of Frances Coles. Unfortunately, there are indications that the suggested involvement of Sadler in the death of Coles slightly skewed the testimony that followed and it would have been preferable had the medical evidence been presented before that relating to Sadler. Sadler's involvement will be considered later.

On day four of the inquest, reported in *The Times* on 24 February 1891, Dr Oxley who attended the scene after being summoned by Constable Hart described the position of the body. Oxley gave the opinion that, 'he did not think a drunken man would have been capable of inflicting the wounds' to the neck of the victim. Dr George Bagster Phillips, Whitechapel Divisional Police Surgeon, who undertook the post mortem examination of Coles' corpse, then gave details of his findings:

On Saturday morning [14 February 1891] I made a minute examination of the incision in the throat. There was an external wound, the edges of the skin being not exactly cut through, there being a portion of about an inch long undivided. In my opinion, there were three distinct passings of the knife across the throat - one from left to right, one from right to left, and the third from left to right. Below the wound there was an abrasion, as if caused by a finger nail. Above the wound there were four abrasions, possibly caused by finger nails. From the position of these marks I opine that the left hand was used. There were some contused wounds on the back of the head, which I am of opinion were caused by the head coming into violent contact with paving stones. I came to the conclusion that death had been almost instantaneous, occasioned by the severance of the carotid arteries and other vessels on the left side. In my opinion, the deceased was on the ground when her throat was cut. I think that her assailant used his right hand in making the incisions in the throat, and that he had used his left hand to hold her head back by the chin; that he was on the right side of the body when he made the cuts. The tilting of the body to the left was to prevent the perpetrator from being stained with blood. There was a complete absence of any struggle or even any movement from pain, but it may have arisen from the fact that the woman was insensible from concussion. It was not a very sharp knife that caused the wounds. I do not think the murder was done by a skilful person. From the appearances after death the woman could not have been drunk at the time of her death.

Sergeant George Bush of the Criminal Investigation Department produced a detailed plan of the murder location showing all the places mentioned in the evidence and the distances from the given points to the scene of the murder. He pointed out that there were eight different routes leading from the archway by which a person might get away, but there were only two entrances to Swallow Gardens itself.

Constable Thompson estimated the length of arch beneath the railway to be something over 40yds. He was right and according to the OS map of 1894-6 the distance was 41yds and Coles' body lay towards the mid point of the archway, or at least not noticeably towards either end. This was a risky location. There were only two points of exit and the site was visible from both ends with the view out of the arch probably not good against the ordinary streetlamp at either end, and although illuminated, the constables needed their lamps to view the body. As such it is a typical Ripper murder location. Thompson further tells us that he was some 80yds from the archway, walking along Chamber Street from Leman Street, when he looked back at the clock on the tower of the Co-operative Stores in Leman Street. This would place him 130yds or so from Leman Street and a distance of approximately 100yds from Coles' body. Policemen walked at a relatively slow stroll and would cover 100yds in a little less than two minutes assuming they were not distracted by investigating doorways and passages.

Thompson was last at the arch from Chamber Street at 2.00am according to his testimony. He then walked as far as Royal Mint Street through Swallow Gardens and then back to Chamber Street, which would have taken the time to around 2.02am. He continued on his beat and when he was again in Chamber Street and around a minute from the arches, he noted the time to be 2.15am. His beat thus took sixteen minutes on that occasion, confirming his estimate of fifteen to twenty minutes. Thus, it seems likely that we can use an estimate of sixteen minutes for Thompson to complete his beat which took in Chamber Street, Prescot Street and small portions of Mansell Street and Leman Street, as well as an excursion through Swallow Gardens from Chamber Street to Royal Mint Street and back with a cursory examination of the other two arches. This total distance of some 800yds Thompson thus covered at a rate of 100yds in approximately two minutes not so very different from my own estimate of police walking time allowing additional time for Thompson to check doors and passageways on route.

Allowing perhaps fifteen seconds from the moment the killer cut Coles' throat until Thompson heard the a man's footsteps, and assuming the footsteps were those of the killer, then Thompson would have arrived at Coles' body a minimum of two minutes after the vessels in her neck were severed. Judging by the post mortem report the carotid vessels on the left side were severed which would have caused the victim to bleed to death very quickly, and within a matter of seconds Coles would have been unconscious. Certainly by the time Thompson arrived at the scene of her murder she would have been dead through loss of blood although her body may still have shown some agonal muscular contractions but progressively not reflex responses thus, the fact that Thompson saw her 'open and shut one eye', was probably not an indication that she was still alive. Although the constable shone his lamp onto the corpse this probably did not evoke a response by which Coles opened an eye. There is no doubt in this instance that the time of death can be accurately determined at a couple of minutes before 2.15am, and this time of death is reliable regardless as to whether or not the footsteps heard by Thompson were those of the killer.

The constable was sure that the footsteps were suddenly audible and that they did not gradually get louder as the man approached or as Thompson caught up with whoever was walking ahead of him, depending on their relative positions. This would imply that that whoever made the footsteps suddenly started walking or suddenly came into earshot for instance by entering Chamber Street from a passageway. Thompson was 80yds away from the arches and the entrance to Swallow Gardens – easily within visual distance of anyone entering Chamber Street, especially since by testimony there was an ordinary street gas lamp situated at the entrance to the arch, which would also have illuminated the immediate vicinity of Chamber Street. The sound of footsteps would have alerted Thompson and he would have looked towards the source of the sound. Thus, had someone emerged from the arches into Chamber Street at 2.15am when Thompson heard the sudden onset of footsteps, he would almost certainly have seen that person. The footsteps that Thompson heard were only at an ordinary pace, which is not indicative of someone fleeing the scene, and in any case the Ripper would most likely have worn rubber soled shoes so as not to betray his presence. If the sound of footsteps did come from Coles' killer then he must have been disturbed by something but it seems that Thompson was the only other person in the vicinity and he was probably too far from the murder scene. If Thompson did disturb the killer then he would hardly have run towards the constable.

I suspect that the footsteps heard by Thompson were not those of the killer, but that those same footsteps also disturbed the murderer from continuing his activities and he left the scene away from the source of the footsteps, by taking a route into Royal Mint Street. He thus narrowly escaped being discovered and would have been frustrated in any attempt to mutilate his victim. Considering that the Ripper murdered Catharine Eddowes after being frustrated in his attack on Elizabeth Stride one could wonder as to whether or not there were any other reported assaults the same night that Frances Coles was murdered.

Constable George Elliott was patrolling in plain clothes outside the Baron Rothschild's refinery in Royal Mint Street when he heard the sound of Thompson's whistle. He attended the scene then went off to Leman Street police station for assistance. Elliott was so close to Swallow Gardens that he 'must have heard' any sound that came from the arch and during the course of the evening he saw plenty of men and women passing through Swallow Gardens but nothing unusual attracted his attention and he did not recollect seeing any man or woman going into the passageway after 12.30am. From his testimony one would imagine that Elliott would have seen anyone leaving Swallow Gardens immediately after Coles was murdered, but he then confounds matters by saying that he was 250yds from Swallow Gardens when he heard Thompson's whistle blow. It is probable that he would have seen nothing from this distance and it is likely that he would have heard nothing less audible than a scream. The Royal Mint Refinery was situated on the south side of Royal Mint Street with the eastern boundary almost opposite the southern entrance to Swallow Gardens, and the western boundary just short of the southern entrance to Little Prescot Street, which led from Royal Mint Street to

Chamber Street and ran parallel to Swallow Gardens also travelling beneath the railway and through arches. The distance from the Royal Mint Street entrance to Swallow Gardens to the western end of the Refinery is around 100yds, which would have been within visual distance, assuming reasonable street lighting. If Elliott was 250yds from the entrance to Swallow Gardens then he was well beyond the Refinery, and almost in Minories if he were to the west along Royal Mint Street or in Cable Street if to the east. If Elliott patrolled around the Royal Mint, and he does not say that he did so, then he would have been much to the south in Cartwright Street and almost in Upper East Smithfield. In any event he would not have been in visual contact with Swallow Gardens.

The first officer on the scene after Thompson had blown his whistle was Constable Fredrick Hart whose beat was around the Royal Mint. He patrolled part of Royal Mint Street, Cartwright Street, Upper East Smithfield, and as far east as Trinity Square, a good 450yds from Swallow Gardens. His beat would have brought him past the Royal Mint Street entrance to Swallow Gardens once on each circuit. According to Thompson it was three to four minutes before assistance arrived, although realistically it was probably less than that. Hart told the inquest that he was also 250yds from Swallow Gardens when he heard the blow of Thompson's whistle and should have been on the scene in less than two minutes if he started running immediately after hearing the alert. Anything less would have been an inappropriate response to a constable requesting assistance. Since Elliott does not mention that Hart was at the scene when he arrived we can assume that he had already arrived and gone to find Dr Oxley at his home in Dock Street – Hart would have returned to Royal Mint Street then made his way west until he reached Dock Street. Why it should have taken Elliott longer than Hart to reach the scene when he was by account the same distance of 250yds away, is a mystery. In any event we can say that Hart arrived after two minutes and Elliott after three minutes, and that both were some distance away from the scene, that is, within earshot, but not within visual contact of the entrance of Swallow Gardens from Royal Mint Street. The point here being that Coles' killer could have left Swallow Gardens by the southerly exit into Royal Mint Street without being seen by either patrolling constable, from there he would probably have taken a westerly route along Royal Mint Street and into Cable Street. By any measure, however, his exit unseen by this route was unbelievably lucky, although Coles' murderer did not need to leave Swallow Gardens directly by the exits into Chamber Street or Royal Mint Street. From inquest testimony it is clear that there were eight different routes by which he could have left Swallow Gardens, the remaining six being into the grounds of the railway goods depot on either side of the passageway, thence towards Little Prescot Street to the west or into the grounds of St Mark's Infants School to the east. Eventually, however, the killer would have to enter either Royal Mint Street or Chamber Street in order to make his escape.

Chamber Street was primarily a residential area and there were houses ahead of Police Constable Thompson when he first heard footsteps at a point 80yds away from the arches. Just past the Catholic School opposite the entrance to Swallow Gardens there were several houses out his line of vision and anyone leaving home for work on a route that took them away from Thompson and along Mansell Street would have immediately appeared on Chamber Street out of sight of Thompson while their footsteps would have been audible ahead of him. Even today there is a sinister aspect to the confined exit from Chamber Street to Mansell Street and anyone exiting from the location of the railway arches in Chamber Street would soon be out of sight as they travelled west. Also, the footsteps of anyone entering Chamber Street from Little Prescot Street would have suddenly become audible in much the same way as those belonging to someone entering from Swallow Gardens, and although they would have been further ahead by some 90yds, the same reasoning applies but they would never come into the view of anyone in Chamber Street. There is no shortage of alternative possibilities and to assume that the footsteps were those of the murderer just because they were heard in the vicinity of a murder immediately after the act is understandable but unjustified. This is of marginal relevance except insomuch as Constable Thompson was concerned. Having witnessed the horror of Frances Coles opening and closing one eye and thus believing her to be still alive, he was apparently haunted for the rest of his life by the fact that he was unable to follow the footsteps that he was convinced belonged to her killer, and thus to Jack the Ripper. His concern in both respects was probably unfounded but in any event, his own life ended tragically when he was stabbed to death in 1900 when trying to clear a brawl in a coffeehouse.

Investigations into the circumstances surrounding Frances Coles' murder were considerably complicated when the police thought they had a suspect. On the day after the murder, Thomas Sadler was arrested in connection with the crime and consequently was also briefly thought to have been Jack the Ripper. This latter consideration by the police is important in view of suggestions by senior police officers regarding possible suspects. Whatever was subsequently thought regarding the identity of the Ripper, the police clearly thought that he was still at large at the time that Frances Coles was murdered.

Thomas Sadler was a married man. He was a sailor, a drunkard who verbally abused anyone who crossed him, and was not averse to getting involved in a brawl or two. He allegedly threatened his wife Sarah on more than one occasion and she gave her opinion of him to Chief Inspector Swanson who interviewed her a week after the death of Coles. Sarah Sadler described her husband as being 'as good as could be' when he liked, and 'rough when he wanted'. 'When he was in drink', said Sarah Sadler, 'he was irritable. After he had smashed the things on one occasion, he was sorry for it. He did not stay out at nights, he used to come home sometimes at eight o'clock, and he generally had the drink before he came in'. Swanson pressed Sarah Sadler as to whether her husband had ever assaulted or threatened her but she declined to answer. There is evidence that he did so a year or more after the murder of Coles. Sarah Sadler's assessment of her husband is very much the impression one gets when reading about his activities and far from being a committed misogynist with a history of violence against women who was ever-eager to use a knife, he actually appears to be a far more sensitive and generous individual beneath the exterior of a quick-tempered roughneck. His character does not make him a murderer and certainly not a serial killer.

Friday 13 was undoubtedly unlucky for Frances Coles, but it was also something of a disaster for Thomas Sadler. His statement to the police details what he remembered of the day but his statement is that of a man trying to recall what he did while in a drunken stupor more than twenty-four hours after events. Sadler's statement contains gaps, no useful timing, and the transposition and merging of events that were undoubtedly misleading at the time and still appear to be so for many investigators today. Fortunately for Sadler, several witnesses including police officers observed him during the course of his travels that evening and were tracked down by his defence council. Sadler's statement was read out at the inquest and I have extracted the salient details, as he gave them. [104]

Thomas Sadler was generally known as Tom Sadler and was employed as ship's fireman. He was discharged from his last ship, the steamship *Fez*, on the evening of Wednesday 11 February – he had not been paid for his voyage at that time but did have an account for his wages of £4 15s 3d that he would collect on Friday morning from the shipping office. Sadler had a drink at *Williams Brothers* at the corner of Goulston Street then, at 8.30pm, he left his baggage at the Victoria lodging home and went into *The Princess Alice* public house where he had another drink. At between 8.30pm and 9.00pm he saw Frances Coles, whom he had known for some eighteen months, in a bar in *The Princess Alice*. He beckoned her over to him and they left together to go drinking at other public houses. On Wednesday night they went together to a common lodging house at White's Row Chambers and stayed the night together. Coles had a half-pint bottle of whisky.

The following day, Thursday 12 February, they left the lodging house together at between 11.00am and noon and, not surprisingly, they then went into several public houses including *The Bell* in Middlesex Street. There followed a discussion about bonnets after which they made their way to a bonnet shop in Nottingham Street and on route they stopped for more drinks. [105] Sadler bought Coles a hat and suggested that she threw away her old one but she did not and instead pinned it to her dress. The couple then went to *The Marlborough Head* public house in Brick Lane where they continued to drink. [106] They left the public house because Sadler had arranged to meet with a man called Nichols in Spital Street. The purpose of this assignation is unknown, but Sadler suggested that he meet up with Coles in a public house, the name of which Sadler could not remember, after his appointment, but as they walked together along Thrawl Street a woman with a red shawl attacked him. The woman struck him on the head and while he was on the ground he was kicked by some men who then ran off 'into the lodging houses'. At this point the intoxicated Sadler realised that his money and watch had been stolen. He was 'penniless' and then had a row with Coles because she did not help him during the attack. Sadler left Coles on the corner of Thrawl Street and was 'downhearted' at the loss of his money because it meant that he could not afford a bed for the night. With this in mind he then went to the London Docks, he had no idea as to timing, and applied for admission so that he could go aboard the *SS Fez*. He was refused admission because he was drunk and then engaged in an exchange of verbal abuse with some dockworkers in the presence of a Metropolitan Police constable. As soon as the police officer had moved away from the scene the dock workers set about Sadler who received his second beating of the night. The dockworkers left Sadler bruised and bloody and they went off along Upper East Smithfield while Sadler stumbled down Nightingale Lane where he reckoned he remained for fifteen minutes nursing his injuries. Sadler then went back to the Victoria lodging house in Upper East Smithfield and applied for a bed, but he was refused admission because he was so drunk. Sadler 'begged and prayed' for a bed but was still declined entry so he left and 'wandered about'. Sadler still had no recollection of times, but ended up in White's Row where he went to the lodging house where he and Coles had slept the night before. He found her in the kitchen sitting with her head on her arms and she 'appeared half dazed from drink'. Sadler asked if she had enough money to pay for a double bed, but she had none. He said that he had some money coming and could she get a bed 'on trust' but Coles said that she could not. Sadler tried to persuade the lodging house deputy to let them have a bed on the strength of the wages that he had yet to collect but he was refused and was eventually turned out leaving Coles behind in the lodging house. Sadler then set off, to the best of his belief, towards the London Hospital in Whitechapel Road in order to get his wounds dressed. On route he met a policeman who asked him where he was going and when Sadler explained what had happened the policeman searched him to see whether he had a knife. Sadler told the constable that he did not carry a knife and in any event a knife was not discovered during the search. The policeman helped Sadler to the hospital gate where he spoke to the porter who was rather reluctant to let him in. Sadler verbally abused the porter who eventually let him in and he went to the accident ward where his wounds were dressed. After establishing that Sadler had nowhere to go the porter allowed him to lie down on a couch in the admissions room. Sadler continued to have no idea as to timing but suggested that he left the hospital at somewhere between 6.00am and 8.00am on Friday morning. Sadler then went straight to the Victoria Home where he 'begged for a few halfpence' without success, and thence to the shipping office to collect his £4 15s 3d wages. What happened after that is not relevant but suffice to say that the police were soon on his trail and after locating him in *The Phoenix* he was questioned then subsequently arrested in connection with Coles' death.

Sadler's testimony was not apparently scrutinised during the inquest but several witnesses were called to testify as to events and sightings involving Sadler and Coles. Generally speaking the witnesses entirely corroborated Sadler's account of events and additionally added chronology to his otherwise timeless night, but there were significant points of confusion and, in view of Sadler's condition that evening, it is perhaps better to rely upon what the witnesses recall rather than what Sadler thought happened. The most significant discrepancies were a gap during which events took place to which Sadler makes no reference, even though they were not of an incriminating nature, and confusion over his visits to the lodging house in White's Row. The gap in Sadler's testimony covers a period from his beating at the docks until he was searched by the constable near to the London

Hospital. A dock labourer, John Dooley and Dock Constable Frederick Session fixed the time of Sadler's brawl at between 1.15am and 1.20am. Police Constable Arthur Sharp searched Sadler in Whitechapel Road at close to 3.30am. It is evidence to the extent of Sadler's condition that he lost almost two hours for which he was unable to give account. In particular, he was unable to recall his encounter with Sergeant Edwards outside the entrance to the Royal Mint at shortly before 2.00am, fifteen minutes before Coles was murdered, or his second visit to the lodging house an hour later.

Sadler was undoubtedly confused as to the order of those events that he could actually recall and either recalled the second assault ahead of his first visit to the lodging house, or recalled his encounter with Coles as being on the occasion of his second visit to the lodging house in White's Row. It is worth clarifying the order of events from the testimony of other witnesses. Sadler actually made two visits to White's Row that night; on both occasions he attempted to secure a bed and on both occasions he was refused entry on the grounds that he had no money and in any case he was too drunk. The first occasion that he entered the lodging house was at around 11.00pm when he saw Frances Coles. He spoke with her, and through his drunken haze reminded her that he had been robbed earlier in Thrawl Street and had no money and asked whether Frances had enough money for a double bed, which of course she had not. Charles Guiver the lodging house watchman advised Sadler to go outside to bathe his wounds and when he returned it was clear that he had a 'gravel rash' from being thrown down on the ground. There was no blood on his clothes at this time and his injures were those sustained earlier in the evening when the woman in the red shawl and her accomplice robbed him in Thrawl Street while Sadler was in the company of Coles. Sadler left the lodging house on the instruction of Guiver some time before Coles left and probably around midnight. The second occasion that Sadler visited the White's Row lodging house was at around 3.00am or forty-five minutes or so after the murder of Coles. Sadler wanted to get in to see if Coles was there but was refused admission and it was suggested that he might like to go to the London Hospital to have his wounds dressed. On this second visit Sadler was clearly more severely injured than he was when he first called at the lodging house and was bleeding from his wounds. This second visit was made after the assault on him outside the London Docks almost three quarters of an hour earlier. In his confusion Sadler mentioned in his statement that he met with Frances Coles at the lodging house at this second visit and not at the first. In fact, he mentions only one visit to the lodging house and not two. As a result of the confusion it has been suggested by some investigators that Sadler was assaulted three times that evening but in fact he was only attacked twice. In any event Sadler certainly took some exercise and staggering between the boundaries of Whitechapel undoubtedly accounted for a significant amount of his time that evening.

With regard to the timing of Sadler's movements we are only really interested in his whereabouts between 2.00am and 2.30am and the first useful testimony comes from Police Constable William Bogan who was outside the main entrance to London Docks at 1.30am on Friday morning when he saw a man who looked like a sailor lying down in the gateway. According to Bogan the man was drunk and had a wound over his left eye. He became abusive and the constable warned him to move on before walking off on his beat. Constable Bogan identified the man as Sadler and he encountered him again at around 2.00am opposite the Mint in Little Tower Hill when accompanied by Sergeant Wesley Edwards. Bogan fixed the time by the Tower clock, which had just struck 2.00am, and on this occasion Sadler had acquired additional injuries. Sadler now had a cut over his right eye and his face was covered with blood, he told the officers that he had been assaulted by some men outside the docks and that he had been kicked in the ribs. According to Edwards he accompanied Sadler towards Minories for a distance of 30yds where he left him. The police officers suggested that it would have taken Sadler between three and five minutes to travel from where they left him to Swallow Gardens and by this time it was ten or twelve minutes past 2.00am according to Constable Bogan, although Edwards reported the time as being somewhat earlier. Sadler makes no mention of this encounter in his statement. Sadler was not seen again until he returned to the lodging house in White's Row at 3.00am in search of a bed for the night, the time being confirmed by Charles Guiver, the night watchman at the lodging house, who threw him out.

It is thus just about physically possible for Sadler to have murdered Frances Coles under the archway to Swallow Gardens but in reality was that likely? That he happened to be in the vicinity of Swallow Gardens was pure coincidence. He was drunk almost to the point of being totally incapable and had been beaten up twice that evening and suffered bruising and significant bleeding from head wounds. Sadler had not previously threatened any harm to Frances Coles and although he was clearly a belligerent character there is no indication whatsoever that he would have hurt Coles had they met, or even that he would have any reason to do so.

One witness conflicted significantly with Sadler's story by saying that he had bought a knife from someone resembling Sadler at around 10.30am on the morning of Friday 13 February. One imagines that Sadler would have sobered up to some extent by this time so we can't attribute the fact that he made no mention of this to his drink-addled mind. Duncan Campbell, a sailor, was staying at the Sailor's Home in Well Street when he was approached by a man who said that he was 'nearly dead' having been 'out all night' and robbed. The man produced a clasp knife from his right hand pocket and offered to sell it to Campbell who gave him 'a shilling and a bit of tobacco for it'. The two parted company after about five minutes and it was half an hour later that Campbell heard of the murder of Frances Coles. He inspected his purchase but found no signs of blood and after washing it noticed that the water was 'slightly salmon coloured', but he did not think it was discoloured by blood, but more likely by rust. After briefly pawning the knife, Campbell eventually took it to the police and told them how he had come by it, and picked Sadler out at an identity parade. Thomas Robinson, the owner of the marine shop where Campbell pawned the knife told the inquest that the following Sunday he had used the knife to cut up his dinner. But the knife was very blunt and needed to be sharpened on a whetstone otherwise 'he could not have cut bread and meat with it' – hardly the sort of weapon to have been used to sever the tough blood vessels of the human neck. The knife was produced in court and the divisional surgeon, Dr Phillips, gave his opinion together with that on Sadler's clothing and wounds, reported in *The Times* on 24 February 1891:

The knife produced would be capable of inflicting all the wounds found on the neck. It was not a very sharp knife that caused the wounds. On Monday, the 16th, I examined the sailor's cap produced. It was saturated with blood. The left and right cuffs of a shirt were stained with blood. The coat had two spots of blood on the right breast and two drops on the right sleeve. There was also a deposit of blood inside the right sleeve. The boots had no blood on them. On Monday, the 16th, I examined Sadler at Arbour-square police-station. I found two wounds on the scalp, and the appearances of the blood on the clothes were consistent with its having come from either of these wounds.

Phillips of course saw the knife *after* it had been sharpened by Robinson, so any opinion as to the sharpness of the exhibit was irrelevant. If such a transaction took place then Sadler would have been at the Sailor's Home in Well Street at between 10.15am and 10.30am. But at 10.30am that same morning, Sadler was stated by Edward Gerard Delaforce, the deputy-superintendent at the shipping office, to have presented his account for payment of wages and was paid some twenty minutes later. The Shipping Office was in Tower Hill or a good ten minute walk from the Sailor's Home assuming the shortest route via Whitechapel Road.

When Sadler was searched by Police Constable Arthur Sharp outside the London Hospital at 3.30am he did not have a knife. However, Sadler did return to the Victoria Home earlier that morning and thus he could have collected a knife from his kit, which was still where he had left it on the Wednesday evening. Having no money and probably being desperate for a drink he could have collected his knife with the intention of selling it, being totally oblivious to the fact that Coles had been murdered. This would have been an unfortunate move on behalf of Sadler who would thus be most unlikely to admit to selling the knife in the knowledge that he would then have to explain why he had done so. It remains, however, rather improbable that Sadler would have sold his knife for a shilling and then gone straight to the shipping office to collect his wages of £4 15s 1d, although he did admit to unsuccessfully begging for a few halfpence at the Victoria home before going to collect his wages. It is difficult to see why Sadler would have gone to the trouble of selling his knife unless he realised that the police would be after him in connection with the murder of Coles – Sadler did remark to Sergeant John Don just prior to his arrest after police found him in *The Phoenix* public house that he, 'expected this' – although it would have made rather more sense to just throw away the knife rather than sell it.

A clear sign of the desperation with which the police were attempting to make a case against Sadler was revealed in a report by Inspector Henry Moore on 2 March 1891.[107] The report detailed enquiries into Sadler's history in the course of which they traced Rose Moriarty with whom Sadler and his wife had lodged thirteen to fourteen years earlier. Moriarty described how Sadler had threatened his wife with a 'dagger-shaped' knife, and how Sarah Sadler sought refuge in Moriarty's room. Since she had seen Sadler with a knife in his hand, Moore thought it 'as well that Mrs Moriarty should have an opportunity of identifying the knife sold to Campbell'. It is of little surprise that Moriarty did not pick out the knife from among others assembled and even if she had done so the likelihood is that her testimony to that effect would have been ridiculed in any subsequent prosecution.

If we are to believe that Sadler was involved in the murder of Frances Coles we have to accept that a beaten and drunken man staggered his way from where he had just left two police officers to Swallow Gardens where he coincidentally bumped into Frances Coles who must have been alone. At that very instant, for there would have been little time for any discussion, Sadler must have produced a sharp knife and without any indication of a substantial reason he cut her throat with some agility and precision in exactly the right place to silence her and cause her to bleed to death. Having inflicted such wounds to his victim Sadler would then have to silently exit the scene with some haste and stealth.

At around 2.00am, some fifteen minutes before Coles was murdered, Sergeant Edwards testified that he saw Sadler drunken and bloodied on the pavement outside the Mint and although great emphasis has been placed on Sadler's inebriation there is also a distinct possibility that he was concussed following the beating during which he received head injuries. This would further contribute to his lack of coordination and memory loss. Dr Oxley told the inquest that; 'If a man were incapably drunk and the knife blunt I don't think he could have produced the wound', because, 'If a man were swaying about I don't think he could control the muscles of his hand and arm sufficiently to cause the wound'. Any scenario that suggests Sadler murdered Coles is totally implausible and not just because of Sadler's condition. Even if Sadler were not drunk and did possess a knife that would cut his meeting with Coles in this way is a coincidence beyond credulity. There is no obvious reason why Coles would have been alone in Swallow Gardens at that hour and it is far more likely that she entered with a prospective client with the intention of earning a few pennies in or around that place and that the man with whom she engaged was her killer.

The inquest jury were not convinced of Sadler's involvement in the murder of Frances Coles and after just thirteen minutes deliberation returned a verdict of wilful murder against some person or persons unknown and Sadler was discharged. Any further hopes that the police may have had that Sadler was Jack the Ripper quickly came to nothing when shipping records were examined and it was convincingly demonstrated that Sadler was not the serial killer. On 7 August 1888 Sadler signed on at Gravesend for a voyage to the Mediterranean aboard the *Winestead*, and did not return to London until 1 October when he was discharged as a crewmember. Unfortunately, the police became obsessed with Sadler and their urgency to so readily embrace him as Coles' killer, if not Jack the Ripper, was a huge distraction from a determined search for the man who actually did kill Coles. In fact the bias that the police exhibited remained prevalent several months later when Sadler was still under observation in December 1891 following the receipt of a letter from his wife alleging that he had repeatedly threatened to take her life. On this occasion the police had an informant in the person of James Moffatt, a retired pensioner, who lodged with the Sadlers. Sadler at this time ran a chandler's shop and apparently 'did good ready money trade, his takings averaging £2.10s per day' and 'devoted his time to the business'. Moffatt was not taciturn in his descriptions of Sadler saying that 'although he had been at sea for many years he had never heard such horrible language as that uttered by Sadler to his wife, and he was obliged to lock his bedroom door every night for in his opinion Sadler was a treacherous and cowardly man'. Sarah Sadler was advised by the police to apply to a magistrate to have her husband's behaviour curbed. Sergeant Boswell interviewed Sarah Sadler five days later and established a patrol in the vicinity and sight of Sadler's house to 'render Mrs Sadler assistance should the occasion arise' and duly 'Mrs Sadler expressed her thanks for the attention and courtesy that she received from the police'. One is inclined to wonder whether or not she would have received quite the same level of attention had the name of her husband been other than James Sadler who, police reports continued to point out as late as January 1893, had been charged with the murder of Frances Coles. In any event, after a brief period of peace between Sadler and his wife she eventually applied to the magistrates after further threats of violence from him on 9 May 1892, and on 16 May 1892 he was bound over in his own recognisance of £10 to keep the peace for six months. On 2 January 1893 Sadler moved from their lodgings at which time his wife suggested that he remain under surveillance – whether or not such was the case is not known.

Frances Coles' fellow prostitute Ellen Callagher gave a description of a man who may have been the killer.[108] Callagher knew Sadler and she had seen him with Coles earlier that evening, but when she saw Coles with a man outside *The Princess Alice* public house on the corner of Commercial and Wentworth Street at 1.30am that man was not Sadler. Callagher's testimony fits broadly with that of other witnesses since Coles had just been turned out of Shuttleworth's eating house in Wentworth Street where Joseph Haswell who worked for Ann Shuttleworth remembered serving her with 1½d worth of mutton and bread before putting her out of the shop at around 1.45am. From there Coles turned right towards Brick Lane. Callagher's testimony as reported in *The Times* on 28 February 1891 stated:

She [Coles] told me that she had just been turned out of Shuttleworth's, where she had been having something to eat. I went by the public house clock [regarding the timing of events]. I walked up Commercial-street towards the Minories with her [Coles], and asked her what she was going to do. A man spoke to me. He was a very short man, with a dark moustache, shiny boots, and blue trousers, and had the appearance of a sailor. It was not Sadler. Because I would not go with him he punched me and tore my jacket. Frances was about three or four yards away at the time. We were both just getting over drunkenness. He went and spoke to Frances then, and I said, "Frances, don't go with that man, I don't like his look." She replied, "I will," and I then said, "If you are going with that man I will bid you goodnight." I left them at the bottom of Commercial-street going towards the Minories, and I went to Theobald's lodging-house, Brick-lane. I watched them till they turned round by the public house into White-street. I first heard of the murder on Friday at 5 a.m., and in consequence of advice I went to Leman-street Police-station and stated what I knew. I was then taken to the mortuary and identified the body as that of Frances.

There was inevitably some doubt as to timing, because Callagher stated that she first saw Coles outside *The Princess Alice* at 1.30am and events progressed from that time, whereas Haswell was adamant that Coles did not leave

Shuttleworth's until 1.45am. Callagher must have met with Coles immediately after she had been turned out of the eating house otherwise she would not have known where Coles had been, so we can assume that Coles did not go into Shuttleworth's after parting company with Callagher. The fact is that Coles and Callagher were together at around fifteen to thirty minutes before Coles was murdered and, according to Callagher, both were propositioned by the same man. The deputy at Theobald's lodging house confirmed to Callagher that she had arrived back there at 2.00am, which would suggest that Coles and Callagher met at around 1.45am and not as early as 1.30am. The fact that the police did not act enthusiastically on the evidence of Callagher suggests that, apart from their distraction with Sadler, they may not have been too convinced by her testimony, and there is evidence to this effect from the only reference in police documents to the testimony of Callagher. A report from Inspector Henry Moore on 3 March 1891 explains:

I beg to report that since yesterday several statements have been taken; but no good result will be obtained from them; except to prove that the statements previously made and evidence given before the Coroner by Ellen Calanna alias Calman is untrue; especially with regard to the assault upon her which resulted in her receiving a black eye. Special report submitted.[109]

Unfortunately, the special report referred to by Moore does not appear in the case records and thus the ambiguity of his statement regarding Callagher's testimony can not be cleared up. Moore's investigation of Callagher's comments at the inquest and his report came after the jury's verdict, but there is no doubt that the police still had Sadler firmly in their sights and it would have taken a very substantial piece of evidence to distract their focus in a more useful direction. This is unfortunate because it is impossible to accurately gauge the weight of Callagher's statement and given the potential value of her supposed observations it is worthwhile looking closely both at her statement and at the subsequent report by Moore.

Callagher's testimony is confusing but according to her account it seems that a man approached her and because she would not go with him, he punched her and tore her jacket. He then approached Coles who apparently agreed with his request. However, Moore clearly interviewed Callagher and possibly others in order to test the credibility of her account. His conclusion was that at least some of her testimony was untrue. I do not wish to fall into the trap of over-interpreting statements but in this case there is room for some latitude. There are four significant elements to what Callagher said; firstly that she and Coles met after Coles left Shuttleworth's; secondly that a man approached them in Commercial Street; thirdly that the man attacked Callagher; and finally that the man went off with Coles. Of these four elements, the most important one is the observation that Coles went off with the man described by Callagher. However, when Moore says that Callagher's statement is untrue, he places emphasis not on the presence of the man and any association that he may have had with Coles, but on the assault by the man on Callagher. Moore is specific in saying that Callagher lied about the assault that left her with a black eye. This is curious because one would have expected

Moore's overview of his further investigations to place emphasis on the presence of the man being false rather than the assault and black eye being untrue. It is thus possible that Moore did not regard all of Callagher's testimony as being untrue, merely those parts of her testimony that refer to the assault upon her. This is logical enough since it would be rather difficult to believe that Coles went off with a man who had just violently assaulted a woman in her presence.

Since there were apparently no other witnesses to this incident, there is only Callagher's word that events took place, with little hope of corroboration. Quite why Callagher would have wished to lie about the assault is anyone's guess, but because prostitutes were regarded with such universal derision she may well have felt the need to give support to her story by embellishing it. Her tale of an assault gives credence to the presence of a violent man and thereby credence to the likelihood that he was the one who murdered Coles. But by embellishing her account she reduced her credibility regardless of whatever other aspects of her story were true. That is a pity because there is a distinct possibility that Callagher did meet Coles as she suggested and that Coles left with the man Callagher described. It is understandable why Callagher would have embellished her story but it makes no sense for her to have invented the whole incident.

Coles' alleged encounter with the stranger took place at some time after 1.45am if we take the timing given by Haswell as being more accurate than that given by Callagher. Indeed, since Coles didn't leave Shuttleworth's in Wentworth Street until 1.45am and then had then to make her way to *The Princess Alice* in Commercial Street before her meeting with Callagher and being propositioned by the man, it is quite likely that it was close to 2.00am before Coles left with the man and parted company with Callagher, who then returned to her lodgings in Brick Lane at around 2.00am. As she left for her lodgings, Callagher saw Coles and the man head off down Commercial Street and into Whitechapel High Street in the direction of Minories. Callagher's reference to White Street is probably Whitechapel High Street since there is no record of a White Street in the vicinity on either the 1873-80 or 1894-96 edition maps of Whitechapel. The distance from the corner of Commercial Street and Whitechapel High Street to Swallow Gardens via Mansell Street, which would be the most likely route for the couple to take, is some 750yds – at an average walking speed it would have taken the couple under ten minutes to complete the journey.[110] Depending upon how flexible one wishes to be with the timing then it is entirely possible that this was Coles' final journey in the company of her killer, since there would realistically be little time for her to become involved with any other man between leaving Callagher and arriving at Swallow Gardens.

There is an intriguing possibility that the description given by Callagher is the best description of Jack the Ripper that we currently have and it does tally with possible sightings in relation two other murders. Callagher described the suspect as being a very short man, with a dark moustache, shiny boots, and blue trousers, and the appearance of a sailor. From time to time, clothes can change and whiskers can come and go, but the height of an individual does not alter. Compare this description with that given by Elizabeth Long who saw Annie Chapman talking with a man shortly before she was killed and described him as standing only a 'little taller' than Chapman. And the testimony of Joseph Levy, one of the witnesses thought to have seen the Ripper standing with Catharine Eddowes, who reported seeing her with a man who was only 'about three inches taller than the woman'. Chapman and Eddowes were both only five feet in height.

Was Frances Coles a victim of Jack the Ripper? Much the same arguments apply to Frances Coles as to Alice McKenzie and there is no logical reason for her murder to be excluded from the series. Had she been discovered with her abdomen opened and her uterus removed then there is no doubt that she would have been regarded as a victim of Jack the Ripper. All the indications are that her killer was disturbed in his activities and was thus unable to carry out whatever intentions he may have had.

Even disregarding mutilations there are significant similarities between the murder of Frances Coles and the other victims of the Ripper. The location was typically that of a public place where there was no guarantee that the killer would not be discovered in the process of committing murder. There were police patrols nearby, but that would not be unusual in any part of the East End at that hour of the night, and the location would be that chosen by a prostitute for the conduct of sexual activity or on route to such. In this instance I suspect that the Ripper and his victim were on route when he seized the opportunity to attack her under the shelter of the railway arch. It is unlikely that Coles would voluntarily perform in the middle of the road and the fact that she had contusions to the back of her head strongly suggests that she hit the ground falling backwards. This need not have been a backwards fall from vertical and could have been sustained by falling backwards, or following an attack from behind by her killer. It seems reasonable to assume that the couple were walking from Chamber Street to Royal Mint Street when the attack took place since her body then lay in the direction in which they were travelling with feet pointing towards Royal Mint Street.

As with other victims, Coles was killed by precisely delivered cuts, predominantly to the left side of her neck, severing the carotid vessels on the left side with unconsciousness following within a minute and death shortly thereafter. Again the victim was not heard to cry out, even though there were policemen within earshot, and there was no evidence of a struggle at the scene. These are significant features of the Ripper's *modus operandi*. The killer inflicted his fatal cuts to both silence and immobilise his victim – even in instances where the windpipe was not severed, the immediate shock of such wounds would cause the victim to slump to the ground in silence.

Phillips suggested that the knife used was not a very sharp knife, which has been consistently misinterpreted to mean that it was a blunt knife. Yet Oxley, who was also involved in the post mortem examination of Coles, suggested that the knife produced at the inquest could not be the murder weapon because it could not have made 'so large and clean a cut'. I think that Phillips meant to convey the impression that the knife used was a sharp knife but not a *very* sharp knife, thereby trying to open up a gap between the murder of Coles and that of the other Ripper victims since he seems to have formed the opinion that Coles was not victim of the serial killer, and thereby prejudged the information before him.

Phillips was of the opinion that Coles' attacker was right-handed and the evidence suggests this. Of the three cuts to the victim's neck, Phillips was also of the opinion that two cuts were made from left to right and one from right to left. We must assume the orientation is that of the victim, as would be appropriate, and not that of the attacker. Phillips believed the cuts to have been made while the victim lay on the ground, with her attacker to her right. He also suggested that the killer tilted her body to the left while making the cuts to prevent himself being covered with blood from her wounds. Oxley also thought that Coles' throat had been cut while she was on the ground but he told the inquest that although there was but one incision of the skin there must have been two wounds because the larynx had been opened in two places and he thought that the wounds had been made by someone standing in front of the victim and not to the right of the victim as Phillips had suggested. The cuts were thus partially across the front of the throat with emphasis on the left side which is where the vessels were severed. There is no mention of vessels on the right side of the neck being divided but clearly the windpipe was at least partially severed. The fact that cuts were made in two directions should not be taken to imply that the killer was ambidextrous. If there were indeed three cuts then it seems likely that the cuts from left to right were inflicted from behind and the cut from right to left was inflicted after the victim had fallen to the ground.

I have no doubt that Frances Coles was a victim of the same serial killer who had murdered five other victims, but it does appear as though she was his last, or at least his last using his established *modus operandi*.

2.4 The murder of Mary Jane Kelly (c1863-88)

On 9 November 1888 the extensively mutilated body of a woman was found lying on a bed at 13 Miller's Court, a single lodging room. The woman was a prostitute and Joseph Barnett, the man with whom she had lived for twenty months, identified her as Mary Jane Kelly.[111] The couple had spit up a few days earlier after a row over her allowing the room to be used by other prostitutes. Kelly bled to death through a wound to her neck and because of the nature of the murder it was immediately linked to others with similar characteristics. Mary Jane Kelly was considered to be another victim of Jack the Ripper, but a detailed analysis of the circumstances surrounding this murder casts doubt upon such an assertion. Kelly was murdered forty days after the slaying of Catharine Eddowes.

Mary Jane Kelly was also known as Marie Jeanette and by the nicknames 'Black Mary', 'Fair Emma', and 'Ginger'. Kelly was probably born in Limerick in 1863 and then she moved from Ireland to Caernarvonshire or Carmarthenshire in Wales in her early childhood. Her father, John Kelly, was employed at an ironworks and Mary Jane met and married a collier by the name of Davies circa 1879.[112, 113] Within two or three years of marrying, Mary Jane's husband was killed in a mining accident at which point she allegedly lived in Cardiff and turned to prostitution as a means of support. She was, according to Barnett, 'in an infirmary there for eight or nine months', although whether she was working there, or a patient is uncertain. From Cardiff, Kelly moved to London circa 1884 and by account she worked in a West End brothel during which time she made a brief excursion to work in France. After a couple of weeks in Paris she returned to London and moved to the East End. Kelly was reportedly around 5ft 7in and generally attractive. No photographic image of Kelly prior to her death exists and her face was so badly mutilated by her killer that even a post mortem image of such would not have proved informative. Kelly wore only a chemise when she was killed. Her clothes were folded neatly on a chair, her boots were in front of the fireplace, and there were indications that other clothing had burned in the hearth.

The wounds to Kelly are detailed in Diagram 7 and the location of the murder is illustrated in Map 7 and a complete tabulation of relevant findings is given in Table 1. Files in the National Archives relate to the murder of Mary Jane Kelly.[114] The photograph of her mutilated corpse at the scene of her murder is reproduced as Illustration 1.[115] The official inquest papers have survived.[116] Kelly's inquest was not as searching as we have come to expect from those for other victims, especially with regard to the medical evidence, and it is fortunate that other documents, notably the post mortem notes made Dr Thomas Bond, have survived to make up the shortfall.[117] The coroner Wynne Baxter did not preside over the inquest into the death of Kelly, this task falling instead to his rival Dr Roderick MacDonald. Had Baxter been in charge then the inquest would almost certainly have been adjourned with further testimony, especially medical evidence, heard at a later session. However, it seems that MacDonald was keen to distance himself from Baxter's approach as he conducted a somewhat truncated inquest that was over as soon as the cause of death had been established. The inquest details were reported the following day in *The Daily Telegraph* on 13 November and MacDonald gave his reasoning to the jury thus:

The question is whether you will adjourn for further evidence. My own opinion is that it is very unnecessary for two courts to deal with these cases, and go through the same evidence time after time, which only causes expense and trouble. If the coroner's jury can come to a decision as to the cause of death, then that is all that they have to do. They have nothing to do with prosecuting a man and saying what amount of penalty he is to get. It is quite sufficient if they find out what the cause of death was. It is for the police authorities to deal with the case and satisfy themselves as to any person who may be suspected later on. I do not want to take it out of your hands. It is for you to say whether at an adjournment you will hear minutiae of the evidence, or whether you will think it is a matter to be dealt with in the police-courts later on and that, this woman having met with her death by the carotid artery having been cut, you will be satisfied to return a verdict to that effect. From what I learn the police are content to take the future conduct of the case. It is for you to say whether you will close the inquiry to-day; if not, we shall adjourn for a week or fortnight, to hear the evidence that you may desire.

The jury did not express a desire to listen to the 'minutiae of the evidence' and delivered their verdict of wilful murder against some person or persons unknown on the basis of one day of testimony.

Because the body discovered in room 13 Miller's Court had such extensive facial mutilations there was inevitably speculation as to the identity of the woman. Barnett testified that he was only able to identify her 'by the ear and eyes', but he was nonetheless 'positive' that it was the same woman he knew. There has been speculation that Barnett did not actually say 'ear and eyes' but 'hair and eyes' and that those reporting his testimony misheard. 'Ear and eyes' was reported in *The Daily Telegraph*, and in the official inquest notes, and 'ears and eyes' in *The Star*, so it is unlikely that all three independent sources misheard, although it is possible that the newspaper reporters took their wording from the same source, that of the official inquest records. From the crime scene photograph of Mary Jane Kelly it is just about possible to discern her features, but could Barnett have more accurately recognised his former partner by her hair or by her ear and how could her eyes be so useful in this regard when her face was gashed in all directions with the nose, cheeks, eyebrows and ears being partly removed? Barnett reportedly did note 'the peculiar shape of the ears' of Mary Jane Kelly and it is possible that this aspect of the identification was mentioned at the inquest but not so recorded or reported. [118] *The Daily Telegraph* on 10 November 1888, described Kelly as 'of a fair complexion, with light hair, and possessing rather attractive features, dressed pretty well', and *The East London Observer* on 17 November 1888, described her as, 'A woman of about 25 years of age – a blonde of medium height'. *The Western Mail* on 10 November 1888 suggested that Kelly's nickname was 'Ginger' indicating that she may have had reddish hair.

Walter Dew, a young constable working in Whitechapel at the time of the murders and later to become Chief Inspector, remembered Kelly as being 'a pretty buxom girl'. Dew also said that he had 'often seen her parading along Commercial Street, between Flower and Dean Street and Aldgate, or along Whitechapel Road', and he recalled her as 'usually in the company of two or three of her kind, fairly neatly dressed and invariably wearing a clean white apron, but no hat'. [119]

John McCarthy, the lodging house keeper had known Kelly for ten months and also 'had no doubt about her identity'. No relatives of Kelly were located, although it is doubtful that they would have been able to provide any reliable evidence of identification. The police seemed in no doubt that the corpse was indeed that of Mary Jane Kelly. Inspector Abberline in a written report on the murder said after the inquest that 'a number of witnesses were called who clearly established the identity of the deceased'.

A lengthy report in *The Daily Telegraph* on 10 November 1888 provides some background regarding the location of Miller's Court:

Entrance to her apartment was obtained by means of an arched passage, opposite a large lodging-house between Nos 26 and 28 Dorset-street, ending in a *cul-de-sac* known as Miller's-court. In this court there are six houses let out in tenements, chiefly to women, the rooms being numbered. On the right-hand side of the passage there are two doors. The first of these leads to the upper floors of the house in which Kelly was living. It has seven rooms, the first-floor front, facing Dorset-street being over a shed or warehouse used for the storage of coster's barrows. A second door opens inwards, direct from the passage, into Kelly's apartment, which is about 15 ft square, and is placed at the rear corner of the building. It has two windows, one small, looking into the yard, which is fitted with a pump. The opposite side of the yard is formed by the side wall of houses, which have whitewashed frontages, and are provided with green shutters. From some of these premises, on the left-hand side of the court, it is possible to secure a view, in a diagonal direction, of the larger window, and also the doorway belonging to the room tenanted by the deceased. In this room there was a bed placed behind the door, and parallel with the window. The rest of the furniture consisted of a table and two chairs.

In fact, Mary Jane Kelly's ground floor room in Miller's Court measured approximately 12ft by 10ft with a single point of entry, two windows, one smaller than the other and having broken panes, and a hearth. Within the room there was a bedstead, two tables, a chair, and a cupboard. Kelly was a prostitute and used the rented room for such purposes – she was unique among her peers in this respect and there is reason to call into question her relationship with her landlord John McCarthy. Kelly did not regard paying the rent as a priority and it is difficult to understand how she had managed to accumulate such large arrears. Joseph Barnett had known Kelly for some twenty months and had lived with her in that room for ten months. Barnett did not approve of her activities as a prostitute and moved out nine days earlier to live in nearby lodgings and then to Grays Inn Road the day after Kelly's murder. At Kelly's inquest Barnett gave evidence to the effect that he had moved out 'because she [Kelly] had a woman of bad character there, whom she took in out of compassion'. Barnett saw Kelly the day before her murder, but insisted that their parting had been on friendly terms.

John McCarthy's servant, Thomas Bowyer, discovered Kelly's body. On the morning of 9 November 1888 Bowyer was told by McCarthy to go and collect the 29 shillings in rent arrears that she owed and at around 10.45am he knocked on the door of 13 Miller's Court. There being no response, Bowyer went to the window and through a broken pane he pushed the curtain aside. He described seeing 'two lumps of flesh laying on the table close against the bed' and on a second examination he 'saw a body of someone laid on the bed, and blood on the floor'. Bowyer went straight back to report to McCarthy who also examined the grisly scene through the window before both went to the police station in Commercial

Street.

It was at 11.15am that Dr Phillips, surgeon to Whitechapel, H Division, arrived at the scene. His contribution to the inquest was brief as reported in *The Daily Telegraph* on 13 November 1888:

I was called by the police on Friday morning at eleven o'clock, and on proceeding to Miller's-court, which I entered at 11.15 [he entered the Court at this time not the room], I found a room, the door of which led out of the passage at the side of 26, Dorset-street, photographs of which I produce. It had two windows in the court. Two panes in the lesser window were broken, and as the door was locked I looked through the lower of the broken panes and satisfied myself that the mutilated corpse lying on the bed was not in need of any immediate attention from me, and I also came to the conclusion that there was nobody else upon the bed, or within view, to whom I could render any professional assistance. Having ascertained that probably it was advisable that no entrance should be made into the room at that time, I remained until about 1.30p.m. when the door was broken open by McCarthy, under the direction of Superintendent Arnold. On the door being opened it knocked against a table, which was close to the left-hand side of the bedstead, and the bedstead was close against the wooden partition. The mutilated remains of a woman were lying two-thirds over, towards the edge of the bedstead, nearest the door. Deceased had only an under linen garment upon her, and by subsequent examination I am sure the body had been removed, after the injury which caused death, from that side of the bedstead which was nearest to the wooden partition previously mentioned. The large quantity of blood under the bedstead, the saturated condition of the palliasse, pillow, and sheet at the top corner of the bedstead nearest to the partition leads me to the conclusion that the severance of the right carotid artery, which was the immediate cause of death, was inflicted while the deceased was lying at the right side of the bedstead and her head and neck in the top right-hand corner.

On 16 November 1888 Dr Thomas Bond prepared a report on his observations of Kelly's body at the crime scene and of his post mortem examination of her corpse. Bond was called in to give opinion on the murder of three victims and in addition to Mary Jane Kelly, he reported on the deaths of Alice McKenzie and Rose Mylett. He also prepared a general report on the Ripper murders for Assistant Commissioner Robert Anderson. There is no doubt that Anderson's action in involving Bond caused irritation that became obvious with later murders. In the case of Rose Mylett, Bond viewed the body and gave a second opinion much to the consternation of the coroner, which precipitated correspondence. Chief Inspector Donald Swanson clarified the situation by stating that:

Mr Bond was employed as an expert to examine and report upon the surgical reports of the four murders ending with Mitre Square, but in these cases he did not examine the bodies. The final body, which he examined, was that of Mary Janet [*sic*] Kelly, but so far as I am aware, the examination was with the consent of Dr Phillips, who was first called by Police, and the reports do not shew that the Coroner's consent was asked for or necessary. Mr Bond did not give evidence before the Coroner.[120]

Conflict between Bond and Phillips was also evident and Bond's document-ation of the factual elements of the murders is probably more useful than his opinions. Bond did not give evidence at the Kelly inquest but his hand-written notes survive and provide valuable information.[121] His comments are as follows:

Notes of examination of body of woman found murdered & mutilated in Dorset St.
The body was lying naked in the middle of the bed, the shoulders flat but the axis of the body inclined to the left side of the bed. The head was turned on the left cheek. The left arm was close to the body with the forearm flexed at a right angle and lying across the abdomen. The right arm was

slightly abducted from the body and rested on the mattress. The elbow was bent, the forearm supine with the fingers clenched. The legs were wide apart, the left thigh at right angles to the trunk and the right forming an obtuse angle with the pubes.

The whole of the surface of the abdomen and thighs was removed and the abdominal cavity emptied of its viscera. The breasts were cut off, the arms mutilated by several jagged wounds and the face hacked beyond recognition of the features. The tissues of the neck were severed all round down to the bone.

The viscera were found in various parts viz: the uterus and kidneys with one breast under the head, the other breast by the right foot, the liver between the feet, the intestines by the right side and the spleen by the left side of the body.

The flaps removed from the abdomen and thighs were on a table.

The bed clothing at the right corner was saturated with blood, and on the floor beneath was a pool of blood covering about two feet square. The wall by the right side of the bed and in a line with the neck was marked by blood which had struck it in a number of separate splashes.

The face was gashed in all directions, the nose, cheeks, eyebrows, and ears being partly removed. The lips were blanched and cut by several incisions running obliquely down to the chin. There were also numerous cuts extending irregularly across all the features.

The neck was cut through the skin and other tissues right down to the vertebrae, the fifth and sixth being deeply notched. The skin cuts in the front of the neck showed distinct ecchymosis. The air passage was cut at the lower part of the larynx through the cricoid cartilage.

Both breasts were more or less removed by circular incisions, the muscle down to the ribs being attached to the breasts. The intercostals between the fourth, fifth, and sixth ribs were cut through and the contents of the thorax visible through the openings.

The skin and tissues of the abdomen from the costal arch to the pubes were removed in three large flaps. The right thigh was denuded in front to the bone, the flap of skin, including the external organs of generation, and part of the right buttock. The left thigh was stripped of skin fascia, and muscles as far as the knee.

The left calf showed a long gash through skin and tissues to the deep muscles and reaching from the knee to five inches above the ankle.

Both arms and forearms had extensive jagged wounds.

The right thumb showed a small superficial incision about one inch long, with extravasation of blood in the skin, and there were several abrasions on the back of the hand moreover showing the same condition.

On opening the thorax it was found that the right lung was minimally adherent by old firm adhesions. The lower part of the lung was broken and torn away.

The left lung was intact. It was adherent at the apex and there were a few adhesions over the side. In the substances of the lung there were several nodules of consolidation.

The pericardium was open below and the Heart absent.

In the abdominal cavity there was some partly digested food of fish and potatoes, and similar food was found in the remains of the stomach attached to the intestines.

The exact time of Kelly's death is almost impossible to deduce from crime scene or post mortem details. The initial examination of the body did not reveal any relevant information – hardly surprising since it was not examined until 1.30pm, almost three hours after discovery. And the inquest was woefully inadequate in not seriously addressing the matter of timing although the police probably had rather more information at their disposal than was made available at the inquest. In a later report Bond made an estimate of the time of death based on his examination of the corpse at 2.00pm on 9 November and his subsequent post mortem examination:

Rigor mortis had set in, but increased during the progress of examination. From this it is difficult to say with any degree of certainty the exact time that had elapsed since death as the period varies from 6 to 12 hours before rigidity sets in. The body was comparatively cold by 2 o'clock and the remains of a recently taken meal were found in the stomach and scattered about over the intestines. It is therefore certain that the woman must have been dead about twelve hours and the partly digested food would indicate that death took place about 3 or 4 hours after the food was taken, so 1 or 2 o'clock in the morning would be the probable time of the murder.[122]

In view of the unclothed and dissected state of the corpse, the extreme blood loss, and the broken window, heat loss from the body would have been relatively rapid but at least any residual warmth and indications of rigor would have been of some predictive value had the body been examined immediately upon discovery. The observation at post mortem examination that the stomach of the victim contained the partially digested remains of a meal of fish and potatoes could also have been of some value but only in general terms because food can remain in the stomach for several hours depending on a number of variables. However, since there is no indication as to when the victim ate this meal then the time of death can not be reliably extrapolated even in broad terms.

It probably would not have taken the killer more than ten to fifteen minutes to commit his awful crime from the moment that the knife made the first wound to Kelly's neck. Judging by reports as to the distribution of blood on the wall and beneath the bed, her head was at the top right corner of the bed when her neck and right carotid artery were severed and she remained in this position while bleeding to death. From the image of the crime scene reproduced as Illustration 1 quite distinct blood splashes can be seen against the wall and after impact the blood has clearly run downwards.

This pattern of blood distribution has been contrived by some into lettering and it has been suggested that the letters 'FM' were formed in Kelly's blood by way of the killer's 'signature'. James Maybrick, the Liverpool cotton broker and alleged author of the Maybrick Diary – the supposed dairy of Jack the Ripper – being the suggested culprit on this occasion and it is suggested that he was driven to murder prostitutes as a consequence of the infidelities of his wife Florence Maybrick whose initials he supposedly daubed next to Mary Jane Kelly's corpse.[123] But there is nothing whatsoever to substantiate this suggestion. The blood splashes exactly correspond to the position in which Kelly's head would have been when the vessels were cut and probably represent the initial spurts when the carotid artery was first opened, there been little to restrict blood flow on this occasion. Had the killer wished to leave a signature by way of bloody writing then I suspect that he would have not have chosen the least accessible corner of the room, since he otherwise had no knowledge that a photograph of the scene would be captured over which Ripperologists could trawl for an eternity. Such was the carnage and distribution of blood and tissues in 13 Miller's Court that with a little imagination it must have been possible to similarly identify much of the alphabet!

After the initial cut, Kelly would have been immobilised by shock, becoming unconscious in less than a minute and, although the rate of blood loss would have lessened as blood pressure dropped, death would have ensued moments later as the body exsanguinated. It appears as though the killer surprised his victim, but even so it would have been necessary for him to restrain her with one hand, possibly with his right hand over her mouth, while inflicting the fatal cut to her neck with a knife held in his left hand. An appreciable amount of blood accumulated in one place – in the bedding and on the floor at the top right corner of the bed – which suggests that the killer waited until his victim had stopped breathing before commencing mutilation.

Kelly at this time was lying on the right side of the bed from which there was no access because the bed was, according to the police surgeon, 'close against' the partition wall. It would make no sense for the killer to reach across the bed in order to perform the mutilations and at some point he pulled the body closer so that it was 'two-thirds over towards the edge of the bedstead nearest the door'. Without knowing the depth and direction of cuts it is difficult to estimate the position of the killer when he carried out his work but it is reasonable to assume that much of it was conducted from the left side of the bed.

In his report to Anderson, Bond mentions that 'the corner of the sheet to the right of the woman's head was much cut and saturated with blood' which he took to indicate that Kelly's face may have been covered with the sheet at the time of the attack.[124] If her face was indeed covered, and this would by no means be a reliable interpretation of the findings, then it could suggest that Kelly was asleep when the killer struck. I have reservations about this and doubt that the murderer would allow his attack to be potentially compromised by a bed sheet.

The timing of the murder is of no value other than to possibly indicate a description of the killer, but without reliable medical guidance, such an estimate is heavily reliant upon witness sightings and as usual confusion prevails. Based upon witness statements, the most likely opportunity for Kelly's murder was between 2.30am and 7.45am, or much later at between 8.45am and 10.30am, fifteen minutes before her body was discovered. As in every other case, there is no way of knowing how accurate were the times stated by witnesses. Spitalfields church clock chimed on the quarter hour, so presumably estimated timings were relevant to that, but in the matters discussed here, a difference of five minutes either way can be crucial.

Two witnesses claim to have seen Kelly as little as forty-five minutes before the body was discovered in Miller's Court. This evidence suggests that she was not killed until between 10.00am and 10.30am on the morning of 9 November and thus much later than the Ripper victims. This supposed later sighting also initiated speculation that Kelly returned to her room in the early hours and discovered the body of another prostitute who was in her room and that she used the opportunity to escape from her identity. This rather presupposes that she would have a desperate need to do such and the presence of mind to exploit the circumstances, neither of which is largely tenable. The extent to which mistaken sightings or timings can throw an investigation off course has already been mentioned and on balance there is no reason to be distracted in this instance. There was not an elaborate deception and the body in the room in Miller's Court was that of Mary Jane Kelly.

By examining witness testimony there were allegedly several sighting of Kelly on the evening of 8 November and in the early hours of 9 November. Witness statements were given by Mary Anne Cox, a 'widow and unfortunate' who lived at

5 Miller's Court, and who had known Kelly for eight or nine months; Elizabeth Prater, the estranged wife of a boot machinist who lived directly above the room in which Kelly was murdered, and who had known the murdered woman for some five months; Sarah Lewis, a laundress of 29 Great Pearl Street who happened to be staying that night at Mrs Keyler's room on the first floor of 2 Miller's Court; and George Hutchinson, an unemployed labourer of the Victoria Home Commercial Street whom Mary Jane Kelly supposedly knew, and who may have been among her regular clients. Hutchinson did not give information to the police until three days after the murder so consequently he did not testify at the inquest.

By interpretation of the statements by Cox and Prater and allowing a little latitude for timing it seems that Kelly returned to her room, somewhat the worse for drink, at around 11.45pm on the evening of 8 November and went inside with a shabbily dressed man who carried a pot of ale in his hand. *The Daily Telegraph* on 13 November 1888 reported what Cox told the inquest:

I last saw her [Kelly] alive about midnight on Thursday very much intoxicated, in Dorset Street she went up the Court a few steps in front of me, there was a short stout man shabbily dressed with her, he had a longish coat, very shabby dark and a pot of ale in his hand, he had a hard billy cock black hat on, he had a blotchy face and a full, carroty mustache [*sic*] his chin was clean.

I saw them go into her room. I said good night, Mary and the man banged the door, he had nothing in his hands but a pot of beer. She answered me I am going to have a song, I went into my room and I heard her sing "a violet I plucked from my mother's grave when a boy". I remained a quarter of an hour in my room, then went out. She was still singing, I returned about one o'clock she was singing then. I washed my hands and went out again she was still singing. I came in at 3 o'clock, the light was out and there was no noise. I did not undress at all that night, I heard no noise, it was raining hard. I did not go to sleep at all I heard nothing whatever after one o'clock.

Kelly, presumably accompanied for at least some of the time with the man, stayed in her room until after about 1.00am at which time she went out again. Prater returned to Miller's Court at about 1.30am on the morning of 9 November and did not see any sign that Kelly was in her room. *The Daily Telegraph* reported Prater's testimony on 13 November 1888:

I stood at the corner by Mr McCarthy's shop till about twenty minutes past one I spoke to no one I was waiting for a man I lived with, he did not come [Prater may actually have been soliciting]. I went up to my room. On the stairs I could see a glimmer through the partition if there had been a light on in the deceased's room. I might not have noticed it. I did not take particular notice – I could have heard her moving if she had moved. I went in about 1.30 I put 2 tables against the door. I went to sleep at once I had something to drink I slept soundly till my kitten disturbed me about 3.30 to 4. I noticed the lodging house light was out, so it was after 4 probably – I heard a cry of oh! Murder! As the cat came on me I pushed her down, the voice was a faint voice – the noise seemed to come from close by – It is nothing uncommon to hear cries of murder so I took no notice – I did not hear it a second time.

The latest sighting of Kelly was made by George Hutchinson at 2.00am. Hutchinson spoke with Kelly who by his account asked him if he could lend her sixpence. But Hutchinson had no money so Kelly moved off and spoke with another man whom she then took back with her to Miller's Court. Hutchinson was surprised to see Kelly in the company of such a man which is apparently why he took such an interest. Hutchinson made a statement to the police:

About 2 am 9th I was coming by Thrawl Street, Commercial Street, and saw just before I got to Flower and Dean Street I saw the murdered woman Kelly and she said to me Hutchinson will you give me sixpence. I said I cant I have spent all my money going down to Romford. She said Good morning I must go and find some money. She went towards Thrawl Street. A man coming in the opposite direction to Kelly tapped her on the shoulder and said something to her. They both burst out laughing. I heard her say alright to him and the man said you will be alright for what I have told you. He then placed his right hand around her shoulders. He also had a kind of small parcel in his left hand with a kind of a strap round it. I stood against the wall of the Queen's Head Public House and watched him. They both then came past me and the man hid down his head with his hat over his eyes. I stooped down and looked him in the face. He looked at me stern. They both went into Dorset Street I followed them. They both stood at the corner of the Court for about 3 minutes. He said something to her. She said alright my dear come along you will be comfortable. He then placed his arm on her shoulder and gave her a kiss. She said she had lost her handkerchief he then pulled his handkerchief a red one out and gave it to her. They both then went up the Court together. I then went to the Court to see if I could see them but could not. I stood there for about three quarters of an hour to see if they came out they did not so I went away.

Description age about 34 or 35. Height 5ft 6 complexion pale, dark eyes and eye lashes slight moustache, curled up each end, and dark hair, very surly looking dress long dark coat, collar and cuffs trimmed astracan [astrakhan] and a dark jacket under. Light waistcoat dark trousers dark felt hat turned down in the middle. Button boots and gaiters with white buttons. Wore a very thick gold chain white linen collar. Black tie with horse shoe pin. Respectable appearance walked very sharp. Jewish appearance can be identified.[125]

In a newspaper report in *The Times* on 14 November 1888, Hutchinson added a little more to the description:

The man I saw carried a small parcel in his hand about 8in. long and it had a strap round it. He had it tightly grasped in his left hand. It looked as though it was covered with dark American cloth. He carried in his right hand, which he laid upon the woman's shoulder, a pair of brown kid gloves. He walked very softly. I believe that he lives in the neighbourhood, and I fancied that I saw him in Petticoat-lane on Sunday morning, but I was not certain. I went down to the Shoreditch mortuary to-day and recognized the body as being that of the woman Kelly, whom I saw at 2 o'clock on Friday morning. Kelly did not seem to me to be drunk, but was a little bit spreeish. After I left the court I walked about all night, as the place where I usually sleep was closed. I am able to fix the time, as it was between 10 and 5 minutes to 2 o'clock as I came by Whitechapel Church. When I left the corner of Miller's-court the clock struck 3 o'clock. One policeman went by the Commercial-street end of Dorset-street while I was standing there, but no one came down Dorset-street. I saw one man go into a lodging-house in Dorset-street, and no one else. I have been looking for the man all day.

One is entitled to wonder why such important details regarding the watch chain were absent from the version recorded by the police, but such deficiency may not be due to Hutchinson. Hutchinson's interest in Kelly and the man she met can not fail to impress. Quite why he was so concerned with their movements is curious and considering that he waited for three days before giving his potentially important observations to the police is an enduring mystery, and calls into question Hutchinson's motives and involvement. In his statement to Abberline, Hutchinson mentioned that he was surprised to see a man so well dressed in Kelly's company, which is why he watched them. Indeed, a man so well attired in the environs of Dorset Street would have attracted a good deal of attention and much of it for the wrong reason. It would be a surprise that he could escape the district with his life let alone with his valuables assuming of course that he was not accompanied by a minder and that he travelled the greater part of his journey on foot, neither of which need necessarily have been the case. A newspaper report suggested that the old mania for 'slumming' in Whitechapel had become fashionable once again and that 'scores of young men' who had never before been to the East End of London prowled the neighbourhood in which the murders had been committed.[126] In any event, the description of the suspect given by Hutchinson is fascinating since this could have been the man who murdered Mary Jane Kelly.

Hutchinson's presence in the vicinity seems to have been witnessed by Sarah Lewis at 2.30am when she approached Miller's Court on route to Mrs Keyler's room. She told the inquest that a man was standing in the street and 'looking up the court as if waiting for some one to come out'. Lewis noted the time by the Spitalfields church clock and she also reported seeing a drunken woman with a man. According to *The Daily Telegraph* on 13 November 1888, Lewis told the inquest that:

I dozed in a chair at Mrs Keyler's, and woke at about half past three. I heard the clock strike. I could not sleep. I sat awake till nearly four when I heard a female's voice shouting "Murder" loudly. It seemed like the voice of a young woman. It sounded at our door. There was only one scream. I took no notice, as I only heard one scream.

Thus, Lewis and Prater both heard a cry of 'murder'. Prater reported hearing just one cry of 'murder' when she addressed the inquest and such was reported both in the official inquest report and in the newspapers. However, in her statement given to the police just prior to the inquest she reported hearing 'screams of murder about two or three times in a female voice'. Prater further reported in her written statement that she 'did not take much notice of the cries as I frequently hear such cries from the back of the lodging-house where the windows look into Miller's Court'. According to the official report of the inquest, Prater was clearly asked to confirm that she heard just one cry so we can assume that either this had actually always been the case or she changed her mind.[127] Number 2, Miller's Court, where Sarah Lewis spent the night, was just across the passageway from number 13 and upstairs on the first floor. It is interesting to note that Prater, who was directly above Kelly's room, heard only a faint cry, whereas Lewis, who was just across the passageway from Kelly's door, heard a loud cry. The volume of sounds is of course highly subjective, but if this cry emanated from Kelly's room then there is a possibility that the door was open at the time and the cry came from someone on the threshold. No further sound was heard from Kelly's room. Lewis remained in the Court until late afternoon and Prater was up at 5.00am and in the public house by 6.00am. She returned to her room at some unspecified time then slept until 11.00am when presumably she was woken by the activity surrounding the discovery of the body. Cox was in her room until at least 6.15am. There is a report in *The Times* on 10 November 1888, that at around 8.00am, Catherine Pickett, a flower seller who also lived in Miller's Court, went to Kelly's room in order to borrow a shawl on account of the rain and morning chill, but she received no response. Pickett had also heard Kelly singing in the early hours but her husband prevented her from going across to Kelly's room to complain.

Prater is quite adamant that she heard no sounds other than the cry of 'murder' and in particular she was not disturbed by noises of furniture being moved around.

It is interesting to note that both Prater and Lewis woke up or were awake without specific reason at around 3.30am and it could be that they were disturbed by noises or activities of which they were not conscious, and other than for reasons of being disturbed by a cat or just waking up because they could not sleep.

Cries of 'murder' in the middle of the night were clearly not a rarity in the East End of London towards the end of the nineteenth century so it is probably not surprising that, because there was only one cry heard by the witnesses, neither took any particular notice. It is noteworthy that these were neither screams, nor cries for help that would be a more instinctive response from a woman who was in fear of her life. Evidence from the crime scene indicates that Kelly did not struggle or put up a defence of any kind during the attack and assuming that she had no opportunity to cry out immediately before the assault then her ability to make a sound of any kind ended when the fatal knife wound cut through her windpipe.

There is a possibility that the cry of 'murder' was made by someone other than the victim – another woman who perhaps discovered Kelly's mutilated body at around 4.00am but was not prepared to stay around and left the scene in panic. Perhaps one of Mary's fellow prostitutes entered the room and discovered the body then left for fear of being implicated in some way. According to inquest testimony in *The Daily Telegraph* on 13 November 1888, Maria Harvey, a fellow prostitute, had spent time with Kelly at 13 Miller's Court earlier that week.

I knew the deceased as Mary Jane Kelly. I slept at her house on Monday night and on Tuesday night. All the afternoon of Thursday we were together. I said, "Well, Mary Jane, I shall not see you this evening again," and I left with her two men's dirty shirts, a little boy's shirt, a black overcoat, a black crepe bonnet with black satin strings, a pawn-ticket for a grey shawl, upon which 2s had been lent, and a little girls white petticoat.

Harvey confirmed to the inquest that she knew Barnett and that Kelly had never spoken to her about being afraid of anyone. She also confirmed that the black overcoat she left in the room was that shown to her by the police.

Assuming that the gas lamp immediately opposite the door to number 13 had not been extinguished by this time then light would have illuminated the otherwise darkened room sufficiently for anyone opening the door to witness the scene of carnage. Maria Harvey had stayed with Kelly before so she would be aware of to how to open the apparently locked door and there is a distinct possibility that she returned to Miller's Court in the early hours of 9 November. However, it is unlikely that anyone opening the door by reaching in through the window could have avoided the pieces of flesh discarded on the table and this alone could have been reason to cry murder.

The fact that it was necessary to break into the door at 13 Miller's Court requires explanation because rather more significance has been made of this than was ever justified, the suggestion being that the killer locked the door behind him and took the key with him when he left. However, the truth is rather different since Barnett and Kelly had lost the key to the door. Barnett told inspector Abberline that the key had been missing for some time, and since it had been lost Barnett and Kelly opened the door by reaching through the broken window and pulling back the catch. 'It is quite easy', Abberline informed the inquest, which may have been the case, but only if one knew the procedure and apparently no one who arrived at the scene realised that the door could be opened by that means. It must also be assumed that the key went missing after the window was broken otherwise the occupants would not have been able to enter their lodgings. There is no indication as to exactly when Barnett and Kelly had the argument that resulted in the windowpanes being broken but McCarthy suggested that they were broken 'a short time ago', whereas Julia Vanturney of 1 Miller's Court suggested that the windows were broken 'a few weeks ago whilst she [Kelly] was drunk'. The key was not necessary to lock the door, the lock being of a sprung latch rather than a dead lock type, but in order to open the door from outside the key was required. It is worth bearing in mind that the key could have been taken by one of Kelly's clients. This would suggest that the client had the intention to return which would imply that her murder resulted from a plan rather than from a spontaneous act. If Kelly was in the habit of sleeping with a table against the door as seemed common and sensible practice given the nature of the neighbourhood, then obviously such would not have been in place when the killer left and could not have been moved without noise if her killer arrived unexpectedly. It is entirely possible that Kelly felt that a sprung latch on the door was sufficient security without the need to reinforce it with furniture.

On the basis of the above witness reports it would seem likely that Kelly was murdered some time between 2.30am and 4.15am if the cry of 'murder' came from the victim or from someone who entered her room, or between 2.30am and 7.45am if the cry was unconnected with Mary Jane Kelly's murder.

As already mentioned, there were reported sightings of Mary Jane Kelly later on the morning of 9 November. Caroline Maxwell, the wife of a lodging house deputy from Dorset Street had supposedly know Kelly by sight for about four months but had only spoken to her twice prior to 9 November. Maxwell said at the inquest that she saw Kelly at around 8.15am then again at 8.45am when she returned from getting her husband's breakfast. At their first encounter Maxwell saw Kelly standing at the entrance to Miller's Court, when Kelly admitted to being ill following too much beer and had vomited in the street, and at the second sighting Kelly was reportedly talking to a man outside *The Britannia* public house on the corner of Commercial and Dorset Street. By Maxwell's account, Kelly admitted to her that she had 'the horrors of drink' upon her since she had 'been drinking for some days past'. Kelly's 'morning sickness' has been used by some to suggest that she was pregnant, but there was no mention of this in Bond's thorough post mortem report and such a condition was unlikely. In a report in *The Illustrated Police News* on November 17, 1888, Maurice Lewis, a tailor who lived in Dorset Street and an acquaintance, or maybe even a client, of Mary Jane Kelly, who had known her for five years, also claimed to have seen her that morning. His supposed sighting of Kelly was between 10.00am to 10.15am when he and friends entered *The Britannia*. Lewis does not say how long he was in *The Britannia* or whether or not Kelly left before him or remained after he had gone.

If Kelly was out and about that morning then she must have left her room before 8.00am when Catherine Picket reportedly called and received no answer.

But there were no further sightings of Kelly that morning in spite of the fact that she would have been on the streets for anything up to two and a half hours. This tends to lessen support for the reported sightings by Maxwell and Lewis. Furthermore, if Maxwell did see Kelly that morning then it is also possible that Lewis saw her as well which meant that just thirty to forty-five minutes lapsed from the reported sighting by Maurice Lewis to the discovery of the body which is probably insufficient time for Kelly to return to her room with the killer, undress and fold her clothes and place them neatly on a chair at the foot of the bed, and for the killer to then indulge in an act of extreme, though not especially skilful, butchery and slip away before Thomas Bowyer peered in through the window. Had the corpse been examined as soon as the police surgeon arrived on the scene at 11.15am instead of over two hours later at 1.30pm, the temperature of the body would have at least given an idea as to whether the murder had just been committed or whether the killer had struck much earlier in the morning.

If the woman seen by Maxwell was Mary Jane Kelly, then it is fair to assume that her stomach was emptied at 8.15am when she had vomited in the street. The woman found in Miller's Court had a partly digested meal of fish and potatoes in her stomach, so if Kelly was strolling around the streets of Whitechapel before 9.00am and was murdered between then and 10.15am then at some point she must also have taken a meal. Bond's deduction that the partly digested stomach contents were the remains of a meal that had been taken some three to four hours prior to death tends to further negate the observations of Maxwell and Lewis, even allowing for the significant error that can result from using the extent of meal digestion as an estimate of time of death.

Furthermore, Bond reported that at 2.00pm on 9 November when he examined Kelly's body, it was 'comparatively cold' and that rigor mortis had set in and 'increased during the progress of the examination'. Bond admitted the difficulty in accurately estimating the time of death from the information he had but estimated that 'the woman must have been dead about twelve hours'. In fact, he was probably right and may even have under estimated the length of time for which she had been dead. The broad rule of thumb suggests that if a body is cold and stiff then it has probably been dead for between 8hrs and 36hrs under average conditions.[128] Where the body lies in a cool environment or if cooling is enhanced, as would have been the case with such a mutilated corpse, then the onset of rigor is further delayed. While it is quite impossible to accurately state the time at which Kelly died, the state of her corpse at 2.00pm suggests that she was murdered much earlier than 9.00am to 10.15am on 9 November. But Maxwell was adamant that she was not mistaken as to timing – her statement was after all given on the same day as Kelly's death. *The Daily Telegraph* carried a further report on 12 November 1888:

The question has arisen whether Mrs Maxwell might not have confounded one morning with another, but when questioned on this point she avers that there were circumstances connected with her own work to enable her to fix it as Friday morning without any doubt or misgiving whatever.

These circumstances were detailed on the same day by an article in *The Times*:

When asked by the police how she could fix the time of the morning, Mrs Maxwell replied, "Because I went to the milkshop for some milk, and I had not before been there for a long time, and she [Kelly] was wearing a woollen cross-over that I had not seen her wear for a considerable time". On enquiries being made at the milkshop indicated by the woman her statement was found to be correct, and the cross-over was also found in Kelly's room.

If Maxwell was right about the timing then the woman she referred to was not the Mary Jane Kelly murdered in Miller's Court. Maxwell described Kelly to a newspaper reporter as, 'a pleasant little woman, rather stout' and Maurice Lewis' description was much the same.[129] Mary Jane Kelly was in fact reportedly 5ft 7in, which was significantly above the average adult female height in 1888. Close scrutiny of the image of what remained of Kelly's corpse suggests that she was not overweight, but unfortunately her height can not even be approximated from the corpse due to an absence of anything within the picture that could be used to scale the image. There is nothing in the official records to substantiate the report in *The Times* that the 'cross-over' identified by Maxwell was found in Kelly's room.

I can only reiterate that witnesses do not know that they are going to be witnesses and consequently the recollection of what they actually see can often be influenced by what they think they should have seen. Lewis's account only ever appeared in a newspaper and Kelly was not in the East End before 1885 so he could not have known her for five years. Maxwell admitted that she had only ever spoken to Kelly on two previous occasions and that she had not seen her for three weeks until Friday 9 November. Maxwell could not have identified the corpse as that of the woman she knew as Mary Jane Kelly because there was precious little left to identify so her observations must be regarded as wholly unreliable. Realistically, it seems far more likely that both Maxwell and Lewis were simply mistaken as to who they saw, when the sighting was made, or who they knew as Mary Jane Kelly.

Assuming that Kelly was murdered in the early hours of 9 November then there is little doubt that her killer would have needed some light by which to work, especially when inflicting an initial wound that could not be accurately delivered in total darkness. Jack the Ripper was a skilled operator even in the dark but Mary Jane Kelly's killer needed light. Assuming that it was lit, some light could have entered the room from the gas lamp directly opposite the door to number 13, since no door is a perfect fit, and although the amount of light from this source or through the closed curtains would have been minimal, the room almost certainly would not have been in total darkness.

When Cox returned to her room at 3.00am she saw no sign of a light from Kelly's window and heard no sound, but Kelly was probably inside her room with a man by this time. Cox also heard no cry of 'murder' in spite of the fact that she claims not to have slept at all that night, although her room was towards the far end of the Court. Both Prater and Lewis were in their rooms when Kelly arrived back with the man witnessed by Hutchinson at around 2.15am. Prater was asleep by this time. There is nothing about the killer's activities within the room that would have resulted in significant noise unless he had accidentally collided with furniture. With regard to the fire in the hearth, Abberline gave his impression to the inquest, documented in the official inquest report:

I have taken an inventory of what was in the room, there had been a large fire so large as to melt the spout off the kettle I have since gone through the ashes in the grate and found nothing of consequence except that articles of woman's clothing had been burnt which I presume was for the purpose of light as there was only one piece of candle in the room.[130]

It is fairly certain that Kelly would not have burned the clothing because some of it belonged to Maria Harvey and it would be worth far more as clothing than as fuel. So Kelly's killer must have set fire to the clothing in the hearth although this remains a rather obscure activity. Burning clothing does not provide a very effective light source and I doubt that such was the reason for the fire. After all, a candle was present in the room and by accounts was less than half used, so if the killer needed light then it is more likely that he worked by candlelight. It is also unlikely that burning clothing would generate a fire that was fierce enough to melt metal – or even a soldered joint – not that there was any evidence that the kettle spout was actually melted on that occasion and it may have been subjected to fierce heat before the night of Kelly's death. It would be far more likely that Kelly's killer lit the fire in order to dispose of some of his own clothing that had become contaminated with blood and other material during the course of his activity, especially if that clothing would have given the police clues to his identity.

Several circumstances of the murder of Mary Jane Kelly do not fit well with the Ripper murders, and elements of the *modus operandi* established in other murders are absent from that of Kelly. The anomalies are as follows:

- The Ripper did not engage with his victims beyond sufficient of an exchange to persuade them to go to a location for sex. If the Ripper was Kelly's killer then he would almost certainly have attacked her the moment they entered her room; seconds after the door had closed behind them and the instant her back was towards him. Having a naked victim or even having any sexual engagement with the victim were not part of the killing ritual for the Ripper; such components were not a part of the fantasies that compelled him to kill.

- There is also the matter of the handedness of the killer. According to the circumstances of death it is likely that Kelly was killed by a left-handed assailant. The killer unavoidably approached Kelly from her left because access from the other side of the bed was not possible. At that time Kelly was on the right side of the bed with her head towards the far corner and faced with such an arrangement, a right-handed assailant would have instinctively wounded the left side of the neck so that he could restrain her head or even place a hand over her mouth with the left hand. The right side of Kelly's neck would have been easier and naturally more comfortable to attack by a left-handed killer. The Ripper murders were almost certainly carried out by a right-handed assailant. Also, in not one of the Ripper murders was there any evidence of an excess of spurting blood. The Ripper's technique was so refined as to avoid this. But in the case of Mary

Jane Kelly blood from her severed right carotid artery had spurted against the partition wall to the right of the bed. No attempt had been made by her killer to limit or direct the flow and it is possible that he may have been splashed with blood as a consequence.

- The removal of Mary Jane Kelly's breasts in this murder is contrary to activities for the Ripper murders. This is a clear sexual and defeminising mutilation, yet in spite of the relative ease with which such could have been performed, even in the darkness, not one of the Ripper victims showed a similar mutilation – not even an attempt to mutilate or even to stab the chest. It is of course a possibility that on this occasion the killer had so much time that he was able to indulge himself with a frenzy of meaningless mutilation with the intention of shocking whoever discovered the body, but otherwise it is a significant anomaly.

- In addition to removing most of the abdominal organs, Kelly's thorax was also opened, the lungs slightly cut, and it seems that the heart was removed from the scene. On this latter point there has been some discussion surrounding the exact meaning of 'absent' in Bond's post mortem report. Opinions are divided as to whether Bond meant that the heart had been removed from the body or removed from the scene. It had certainly been removed from the body since Bond makes specific mention that the pericardial sac had been ruptured to gain access to the heart – this was accessed from below the rib cage and without the killer cutting through the ribs. Whether the heart was removed from the murder scene is arguably of less importance but most likely it was, otherwise further mention would have been made of the organ, specifically, where in the room it had been discarded. Importantly there was no specific and focussed mutilation – virtually every abdominal organ was removed and spread about the scene in a completely random fashion.

There have been speculative suggestions that one femur of the victim was split longitudinally but there is actually no evidence for this and in particular Bond makes no mention of such an injury in his comprehensive report. Such an injury would probably call for the use of a rather heftier instrument than a very sharp knife and if the killer had such to hand then he would certainly have used it rather more freely than just to split one bone. The crime scene images of Mary Jane Kelly's corpse may also be misleading since at first glance it seems as though the shaft of her right femur has been stripped of skin and muscle. However on closer examination this is not the case and what appears to be exposed clean bone is in fact a strip of skin along the top of the thigh – several cuts can clearly be seen in the skin. It is, however, another image of the corpse taken from the right side of the bed that has given rise to suggestions that the head of the femur has been split. After examining a good quality reproduction of this image I can see no convincing evidence to indicate that exposed bone let alone bone marrow is depicted in the image.

Much can be gleaned from a minute examination of the original images of Kelly's corpse, largely reinforcing Bond's post mortem description, and digital enhancement reveals more detail than is visible at first sight and in published images, including that reproduced later in this book. Kelly's killer undoubtedly hacked at her face and deep cuts are visible more especially on the left temple, on the forehead and across the right eye, on the right cheek, and across the left side of the chin. The upper portion of the nose has been cut off and the left nostril distorted below that on the right. Kelly's lips are visible but the right eye appears closed. Although these mutilations are extensive, they are probably not sufficiently so to prevent identification of Kelly by someone who knew her well and if the killer wished to make his victim totally unidentifiable he would have removed her features completely. Extensive lacerations are apparent to the right side of the neck – the left side is not visible in the image – and the ventral aspect of the thorax has been almost completely stripped of skin from the collar bones downwards, both breasts being separately removed in the process. The abdomen has been extensively eviscerated such that Kelly's left forearm and hand are positioned in a largely empty abdominal cavity. Just above Kelly's wrist can be seen the lower aspect of the thorax which is open – the diaphragm should cover the base of the thorax but it has been cut away with what appears to be lung tissue visible just inside the thorax. There is no doubt that the thorax was opened and the thoracic organs disrupted. Mutilation extends to include the external genitalia and thighs of the victim with complete removal of pelvic organs such that there is no discernable structure remaining. There are deep lacerations to Kelly's upper and lower left arm – the right arm is not visible – and in addition to the extensive removal of skin and muscle from the inner thighs of the victim there is a wound to the right calf and appreciable daubing of blood over the skin, apparently representing the killer's finger marks. Organs and severed tissues are distributed around the corpse but none are identifiable from the image.

In general terms, the mutilation of Kelly's body seems to have been undertaken with considerably less skill than that employed with certain other victims and it does rather fall into the category of crude butchery. Anyone who had read the inquest details in the newspapers would have had an approximate idea of the state in which Catharine Eddowes' body was left, and to an imitator, the removal of any organ would be good enough, especially for someone not too familiar with anatomy. Otherwise, why was the uterus not taken from the scene in this instance? In a sense, the mutilation of Mary Jane Kelly was no more than a rather crude approximation of the mutilation of the other victims.

Dr Thomas Bond was of the opinion that Kelly was one of the Ripper victims, but this assertion was based upon a comparison of what he had seen at the post mortem examination of Kelly with no more than the notes on the previous victims. In a general report on the murders submitted to Anderson Bond further asserted that in each case the mutilations were inflicted by someone with no anatomical or technical knowledge and he could not on that basis even implicate 'a butcher or horse slaughterer or any person accustomed to cut up dead animals'.[131] This was a risky conclusion to reach since he had not seen the corpses of the other victims and his opinion was probably much swayed by the mutilated remains of Kelly. On the balance of information available there is indeed little to suggest that Kelly's murderer possessed any anatomical or technical skill whatsoever.

With regard to the logistics of Kelly's death there are only two realistic scenarios for how she and her murderer came together; one involves Kelly meeting her killer and taking him back to her room and the other involves the killer entering her room while she slept. In either case the fact that Kelly had drunk to excess the previous evening would only have assisted the killer's objective. There were no reports of noise coming from the room and no indications that a struggle took place. There were negligible identifiable defensive wounds to Kelly, apart from a minor superficial cut to the thumb that had bled, and abrasions to the back of the hand that were not typically defensive in nature but could have been inflicted as Kelly put up a reflex defence. Thus, she was either killed while she slept, or taken by surprise and instantly overpowered. The deep lacerations to Kelly's forearms were clearly inflicted after death as evidenced by a lack of bleeding that would be associated with such deep cuts had they been sustained while the victim was alive, at least as far as can be seen in the crime scene photograph of her body.

Kelly's position on the far right of the bed at the time the fatal wound was inflicted could be taken to suggest that someone else was on the bed beside her just prior to her death. This is possible, but unlikely and would result in a number of logistical difficulties that would make an attack unnecessarily complicated.

If Kelly did not take the murderer back to her room then the assailant must have entered the room and attacked her while she slept. It was certainly possible for someone to enter the room and kill Kelly in this way, but that person could not have been a total stranger because he must have either stolen the key on a previous visit or must otherwise have knowledge of how to open the locked door through the broken window. Barnett and Kelly were surely not the only people who knew how to unlock the door; Kelly's fellow prostitutes whom she allowed to use the room together with several men whom they each took back to the room must also have known how to gain access. Assuming that Kelly was in a deep sleep and lacking the additional security of a table against the door, undisturbed access might be easy enough. Light would flood into the room from the gas lamp on the wall outside immediately opposite the door and the killer would have sufficient light by which to inflict a fatal wound to the neck. This done he could close the door and continue unhindered and in relative silence. Of the alternatives, however, it seems on balance more likely that Kelly invited the killer back to her room.

There is little doubt that it was Mary Jane Kelly who was murdered in the room at number 13, Miller's Court some time between 2.30am and 4.15am on the morning of Friday 9 November 1888. Certain characteristics of the murder suggested that it might be another in the series committed by Jack the Ripper, but upon close examination there are significant departures from the conduct of the Ripper murders and it seems highly probable that Kelly was not after all the most publicised victim of the notorious serial killer. She was likely killed by someone she invited into her room and not by someone who entered the room without her knowledge. The fatal wound to the neck was inflicted either while she slept or after being taken by surprise since there was no evidence of a struggle. Kelly bled to death in a matter of minutes from a severed right carotid artery. There are indications are that the killer, who was probably left-handed, and had no particular skill or anatomical knowledge, mutilated Kelly's body in order that it might resemble the work of the Jack the Ripper. Before leaving the scene he burned in the hearth some of his own clothing that had become contaminated with material from the victim's body, together with other items that he found in the room. His work completed the killer slipped unseen into the darkness of the early hours.

The man with a carroty moustache and holding a pot of beer witnessed going into Kelly's room with the victim at midnight was not her killer since Kelly was seen later by another witness George Hutchinson. If we rule out Hutchinson as a suspect and can rely upon his evidence then Kelly was most likely murdered by the man who accompanied her back to her room at around 2.15am; the man seen and described by Hutchinson as of 'respectable appearance'. This fits reasonably well with Bond's crude estimate of the time of death which could have been out by at least a couple of hours but provides an indication that death occurred in the early hours rather than later that morning. Abberline gave credence to Hutchinson's story and specifically stated in his report of 12 November, 'I am of opinion his statement is true'.[132] While Hutchinson gives a good description of the suspect there is little else from his statement that indicates whether the man was Kelly's killer or merely another client. Did Hutchinson's description of the encounter between Kelly and the man suggest that they knew each other? Did the fact that he held the bag tightly in his left hand suggest that he was left-handed or would the fact that he placed his right arm around her shoulders suggest the opposite? Why would a man so dressed and displaying elements of wealth risk being alone in such a violent area unless confident that he would not be accosted? The questions are as tantalising as the answers are elusive.

Whoever killed Mary Jane Kelly was not Jack the Ripper. But the Ripper murders must have provided a very tempting opportunity for anyone with murder in mind, even though there was a very significant risk that in the course of attempting to conduct a copycat killing one would be credited with several others.

3: The characterisation of the Whitechapel serial killer

This section draws together information from all aspects of the Ripper murders and examines how the killer operated and what kind of a man could be capable of committing such horrific crimes.

3.1 The *modus operandi*

3.1.1 The approach and attack of the killer

The prostitutes of Whitechapel could hardly be regarded as delicate examples of womanhood. They were frequently involved in fights, especially when drunk, and often carried scars and bruises as a consequence. The average street prostitute would be expected to put up a strong and vociferous fight if given half a chance, but the Ripper's victims were not afforded such an opportunity. His approach was cool and clinical and it is highly unlikely that his killing routine was conducted in such a way that the victim for one moment realised what was about to happen. A peculiarity of the Ripper murders is that in each case there was no indication that the victim was able to muster any defence to the attack. In no instance was there evidence of a struggle, no screams were heard, and each victim died quickly on the spot where they were attacked. On this basis, it seems unlikely that the Ripper would have wrestled his victims to the ground and he would not have engaged in an initial assault of any kind. Each attack involved a precisely delivered knife cut to the side of the neck that severed the carotid artery leading to unconsciousness probably within in a minute, depending upon whether vessels were completely or partially severed on one or both sides of the neck. Death from exsanguination followed shortly thereafter.

The balance of probability suggests that during the course of several attacks at least one assault will not go according to plan giving the victim the opportunity for a defensive response, to scream, or to retaliate. Not so with these murders and there are no indications that the Ripper's knife missed the target at the first attempt in any attack. This is an extraordinarily risky way to kill someone and highly prone to failure because of the small target area and relative ease of defence by the victim if given the slightest opportunity, especially if the initial wound does not find the target. Although throat slashing was to some extent part of the culture of the day, this method of killing could not be used by anyone of a hesitant disposition and does require skill, accuracy, and certainly some degree of anatomical knowledge. Cutting the front of the throat, as is often the case in suicidal injuries, carries no guarantee of instant success because, while the trachea will usually be severed, the major blood vessels often escape injury, at least with the first cut. Also, forcing the head back to allow for a cut across the front of the throat tends make the carotid vessels less accessible to all but the deepest cuts.

The fact that the killer managed to practice his craft with such deadly efficiency warrants closer examination and several clues as to his likely approach are apparent among the tabulated crime scene and post mortem details for the Ripper victims as given in Tables 1 and 2.

The salient points are as follows:

- The distribution of blood was limited to the point where the victim died. There was no widespread spurting of arterial blood and the victim's clothes were not covered in blood except where it had soaked into the back of garments while victims lay on the floor after the attack.
- Almost all of the blood loss occurred when the victims were lying on the ground
- Victims died at the spot where they were attacked and none was moved from another location
- There were no signs of a struggle, no defensive wounds to the hands or wrists of the victims, and no screams for help. With the exception of Frances Coles, none of the bodies showed any bruising or abrasions to the back of the head or elbows to indicate that they had fallen backwards and hit the ground
- The throat of each victim was severed from left to right with death from exsanguination.
- One cut appears to have been sufficient to fatally wound each victim although in some instances there were additional cuts to the neck. The wounds to the throat preceded all other mutilations.
- There were no preliminary stabbing wounds, or any other immobilising injuries apart from indications of strangulation of Chapman.
- At least two of the victims were discovered with their legs drawn up towards the body

Each of these factors makes a small contribution to forming an opinion as to how the killer may have approached and murdered his victims. This does not mean to say that the circumstances were exactly the same on each occasion because there were inevitably variables over which he had no control. But his technique was sufficiently adaptable and a plausible scenario can be constructed as to how he managed to kill so successfully.

Firstly, it is evident from the information examined thus far that the killer was right-handed. Whether the attacks were made facing the victim or from behind, it is almost certain that the left side of the neck would be targeted by instinct with the left hand employed to steady the victim or to stifle any screams that she may have attempted. Cuts to the neck ran from left to right of the victim, although in the case of Mary Ann Nichols, the surgeon suggested otherwise, which was somewhat contrary to his reported findings, and in the case of Frances Coles, the surgeon suggested that one of the three cuts may have been made from right to left of the victim, which is also a doubtful interpretation.

It is unlikely that the killer inflicted the cuts to the neck while facing the victims. Such deep wounds would be difficult to inflict from the front with a knife held in one hand while attempting to secure and silence the victim with the other hand. Any assault from the front would forfeit some element of surprise, and in a fraction of a second the intended victim could respond with defensive arm or body movements. A face-to-face approach by the killer would almost certainly not have been successful on six occasions out of six. It also seems unlikely that the victims were wrestled to the ground before inflicting the neck wounds. This approach would very likely result in a struggle with screams and defensive manoeuvres from the victim.

It is far more likely that the killer attacked his victims from behind, first by placing the left hand or arm across the mouth to both silence and steady the victim and then cutting across the victim's throat from left to right with a very sharp knife held in the right hand. The victim would be taken completely by surprise and would be immediately immobilised. Her legs would give way and she would sink quickly to the ground assisted by the killer. Her position on the floor would be almost where she stood and the fact that Elizabeth Stride's legs were drawn up would also support this.

It would not be necessary for the killer to sneak upon his victim in order to employ this means of attack. In fact to pounce from the gloom would be fraught with too many variables and the Ripper appears to have been a rather more cunning operator than that. It is highly unlikely that he lurked in the shadows until a target walked by, but rather more likely that he found a prostitute and engaged her in conversation on the pretence of placing some business her way. They would then set off to a secluded location for sex and on route the killer would capitalise on a suitable moment to attack her. A killer who intends to mutilate his victim needs time in which to operate and must select a location that will afford the minimum risk of being disturbed. Because the Ripper went with his victims rather than leading them, he would not know in advance the location of his attack, thus on each occasion he made an instant decision in this respect and may not always have judged wisely. When the decision was made, and with the woman momentarily distracted, he would step behind her and make his attack. The element of surprise would be easier to achieve while walking along than when the destination was reached. This approach minimised the risks for the killer and afforded him a high level of control through all phases of the attack. The killer's ability to strike so effectively was devastating and the fact that Elizabeth Stride still clutched a packet of cachous in her hand as she bled to death is a frightening testimony to the speed and efficiency of his technique. There is no evidence to suggest that the Ripper directly engaged in a sex act with any of his victims, nor that such was ever his intention.

3.1.2 An analysis of the neck wounds

The diagrams 1-7 give a representation of the approximate size and location of the neck wounds for each Ripper victim and for Mary Jane Kelly. In some cases several cuts were made to the neck but only the major wounds described at post mortem examination are illustrated, the relative depth of each wound being represented by the width of the cut area.

There is a belief prevalent among writers on the Ripper murders, largely based upon the impressions of contemporaneous investigators, that because blood was not widely distributed at the murder scene of any of the victims, the wounds must have been inflicted while the victim lay on the ground. While this is certainly a possibility it need not necessarily be true and tends to ignore the practicalities of such an approach. A cut to the side of the neck that is deep enough to puncture the carotid artery would certainly lead to severe and rapid loss of blood under arterial pressure and there is undoubtedly the potential for that blood to become significantly distributed in the vicinity of the murder. Upon the absence of any spraying of blood is based the assertion that the throat of each of the Ripper victims must have been cut while they were prostrate on the ground because so little blood was found any distance from the victim. However, it is evident from the murder of Mary Jane Kelly that blood spurted from her neck while she lay on the bed, and to such an extent that it splashed against the wall adjacent to her body. Dr Thomas Bond commented in his report on the scene that; 'The wall by the right side of the bed and in a line with the neck was marked by blood which had struck it in a number of separate splashes'. In other words, even though Mary Jane Kelly was undoubtedly lying down when the fatal wound to her neck was inflicted, there was appreciable spurting of blood and had the wall not been in the way then her blood would have travelled a significant and noticeable distance from her body. The police surgeons who examined the bodies of the Ripper victims generally concluded that each woman had been thrown or forced to the ground by her assailant whereupon her neck had been cut. However, neither the practical considerations of this, nor the alternative possibility that the initial wound may have been inflicted with victim and assailant upright, appear to have been seriously considered.

There is no doubt that blood does spurt from severed arteries but the extent to which such happens is governed by several factors not least of which are the degree to which the artery is severed and the depth of the artery within the tissues. It must also be noted that spurting falls off quite quickly as blood pressure drops and the greatest projectile volume would follow the initial cut. Thereafter, as blood pressure falls, so too would the projected distance. Clearly, an artery that is completely severed will be able to void more blood than one of similar size that is only partially cut through thus the greatest projection would come from an initial cut to a moderately sized artery such as a carotid artery that was completely severed. However, the situation is not quite as simple as one might imagine and the idea that blood gushes from severed arteries with all the maintained force of a high-pressure hose prevails, but without foundation. The pulse pressure of blood in the arterial system falls instantaneously with the shock of a traumatic injury such as a wound to the neck would induce.[1] When initially severed, blood from a major vessel such as the common carotid artery can spray for a maximum distance of the order of half a metre, but there will only be effective spurting of blood if the open end of the vessel can void externally which is rarely the case and especially relevant in the neck. The hypothetical initial spurt depends on the open proximal side of the vessel, the side retaining connection to the heart, being unobstructed and thus free to void to the maximum extent. With specific regard to the carotid artery, if the head is inclined away from the side of the wound then the wound will be open and the blood can flow more freely and may even spray, but if the head is inclined, or deliberately held towards the side of the wound then the passage of blood from the artery will be restricted and may even continue to flow internally, even into the windpipe if that is severed, with the result that a pressurised oozing of blood, rather than spurting and spraying results.

Clearly, blood can still spurt from a neck wound even though the victim is on the ground, although the arc followed by the spurt would be shortened due to the low distance from the ground thus the blood would not appear to travel as far. Descriptions of blood distribution for Ripper victims do not suggest spurting even when the victims were on the ground, the pattern being one of pooling rather than spurting. A very sharp knife of the kind used by the Ripper would make a thin deep cut and if the killer were to hold the wound closed through his grip on the victim's head then blood would indeed ooze rather than spurt. In this way, the Ripper could quite easily have suppressed the extent to which blood flowed from a victim's neck merely by forcing her head over to the cut side, effectively closing the wound for the few seconds that it would take for him to get out of the way so that he would not be covered in blood. In fact the reflex response of the victim to a sharp knife cutting into the neck would be to bring the head down to the shoulder on the same side as the injury as a defensive response – at least for the instant in which the muscles were intact. Forcing the victim's neck to the left, which could be easily and naturally done from behind, while holding the head with the left hand would close the wound sufficiently to prevent projectile blood loss until the victim was on the ground where bleeding could similarly be controlled. Obviously the Ripper was not concerned by the extent to which he splashed the floor with his victim's blood, but he would have been concerned about his clothing becoming contaminated. His technique was either designed to avoid such contamination or such was a fortuitous consequence. I believe that the killer deliberately minimised the extent to which he became contaminated with the blood of his victims. After murdering each woman he would have to walk among the population, possibly in full view of police constables, and any sign of blood about his person would undoubtedly have led to some awkward questions.

In connection with the murder of Frances Coles, Phillips suggested that the body was inclined to the left when the killer struck in order to minimise the extent to which he was covered in the victim's blood. This is the only reference to what I believe is a technique used by the Ripper throughout the murder series but unfortunately it was only contemporaneously considered for the last victim, and impossible to retrospectively verify for the others. Although Phillips suggests that Coles was wounded while lying on the ground it would be even easier to employ the same technique to restrict contamination from blood spray in an upright victim. It can not be over emphasised that the Ripper was a skilled practitioner of his craft. He was not new to the business of killing; he selected his victims, engaged with them, and dispatched each with clinical efficiency. He ensured that the first cut to the throat was precisely delivered to immediately render his victim immobile and silent with death inevitable. It is unlikely that the murderer would be completely free from contamination with his victim's blood, but his technique was so precise that even this aspect was minimised.

That the cuts to the neck were deep was not through any attempt to sever the head from the body, as seems to have been a popular misinterpretation, but a consequence of the killer's need to make a thoroughly lethal cut to the neck to ensure that his victim died as quickly as possible. He did, of course, not do this out of consideration for his victim, but in order to ensure that there was no possibility of her struggling or reviving. In instances where there is more than one cut to the neck, it seems that the shorter cut was made initially, and to the left of the neck, and the larger cut secondary to that and across the throat. The immobilising and frequently lethal cut was probably made when the Ripper initially attacked his victim from behind and while each was standing, and it is possible that the secondary cuts were made after she had collapsed to the ground.

In addition to severing the coronary artery a deep cut to the side of the neck would almost certainly cut through the vagus and phrenic nerves, responsible for innervating the heart, lungs, and diaphragm. Not only would the victim then suffer a rapid blood loss leading to irreversible shock but the heart beat and breathing would both be compromised. Loss of blood supply to the brain would lead to death within a couple of minutes with unconsciousness after about thirty seconds.

3.1.3 Strangulation, scratches and marks

It is of some surprise that even with the amount of information currently available several authors persist in suggesting that the Ripper victims were strangled or suffocated prior to wounding as part of the killer's *modus operandi*. There is only one instance in which there is any evidence to suggest that the Ripper attempted to throttle a victim prior to wounding her neck and I suspect that on this occasion such an activity was an adaptation to altered circumstances rather than part of the routine.

Although I have already argued in favour of the neck wounds being inflicted while the victims were standing or in the process of being pulled backwards, it is necessary to further examine the Ripper's technique with regard to the mechanics of the attack. A major problem for those who suggest that the Ripper wounded his victims only after they lay prostrate upon the ground is the need to account for the means by which they came to be in that situation and this can be a stumbling block. For cuts to the neck to be inflicted while a victim is lying on the ground it is obvious that the victim must be invited or forced to be in such a position in the first place. One might imagine that in the conduct of her profession, a prostitute would need little encouragement to lie on the ground, but the streets were wet and filthy and there is rather more likelihood that the act was performed upright, against a wall for instance. Prices inevitably reflected this giving rise to the slang reference to a prostitute as a 'twopenny upright' which reflects both the price and the attitude of the encounter. The woman with her back to the wall for support would lift her skirts for access; the fact that the clothing was always of a loose fit facilitated this which is why the Ripper could so easily lift the skirts of his victim's to well above the waist for mutilation. Thus, if a victim were reluctant to lie down in the mud then she must have been forced to do so by violent actions; either by suddenly hitting the victim or by some means restraining her and forcing her to the ground, hence the strangulation theory. But it is difficult to see how this might be employed with the absence of any sign of a struggle, or any cries for help.

The factors relevant to the strangulation of victims can be tabulated as follows:

Victim	Number cuts to throat	Marks on face and/or neck	Indications of strangulation	Body close to wall	At location for sex or on route
Nichols	Two	Bruising consistent with hand over face	None	Yes	Probably on route
Chapman	Two	None on neck; some on chin and side of jaw	Face swollen; tongue swollen; consistent with suffocation not necessarily strangulation	Yes	At location
Stride	One	None	None	Yes	At location
Eddowes	One	Abrasions left cheek	None	Yes	Probably at location
McKenzie	Two	None	None	Yes	Probably on route
Coles	Two possibly three	Possible finger nail marks.	None	Possibly	Probably on route

It would be almost impossible to throttle a victim with one hand, and difficult even with two hands if the victim were able to move backwards. Thus, to avoid a struggle and the risk if failing in the attempt, the favoured approach would have to be with the victim against a wall. If we for a moment entertain the possibility that partial strangulation was part of the Ripper's technique then the precise mechanics of the assault need scrutiny. Assuming that the killer is in front of and face to face with the victim who is, by consent, with her back against a wall and ready for action, then the perfect orientation would indeed be arranged. The killer would place his hands around her neck before she could utter a sound and maintain pressure with his fingers until she fainted and collapsed to the floor. At this point he would produce a knife and, working from the right side of her body, cut her throat on the left side initially, then again where more than one cut is inflicted. This proposed method is logistically plausible and it is true that most of the victims were killed close to a wall. It is also true that in some instances there are marks on the neck of the victim that could be interpreted as indicating and attempt at strangulation by the attacker. But this is not the means by which the Ripper victims were murdered.

If the killer used this technique as a part of his routine then there would be far more significant injuries to the throat of each victim that were consistent with strangulation, and this is not the case. Looking at Table 1 and Table 2 there are just two instances of some evidence of strangulation among the ten Whitechapel murder victims evaluated. If the evaluation is restricted to those that I believe to be victims of the same serial killer then there is just one instance, that of Annie Chapman, whose injuries were more consistent with suffocation.

Homicidal strangulation using the hands applies great pressure to localised areas frequently with associated bruising and damage to internal structures of the neck as well as to the overlying skin. The mechanism of death from throttling relates to the compression of the neck and the application of pressure to the airway, jugular veins, carotid arteries or sinuses, or to nerves.[2] When pressure is prolonged, then the classic signs of venous obstruction will be seen, with blueness, swelling and congestion of the face, petechial haemorrhages in the eyes and face, and sometimes bleeding from the nose and ears. Internally, if pressure has been sustained, congestion and blueness may be seen in the tongue, pharynx and larynx.

There definitely were marks on the neck for some of the Ripper victims but according to the medical examiners these were a consequence of grasping the chin while the throat was being cut – an even more difficult scenario to accommodate. Inquest evidence suggested an attempt to suffocate Chapman, but there was no physical evidence of strangulation upon her neck. Throttling is a very physical act and tends to leave quite significant bruising, damage to laryngeal cartilages, and abrasions but no such pathology was seen in this instance.

The absence of any noise from the victims has also been used as evidence to suggest that Ripper victims were strangled at least to insensibility in preparation for wounds to the throat. That could possibly be true, but a direct cut to the throat would be far less complicated and much more effective in silencing a victim even if the windpipe were not severed. The shock alone of inflicting such a traumatic injury would ensure the victim made no sound and it is almost certain that each would have instantaneously collapsed as their legs gave way beneath them. Phillips certainly confirms this to be a reason for the absence of any noise in relation to the death of Alice McKenzie. It is implausible that the killer would choose a complex method of killing that involved partial strangulation from the front followed by throat severance on the ground when there was no need whatsoever to do so. The case for such has nowhere near been proved and it is far easier to envisage and alternative and much simpler method of attack from behind while standing.

The killer was inevitably in a hurry with each murder and needed to quickly silence a compliant victim so he was unlikely to have become embroiled in a complex series of manoeuvres that may or may not have worked and had a great potential for failure. It is unlikely that manual strangulation would be possible from anything other than a frontal assault and immediately there are complicating circumstances in that the greater part of the element of surprise has been lost and the victim has an opportunity to struggle. Her fingers would grasp at her neck and her nails would dig into her flesh and into that of the killer and she would kick and punch her assailant in a desperate fight for life. In the case of Stride it is beyond belief that she could have held onto a packet of cachous in preference to putting up a defence to being throttled. Stride was felled instantaneously where she stood.

There is no evidence to suggest that the Ripper routinely throttled or suffocated his victims as part of his *modus operandi*, and in any event it would be a clumsy and time consuming approach not in keeping with the practice of a clinically efficient killer. There were certainly departures from his usual routine and the indications of suffocation to Chapman are not entirely consistent with the circumstances of the other murders, but it would be quite likely that events did not always go entirely to plan and that the killer would need to improvise.

3.1.4 What type of knife did the killer use?
Expert testimony at the inquests of all six Ripper victims indicates that the killer used a sharp or very sharp knife to wound and mutilate his victims. The length of the knife was estimated overall to be between 5in to 8in in length, possibly with a thin blade. A murder weapon was not left at the crime scene in any instance so it is reasonable to assume that the killer used the same knife in each murder. A very sharp 5in to 8in bladed knife would be an extremely dangerous item to carry around and if the owner were to avoid self-inflicted wounds then the blade would have to be protected in some way. If sheathed, such a knife could be concealed in the killer's pocket or elsewhere about the body. It could even be wrapped in cloth and held, or concealed in a bag carried by the killer but these would tend to complicate the act of killing and thereby potentially jeopardise the advantage of a surprise attack. The Ripper favoured a simple approach, which had much to do with the fact that he was never caught in the act. There is no doubt that the knife was sharp – it easily cut through the skin, the laryngeal cartilages of the neck and through muscle and the tough mesenteric connections between abdominal organs as well as leaving cut marks on vertebral bone. The killer must have honed his knife to the sharpness of a cutthroat razor and probably by using the same process.

The absence of stab wounds to any of the victims is a highly significant feature of the Ripper killings and a forceful reason why the murder of Martha Tabram can be excluded from consideration as one of the series. However, the fact that there were no stab wounds does not mean that the knife did not have a pointed end, since in all probability it did have. The only reported stab wounds to any Ripper victim were those to the groin and liver of Catharine Eddowes. Inquest testimony indicated that the blade in this instance was sharp and pointed and at least one inch in width – the depth of the stab was not reported and most knives have a gradually tapering blade. It would be reasonable to assume that a 6in by 1in bladed knife would make a manageable implement for the killer's purposes.

The cutthroat razor was a popular weapon of the day; they were numerous and many a murder was committed as the implement lived up to its name. Any man who shaved owned at least one cutthroat razor, and there are several distinct advantages in using such as a murder weapon; it is relatively small, easily concealed, and very sharp with a protected blade. In many respects a cutthroat razor would have been an ideal implement for the Ripper to employ and the cuts to the throat of each victim could have been inflicted with such a weapon in skilled hands. However there are major disadvantages with such a weapon, not least of which is a significant risk of self-inflicted injuries. A cutthroat razor is difficult to hold for any length of time, especially when used on tough tissues because the blade has to be supported, and it would not have been a very effective implement for mutilation on the scale undertaken by the Ripper. Also, because a cutthroat razor has no point, it would be difficult to use to make entry wounds through the abdominal skin and muscle. The conclusion of those who examined the bodies was that a pointed blade must have been used and it is difficult to disagree with this.

Phillips gave an opinion at the inquest into the death of Annie Chapman that the wounds could have been inflicted by a post mortem knife, but not a type that might be carried by a doctor in 'the ordinary surgical case'. He thought that a slaughterer's knife was also a possible candidate, but those used by cobblers and others in the leather trade would be unlikely to have a long enough blade. There is a suggestion that Major Henry Smith, the acting Commissioner of the City Police, showed shochet knives, used in Jewish ritual slaughter, to the medical men involved in the post mortem examinations of the Ripper victims, but such were considered not to have been used by the killer because they had curved blades and that used by the Ripper was straight.[3]

3.2 Was the killer skilled in anatomy and dissection?

On this issue it is important to follow opinions of the day, since those investigating the Ripper murders knew the standards of education within the population, the nature of the workforce, and the minutia of everyday life.

With a couple of exceptions, the doctors who examined the bodies of the mutilated murder victims were of the opinion that the killer had some anatomical knowledge and dissection skills that allowed him to precisely locate and remove organs. The level of skill has largely been dealt with when examining the specific murders but in the case of Catharine Eddowes in particular there is strong evidence of some dexterity with a knife and knowledge of anatomy, whereas the extensive mutilation to Mary Jane Kelly's body seemed to have been a far less skilful slash and grab exercise.

With regard to the fatal neck wounds, in each of the Ripper murders the killer clearly had knowledge of the neck vasculature in order to inflict such devastating wounds precisely and consistently and this is a much underestimated factor. There is a tendency to think that, just because murder was commonplace on the vicious streets of the East End, throat cutting was also frequently encountered. In a general way this is probably true, but the fundamental difference between common throat cutting and the technique employed by the Ripper was his absolute clinical precision. An inexperienced throat cutter would instinctively target the front of the neck, which would inevitably sever the windpipe, but only infrequently cut the major carotid vessels unless the cut was extraordinarily deep across the throat. The consequence of this would be that, although silent, the victim would bleed to death relatively slowly. Only with knowledge that the major blood vessels to the brain run up either side of the neck and relatively deep within the tissues, would a killer be able to specifically deliver the lethal cut.

If there is any doubt as to how unusual this was then we can look to the comments of an experienced judge who sat at the trial of Robert Wood, the man accused, and found innocent, of the murder of Emily Dimmock in 1907. Dimmock was not a victim of Jack the Ripper and the same overall *modus operandi* was not employed, but her throat was cut and she quickly bled to death from a single wound. Mr Justice Grantham in summing up at the end of the trial, made it absolutely clear how unusual such a means of death was, even in late Victorian times:

That the unfortunate woman [Dimmock] has been done to death there is no doubt. She had been murdered in a most remarkable way. There is no doubt also that the murder was committed by someone who, if not adept at murder, at any rate had some knowledge of how to put a person quickly to death. I have tried a great many murder cases, but I have never tried one in which apparently a woman had been murdered in her sleep by one blow [cut] delivered with great force, and apparently done so without a struggle, and apparently by a person who lay between her and the wall. This poor young woman was murdered almost in her sleep, without ever waking again in this world, by one blow inflicted with such great force and skill, which nearly severed every muscle of her neck, as almost cut to the spinal cord. I have tried many murders during my time, but none has struck me so forcibly as this in which the victim was murdered by one blow.[4]

The limited state of knowledge and of education available to the general population towards the end of Queen Victoria's reign should not be under-estimated. Mammalian anatomy was simply not a feature of everyday knowledge and while many people in 1888 may have known what a kidney looked like, since offal was commonly eaten, it would be unreasonable to assume that they could locate and remove the organ in a human body. Such a situation is even less likely for the uterus; the organ would have been neither well known nor easily recognised by much of the male population at that time. The suggestion that anyone could have removed targeted organs is far from true and even today in a reasonably well-educated society there are not too many people who can precisely locate body organs *in situ* as opposed to pointing to them on a diagram.

While possessing some anatomical and dissection skills, the murderer did not necessarily need to be a doctor or student of medicine. Many trades of the day involved skill with a sharp knife and those working in an abattoir would be well acquainted with exsanguination via vessels in the neck and the anatomical location of organs. The arrangement of organs in the pig for instance is pretty much the same as that in a human, although it must be said that such a worker would be familiar with the location of the edible kidneys, but not necessarily with the whereabouts or appearance of the uterus.

There is no doubt that the fatal wound inflicted by the Ripper is very similar to that employed by the shochet in the ritualistic slaughter of animals or shechita in accordance with Jewish law. By this means slaughter is effected using a quick, deep stroke across the throat with a perfectly sharp blade with no nicks or unevenness. This method is supposedly painless, causing unconsciousness within seconds, the animals frequently collapsing immediately. A slaughterman of any persuasion would kill the beast by cutting the throat in order to void blood from the body but by conventional means, and entirely as a consequence of expediency, the animal would first be poleaxed into unconsciousness.

3.3 Geographical distribution of the murders

The six Ripper murders were all committed within a well-defined area and although that does not necessarily mean that the killer lived within that area, it is almost certain that he knew the Whitechapel district well enough to be aware of his location at any time and the best routes of escape.

An examination of the time at which each of the murders was committed reveals a broad pattern in that the further north the murder, the later in the night it took place, which would suggest that the killer travelled from a location in the south of the district. This is of course highly speculative and is based upon the rather simplistic idea that whenever the Ripper went out with murder in mind, he commenced at the same time on each occasion and wandered the streets until he found a suitable victim, and that his progress through the streets of Whitechapel took him further north with the passage of time. It is reasonable to assume that the Ripper started his search after midnight and on some occasions he found a victim almost immediately while on other occasions it took somewhat longer. Having started the evening with a murderous imperative, his urges would need to be satisfied so that it is only with the onset of dawn that he would have to admit defeat. As we have already seen in the case of Annie Chapman, the Ripper's urge to kill was so strong that even the emerging daylight was no deterrent, the risk of being seen and subsequently identified increasing markedly without the cover of darkness. It is almost certain that the Ripper did not find a suitable victim under favourable circumstances on every occasion that he set out to kill. Thus, he must have encountered, and probably even engaged with, several potential victims between the murders and some unknowingly had a lucky escape for one reason or another. The Ripper practised his craft with an all-or-nothing approach which is why no women were merely wounded and not killed by his knife. The boldness of each attack and his proximity to being caught in the act says much about the fragility of opportunity – if these were the best opportunities for murder then there must have been many more occasions on which he was frustrated.

If we take the arbitrary reference point of Royal Mint Street and Cable Street which run into each other on the southern boundary of Jack the Ripper's area of activity then we can examine the relative distances of each murder scene from this reference point. The distances are given for each victim in the table below. All measurements are straight line distances from Royal Mint Street or Cable Street to the murder scene for each victim. It is likely that Frances Coles met her killer in Commercial Street and walked with him to the scene of her murder in Swallow Gardens, just off Royal Mint Street, so out of interest I have also included the distance from where Coles died to where she met her killer. There are two distinct bands of activity running parallel to Royal Mint Street and Cable Street. The first band includes the murders of Nichols and Chapman, which were the first two victims, and is the most distant from the Royal Mint Street/Cable Street and also the latest after midnight; and the second band includes three of the four remaining victims. Coles, the final victim, was killed just off Royal Mint Street although she met her killer precisely in the second band.

Victim	Location	Distance north from Royal Mint Street / Cable Street (direct)	Time of death – latest estimate in all cases
Chapman	Hanbury Street	0.72 miles	05.45am
Nichols	Buck's Row	0.63 miles	03.45am
McKenzie	Castle Alley	0.36 miles	12.45am
Eddowes	Mitre Square	0.24 miles	01.45am
Stride	Berner Street	0.19 miles	01.00am
Coles	Swallow Gardens	0 (0.36 miles)*	02.15am

* Coles probably met her killer in Commercial Street so the distance from the corner of Whitechapel Street and Commercial Street to Royal Mint Street/Cable Street is included for comparative purposes.

These data, limited though they may be, are interesting because one can quite reasonably speculate that a killer who embarks upon a series of murders may be inclined to kill his first victims some distance from his home. Then, as he becomes more confident and arrogant he murders victims closer to his home. It is very tempting to speculate that so confident was the Ripper that he would not be caught that he actually murdered his final victim audaciously close to his own home.

I do not think that there is any relevance in the distance between the murders of Stride and Eddowes on the same evening. The distance from Berner Street to Mitre Square was about three quarters of a mile as determined by Fredrick Foster, architect and surveyor, and a walking time of just twelve minutes by 'the nearest route that anyone unaccustomed to it would take'.[5] The Ripper clearly had an imperative to kill again that night and to mutilate and it would seem logical that he went away from the scene of the first murder and also further away from his home in search of another victim. To murder on his way home would not make sense to an intelligent killer. A route away from Mitre Square via Goulston Street is also of little significance – he could go anywhere from that point although if bloodstained or carrying human organs he would need to avoid major thoroughfares such as Whitechapel High Street, Leman Street, or Commercial Road. He would be aware of fervent police activity in Aldgate and the obvious need to circumvent the area, and if he were intent upon returning south then a route via Mansell Street and Chamber Street, would take him along poorly lit streets and well away from activity surrounding either of the murders that night. There can be little doubt that the Ripper knew the streets and knew the best routes to take in order to reach safety.

There is an unlikely possibility that the killer came into London by train in the evening and roamed the streets all night with murder in mind before leaving by train in the morning. Although the distribution of murder scenes is generally within easy access from Liverpool Street Station, or Broad Street Station as it was then known, neither the time nor distance relationships of the murders have any meaningful distribution. There are other reasons why this is an unlikely scenario. Firstly, the killer would not be able to return to base as soon as a murder was committed and would be forced to continue roaming the streets; this would be very risky if he happened to be bloodstained. And secondly, he could not risk mixing with travellers at the station or on the train with the probability that he may be covered with the bloody consequences of his endeavours. While abattoir workers would frequently be so contaminated, they would not be in the habit of catching an early morning train out of the city and the risk of attracting attention would be far too great given the increased vigilance that prevailed.

3.4 What kind of a man was Jack the Ripper?

There were undoubtedly serial killers before Jack the Ripper and many more have been identified since. They are savage and insouciant individuals who ruin many more lives than those they bring to a premature end. The women killed by the Ripper were considered less worthy in Victorian society because of the path their lives had taken and sadly their passing affected few but themselves. These women were already victims of a society that brought them to the edge of life and derided them for following the only course by which they could earn enough pennies to drink themselves into oblivion and thus lessen the pain of facing the next day. The Ripper probably did bring them some kind of an early relief, but the choice was not theirs and they were murdered for nothing more than the self-gratification of a psychopathic mind. The manner in which the victims were killed and mutilated shows a complete absence of any empathy or sympathy, both of which are principle characteristics of psychopathic behaviour.

The Ripper targeted women and his crimes had a sexual component, and although there is no evidence that sexual activity was a factor during the murders, it probably was at some point afterwards. Whether or not the Ripper actually targeted prostitutes because they were prostitutes is, however, uncertain. The fact that his victims were all prostitutes did not mean that he specifically targeted such or that it was essential that the women he killed and mutilated were of that profession. The Ripper's objective was certainly to murder women and the time and location of his crimes virtually dictated that the only women he would be likely to encounter would be street prostitutes or indigent women which would pretty well amount to the same. These women were vulnerable and easy targets for a serial killer, but if the Ripper specifically targeted prostitutes other than for reason of pragmatism then there must have been some psychological trauma in his life that caused him to do so. Perhaps he had contracted venereal disease from a street girl, perhaps his mother was a prostitute, or maybe he was sexually inadequate and targeted a stereotype that he considered worthless. If contracting syphilis from a prostitute was indeed a significant factor this would be more likely to act as a trigger in someone with a pre-existing psychopathological condition, than it would be a motivational reason for killing.

There is no doubt that these murders were sexually motivated and conducted by a man who hated women. The removal of the uterus, an organ strongly symbolic of womanhood and motherhood, was a significant defeminising mutilation and could have been the primary objective in each murder. After defeminising and depersonalising his victims the killer left their mutilated bodies on display to shock whoever subsequently discovered their remains. That each victim was fully clothed at the time of the attack, with no evidence of attempted sex prior to, during, or after any of the killings, indicates that sexual gratification at the scene was not an objective. The sexual component probably related more to the killer's fantasies and these compelled him to kill and mutilate. The trophies that he took may have featured heavily in whatever rituals were subsequently performed.

Cutting and stabbing are very different types of wounding. To stab someone is to want that person dead, and to stab someone repeatedly is to, in a sense, want the person *very* dead, which is why frenzied attacks often involve far more stabbing than is actually necessary to kill someone. Cutting wounds suggest a far more complex motive, and to inflict such in life or after death reflects a desire to inflict pain, to maim, and disfigure the victim. By cutting the flesh, the perpetrator is prolonging the pain of the attack as well as disrupting or dismantling the integrity of the victim's body thus removing their identity as a person or as a human being. With regard to the issue of pain, the fact that the victim may be dead when the wounds are inflicted is irrelevant. It is likely that the Ripper would have readily inflicted the wounds with the victim alive but in the interests of expediency, it was better for them to be silent ahead of the onslaught. Realistically, they would most probably have been alive but unconscious as mutilation commenced. Such attacks clearly display intense hatred and the facial mutilations further indicate that the killer not only wants the victim dead but also depersonalised. Most importantly, the Ripper was an experienced killer; Mary Nichols could not have been the first person that he killed although there is, as yet, no evidence that he 'practiced' on other victims prior to his first murder.

The Ripper was successful with apparently his first attempt in Whitechapel and that theme continued until the murders ceased. He operated in a London that was very different in most respects from that today yet not so different in other ways. Whitechapel was a dangerous area by any standards and anyone entering the 'labyrinth' without experience of self-preservation would quickly fall victim to violent thieves or drunken brawlers. The Ripper fitted into the background and was experienced enough and sufficiently familiar with the environment to conduct himself with safety. Even at night the streets of Whitechapel were relatively busy mostly with vagrants, drunks and prostitutes and those searching for the services of the latter. To counter this there was a considerable police presence, with constables on beats that they patrolled all night long. There was every chance that an inexperienced multiple murderer would have been apprehended or at the very least be interrupted in his activities, but this was not the case with the Ripper – a testimony to his abilities and not a consequence of chance alone. The Ripper knew where to operate, which victims to select, how to approach them, when to kill them and how to kill them; he moved with ease in the district and appeared to know it well if perhaps not very well. He was comfortable in the destitute areas of Whitechapel, and although I doubt that he lived there, he must have had contact with the area at some time in his life with sufficient frequency to allow a degree of familiarity. It is also worth noting that not all areas of Whitechapel were dilapidated slums accommodating the worst that Victorian society had to offer. Charles Booth's poverty map of 1889 shows that there were many streets housing 'lower class vicious semi criminal' types but these were frequently juxtaposed with areas in which lived 'fairly comfortable' and 'middle class well-to-do' residents.[6] Dr George Phillips resided at 2 Spital Square, Spitalfields and Dr Frederick Blackwell at 100 Commercial Road – both in close proximity to Whitechapel murder sites.

The Ripper's social interface was such that he was able to engage with his victims and walk with them until the opportunity arose for him to kill them. Even during the hysteria that gripped Whitechapel he was completely disarming to his victims and their suspicions were not aroused by his behaviour, which suggests that he was calmly in control and able to put his victims completely at ease. It is fairly typical of the psychopathic personality that such individuals are superficially charming while being persuasive and manipulative. They often have an over inflated impression of themselves, are frequently grandiose, and quite unable to process emotional information in the same way that others do. Severin Klosowski, a Ripper suspect who is examined in a later chapter, exquisitely exemplifies such a persona. It is impossible to know whether or not the Ripper knew any of the victims, but if he did so then it was by accident. He did not spend time with them other than immediately prior to killing them. The Ripper probably did not frequent pubs, especially prior to the murders and almost certainly would not have been the worse for alcohol. His murderous technique required too much precision and his control would be at risk if he were drunk. It would also be risky for him to be seen in the company of his victims or of any other women prior to the murders so I doubt that he would have engaged in any social activities in Whitechapel. It is far more likely that he set out at around midnight on each occasion with the sole intention of murdering and mutilating a woman.

Jack the Ripper worked alone; he was a man who liked to be in control and had no need for an accomplice and the involvement of another person would surely have compromised his activities. That he murdered victims in Whitechapel suggests that he probably lived close by. He lived alone in his own accommodation so that he could come and go at all hours of day or night without having to give explanations. Although the Ripper almost certainly found personal relationships difficult and was probably sexually inadequate, he must have been superficially plausible and assertive. He was a confident killer who could easily dupe his victims and manipulate them into a situation that left them vulnerable to attack and allowed him to commit murder without a defensive response. The Ripper planned his attacks and targeted strangers.

Jack the Ripper was not a madman, he was well aware of what he was doing and did not wish to get caught. He was a psychopathic killer with a deep hatred of women and psychosexual factors directed his actions; he was a sexual psychopath and the manner of the mutilations and disproportionate use of violence are further evidence in support of this. Whether or not there are indications from his early life or everyday adult life we shall probably never know, but it is almost certain that he would have a propensity towards antisocial behaviour, which may or may not have included violence, and which would quite readily manifest in his dealings with other people. Psychopathic traits have been studied intensively for many years and are well documented; those affected having a well defined condition with underlying morphological brain pathology for which there is as yet no treatment.[7] Part of the biochemistry of psychopathy is related to neurotransmitter and hormonal imbalance with reduced levels of serotonin and elevated levels of testosterone being important. The role of testosterone is significant in determining that most psychopaths are male. Whether psychopaths are born or made remains a moot point but elements of both may be necessary for the condition to fully develop.

There is an intriguing possibility that the Ripper may have been a member of Queen Victoria's Army. Such an eventuality would account for three important factors pertaining to the Whitechapel serial killer. Firstly such an individual would probably have experience in killing and possibly even by the method employed by the Ripper. There were so many wars and skirmishes during the second half of the nineteenth century that a soldier in the Victorian army would almost certainly have seen action at some time during his period of service. Secondly, the sudden onset of the murders, the subsequent infrequency, and final cessation could be related to postings and active service, and even to death in service. And thirdly the Tower Barracks was positioned in exactly the locality one might expect the Ripper to operate from. This is a simplistic overview that ignores logistics but certainly warrants further exploration. The killer need not necessarily have been a serving soldier but could have gained experience in his craft from previous service. It is a disturbing fact that many multiple and serial killers identified over the past half a century have had military training or have been at some time engaged in military service. The army teaches individuals how to kill and after active service they know how to kill, and the aversion to killing, once removed, may never return.

After the murder of Mary Jane Kelly, who at the time was regarded as a victim of the serial killer, Dr Thomas Bond gave his impressions of the type of man who was responsible in his overview of the Ripper murders to Assistant Commissioner Robert Anderson:

The murderer must have been a man of physical strength and of great coolness and daring. There is no evidence that he had an accomplice. He must in my opinion be a man subject to periodical attacks of Homicidal and erotic mania. The character of the mutilations indicate that the man may be in a condition sexually, that may be called satyriasis. It is of course possible that the Homicidal impulse may have developed from a revengeful or brooding condition of the mind or that Religious Mania may have been the original disease, but I do not think that either hypothesis is likely. The murderer in external appearance is quite likely to be a quiet inoffensive looking man probably middle aged and neatly and respectably dressed. I think he must be in the habit of wearing a cloak or overcoat or he could hardly have escaped notice in the streets if the blood on his hands or clothes were visible.

Assuming the murderer to be such a person as I have just described he would probably be solitary and eccentric in his habits, also he is most likely to be a man without regular occupation, but with some small income or pension. He is possibly living among respectable persons who have some knowledge of his character and habits and who may have grounds for suspicion that he is not quite right in his mind at times. Such persons would probably be unwilling to communicate suspicions to the Police for fear of trouble or notoriety, whereas if there were a prospect of reward it might overcome their scruples.[8]

Bond's report is interesting as one of the first recorded 'offender profiles' and as such it was probably not a bad attempt, although I doubt that anyone knowing the killer would have necessarily suspected his activities as such.

The single most obvious mistake made by investigators is to identify an individual who circumstantially fills the role of serial killer and then attempt to fit the evidence to that individual. This is a highly biased approach and usually results in those bits of information that do not fit well being excluded or written off as unimportant. A fundamental flaw with this approach is the assumption that anyone can be a serial killer and even more incredulously, that anyone can clinically and coldly cut the throat of another human being and inflict horrendous mutilations. Such is simply not the case and it takes a very special kind of person indeed to be, not just a multiple, but a serial killer. In other words, authors continue to regard the ability to kill component as being of secondary importance.

3.5 Witness sightings and descriptions

When witnesses give descriptions they almost inevitably differ from each other and are at variance with actuality. This is a much greater problem where subjective interpretations are given and less so when witnesses have a definite choice, assuming that their powers of observation, and very often recollection, are reliable. For instance when describing someone's height there are really only three categories that can be readily estimated; those of average height, shorter than average, or taller than average. These are relatively reliable criteria since we all form an opinion as to what constitutes average height during the course of our everyday encounters with other people. We quickly learn to compare with this height and can thus say what differs from average. However, as soon as we are called upon to estimate the actual height of an individual we can easily be several inches out which can make such attempts to gain more precise estimates somewhat misleading. Thus a witness may describe a man as being taller than average but without knowing what constituted average height in measured terms they may then report his height at 5ft 7in which would have been close to average for an adult male at the end of the nineteenth century. Relative descriptions and presence or absence descriptions are far more reliable, thus whether or not a man had a moustache is likely to yield an accurate description but the colour or dimensions of that moustache may be less so. General appearance is also subjective and a description of clothing worn is likely to vary between witnesses and may also be distant from reality. Also clothing can change from occasion to occasion although this was less likely among the very poor, but of all the parameters, an estimate of age is probably the least reliable, unless broadly categorised into decades. Unfortunately, witnesses are only called upon to give descriptions after the event. They obviously have no forewarning that they need to take more than a passing interest in what goes on around them and unless someone attracts their attention they will only have vague recollections that may become distorted under the pressure to be accurate.

Apart from the victims, several other prostitutes must have encountered Jack the Ripper over the duration of the Whitechapel murders. It is highly likely that he engaged with more women than those he murdered but the circumstances enabling him to prosecute his objective can not have been favourable on every occasion. It is thus possible that there were several other witnesses who had direct contact with a man they suspected of being the Ripper but the likelihood that any would come forward would have been remote. Fear silenced them; after encountering a man that they believed to be a cold and callous killer they would not be inclined to volunteer information to the police. Their status would not afford them much right to protection, not that their lives were amenable to such and a prostitute in fear of her life would have no place to hide and no sanctuary for protection. Not to get involved in the first place would be by far the better course of action.

Some years after the Ripper murders ceased an article appeared in *The People's Journal* which was purported to be based upon a report of Sergeant Stephen White who was in the Whitechapel H Division at the time of the

Whitechapel Murders.[9] It was reported that White was one of several policemen in plain clothes and patrolling the streets at the time of the murders:

For five nights we had been watching a certain alley just behind the Whitechapel Road. It could only be entered from where we had two men posted in hiding, and persons entering the alley were under observation by the two men. It was a bitter cold night when I arrived at the scene to take the reports of the two men in hiding. I was turning away when I saw a man coming out of the alley. He was walking quickly but noiselessly, apparently wearing rubber shoes which were rather rare in those days. I stood aside to let the man pass, and as he came under the wall lamp I got a good look at him.

He was about five feet ten inches in height, and was dressed rather shabbily though it was obvious that the material of his clothes was good. Evidently a man who had seen better days, I thought, but men who have seen better days are common enough down east, and of itself was not sufficient to justify me in stopping him. His face was long and thin, nostrils rather delicate, and his hair was jet black. His complexion was inclined to be sallow, and altogether the man was foreign in appearance. The most extraordinary thing about him, however, was the extraordinary brilliance of his eyes. They looked like two very luminous glow worms coming through the darkness. The man was slightly bent at the shoulders, though he was obviously quite young – about 33 at the most - and gave one the idea of having been a student or professional man. His hands were snow white and the fingers long and tapering.

As the man passed me at the lamp I had an uneasy feeling that there was something unusually sinister about him, and I was strongly moved to find some pretext for detaining him; but the more I thought it over, the more I was forced to the conclusion that it was not in keeping with British police methods that I should do so. My only excuse for interfering with the passage of this man would have been his association with the man we were looking for, and I had no grounds for connecting him with the murder. It is true I had a sort of intuition that the man was not quite right. Still, if one acted upon intuition in the police force, there would be more frequent outcries about interference with the liberty of the subject, and at that time the police were criticised enough to make it undesirable to take risks.

The man stumbled a few feet away from me, and I made that an excuse for engaging him in conversation. He turned sharply at the sound of my voice, and scowled at me in surly fashion, but he said 'Good night' and agreed with me that it was cold.

His voice was a surprise to me. It was soft and musical, with just a tinge of melancholy in it, and it was the voice of a man of culture - a voice altogether out of keeping with the squalid surroundings of the East End.

As he turned away, one of the police officers came out of the house he had been in, and walked a few paces into the darkness of the alley. 'Hello! what is this?' he cried and then he called in startled tones for me to come.

In the East End we are used to some shocking sights but the sight I saw made the blood in my veins turn to ice. At the end of the cul-de-sac huddled against the wall there was a body of a woman, and a pool of blood was streaming along the gutter from her body. It was clearly another of those terrible murders. I remembered the man I had seen, and started after him as fast as I could run but he was lost to sight in the dark labyrinth of East End mean streets.

The location described by White does not match any of the murder scenes because none of them was a cul-de-sac. The closest possibilities are Mitre Square, where Catharine Eddowes was murdered, and Castle Alley which is not at first sight a thoroughfare, where Alice McKenzie was killed. However, McKenzie was murdered in July and it was not a 'bitterly cold' night. Also from White's description there was considerable police activity indicating that the occasion described was in the midst of the Ripper murders.

Sergeant White did not give testimony at any of the inquests, including that of Catharine Eddowes and his observations are not mentioned in any correspondence which renders them especially difficult to accommodate since they would have been crucial in providing the best and most reliable description of a suspect.

Howells and Skinner point out in their examination of this issue that White may have maintained a low profile and his observations suppressed because he was a Metropolitan Police Officer operating under cover in the City of London thus outside of his jurisdiction, although clearly he would have told his immediate superiors.[10] While true this is difficult to accept as a reason why no reference to his encounter with a suspect appears anywhere other than in *The People's Journal* just over a week after White's death. It is evident that White's observations suffer more than a little from journalistic embellishment and curious that the article was published some thirty years after the death of Catharine Eddowes. Taking all aspects into considered there is good cause to regard this article and the description given with scepticism.

Three witnesses reported seeing different victims with a man described as being of below average height moments before each victim was murdered. In one instance, the witness Joseph Levy who saw a suspect in the company of Catharine Eddowes reported that the man with whom she stood was three inches taller than she was and that he estimated her height to be around 5ft 0in. He was indeed accurate with his estimation of Eddowes' height and we are thus entitled to regard his estimate of the height of the man in her company as being 5ft 3in at most. The fact that for three of the six murders, witnesses saw a man of shorter than average stature in the company of the victim just prior to her murder has to be regarded as more than coincidence. Since suspects were only witnessed for four of the six murders then in three out of four murders a similar suspect was observed. The murder for which a shorter than average suspect was not observed was that of Elizabeth Stride and I have already examined at length the confusion surrounding sightings of Stride in the company of various men prior to her demise and to the point at which I believe that she may not have actually been observed in the company of her killer. This is not a case of making the story fit the hypothesis, but is an interpretation of what is reported and not of what is supposed. A summary of the three sightings is given in the following table:

Victim	Witness	Height of Suspect	Age	Whiskers	Other
Chapman	Elizabeth Long	Shorter than average	Over 40	No detail Unseen	Dark Foreigner
Eddowes	Joseph Levy	Shorter than average perhaps 5' 3"	No detail	No detail Unseen	No detail
Coles	Ellen Callagher	Shorter than average	No detail	Moustache	Dark Shiny boots Blue trousers Appearance of a sailor

The man seen by Joseph Levy was also, presumably, the same as the man witnessed by Joseph Lawende who became an important witness as far as the police were concerned even though he consistently maintained that he would be unable to identify the man in the event that he were called upon to do so. There is no direct statement evidence or inquest testimony as to what description Lawende gave to the police, although the description that they issued subsequently may reflect his impression of the man seen with Eddowes. One reported description was of a man of shabby appearance, about 30 years of age and 5ft 9in in height, of fair complexion, having a small fair moustache and a cap with a peak.[11] This description was issued shortly after the murder but on the grounds of height alone it can not have been based upon any input from Levy. A further report gives the description as about 30 years of age, medium build, 5ft 7in or 5ft 8in tall, with a fair complexion and a fair moustache, wearing a pepper-and-salt loose jacket, red neckerchief and grey cloth cap with a peak. He had the appearance of a sailor.[12] But again on the grounds of height, which would be regarded as average, this man does not fit with the description given by Levy and in the absence of any direct and immediate testimony its value is doubtful.[13] Lawende was used by the police in an attempt to identify suspects but there is no evidence to suggest that any other witness was similarly used.

The police, it seemed, were frequently inclined to take a blinkered view on the range of information available to them, focussing only on that which was specious and ignoring that which appeared less relevant. On more than one occasion such a narrow perspective placed the emphasis of their investigation on the wrong evidence, which may have distracted them from pursuing more relevant leads. The evidence of Schwartz in the Elizabeth Stride investigation and the arrest of Thomas Sadler in connection with the murder of Frances Coles were two distractions that took the thrust of the police investigation away from where it should have been focussed.

It is inconceivable that no one saw Jack the Ripper during the course of the six murders that I believe he committed. There are possible suspect sightings in four of these murders and the odds are in favour of the serial killer being observed in at least one instance. When we take into account that an individual of less than average height was seen, not just in the vicinity of, but actually talking to each of three of the victims shortly before their murder, then there is justification for concluding that the same man was likely to have been involved.

In addition to the matter of height, two of the three witnesses describe the man as being dark and in one instance he has a moustache. Other witnesses do not contradict these observations; they merely did not get a good enough sight of the man to confirm them. So we have the description of a suspect who is shorter than average height and who may be of dark complexion and hair, and with a moustache. Additional testimony suggests that on one occasion at least, he wore shiny shoes and blue trousers and had the appearance of a sailor and on another occasion it was reported that the man looked foreign.

4: The suspects

4.1 The Macnaghten report

With regard to a list of suspects, the then Chief Constable Melville Macnaghten provided a few generations of Ripperologists with a misleading basis upon which to theorise by virtue of his Memorandum of 23 February 1894.[14] Along with the canonical list of victims, there is also a canonical list of three suspects in the form of Montague John Druitt, Aaron Kosminski, and Michael Ostrog. To this list can also be added Francis Tumblety, Severin Klosowski alias George Chapman, and Walter Sickert. Many others have also been suggested, but until any substantial evidence against them emerges, they remain of marginal interest and are not considered here.

Although Ostrog possibly came to the attention of the police as a Ripper suspect while the murders were still being committed, prior to Macnaghten's Memorandum, there is no evidence to indicate that Druitt or Kosminski had been considered as suspects while they were alive or free in the community. Thus, it would be more realistic than cynical to suggest that, since the chances of the police identifying the Ripper after the murders had ceased had slipped from difficult at best, to somewhere over the horizon at worst, the Chief Constable felt safe in making not entirely justifiable accusations against individuals who were not in a position to defend themselves.

There are in fact two versions of the Macnaghten Memorandum; one, discovered in the possession of Macnaghten's daughter, Dowager Lady Christabel Aberconway, which was a part typewritten, part handwritten copy of the original documents which were lost, and the second version was found in the files at Scotland Yard.[15] The two versions differ in some important respects and there is also no evidence to confirm whether the Memorandum was ever sent to the intended recipient or otherwise used. The copy held by Macnaghten's daughter was probably a draft of that on file at Scotland Yard. It has been pointed out that almost every personal comment included by Macnaghten had been deleted from the Scotland Yard version so that the report appears to be a statement of informed police opinion whereas in reality it was more a record of Macnaghten's personal interpretations and conclusions.[16] Unfortunately, a document that should be read with a considerable amount of caution has, since its discovery in 1959, become something or a cornerstone in Ripperology. While it is important to take seriously the opinion of the investigators of the time because they viewed the crimes in context and were also probably privy to information that is no longer available or that was never made known, with the passage of time comes the benefit of hindsight, and this with the aid of the powerful vision of present day techniques in criminology.

The approach of Macnaghten in reaching his conclusions is not entirely logical. While it may have been politically expedient to suggest that the killer had since died or been incarcerated, his beliefs were most likely reached on the back of weak circumstantial evidence coupled with the fact that the murder series apparently ceased. Thus it was the case that these suspects were chosen because there were supposedly, and in Macnaghten's opinion, no more murders, and it was not the case that there were no more murders because the killer had been identified and was no longer in circulation. After all, Macnaghten probably guessed that whatever he said would be difficult to disprove, although history has not necessarily demonstrated that to be the case. Macnaghten based his accusations on the canonical list of victims which he in fact compiled, but again this was probably more a matter of expediency than an objective examination of the facts because if McKenzie and Coles are included then two of Macnaghten's suspects fall from the list immediately – one because he was no longer alive when McKenzie met her fate and the other because he was incarcerated before Coles bled to death in Swallow Gardens. Macnaghten mentions four other Whitechapel murders including those of McKenzie, and Coles in his report, but while not specifically excluding them from the series he does not give any reasons as to why they are not unreservedly included. Apart from the canonical victims Macnaghten clearly had a theory that may have influenced the way that he interpreted the significance of the victims and their inclusion in his list, as the following paragraph from the Scotland Yard version of the report illustrates:

It will be noticed that the fury of the mutilations increased in each case, and, seemingly, the appetite only became sharpened by indulgence. It seems, then, highly improbable that the murderer would have suddenly stopped in November '88. A much more rational theory is that the murderer's brain gave way altogether after his awful glut in Miller's Court, and that he immediately committed suicide, or, as a possible alternative, was found to be so hopelessly mad by his relations, that he was by them confined to an asylum.

This statement is highly skewed in favour of one suspect, Montague Druitt, whom Macnaghten clearly held 'strong opinions' about according to the Lady Aberconway version of the report. As well as illustrating perfectly why it is so important to establish exactly how many victims were attributable to the same killer, Macnaghten's conclusions are a good example of a biased and subjective approach in which the theory is established first of all and the facts bent to fit around the belief. Macnaghten's logic is shaky for a number of reasons not least of which is his assertion that the mutilations increased in ferocity with each murder. The fact that they appeared to do so was entirely a consequence of the amount of time that the killer was able to spend with each victim and completely unrelated to intent, and I have no doubt that had the Ripper not been disturbed after killing Nichols then she would have been completely eviscerated. Furthermore, Macnaghten's theory is greatly influenced by what took place in Miller's Court, but if Mary Jane Kelly is excluded from the list of the Ripper's victims and McKenzie and Coles included then his precipitous crescendo theory falls apart.

In attempting to dismiss McKenzie and Coles, Macnaghten suggests that both were stabbed in the throat rather than having their throats cut, and by merely mentioning Sadler in relation to the murder of Coles he strongly implies that he still regarded the ship's fireman as prime candidate for her killer. Also, there is no documented evidence to suggest that serial killers *never* stop killing by conscious decision. There are no rules governing psychopathy and in any event there are many reasons why a killer may unavoidably stop killing, or stop killing in the same location, the least likely of which is by suicide.

The rather approximate nature of Macnaghten's report and the numerous errors and inconsistencies within it tend to suggest that he was not entirely up to speed with events that occurred several years previously and mostly at a time that pre-dated his appointment to the force in 1889. The fact that he obviously had full access to documents and to the opinions of the investigating police officers does not make his conclusions any more convincing. Whatever Macnaghten may have thought, his opinion was not necessarily shared within the constabulary as Frederick Abberline illustrated in interviews with the *Pall Mall Gazette* in 1903, eleven years after his retirement from Scotland Yard. [17] Abberline refuted commonly held beliefs saying that:

You can state most emphatically that Scotland Yard is really no wiser on the subject than it was fifteen years ago. It is simple nonsense to talk of the police having proof that the man is dead. I am, and always have been, in the closest touch with Scotland Yard, and it would have been next to impossible for me not to have known all about it. Besides, the authorities would have been only too glad to make an end of such a mystery, if only for their own credit.

I know it has been stated in several quarters that "Jack the Ripper" was a man who died in a lunatic asylum a few years ago, but there is nothing at all of a tangible nature to support such a theory'.

4.2 Montague John Druitt (1857-88)

Diligent research has unearthed much about Druitt's life and readers are referred elsewhere for details.[18] However, among the information available there is no sound reason why Druitt should have been regarded as a serial killer other than supposed suggestions that his own family were suspicious of what he might be up to. The Scotland Yard version of Macnaghten's thoughts on Druitt reads as follows:

(1) A Mr M J Druitt, said to be a doctor & of good family, who disappeared at the time of the Miller's Court murder, & whose body (which was said to have been upwards of a month in the water) was found in the Thames on 31 Decr., or about 7 weeks after that murder. He was sexually insane and from private inf. I have little doubt but that his own family believed him to have been the murderer.

The Lady Aberconway version of the Macnaghten Memorandum carries a slightly different assessment insofar as the last statement is concerned, stating that; 'From private information I have little doubt but that his own family suspected this man of being the Whitechapel murderer; it was alleged that he was sexually insane'.

Druitt graduated from New College, Oxford in 1880 with a third class honours degree in Classics and then took up a teaching post at Valentine's boarding school in Blackheath. In 1882 Druitt was admitted to the Inner Temple as he embarked upon a career in law and by 1887 he was recorded as a special pleader for the Western Circuit and Hampshire, Portsmouth and Southampton Assizes. He continued to work at the boarding school while also working as a lawyer, and indications are that he was financially secure. But there are suggestions that he was in 'serious trouble at the school' according to newspaper reports of the testimony of his elder brother William and as a consequence he was dismissed on or about Friday the 30 November 1888 and on 31 December his body was found floating in the Thames at Chiswick.[19] A search of Druitt's pockets revealed, apart from several large stones, some cash, cheques, a first class season ticket from Blackheath to London, the second half of a return Hammersmith to Charing Cross rail ticket dated Saturday 1 December 1888, and other miscellaneous items. In any event, there was sufficient to allow the police to identify the body. Newspaper reports provide the usual level of confusion as to the order of events but it seems from the most comprehensive but rather inaccurate report of the inquest that Druitt's brother William learned from a friend on 11 December that Druitt had not been heard of at his chambers for over a week.[20] The brother then went to London to make enquiries and found out about Druitt's trouble at the school and from there went to Bournemouth. In Druitt's lodgings William reportedly found a letter addressed to him, although other reports suggest there was also a letter addressed to Mr Valentine at the school. Whatever the true circumstances, William read the letter, which was a suicide note, and at this point he would almost certainly have contacted the authorities. The letter was read out in court by the coroner and was reported as saying to the effect that; 'Since Friday I felt like I was going to be like mother and the best thing for me was to die'.[21] Another local newspaper gave a slightly different version reporting that Druitt suggested that; 'what he intended to do would be the best for all parties'.[22]

The sequence of events following Druitt's dismissal from the boarding school is difficult to accurately establish from the information to hand and is probably only of secondary importance. However, it seems that after his final departure and pay-off from the school at Blackheath, Druitt returned to his lodgings in Bournemouth, clearly in a distressed state. That Druitt had the unused return portion of a rail ticket dated 1 December strongly suggests that he died on that day, or shortly thereafter, but that need not necessarily be the case. Druitt was obviously very disturbed and in that condition rational behaviour does not always prevail. If the return ticket is an indication of the day on which he took his life then it seems likely that, having written a suicide note in his lodgings, he left Bournemouth for London where he bought a return ticket from Charing Cross to Hammersmith. It is likely that he did not intend to commit suicide that day, or possibly that he did intend to but bought a return ticket just in case he changed his mind, in any event, at some point he loaded his coat with stones and jumped into the Thames. Quite why Druitt went to Hammersmith is unclear. If Druitt chose the newly constructed Hammersmith Bridge from which to jump then his body moved upstream and given the tidal currents in the Thames that need not be a great surprise, but there were plenty of other bridges that he could have employed. Initially his body would have sunk but with time the gasses produced by putrefaction would have made his corpse buoyant to the point that it would float to the surface – a very sad end to someone who was by account, 'well known and much respected in the neighbourhood. He was a barrister of bright talent, he had a promising future before him and his end is deeply deplored'.[23] A verdict of suicide while in unsound mind was returned at the inquest, which permitted his burial in consecrated ground.

Mental instability was an established trait within Druitt's family; his grandmother committed suicide and his mother suffered from depression and paranoid delusions and by account attempted suicide on at least one occasion. She was admitted to an asylum in July 1888 and this may have been a significant factor in Druitt's own state of mind, hence the reference in his suicide note that he feared he would end up like his mother. Supporters of Druitt as the Whitechapel serial killer have not overlooked the fact that this date coincides with the commencement of the canonical murder series. With regard to the 'serious trouble' that led to his dismissal from the private school at Blackheath we are deeply into the realms of speculation for there is no documentation or informed opinion to indicate the basis for his dismissal. Certainly today 'serious trouble' would be interpreted as fraudulent or sexual impropriety, but since Druitt was apparently fairly well placed financially his sexual conduct has come under scrutiny. Because Druitt was not married and employed at a boy's boarding school, there have been suggestions that he may have been engaged in homosexual acts against the boys in his charge. Clearly any suggestion that such accusations would be made public would be sufficiently great to lead Druitt to commit suicide because this would also impact significantly on his career as a lawyer. Druitt would not have been the first or the last to commit suicide with the Sword of Damocles hanging in the air, although this doesn't entirely ring true with the statement in Druitt's suicide note where he said that he felt he was 'going to be like mother'.

Macnaghten refers to Druitt as a doctor, which of course he was not, and he also puts into writing other errors that suggest that he may not have been a man who checked his recollections before he conveyed them to others. Consequentially, any suggestions that Druitt may have had medical knowledge and thus anatomical and dissecting skills are unfounded. Certainly Druitt's father, uncle and a cousin were all doctors but that doesn't really provide a strong enough link other than to suggest that he may have had access to anatomy books. Looking at pictures in a book is a very far cry from cutting into living flesh with a sharp knife, and the desire to mutilate needs to be in place well before the killer acquires the skill to perform. There are no details to explain why Druitt ever came to the attention of the police in connection with the Whitechapel murders, and he doesn't even appear to have any links with Whitechapel or the East End of London. Clearly someone must have informed the police accordingly, or more likely, Macnaghten had a private source, judging by his reference to 'private information', by which someone had accused Druitt of being 'sexually insane'. If Druitt was accused of sexual impropriety then it would almost certainly have been related to the boys in his charge and thus his 'insanity' would have been of a homosexual nature. It could be that this is the information that reached Macnaghten's ears, but how such then interprets into the random and callous murder of female prostitutes is anyone's guess. As to the informant, it seems unlikely that any of Druitt's family would have directly conveyed unsubstantiated suspicions to the police, because to do so after his death could only cause self-inflicted pain and would be ultimately pointless. Druitt was certainly Macnaghten's favoured suspect but it is very difficult to understand why on the basis of the information that is available.

The only other indication that Druitt may have been Jack the Ripper is related to the fact that his death was coincident with cessation of the canonical murder series, which is hardly conclusive. On 31 March 1903 Inspector Abberline, who had by this time retired from the police force, responded in the *Pall Mall Gazette* to a report in 'a well known Sunday newspaper'. He said of the case against Druitt:

Soon after the last murder [Kelly] in Whitechapel the body of a young doctor [*sic*] was found in the Thames, but there is nothing beyond the fact that he was found at that time to incriminate him. A report was made to the Home Office about the matter, but that it was "considered final and conclusive" is going altogether beyond the truth. Seeing that the same kind of murders began in America afterwards, there is much more reason to think the man emigrated. Then again, the fact that several months after December, 1888, when the student's body was found, the detectives were told still to hold themselves in readiness for further investigations seems to point to the conclusion that Scotland Yard did not in any way consider the evidence as final.

It is interesting to note that Abberline's interview with the *Pall Mall Gazette* was no more than a couple of weeks after the ex-Chief Inspector had latched onto a new suspect for the serial murders in the person of Severin Klosowski, alias George Chapman. Klosowski fulfilled many of the requirements for a psychopathic killer that Druitt quite clearly did not possess and he was hanged in the spring of 1903 for the serial murder of three women unconnected with the Whitechapel series. I shall look at Klosowski later, but Abberline considered him a far more convincing suspect than Druitt – or at least he did in 1903. Whether Abberline considered Druitt to be a stronger suspect ten years earlier is of academic importance only.

Because Druitt died sometime before 31 December 1888, he could not have been responsible for the murders of Alice McKenzie or Frances Coles. All other factors aside, for this reason I am of the opinion that he could not have been Jack the Ripper.

4.3 Aaron Kosminski (c1864-1919)

Aaron Kosminski is the favourite suspect of many Ripperologists but yet again the case against him has been built on circumstantial evidence and opportunity after his appearance on Macnaghten's list of suspects. Kosminski came to be on Macnaghten's list largely through the suspicions of Sir Robert Anderson and there are several references by Anderson to the fact that Jack the Ripper had been 'safely caged in an asylum' without ever actually mentioning Kosminski by name.[24] Anderson's reference to the suspect being from 'certain low-class Polish Jews' was one of several clues as was the suggestion that the suspect had been confronted by a witness after which time the murders ceased; although it should also be said that this identification was probably not until early in 1891 or over two years after the last of the canonical victims was murdered and thus can hardy be regarded as contributing to an immediate cessation of the murder series. However, why Kosminski was a suspect in the first place is unknown since there is no suggestion that he was otherwise known to the police. The Scotland Yard version of Macnaghten's Memorandum describes Kosminski thus:

(2) Kosminski, a Polish Jew & resident in Whitechapel. This man became insane owing to many years indulgence in solitary vices. He had a great hatred of women, specially the prostitute class, & had strong homicidal tendencies; he was removed to a lunatic asylum about March 1889. There were many circs connected with this man which made him a strong 'suspect'.

In the copy of the Aberconway version of the report Macnaghten stated that; 'This man in appearance strongly resembled the individual seen by the City PC near Mitre Square'.

Researchers have pursued Kosminski through the records and a significant amount of information about the Polish immigrant has come to light. Sugden gives a comprehensive review of what is known about Kosminski and there would be little point in duplicating that here.[25] However, it is fair to say that although some pieces of the jigsaw of Kosminski's life have been pieced together there remains no evidence to suggest that he was a psychopath as Macnaghten's reference to 'strong homicidal tendencies' would tend to suggest, nor any indication that Kosminski was anything other than a harmless polish immigrant who masturbated to insanity and ultimately became a vagrant!

'Solitary vices' is of course a euphemism for masturbation and the work of Dr William Acton leaves us with little doubt that masturbation was regarded as the way to a young man's mental ruin, a misconception that almost certainly continued to prevail even during the late nineteenth century.[26] Quite how the police came by such information is a mystery, but Kosminski is clearly rated highly as a Ripper suspect in Macnaghten's estimation so we must assume that the Chief Constable had more information available than has thus far come to light.

Kosminski was born in Poland and came to England in 1882 when aged 17 and was a hairdresser by profession. He was unmarried and in 1890 he probably lived with his sisters and brother-in-law, Woolf Abrahams, at 3 Sion Square which was located at the northern end of Mulberry Street and connected with Union Street which ran between Commercial Road and Whitechapel High Street. On 12 July 1890 Abrahams had Kosminski admitted to Mile End Old Town Workhouse on the grounds of insanity. On 15 July 1890 Kosminski was discharged into the care of his 'brother', which may have been Woolf Abrahams, or another brother-in-law, Morris Lubnowski, whose address was 16 Greenfield Street. Early the following year on 4 February 1891 Lubnowski had Kosminski re-admitted to Mile End Old Town Workhouse and three days later on 7 February he was discharged to Colney Hatch Asylum. Records at Colney Hatch suggest that Kosminski had been insane for five years, or from 1886, and that he suffered from 'self-abuse'. Specifically though, Kosminski was not regarded as a danger to others. On 19 April 1894 Kosminski was admitted to Leavesden Asylum where he remained until his death on 23 March 1919. The certifying medical officer recorded Kosminski as being 'guided' by 'an instinct that forms in his mind' and that he refused food from others because he is told to do so, and that he ate 'out of the gutter' for the same reason. Kosminski was reported as being very dirty and unwashed and that he had not attempted any kind of work for years. During his hospitalisation Kosminski was variously described as having 'hallucinations of sight and hearing', and as being 'very excitable' and 'troublesome at times'.

By the time Kosminski was incarcerated in Leavesden in 1894 he was indeed in a sorry state, but there is no indication as to what he was like six years earlier, although it is unlikely that his relatives would have had him admitted to the workhouse in the first place in July 1890 without good reason. There are no documented details to suggest that Kosminski was involved in a life of crime or that he did at any time actually inflict physical harm on anyone, so it is mystifying that Macnaghten should label him as a homicidal maniac with a great hatred of women, especially prostitutes. But in any event, the case against Kosminski vaporises if Frances Coles was a victim of the Ripper since records show that he was confined in Colney Hatch a week before Coles was murdered in Swallow Gardens.

Even without this contradictory evidence there is no suggestion that Kosminski had any knowledge of human anatomy or of the skills necessary to dissect organs from a human corpse. Also, at the time of the murders, Kosminski would have been living with his relatives and had he returned home in the early hours, on more than one occasion, covered in blood and with a uterus in one pocket and a very sharp knife in the other, I have little doubt that someone within the family would have noticed. Such would of course be a good enough reason for Woolf Abrahams to have Kosminski institutionalised, but had Abrahams detailed his reasons I think that the police would have been informed and would undoubtedly have taken a much greater interest in Kosminski far earlier than was actually the case.

That a witness was supposedly used to identify Kosminski as Jack the Ripper is a further, although ultimately irrelevant, complication that adds rather more to the confusion than it clarifies. However, through this supposed identification, Kosminski was unique among the major Whitechapel murder suspects in that he was the only one against whom there was any suggestion of evidence linking him to the scene of a crime, and the assertions by Anderson and Swanson that Kosminski was Jack the Ripper rest firmly upon such witness identification. Although there is no direct mention of the name of the witness in police or in any other records there are sufficient indicators to suggest that the witness was Joseph Lawende who claimed to have seen Catharine Eddowes in the company of a man in Duke Street at the entrance to Church Passage shortly before she was murdered in Mitre Square. The only other contender as a witness is Israel Schwartz who saw a contretemps supposedly in Berner Street shortly before the death of Elizabeth Stride that same evening, but Schwartz does not fit so well with what researchers have gleaned about the identity of the witness and he is the less likely candidate. In fact, it is interesting to note that in spite of the apparent weight placed on Schwartz as a witness, he does not seem to have been used in an attempt to identify any suspects. We have already noted that Schwartz probably did not give evidence at the inquest, which many researchers have suggested was for his own protection because he was such an important witness. It is reasonable to speculate that if he was that important why was he apparently never used to identify suspects? There are several possible explanations for this; perhaps he was used but we simply do not know about it; he could have moved away and the police lost track of him; or it is possible that the police placed far less importance on his evidence than do many present day authors.

But the witness identification of Kosminski is another distraction that takes us nowhere, especially when one also considers that Lawende was quite adamant after the murder of Catharine Eddowes, that although he was sure he saw Eddowes with a man just before she was murdered he could not give a description of the man and would not be able to recognise him again. Whether this was a ploy, a device concocted at the time to throw attention away from Lawende, is pure speculation, but if Lawende did catch a glimpse of someone whom he was sure he would be unable to recognise again then we have to believe that two years later he identified Aaron Kosminski as the man engaged in conversation with Catharine Eddowes in the early hours of 30 September 1888. This should also be regarded as another contradiction from Macnaghten who suggested that; 'No one ever saw the Whitechapel murderer, many homicidal maniacs were suspected, but no shadow of proof could be thrown on any one'! And there is yet another discrepancy between Macnaghten's memory and the facts when he states, in the Aberconway version of his report, that the suspect was seen by, 'the City PC near Mitre Square'. A suspect was not reportedly seen by a City constable near to Mitre Square prior to the murder of Catharine Eddowes, unless Macnaghten referred to reported recollections of Sergeant Stephen White, although White was a Metropolitan Police Officer. [27]

During the course of tracing the documented life of Kosminski it became apparent from asylum records that another Jew, 23-year-old Aaron Davis Cohen was arrested in December 1888 and found to be insane.[28] Cohen was first committed to Whitechapel Workhouse and then to Colney Hatch where he died in the autumn of 1889. Cohen was apparently violent and his committal was the result of police action. His arrest at that time would have explained the apparent immediate cessation of activity of the serial killer and in many ways, even though little is documented about Cohen, he is a better suspect than Kosminski and yet, he does not appear to have been a prime suspect and did not appear on Macnaghten's list. This of course assumes that there was no confusion of identities. Kosminski did not die 'shortly after committal' as Superintendent Donald Swanson suggested in annotations he made in a copy of Assistant Commissioner Robert Anderson's memoirs, whereas Cohen died within a year of being arrested. And Cohen may or may not have hated prostitutes but he certainly employed them and was arrested in a brothel.[29] In any event, Cohen's incarceration in December 1888 excluded him as a suspect in the death of Alice McKenzie seven months later and Cohen's death in October 1889 was four months before that of Frances Coles. There is no evidence to support the suggestion that either Aaron Kosminski or Aaron Davis Cohen was Jack the Ripper.

4.4 Michael Ostrog (c1833-?)

Ostrog is the last of the suspects mentioned by Macnaghten and warrants attention more because of the inaccuracies and misconceptions reported by the Chief Constable than the suggestion that he had anything to with the Ripper murders for surely he did not. In fact, once again it is difficult to see why he appears on Macnaghten's list. In the Scotland Yard version of his report, Macnaghten described Ostrog as follows:

(3) Michael Ostrog, a Russian doctor, and a convict, who was subsequently detained in a lunatic asylum as a homicidal maniac. The man's antecedents were of the worst possible type, and his whereabouts at the time of the murders could never be established.

In the Aberconway version of his report, Macnaghten also included the statement to the effect that; 'This man was said to have been habitually cruel to women & for a long time carried about with him surgical knives & other instruments'.

At least there is evidence of psychopathic tendencies insomuch as Ostrog was a petty thief and a conman who by account had numerous aliases and passed himself off as a doctor, a surgeon, or the exiled son of the King of Poland. He was, however, not very successful at crime and was reportedly mentally unstable with delusional tendencies so it is doubtful that ultimately he would have been successful at anything in life, including callous and clinically executed multiple murder. Sugden has uncovered much of what is known about Ostrog and I again refer readers to his book for a more comprehensive background.[30]

Ostrog seems to have spent his life in and out of prison and hospital and first appeared in England, in Oxford, in August 1863 when he was sentenced to ten months in prison for theft. From then until 1888 Ostrog pursued his unsuccessful life of crime, which was largely a catalogue of theft and deceit that placed him in Oxford, Cambridge, Bishop's Stortford, Tunbridge Wells, Devon, and Gloucestershire, and many other places besides, when not in prison. In 1874 the *Buckinghamshire Advertiser* recorded his conviction for theft and receiving and there is a useful description of their impression of Ostrog:

Ostrog is no ordinary offender, but a man in the prime of life, with a clever head, a good education and polished manners, who would be certain to succeed in almost any honest line of life to which he might devote himself, but who, nevertheless, is an inveterate criminal. With natural and acquired abilities such as a few men posses, and having before his eyes a warning in the shape of seven years' penal servitude to which he has been sentenced at Maidstone for felony, he nevertheless risked his liberty and forfeited a position which he had obtained in respectable society, by pilfering a few books and a silver cup, worth to him about £5. The case is altogether a psychological puzzle. It is impossible to gauge the mental condition of a man of such intellectual and personal advantages, who would run the risk of ten years' penal servitude for such a miserable mistake.[31]

A description of Ostrog appears in the *Police Gazette* in August 1883 when he was wanted by the Metropolitan Police for failing to report after he was released from prison on licence. Ostrog is described as: five feet eleven inches tall with dark brown hair, grey eyes and a dark complexion, and he was considered to be fifty years of age. Ostrog surfaced again in 1887 and in September of that year he was admitted to Surrey County Lunatic Asylum in Tooting and discharged as 'recovered' on 10 March 1888.[32] Another notice appeared in the *Police Gazette* on 26 October 1888, Ostrog having again failed to report, but on this occasion the notice ended with the sentence; 'Special attention is called to this dangerous man'. Thus, Ostrog is the only one of the three suspects listed by Macnaghten to have been actively sought by the police during the Ripper murders, although this may be purely coincidental. Ostrog does not appear again in English records until he was arrested in April 1891 for failing to report to the police and the following month he was certified as insane with 'delusions of exaggeration' and committed to Banstead Asylum in Surrey as a lunatic found 'wandering at large'.[33] At that time, Ostrog was also regarded as suicidal but not dangerous to other people, although his physical condition was recorded as 'much impaired'. Two years later on 29 May 1893 Ostrog was discharged as 'recovered'. Curiously, the period of Ostrog's incarceration in Banstead would be the time at which Macnaghten referred to Ostrog as being 'detained in a lunatic asylum as a homicidal maniac', a description somewhat at odds with official records. In any event there was a belief by some at the time that Ostrog feigned madness in order to escape longer prison sentences and in that regard he certainly seems to have been successful. Ostrog continued to offend until his last recorded court appearance in 1900 when he was sent to prison for 5 years, although his health by this time was clearly deteriorating. Ostrog did not complete his sentence and was released on licence from Parkhurst on 17 September 1904. At this time he was described as a shade less than 5ft 9in tall and he may have been in his early seventies. At the time of the murder of the canonical victims, Ostrog was reportedly 5ft 11in which was considerable above the average height for an adult male in the late eighteen hundreds.[34] Bearing in mind the extent to which witnesses notice height it is highly likely that anyone seeing Ostrog in the company of any of the victims would have reported him as being well above average height. In fact, none of the witnesses ever reported seeing such a suspect.

Crucially, research has shed light upon an important period of Ostrog's life; the time from 1888 until 1890 that included most of the Whitechapel murders. Macnaghten suggested that Ostrog's whereabouts at this time could not be established although in 1894 he must have known that this particular suspect was slipping from his list because Ostrog protested at a court hearing that in 1889 he was in a lunatic asylum in France, a claim that was subsequently substantiated by French police. For Ostrog was indeed in France in 1888. Research has clearly shown that police in Paris arrested him on 26 July 1888, and on 14 November 1888 he was charged under the name of Stanislas Lublinski, and convicted of theft in Paris and sentenced to two years in prison.[35] Thus, even at the time Macnaghten compiled his report there was obviously some doubt as to whether Ostrog was actually in England when the canonical victims were killed and he is likely to have been in prison when at least one of the subsequent victims was murdered. In fact, because there is so much doubt surrounding Ostrog's whereabouts, even to the extent that Macnaghten makes mention of the fact, it is difficult to understand why he appears with such high profile. Again it is tempting to think that Macnaghten would not have considered Ostrog so strongly unless he had good reason to do so but frankly that argument has been applied to all three suspects and loses validity each time it is employed. It is academic as to whether or not Ostrog had any anatomical knowledge or dissection skills, or whether his personality demonstrated psychopathic tendencies. Whatever abilities he may have had they did not extend to the point at which he could be in two places at the same time and Ostrog has effectively been excluded from any possibility of being the serial killer in the midst of the Whitechapel murders.

Had there been just one version of the Macnaghten report, the 'personal' version held by Lady Aberconway, then it would have been fair to regard this as a draft version that was intended to form the basis of a formal document that would record official police opinion at the time and as such it would be checked for accuracy before being released for scrutiny. However, the fact that a second, amended, version of the original was found among the files at Scotland Yard is troublesome because it indicates that the original version was looked over and amendments were made thus there was an opportunity to validate the facts according to Macnaghten's memory. That such was not undertaken unfortunately throws the value of the whole document into doubt since it contains so many errors that it must be regarded as a document of peripheral interest rather than a cornerstone of research into the Whitechapel murders. Crucially, the list of Ripper victims given by Macnaghten can not be regarded as reliably attributable to the same killer any more than the list of suspects can be regarded as tenable. Fortunately the document would have had no impact at the time since it was not as far as is known released and thus was not influential, and in any event the Ripper murders had ceased by the time it was written. The Macnaghten report has proved to be a red herring as far as latter day research is concerned and doubtless will continue to be so.

4.5 Francis Tumblety (c1833-1903)

Francis Tumblety only came to light as a Ripper suspect in 1993 when Stewart Evans came across a letter written by Special Branch Ex-Chief Inspector John Littlechild to a journalist called George Sims. The typewritten letter was dated 23 September 1913 and was apparently in response to a request by Sims for information on someone referred to as 'Dr D'.[36] At the time Littlechild had retired from Scotland Yard to pursue a career as a private investigator. From the outset we have to regard Tumblety as a marginal suspect and he did not appear on the Macnaghten list but he is nonetheless interesting. There are several elements that are useful contributions to a circumstantial case for Tumblety being Jack the Ripper although inevitably there is nothing that connects him directly with any of the murders. Littlechild suggests that he does not know of a 'Dr D' and that 'T' could be mistaken for 'D' in speech which is why he responded to Sims with what he knew about Tumblety.

The Littlechild letter alone is of limited value other than to bring Tumblety to our attention and give a few pointers, but it is clear from an article in the *Rochester Democrat and Republican* that Tumblety was at the time linked with the Whitechapel murders.[37] Such a contemporary article is of great interest, but of less value given the rather subjective nature of the reporting; however, there are several first hand observations relating to Tumblety that cause raised eyebrows now in much the same way that they must have done late in 1888.

From the opinion of Littlechild it is evident that Tumblety was an 'American quack' who was 'at one time a frequent visitor to London and on these occasions constantly brought under the notice of police, there being a large dossier on him at Scotland Yard'. There is no evidence to suggest that Tumblety practiced his quackery while in England but this does tend to suggest that he may have had some genuine medical and anatomical knowledge and maybe even dissection skills. Perhaps the most significant revelation comes from an American lawyer, Colonel Dunham who was 'well acquainted with Tumblety for many years'. Dunham's opinion on Tumblety was reported in the *Rochester Democrat and Republican* article:

'The man's real name,' said the lawyer [Dunham], 'is Tumblety, with Francis for a Christian name. I have here a book published by him a number of years ago, describing some of his strange adventures and wonderful cures, all lies, of course, in which the name Francis Tumblety, M.D., appears. When, to my knowledge of the man's history, his idiosyncrasies, his revolting practices, his antipathy to women, and especially to fallen women, his anatomical museum, containing many specimens like those carved from the Whitechapel victims - when, to my knowledge on these subjects, there is added the fact of his arrest on suspicion of being the murderer, there appears to me nothing improbable in the suggestion that Tumblety is the culprit.'

Dunham asserted that Tumblety was 'not a doctor, but an arrant charlatan', and described him as being charismatic and 'a Titan in stature, with a very red face and long flowing moustache, he would have been a noticeable personage in any place and in any garb'. 'The fellow was everywhere', said the Colonel, 'I never saw anything so nearly approaching ubiquity'. On one occasion Dunham and his lieutenant colonel accepted Tumblety's invitation to a late dinner – symposium as Tumblety called it – in his rooms:

[188]

He had very cosy and tastefully arranged quarters in, I believe, H. street. There were three rooms on a floor, the rear one being his office, with a bedroom or two a story higher. On reaching the place we found covers laid for eight - that being the 'doctor's' lucky number, he said - several of the guests, all in the military service, were persons with whom we were already acquainted. It was soon apparent that whatever Tumblety's deficiencies as a surgeon, as an amphitryon he could not easily be excelled. His menu, with colored waiters and the et ceteras, was furnished by one of the best caterers in the city. After dinner there were brought out two tables for play - for poker or whist. In the course of the evening some of the party, warmed by the wine, proposed to play for heavy stakes, but Tumblety frowned down the proposition at once and in such a way as to show he was no gambler. Some one asked why he had not invited some women to his dinner. His face instantly became as black as a thunder cloud. He had a pack of cards in his hand, but he laid them down and said, almost savagely: 'No, Colonel, I don't know any such cattle, and if I did I would, as your friend, sooner give you a dose of quick poison than take you into such danger.' He then broke into a homily on the sin and folly of dissipation, fiercely denounced all woman and especially fallen women.

Then he invited us into his office where he illustrated his lecture, so to speak. One side of this room was entirely occupied with cases, outwardly resembling wardrobes. When the doors were opened quite a museum was revealed - tiers of shelves with glass jars and cases, some round and others square, filled with all sorts of antomical [sic] specimens. The 'doctor' placed on a table a dozen or more jars containing, as he said, the matrices of every class of women. Nearly a half of one of these cases was occupied exclusively with these specimens.

Of course, there is no way of knowing whether or not any of the specimen jars actually contained uteri (matrices) and if they did whether or not they were human, but it is interesting to relate this alleged collection of specimens with the removal of the uterus from two of the Ripper's victims and with the enquiry to the sub-curator of the Pathological Museum that the coroner Wynn Baxter detailed at the inquest into the death of Annie Chapman. It is worth reiterating what Baxter said in this regard:

I received a communication from an officer of one of our great medical schools, that they had information which might or might not have a distinct bearing on our inquiry. I attended at the first opportunity, and was told by the sub-curator of the Pathological Museum that some months ago an American had called on him, and asked him to procure a number of specimens of the organ that was missing in the deceased. He stated his willingness to give £20 for each, and explained that his object was to issue an actual specimen with each copy of a publication on which he was then engaged. Although he was told that his wish was impossible to be complied with, he still urged his request. He desired them preserved, not in spirits of wine, the usual medium, but in glycerine, in order to preserve them in a flaccid condition, and he wished them sent to America direct.

Although this issue has already been largely dismissed, from what is known of Tumblety such a request would be very much in character and it certainly provides a point of great interest and speculation while being evidence of nothing. Tumblety was indeed in the country a few months before the murder of Annie Chapman – he arrived in Liverpool in June 1888 and did not leave again until 24 November that year when he fled to France.

Tumblety apparently told Dunham that when he was 'quite a young man he fell desperately in love with a pretty girl, rather his senior, who promised to reciprocate his affection' and after a brief courtship he married her.[38] But all did not go well and the honeymoon was not over before Tumblety 'noticed a disposition on the part of his wife to flirt with other men', which culminated in Tumblety discovering his wife and another man entering a gloomy house in the worst part of town. Tumblety then apparently learned that before their marriage his wife had been a prostitute working in that and many similar houses and at that point he 'gave up all womankind'. This is an odd tale and even if true it probably represents more of an excuse than a reason for his homosexuality. Tumblety was homosexual and Littlechild confirms that he was 'arrested at the time of the murders in connection with unnatural offences and charged at Marlborough Street, remanded on bail, jumped his bail, and got away to Boulogne'. Tumblety was in fact arrested and charged on 7 November with homosexual offences of gross indecency with four men; Albert Fisher on 27 July 1888, Arthur Brice on 31 August 1888, James Crowley on 14 October 1888, and John Doughty on 2 November 1888. Tumblety appeared at Marlborough Street Police Court on 16 November in connection with the charges and was bailed but absconded before any further appearance.[39] Tumblety then fled to France under the name of Frank Townsend and then to America on the steamship *La Bretagne*. There have been suggestions that Tumblety was actually charged in connection with the Whitechapel murders, but if such were the case he almost certainly would not have been given bail and there would surely have been attempts to extradite him from America once his whereabouts were known, which was pretty soon after *La Bretagne* docked in New York. When New York City's Chief inspector Byrnes discovered that Tumblety was living at 79 East Tenth Street at the home of a Mrs McNamara, he placed him under surveillance, but could not arrest him because, 'there is no proof of his complicity in the Whitechapel murders, and the crime for which he was under bond in London is not extraditable'. In America Tumblety was pursued by the press until he managed to slip from public view, but strangely the British press did not carry any reports about his activities. In July 1880 a New York lawyer, William Burr encountered Tumblety when defending a Mrs Lyons and her son against whom Tumblety had made charges of larceny. Burr gave his impressions of Tumblety to the *Rochester Democrat and Republican*:

I had seen him before that time hovering about the old postoffice building, where there were many clerks. He had a seeming mania for the company of young men and grown-up youths. In the course of our investigations about the man we gathered up many stray bits of history about him, but nothing to make a connected life story. He had a superabundance of cheek and nothing could make him abashed. He was a coward physically, though he looked like a giant, and he struck me as one who would be vindictive to the last degree. He was a tremendous traveller, and while away in Europe his letters to young Lyon showed that he was in every city of Europe. The English authorities, who are now telegraphing for samples of his writing from San Francisco, ought to get them in any city of Europe. I had a big batch of letters sent by him to the young man Lyon, and they were the most amusing farrago of illiterate nonsense. Here is one written from the West. He never failed to warn his correspondents against lewd women, and in doing it used the most shocking language. I do not know how he made his money. He had it before he became acquainted with the Lyon family, and was a very liberal spender. My own idea of this case is that it would be just such a thing as Tumblety would be concerned in, but he might get one of his victims to do the work, for once he had a young man under his control he seemed to be able to do anything with the victim.[40]

We thus have a strong image of Tumblety as a man with psychopathic characteristics and this last observation by Burr is intriguing. It seems that if Tumblety wanted to kill someone he may not have had to do the work himself. One is then immediately drawn to Tumblety's homosexual associates and the complex possibility that Jack the Ripper may have been under the control of, or in the employ of, Francis Tumblety. That Tumblety himself committed any of the Ripper murders is extremely unlikely. One only has to look at the descriptions of him to realise that he had a physical appearance that was hard to disguise and a flamboyance that he would find hard to suppress. In the locale in which the Ripper operated the likes of Tumblety would be immediately noticeable and none of the witnesses to suspects at any of the murders reported seeing an individual that fits anything like the description of Tumblety. His height, ruddy complexion, and prominent moustache would have been obvious to any witnesses and he was fifty-six at the time of the murder of the canonical victims. Furthermore, he was in America after the death of Mary Jane Kelly and could not have been directly involved in the subsequent slaying of Alice McKenzie or Frances Coles. Given the existance of evidence suggesting that Tumblety had a connection with the Whitechapel murders it is a little surprising that he did not appear on Macnaghten's list, especially regarding the credentials of those who *were* on the list, but it could be that he was excluded by the police for reasons of which we are not aware. There is only a weak circumstantial case against Tumblety based upon subjective comments reported in newspapers, none of which have been substantiated. Tumblety remained in America and died in St Louis in 1903.

4.6 Severin Klosowski (George Chapman) (1865-1903)

Severin Klosowski was a Polish immigrant who called himself George Chapman from 1895 until his judicial execution in 1903. Klosowski did not come to the attention of the police until 1902 when he was arrested for the murder of Maud Marsh and thus could not have been considered as a Ripper suspect until that time. Marsh was one of three women whom Klosowski poisoned to death with tartar emetic and his credentials as a serial killer naturally brought him into consideration for involvement in the Whitechapel murders both at the time of his arrest and during the years since.

Klosowski did not cooperate with the police after his arrest and everything that is known about him has been built up from the trial testimony of witnesses and from documents found in his possession after he was arrested. Indeed, much of what we know about Klosowski comes from the details of his murder trial. Hargrave Adam compiled an account of the trial from official Central Criminal Court Papers and other sources and we must be indebted to this work, which seems largely accurate regarding the documented facts surrounding Klosowski, although rather less than accurate when interpreting the information and considering him in connection with the Whitechapel murders.[41] With regard to information compiled from trial details, there were effectively three opportunities for evidence to surface and for witness statements to be made. The Coroner's Inquest opened on 28 October 1902 with the fourth sitting on 18 December 1902, although this dealt mainly with identification of the deceased, medical details and the cause of death. The Police Court Proceedings at Southwark Police Court commenced on 27 October 1902, lasting until 11 February 1903, to be followed quickly by the murder Trial at The Central Criminal Court, which commenced on 16 March 1903 and ended three days later.

Although little is known about Klosowski before he emigrated from Poland, the items of documentation that he retained provided something of a sketch of his life during that time. The documents were translated and submitted at the trial, and are in the form of written statements as to Klosowski's training as a surgeon and to his apparent good standing. Of course, from what we now know of Klosowski there exists the possibility that some or maybe all of the documents are forgeries but the court at his murder trial took the documents at face value so we are probably entitled to do the same. The documents represented Klosowski's references.

An extract from Klosowski's birth certificate issued in Kolo, Poland reveals that Severin Klosowski was born into the Roman Catholic faith on the morning of 14 December 1865. From other documents it is apparent that he attended the Krasseminsk School from October 1873 until June 1880 when he left aged almost fifteen years. From December of that year until June 1885, aged almost nineteen years, Klosowski was an apprentice surgeon under the supervision of Moshko Rappaport, the senior surgeon and proprietor of surgery in the village of Zvolen in Poland. In October of his final year in pupillage, Klosowski obtained a certificate to say that he had completed four and a half years of practicing surgery and 'under the doctor's instructions had rendered very skilful assistance to patients – ie., in cupping by means of glasses, leeches, and other assistance comprised in the science of surgery'. The position of surgeon is thus more akin to that of barber-surgeon, or *feldscher* as it was known in Poland and one wonders as to the depth of Klosowski's surgical abilities. Adam points out that Klosowski's skills probably included those of a hairdresser, which was Klosowski's first form of employment when he moved from Poland to Whitechapel. From October 1885 until January 1886 Klosowski received instructions in practical surgery at the Hospital of Praga, Warsaw, where his general conduct was described as 'good'. He was at this time employed by a Mr V Olshanski, who also provided a reference to the effect that Klosowski was his assistant surgeon from 20 August 1885 until 1 February 1886, and then entered the service of Mr D Moshkovski until at least 15 November 1886. On 24 November 1886 a passport was issued to Klosowski allowing him to travel within Poland. The passport was of one year duration and carried a general description of the bearer: Age 21; born in 1865; height, medium; hair, of a dark shade; eyes, blue; nose and mouth, medium; chin and face, longish; birthmarks, none. There is no mention of a moustache.

A document dated 5 December 1886 and from the Ministry of the Interior, Medical Administration Warsaw, is in connection with Klosowski receiving the degree of a Junior Surgeon. The Medical Administration saw no reason to oppose Klosowski receiving such a degree but there is no evidence to suggest that such was ever approved and bearing in mind all the other documents in Klosowski's possession one imagines that certification would have been among them had the degree been granted.

There are two statements that are worthy of brief attention. On 18 November 1882 the Magistrate of the County of Zvolen stated in writing that; 'Severin Klosowski, resident in the village Zvolen, is a well-behaved man and was never found guilty of any crime whatever'. And on 26 April 1886 the Warsaw Police department provided a statement to the effect that; 'In accordance with the application of Severin Klosowski, and in consequence of inquiries ordered to be made, the present certificate is issued from the office of the Chief of Police of Warsaw to the effect that while residing in Warsaw was not observed by the police to be concerned in any improper conduct whatever'. Both of these statements were probably given in response to routine enquiries either from surgical bodies to which Klosowski applied, or possibly in connection with his passport application, although they could equally well suggest that there was some doubt concerning his conduct that led to such references being sought. The magistrate's comment that Klosowski 'was never found guilty of any crime whatever' is a little ominous and, assuming that the statement does not gain unduly from translation, then a slightly more sinister nuance could be associated with such a comment.

The very last piece of translated documentation was a receipt from the Treasury of the Warsaw Society of Assistant Surgeons for hospital fees and was dated 28 February 1887, and confirmed him to be paid up until 3 March 1887. This is the last dated proof of Klosowski's presence in Poland. There are suggestions that Klosowski joined the army at some point in his career, but there is no direct evidence to support this. Indeed, one witness testified to the contrary; Wolff

Levisohn stated that '[Klosowski] could not have been a soldier, because he was too young when he came over here [England]'. In addition to the receipts the police found 'a book containing 500 household prescriptions' with the name S Klosowski written on the front, and two medical books that had been sold to Klosowski by the same chemist who sold him tartar-emetic.

The receipt issued at the end of February 1887 suggests that Klosowski must have been resident in Poland at least into early March 1887 but the picture of a rather restless individual is starting to form, and sometime shortly after issue of the receipt for hospital fees he emigrated to England. The exact date of Klosowski's entry into England is not known but he was in London possibly as early as 1887 and certainly by 1888. Ethel Radin gave evidence that Klosowski was assistant hairdresser to her husband, Abraham, for five months in his shop in West India Dock Road fifteen years previous to the time she gave evidence. Her timing was vague but this could have been Klosowski's first employment in England and he was quick to put his medical skills to good use by helping to nurse Radin's sick baby back to health.

In 1888 Wolff Levisohn, a travelling salesman in hairdresser's appliances met Klosowski in a barber's shop in the basement of *The White Hart* public house at 89 Whitechapel High Street. Levisohn gave evidence at the Police Court and Criminal Court trials and his evidence is important in building up a picture of Klosowski's whereabouts and to some extent his character. Levisohn said that Klosowski, in the course of conversation which began by reference to medicine, said that his name was Ludwig Zagowski and that he came from Warsaw. Levisohn told the court that at this time Klosowski 'spoke Polish, mixed with a little Yiddish' and was an assistant hairdresser at the shop beneath *The White Hart* until 1889 at which time he became proprietor. According to Levisohn, Klosowski stated that he had been a *feldscher*, which Levisohn interpreted to be a doctor's assistant, at the Praga Hospital in Warsaw and that 'he appeared to be very clever with medicines'. Levisohn had himself been a *feldscher* and at some point Klosowski had asked him to get some medicine, a request that Levisohn declined on the grounds that he did not 'wish to get twelve years'.

Levisohn confirmed that initially Klosowski was living by himself, but 'after a time he was joined by a wife and two children'. He apparently did not support them and now and again Levisohn and another man 'gave the woman coppers'. Levisohn ceased to see Klosowski between 1890 and 1894 but then found him working as an assistant hairdresser at 5 West Green Road, South Tottenham. The wife and two children were no longer with him at this time but there was another woman and Klosowski apparently rented a shop in South Tottenham on weekly payments, before later moving to another shop opposite Bruce Grove Station which was also apparently his own business. Levisohn did not see Klosowski again until he was in custody but remarked that while living in Tottenham, Klosowski 'could talk little English'. Levisohn was not enamoured of Klosowski and at the Police Court Proceedings on 7 January 1903, in answer to a question from the defence counsel as to what sort of man he was, Levisohn replied:

He was a "la de da" then, with black coat patent boots, and high hat. There he sits. He has not changed a bit; he has not a grey hair in his head. At Tottenham he had two wives – one was English and the other foreign. The latter was not his Polish wife.[42]

Why Klosowski adopted the alias Ludwig Zagowski for the benefit of Levisohn is uncertain although the choice of name does bear a close resemblance to that of his Godfather Ludwig Zyanski. Perhaps he felt the need to conceal his real name from a fellow countryman. In any event, Levisohn's observation regarding Klosowski's command of English is important when considering that some witnesses relevant to the Ripper murders overheard victims talking with suspects and in the case of the murder of Frances Coles in 1891, Ellen Callagher may even herself have spoken to the killer. If Klosowski could speak only a little English by 1894 it follows that he would have been able to speak even less in 1888 shortly after arriving in England and indeed he and Levisohn communicated in Polish and Yiddish. The use of a common language probably isn't necessary when engaging the services of a prostitute but an absence of English or even a heavy foreign accent would have been noticeable to anyone encountering a suspect who demonstrated such.

Klosowski probably lodged with the Radins at West India Dock Road while working for them, but he almost certainly did not live-in at the hairdressers below *The White Hart* in Whitechapel High Street. Levisohn thought that he may have been living in Greenfield Street near Commercial Street but did not visit him there, and it is likely that he was correct in his assessment, at least in 1890. Prior to that Klosowski probably lived at Cable Street while working at *The White Hart* although the *Post Office London Directory* of 1889 lists Klosowski as running his own hairdressers shop from 126 Cable Street and in all probability he was living there during 1888 at the time of some of the Whitechapel murders.

From what Levisohn says it is apparent that Klosowski was already married when he left Poland and that his wife and two children joined him briefly before moving out. Such, however, did not stop Klosowski from marrying again and in October 1889 he married a Polish girl Lucy Baderski. The woman's brother told the Criminal Court that he thought his sister and Klosowski were then living in Cable Street but that six months later they moved to Greenfield Street, Whitechapel. In September 1890 Lucy gave birth to a son and Klosowski had become proprietor of the barber's shop beneath *The White Hart* in Whitechapel High Street, but on 3 March 1891, Klosowski's son died from 'pneumonia asthenia'. At this time they were living at 2 Tewkesbury Buildings, Whitechapel, and they were still there in April when the 1891 census was conducted. Shortly thereafter the couple emigrated to New York; a move perhaps triggered by the death of their son. Klosowski worked as a barber in Jersey City but all was not well with the couple and Klosowski reportedly threatened his wife with a knife.[43] In February 1892, less than a year after moving to America, a pregnant Lucy returned to London without her husband and on 15 May she gave birth to a daughter. By the end of the month Klosowski had also returned and the couple had a short-lived attempt at reconciliation before going their separate ways. Lucy survived her encounter with Klosowski but others would not be so fortunate.

In 1893 Klosowski found himself a new woman by the name of Annie Chapman, who should not be confused with the Hanbury Street Murder victim of the same name. Klosowski and Annie Chapman lived together for about a year before he became bored with the arrangement and brought home another woman with the suggestion that the three of them live together. Shortly thereafter the now pregnant Annie moved out but at least survived to tell the tale and she testified against her former 'husband' on the second day of the murder trial. Klosowski used Annie's surname and became George Chapman, and did not again admit to being Severin Klosowski.

In 1895 Klosowski met a woman by the name of Mary Isabella Spink whom he 'married' in order to present a facade of respectability to the owner of the lodging house in which they lived. Shortly after the 'marriage' Klosowski and Spink moved to Hastings where he opened a barber's shop. Although outwardly the couple seemed to get on, there are suggestions that Klosowski repeatedly beat Mary with the result that she often appeared bruised with marks on her throat.[44] On 3 April 1897 Klosowski purchased one ounce of tartar emetic from a chemist's shop in the High Street, Hastings and later that year the couple returned to London where he took out the lease of *The Prince of Wales* public house in Bartholomew Square off City Road. Mary's health suddenly deteriorated and she suffered violent stomach pains, vomiting and diarrhoea and progressive emaciation, and died on Christmas Day 1897. The attending physician recorded the cause of her death as phthisis, or pulmonary tuberculosis.

A few months later Klosowski placed an advertisement for a barmaid to which Bessie Taylor responded. Bessie was given the job and before long she and Klosowski were 'married' following another deception and sham ceremony. Bessie then appears to have suffered much the same violent abuse as her predecessor before following a similar fate. On 13 February 1901 Bessie Taylor was dead and the doctor certified her death as being due to intestinal obstruction, vomiting, and exhaustion.

In August of that year Klosowski hired Maud Marsh as his new barmaid and they also were 'married' in what was fast becoming a routine, but by the following summer Klosowski already had designs on her replacement and so began Maud's demise. But on this occasion his activities came under suspicion when Maud's father requested a second opinion when the attending physician, the same doctor who attended Taylor, was bewildered by her symptoms. On 21 October the doctors concluded that Maud was suffering from the effects of an acute irritant poison, but unfortunately for Maud their diagnosis came too late and she died the following day. The doctors refused to make out a death certificate and a post mortem examination was carried out.[45] Toxicological investigation of Maud's stomach contents revealed that she had ingested significant amounts of antimony and the impurity arsenic, and subsequent analysis of the antimony content of her body tissues revealed that she had died from antimony poisoning.[46] The bodies of Mary Spink and Bessie Taylor were thus exhumed and subjected to thorough post mortem examinations and toxicological investigation. The state of preservation of the bodies was remarkable, and in spite of the fact that Mary Spink had been interred for almost five years and Bessie Taylor for about twenty-one months, there were almost no signs of putrefaction. Within the tissues of each corpse were found significant levels of antimony.

William Davison, the chemist who sold the tartar emetic to Klosowski from his shop in Hastings gave a little further insight when testifying at the murder trial.[47] Davidson agreed that he found Klosowski an intelligent man to converse with, which suggests that by 1897 Klosowski's command of English had progressed to such an extent that he could have a conversation with his local chemist. However it must also be born in mind that Davidson was to some extent protecting his own position since there were veiled accusations that he had sold the poison to Klosowski without due precautions, and he may well have given him a rather better character assessment than he perhaps deserved. Davison, however, insisted that he knew Klosowski well; the Pole had after all 'shaved him on many occasions' when he visited the barber's shop. And he had also sold Klosowski two 'old editions of medical books', neither of which especially dealt with poisons. Davison, who was a registered and qualified chemist, was of the opinion that Klosowski, whom he knew as Chapman, 'had a good knowledge of medicines'; he knew him well and had 'several transactions with him', which is why he let him have such a large quantity of tarter emetic even though he knew that he was not a practicing medical man. In any event Klosowski clearly had little difficulty in duping Davison into selling him an ounce of tartar emetic for two-pence. Davidson told the court that one-sixth to one-quarter of a grain of the compound was the prescribed dose as a diaphoretic and in larger doses it was an emetic. In the chemist's estimation two grains of tartar emetic might be fatal and twelve grains would certainly be so. One ounce contains 480 grains so Klosowski certainly had plenty of material to work with. In spite of the very small doses required for therapeutic use it would have been possible to accurately measure and dissolve and further dilute the tartar emetic to the required strength for whatever purpose. Although Klosowski was unlikely to have been concerned with such refinements, he did realise that the poison was cumulative and that by administering small amounts over a period of time it would be effective and draw little immediate attention to his activities.

Antimony has long been used as a poison and there is a suggestion that the metal was called *anti-moine* because a number of monks were accidentally killed by it. Antimony is a poison that accumulates in body tissues and thus can be administered in small amounts, barely detectable to the victim, that accumulate with time to fatally toxic levels. Elemental antimony is a very effective purgative and tartar emetic, or antimony potassium tartrate, was employed as an emetic, expectorant and vermicide, according to the dosage, but was increasingly less used by the end of the nineteenth century as more efficient and less toxic alternatives were discovered. Tartar emetic was sold as a condition powder to 'cleanse the system' and, by administering repeated small doses, sufficient of the poison is absorbed to cause effects similar to those of arsenic poisoning. Tartar emetic was something of an ideal poison because it is colourless, odourless, virtually tasteless and readily soluble in water. One other interesting aspect of antimony poisoning is the fact that it is an excellent preservative and prevents bacterial activity leading to the decomposition of the victim's corpse – a factor that contributed to Klosowski's activities as a multiple poisoner being discovered.

At the end of the fourth day of Klosowski's trial on 19 March 1903, the jury retired at five o'clock and returned just ten minutes later with a guilty verdict in respect of the murder of Maud Marsh. Mr Justice Grantham passed sentence:

Severin Klosowski, for I decline to call you by the English name you have assumed, the only satisfactory feature in this case that we have just completed is that I am able to address you as a foreigner and not as an Englishman. The jury have come to the only conclusion which I am sure every one who has heard the case would have come to. It is not necessary for me to go through the harrowing details of the case, or refer again to the frightful cruelty you have been guilty of in murdering year by year women on whom you have gratified your vile lust. I have but one duty to perform – and it is not necessary for me to say any more – it is the duty of sentencing you to death. [48]

Klosowski was executed by hanging at Wandsworth on 7 April 1903 and as the police investigated his background they discovered several other clues to the personality of the murderer and by the time he came to court they added the crimes of fraud and arson and even without the evidence of the serial murder of three woman, Klosowski clearly displayed psychopathic characteristics. Not surprisingly the police started to entertain the possibility that he may have been involved in the Whitechapel murders, but Klosowski did not admit to anything, even after being sentenced to death.

That Klosowski did not appear on Macnaghten's list of suspects confirmed that in 1894 the police were not aware of his activities but as soon as his history unfolded he came under intense scrutiny. No lesser authority than Ex-Chief Inspector Frederick Abberline came to regard Klosowski as principal suspect. Abberline probably knew more about the Ripper murders than any other officer and although Klosowski was arrested a decade after Abberline's retirement from active police service, there is no doubt that the Ex-Chief Inspector remained informed as to developments even after leaving the force. Abberline gave an interview to the *Pall Mall Gazette* reported on 24 March 1903 and said:

I have been so struck with the remarkable coincidences in the two series of murders, that I have not been able to think of anything else for several days past - not, in fact, since the Attorney General made his opening statement at the recent trial, and traced the antecedents of Chapman before he came to this country in 1888. Since then the idea has taken full possession of me, and everything fits in and dovetails so well that I cannot help feeling that this is the man we struggled so hard to capture fifteen years ago.

My interest in the Ripper cases was especially deep. I had for fourteen years previously been an inspector of police in Whitechapel, but when the murders began I was at the Central Office at Scotland Yard. On the application of Superintendent Arnold I went back to the East End just before Annie Chapman was found mutilated, and as chief of the detective corps I gave myself up to the study of the cases. Many a time, even after we had carried our inquiries as far as we could - and we made out no fewer than 1,600 sets of papers respecting our investigations - instead of going home when I was off duty, I used to patrol the district until four or five o'clock in the morning, and, while keeping my eyes wide open for clues of any kind, have many and many a time given those wretched, homeless women, who were Jack the Ripper's special prey, fourpence or sixpence for a shelter to get them away from the streets and out of harm's way.

As I say, there are a score of things which make one believe that Chapman is the man; and you must understand that we have never believed all those stories about Jack the Ripper being dead, or that he was a lunatic, or anything of that kind. For instance, the date of the arrival in England coincides with the beginning of the series of murders in Whitechapel; there is a coincidence also in the fact that the murders ceased in London when 'Chapman' went to America, while similar murders began to be perpetrated in America after he landed there. The fact that he studied medicine and surgery in Russia before he came here is well established, and it is curious to note that the first series of murders was the work of an expert surgeon, while the recent poisoning cases were proved to be done by a man with more than an elementary knowledge of medicine. The story told by 'Chapman's' wife of the attempt to murder her with a long knife while in America is not to be ignored.

It is a remarkable thing, that after the Whitechapel horrors America should have been the place where a similar kind of murder began, as though the miscreant had not fully supplied the demand of the American agent.

There are many other things extremely remarkable. The fact that Klosowski when he came to reside in this country occupied a lodging in George Yard, Whitechapel Road, where the first murder was committed, is very curious, and the height of the man and the peaked cap he is said to have worn quite tallies with the descriptions I got of him. All agree, too, that he was a foreign-looking man, - but that, of course, helped us little in a district so full of foreigners as Whitechapel. One discrepancy only have I noted, and this is that the people who alleged that they saw Jack the Ripper at one time or another, state that he was a man about thirty five or forty years of age. They, however, state that they only saw his back, and it is easy to misjudge age from a back view.

There are a few errors in Abberline's account but they do not undermine the basis for his belief that Klosowski was responsible for at least some of the Whitechapel murders.

Many investigators, Abberline included, have placed great emphasis on the fact that a murder similar to those of the Whitechapel series was committed in Manhattan at the time that Klosowski may have been living in Jersey City with his wife. The victim was sixty-year old Carrie Brown and she was murdered in a hotel room on the night of 23-24 April 1891. However, from the limited details that have come to light about the murder of Brown there do not seem to be any similarities with the Whitechapel Ripper murders other than the fact that she was a prostitute and her body was mutilated. There is insufficient verifiable detail to warrant Brown's inclusion in the tabulated crime scene and post mortem findings, the only information coming from limited press reports.[49] Information suggests that Brown was strangled first then mutilated after death and that a bloodstained, black-handled table-knife, with a ground or broken blade was found on the floor of the room in which she died. The report suggests that Brown was mutilated by a deep gash that extended from her breast to the lower part of her abdomen and she had been disembowelled, her entrails torn from the body and scattered over the bed. There were also two deep cuts crossing each other on the back in the form of an exact cross. The victim's tongue was out and swollen and her eyes bulged from their sockets.

I believe that this was not the work of Jack the Ripper for the following reasons:

- There was no mention that Brown's throat had been cut. Given that this was a characteristic wound in all Ripper murders the newspaper report would have said if such a wound had been inflicted.
- Brown was murdered indoors, which we have already seen in connection with the murder of Mary Jane Kelly was not the Ripper's style.
- Brown was strangled to death in preference to being exsanguinated
- The mutilation does not sound like the work of a skilled operator

- The knife used to mutilate Brown was not of a type used by the Ripper and he would not have left it at the scene
- The specific mutilation in the form of a cross on Brown's back was not a signature component of Jack the Ripper

At sixty, Brown was much older than Ripper victims, but I do not think that such is necessarily a significant difference. There are fewer similarities between the murder of Brown and the Ripper victims than there are between Mary Ann Kelly and the Ripper victims. It is probably also worth remembering that Francis Tumblety was back in the USA by this time but only Klosowski seems to be regularly mentioned in connection with the murder of Brown. There are also vague allusions to other murders in the New York locale at around the same time, but the details of such are sparse and it seems as though the only slaying of significance was that of Carrie Brown.

Obviously, when considering Klosowski as a suspect for the role of Jack the Ripper it is crucial to establish his whereabouts during the period over which the murders were committed and Levisohn's evidence places Klosowski as resident in Whitechapel from 1888 to the spring of 1891 and prior to his temporary move to America. Although certain dates of Klosowski's places of work and residence overlap in the recollection of witnesses there is no doubt that he was perfectly placed within the Whitechapel district either at work or at leisure to have committed each of the murders that I have attributed to the same serial killer. From Mary Ann Nichols through to Frances Coles, Klosowski was in the vicinity of Whitechapel; but that alone does not make him Jack the Ripper.

Although Klosowski showed some evidence of violence toward women there is no evidence that he ever used a knife to inflict injury and there is only one instance of him threatening a woman with a knife. This incident occurred when Klosowski and Lucy were in America and was reported in *The Daily Chronicle* on 23 March 1903, the week after conclusion of the murder trial:

Klosowski's real wife, Lucy Klosowski [Baderski], who was present at the Central Criminal Court last week, has made a startling statement as to what occurred in the New Jersey shop. She states that on one occasion, when she had had a quarrel with her husband, he held her down on the bed, and pressed his face to her mouth to keep her from screaming. At that moment a customer entered the shop immediately in front of the room, and Klosowski got up to attend him. The woman [Baderski] chanced to see a handle protruding from underneath the pillow. She found to her horror, that it was a sharp knife, which she promptly hid. Later, Klosowski deliberately told her that he meant to have cut her head off, and pointed to a place in the room where he meant to have buried her.

This story was reinforced to some extent by the recollections of Detective Sergeant Arthur Neil in his Autobiography.[50] Neil referred to the fact that Lucy Baderski picked out her husband in an identity parade shortly after his arrest in 1902 after which Klosowski denied knowing who Lucy was. In response to his protests she reportedly remarked; 'You remember the time you nearly killed me in Jersey City!' Lucy Baderski did not testify at the murder trial but whether this is a consequence of her marriage to Klosowski is not known – the marriage was in any event possibly bigamous according to the observations of Levisohn. Much emphasis, probably a disproportionate amount of emphasis, has been placed by investigators and writers on the relevance of this incident reported by Baderski as evidence that Klosowski was Jack the Ripper, but the logic is weak. The incident was not reported as testimony and in any event is not first hand information and thus has the potential for embellishment. And even if the incident were accurately reported, owning a knife and threatening to use a knife are not the same as cutting the throat of another person and it is doubtful that this report could constitute more than a fragment of circumstantial interest. It is fair to say that, as a hairdresser and barber, Klosowski clearly worked around cutthroat razors and knew how to keep them very sharp, and although he clearly owned a knife at some time, he would have been far from unique in that respect.

Klosowski's medical training is in doubt and it is very difficult to assess what knowledge he obtained during the course of his pupillage as an assistant surgeon. The fact that he apparently assisted at cupping by means of glasses and leeches does rather suggest that his training was on the boundary of Dark Ages medicine but these techniques were associated with the practice of bloodletting for which barber-surgeons were somewhat notorious.[51] Bloodletting was regarded as something of a panacea treatment; the idea being that many illnesses were a problem of an excess of 'bad blood' and that removing or reducing the source of the problem would alleviate the condition. The procedure was primarily concerned with venepuncture, but where veins flow arteries are rarely far away, although it is highly unlikely that the vessels of the neck would be used for such purpose. It was not unheard of for surgeons to overdo the 'cure' to the point at which the patient bled to death either at one 'treatment' or by degrees. If Klosowski knew about bloodletting, and it is likely that he did, then he would have some fundamental appreciation of the consequences of blood loss and how such may be quickly effected. A bloodletting kit would consist of a very sharp knife or two with which to puncture the vessel and various cups and bowls in which to collect the blood. There is no evidence that Klosowski had such a collection of instruments but as an assistant surgeon aspiring to become a surgeon, one might expect him to have his own knives and cups.

I cannot help but think that, had Klosowski been responsible for the Whitechapel murders, he would have been engaged in other bloody work by some means. Klosowski was a man who could provide evidence of his medical background, dubious though it may have been, and it would have been too great a temptation for him to legitimately bleed other victims, had mutilation, the cutting of flesh and exsanguination been practices that gave him gratification. I think Klosowski was another type of killer; every bit as callous as Jack the Ripper, but different. The fact that Klosowski did not admit to being Jack the Ripper was of course of no surprise – he did not admit to killing Mary Spink, Bessie Taylor or Maud Marsh, so he would hardly admit to umpteen other slayings.

Klosowski would certainly have had the opportunity to wander the streets late at night in search of victims in 1888. He was single until October 1889 when he married Lucy Baderski after, according to her brother Stanislaus Baderski, the couple had been together for 'four or five weeks'. However Stanislaus Baderski was inclined to be a little inaccurate with other recollections especially with regard to timing so it could be that Klosowski and Lucy Baderski knew each other for longer than he suggested but not during 1888. It is possible that Klosowski and Lucy were together when Alice McKenzie was murdered on 17 July 1889 and they definitely were when Frances Coles was killed on 13 February 1891, this latter event being just two weeks before the death of the Klosowski's son.

Klosowski was a compulsive womaniser with no male friends and seemingly driven by a healthy sexual appetite – possibly bordering on satyriasis that Thomas Bond mentioned in his profile of the Whitechapel serial killer. From his history it is apparent that he quickly became bored with one woman, whether 'married' to her or otherwise, and moved onto the next. But the need for multiple and sequential sexual partners was not the motive for Klosowski killing his three 'wives'; there was no need for him to do that. He could rather more easily have just walked away from the relationships or made their situation so intolerable that they would leave with next to no consequences. Klosowski could never have legally married any of his three victims, but presumably in order to secure a regular sexual partner he conned each into 'marriage' probably with a view to walking away from the relationship at some point in the future when he tired of it. In any event if he knew that he did not wish to associate with any one woman for long then why did he 'marry' them? His 'marriages' could not have been for financial gain even though Mary Spink did have a £500 legacy, and although Bessie Taylor came from an affluent family, Klosowski killed her before she had inherited anything. So what was his motive and why did he suddenly decide that he was going to poison them? The rather sad answer is that Klosowski killed because he could and he did so with psychopathic callous indifference.

There have been suggestions that because of a strong sex drive Klosowski may have sought out and used prostitutes, but there is no evidence for this and it is an unsubstantiated leap in logic. Prostitutes in the nineteenth century were almost inevitably infected with venereal disease and there would be a strong likelihood that any man employing prostitutes on a regular basis would himself become infected and transmit the disease. As a useful consequence of Klosowski's activities we have clinical and post mortem information from three of his sexual partners none of whom exhibited any signs of such disease. It could, however, also be argued that the biocidal activity of antimony would have been a very effective 'cure' for bacterial infections and thus during the period over which the toxin was administered, the process of poisoning the victim also cured any infections!

The Ripper sought out prostitutes to kill them not for sexual encounters in the conventional sense, so his activities are not necessarily directly anything to do with his sex drive. When drawing comparisons between Klosowski and Jack the Ripper authors frequently fall into the trap of suggesting that there are many similarities between the two and thus there is a strong possibility that one must be the other. But the shared trait was that of a psychopathic disposition, the characteristics of which are manifest in both men. Confidence and plausibility are as much trademarks of a psychopathic character as are an absence of guilt and empathy. Klosowski and the Ripper were both plausible individuals who were able to put their victims at ease while having in mind the intention to bring each victim's life to a premature end. Klosowski fooled not only his victims but also their relatives. Robert Marsh, Maud's father, admitted to finding Klosowski 'pleasant and agreeable', and he could see that his daughter was 'very happy with him'. Psychopaths are frequently extrovert characters who are supremely confident that they will never be caught because they think that they are cleverer than everyone else. It is such confidence that allows them to talk their way out of tight situations for they are consummate liars who worry little that the tangle of deceit they construct may not always make sense and may very often be contradictory. Adam summed up Klosowski when he said that; 'Being an accomplished liar, he was also, as so often follows, a braggart'. Over confidence was Klosowski's downfall and he made foolish mistakes that rendered his conviction easy, but he didn't think that he would be caught so why should he need to be cautious about his actions?

So was Klosowski Jack the Ripper? Abberline seemed to think so and there are undoubtedly several factors to support the possibility. Not least of these was the fact that he was a convicted serial killer and although he was not the only suspect to display qualities consistent with a psychopathic character, he was the only suspect against whom there was certain evidence of murderous activity. Thus, he did have the ability to kill another human being and to do so on more than one occasion. We also have a man who had received some training in surgery and medicine and thus would have acquired some basic knowledge of anatomy but probably not any dissection or invasive skills beyond venepuncture. Klosowski certainly appears to have become familiar with toxicology although in this instance a little knowledge definitely proved to be a bad thing for Klosowski. Klosowski was certainly violent towards the women with whom he had relationships, but it can not be said that he hated women and there is no evidence to suggest that he had any involvement with prostitutes so we do not know of his opinion on them.

As to Klosowski's whereabouts at the times of the Ripper murders, there is no doubt that he was in Whitechapel when each was committed, including those of Alice McKenzie and Frances Coles, and he would have been in walking distance of each crime. In particular, Klosowski's lodgings in Cable Street would have left him well placed for murdering Nichols, Stride, and Eddowes in 1888, and the distribution and times of these murders has already been considered in relation to the location of a likely base from which the Ripper could have operated. In fact, Klosowski was the only one of the suspects considered thus far who could have committed all six murders. There is also a possibility that he may fit with some witness descriptions of the Ripper, including that given by Ellen Callagher in relation to the death of Frances Coles; although according to Klosowski's passport his average height would have been rather taller than the suspect observed by Callagher and others.

However, the most persuasive argument against Klosowski being Jack the Ripper is the difference in the mode of killing – poisoning is very different from throat cutting and clearly this point was raised at the time. In a follow-up article in the *Pall Mall Gazette* Abberline responded to 'the question of dissimilarity of the character in the crimes' by saying:

I cannot see why one man should not have done both, provided he had the professional knowledge, and this is admitted in Chapman's case. A man who could watch his wives being slowly tortured to death by poison, as he did, was capable of anything; and the fact that he should have attempted, in such a cold-blooded manner to murder his first wife with a knife in New Jersey, makes one more inclined to believe in the theory that he was mixed up in the two series of crimes. What, indeed, is more likely than that a man to some extent skilled in medicine and surgery should discontinue the use of a knife when his commission - and I still believe Chapman had a commission from America - came to an end, and then for the remainder of his ghastly deeds put into practice his knowledge of poisons? Indeed, if the theory be accepted that a man who takes life on a whole-sale scale never ceases his accursed habit until he is either arrested or dies, there is much to be said for Chapman's consistency. You see, incentive changes; but the fiendishness is not eradicated. The victims, too, you will notice, continue to be women; but they are of different classes, and obviously call for different methods of despatch.[52]

Abberline's mention of 'a commission' is another reference to the request from America for uteri, which he is convinced Klosowski was involved with. However, I think that Abberline missed the point. There is certainly no absolute set of laws that govern psychopathic behaviour. While a killer such as Jack the Ripper would be unlikely to stop killing voluntarily, assuming that he had no control over the urge to kill, that does not mean to say that such could *never* happen. Although it is more likely that external factors would prevent such a murderer from undertaking further atrocities it is not out with the bounds of possibility that voluntary cessation of killing could occur.

Overall, I have great reservations about Klosowski's involvement in any murders beyond those with which he was associated, and of these doubts the fundamental change in the *modus operandi* is the greatest obstacle. There is no doubt that serial killers can change their technique, but there is usually still a fundamental theme that remains. This is not simply about a shift from throat cutting to poisoning, the differences are far more complex than that, and if Klosowski were Jack the Ripper then we would have to accept that he had moved from committing very quick, sexually motivated, public slayings of complete strangers – the type of killing that gets an immediate media response and terrorises the population – to the concealed and protracted murder of victims that he knew personally, with the complete absence of any publicity or terror factor, and upon the presumption that he would not be discovered. Witnessing the point of death was probably a significant moment for the Ripper but we know from testimony that Klosowski refused to be present when Mary Spink died and was probably similarly absent at the moment life became extinct for Bessie Taylor and Maud Marsh. The differences are great, but although on balance I do not think that Severin Klosowski was Jack the Ripper, he can not be excluded entirely from consideration.

4.7 Walter Sickert (1860-1942)

The appearance of the painter, draughtsman and graphic artist Walter Sickert on these pages is a good example of how once implicated in the Jack the Ripper story an individual can soon become a suspect. I can only repeat that it is simply not good enough to find a suspect and build up a circumstantial case against that individual without paying any attention to the very necessary requirement that the suspect must have an ability to kill serially. It takes a very special kind of person to be a serial killer.

Walter Richard Sickert was born in Munich, the son of a Danish father and a English mother. Both his father and his grandfather were painters. Sickert moved to London aged eight when his father, Oswald, realised that his sons would be required to serve in the German army if they stayed in the country of their birth. After a brief career as an actor working at minor roles under the actor and impresario Sir Henry Irving among others, Sickert studied for a while at the Slade School of Art before joining James McNeill Whistler to work in the American artist's studio. Sickert soon became a leading figure in the art world with an eclectic and enigmatic output that reflected his ever changing approach to art. His status afforded him the freedom to be an eccentric rebel and he was noted for a lack of conformity to either the accepted establishment or to the shifting trends of bohemian artists, frequently changing his appearance so that he fitted with neither group. In 1929 the *Daily Express* wrote of Sickert: 'Few artists are more ready to change their names, their beard, and the titles of their pictures'.[53]

Sickert was certainly not a suspect for the Whitechapel murders or indeed for any other murder during his lifetime, but he inadvertently ensured later implication when he recounted his experiences and beliefs to an acquaintance, Florence Pash, and a relative, Joseph Gorman Sickert. The Pash version of events was retold by Jean Overton Fuller in 1990 and the Gorman Sickert version of what Walter Sickert thought he knew was retold with considerable embellishment in a loosely fabricated and unsubstantiated yarn about a Masonic conspiracy by Stephen Knight in 1976.[54] More recently Patricia Cornwell claimed that she had solved the case by stating emphatically that Walter Sickert was indeed Jack the Ripper and from that improbable stance set out to prove his guilt.[55]

By these accounts, Walter Sickert's involvement in the Whitechapel murders lies within a tangle of overlapping tales in which royalty is also implicated, and, as with many aspects of Ripperology, there may just be an element or two of truth somewhere deep within the seemingly endless supposition. In order to examine whatever role Sickert might have had in the Whitechapel murders it is necessary to look at the evolution of a variety of stories.

Generally speaking, any royal conspiracy theory makes a better work of fiction than it does a portrayal of the facts, but central to this tale is Prince Albert Victor Christian Edward who was the son of Albert Edward and the grandson of Queen Victoria. Prince Albert Edward, the Prince of Wales and future Edward VII, was known as 'Bertie' and his son, Prince Albert Victor, was known as 'Eddy'. Prince Albert Victor was born on 8 January 1864, served in the army in India from 1889 to 1890, was created the Earl of Athlone and Duke of Clarence and Avondale in

1890, and died of pneumonia on 14 January 1892 aged 28. He was by all accounts a lazy, apathetic, dullard who occupied his time with aimless pursuits, and given that he was also heir to the throne there is no doubt that his behaviour caused consternation among the royal hierarchy.[56]

There are several stories and versions of stories relating to Prince Albert Victor and Jack the Ripper but these all seem to have emanated from a single source, one Dr Thomas Stowell (1885-1970), a surgeon, whose illustrious career involved appointments at St Thomas's Hospital and the Royal Free Hospital in Liverpool among others. Even though Stowell did not go into print with his ideas until an article published in the *Criminologist* in 1970, the suggestion that Prince Albert Victor was Jack the Ripper appeared a few years earlier in the translation of a book by Philippe Jullian.[57] The English translation of Jullian's book appeared in 1967, but the original French text was published in 1962, eight years before Stowell's article in the *Criminologist*.[58] However, Stewart Evans has demonstrated that Stowell may still have been the source of Jullian's suggestion even though the French historian appeared in print before the surgeon, and this was largely due to a conversation that Stowell had with Ripperologist Colin Wilson back in 1960. Stowell apparently told Wilson of his belief that Prince Albert Victor was Jack the Ripper and because there was no suggestion that Stowell's theory was a secret, Wilson conveyed the details to others and Evans neatly demonstrated that Jullian most probably learned of Stowell's theory by word of mouth. In any event it seems likely that Stowell was the originator of the myth although in his own article in the *Criminologist* Stowell does not name Prince Albert Victor directly but refers to the suspect as 'S' with very heavy inference as to the individual's identity. When the furore surrounding his theory erupted Stowell wrote a letter to *The Times* to deny that his suspect was indeed Prince Albert Victor. Stowell died shortly afterwards on 8 November 1970. Stowell's story did not suggest a role for Walter Sickert; the artist was not implicated in this account and Stowell's reference to 'S' as the murderer was not a reference to Sickert.

So, what was the basis for Stowell's theory? According to Stowell, Caroline Acland, the daughter of Sir William Withey Gull (1816-90) physician in Ordinary to the Queen, told him that her father's diary contained an entry for November 1889 to the effect that Prince Albert Victor was dying from syphilis of the brain. Stowell did not of course mention any names in his article in the *Criminologist* but the implication was that Prince Albert Victor may have suffered from some consequential mental incapacity as a consequence. This alone was clearly insufficient basis to suggest that he was Jack the Ripper, so Stowell probably had additional information to support his theory. Evidently, Stowell was asked by Caroline Acland to go through her father's papers, probably sometime during the 1920s, and the likelihood is that Stowell saw something among these documents that caused him to think that either Gull or Prince Albert Victor was Jack the Ripper. This must remain speculation, as are other suggestions that Gull was forced to incarcerate his royal patient. Reports that the physician suffered from lapses of memory and on one occasion found blood on his shirt that he was unable to explain must also be regarded with caution. In his article Stowell suggests that; 'on more than one occasion Sir William Gull was seen in the neighbourhood of Whitechapel on the night of a murder', but there is nothing to substantiate this tantalising assertion so it can not be afforded credence. Stowell was well into his eighties when the article appeared, some fifty years after documents were made available to him, and with such a lengthy time scale there is always a risk that what should be an accurate recollection is little more than a vague reminiscence and it is probably understandable that none of his memories can be reinforced by documentation. However there is another rather damning discredit to Stowell's theory and it relates to what is known about Prince Albert Victor's movements during the Whitechapel murders. Eddy does not appear to have been in London at the time that any of the canonical victims was murdered.[59] No one has yet presented any convincing evidence to show that Prince Albert Victor was Jack the Ripper, not that such a fundamental requirement has prevented the myth from prevailing and growing. Indeed, news coverage after attention was drawn to Stowell's article ensured that the story of Jack the Ripper was firmly back in the public eye and there was thus a bandwagon to be jumped upon.

The next development was the Masonic conspiracy which was aired in a television documentary in 1973, then in 1976 the journalist Stephen Knight published a book in which he suggested that a relationship between Prince Albert Victor and a shop-girl named Annie Crook was the basis for the Jack the Ripper murders.[60] This is the point at which Walter Sickert becomes involved for the first time. The foundation for Knight's book was an interview that he undertook with Joseph Gorman Sickert who claims to be the illegitimate son of Walter Sickert and Alice Margaret Crook, the daughter of Annie Crook. According to Knight's interpretation of the story as told to him by Gorman Sickert, Prince Albert Victor's mother, Princess Alexandra, wrote to the painter Walter Sickert asking that he instruct the young prince and nurture his artistic abilities which, she apparently felt, was one way in which the Heir Presumptive could express himself and hopefully learn to understand more about the people whom he would one day rule. Needless to say such an arrangement was secret and necessitated deceptions, entered into with the connivance of Eddy's coachman John Netley. Walter Sickert supposedly already had royal credentials, since both his father and grandfather were artists to the Royal Court of Denmark from where Princess Alexandra had arrived twenty years previously, so the choice of Walter Sickert, who was just some four years senior to Prince Albert Victor, would have been logical enough. Knight suggested that Sickert rented a studio at number 15 Cleveland Street, Marylebone, and across the road there was a tobacconist's shop at number 22 where Annie Elizabeth Crook worked as an assistant while lodging further along the road at number 6 Cleveland Street.

According to Knight, in the summer of 1884 Sickert introduced Prince Albert Victor to Annie Crook, a Catholic girl who supposedly frequently modelled for the artist at his studio. The Prince then fell in love with Annie, who, it is suggested, bore a strong resemblance, to his own mother, Princess Alexandra. By account Annie Crook was not especially attractive but clearly the Prince had a different perspective and the painting lessons soon turned into trysts with the inevitable consequence that Annie almost immediately became pregnant. Annie named her daughter Alice Margaret and she supposedly received both Anglican and Catholic baptisms. Annie apparently continued to live in the basement at 6 Cleveland Street and to work in the shop. It is then suggested that a girl by the name of Mary Kelly who also worked as an assistant at the Tobacconist's shop in Cleveland Street, was paid by Sickert to give up her job and move into the basement of number 6 Cleveland Street to act as a paid nanny.

Knight suggested that, on the basis of the interpretation of Joseph Gorman Sickert's story, Prince Albert Victor and Annie Crook were married in a Catholic ceremony at St Saviour's private chapel at which both Walter Sickert and Mary Kelly were witnesses. Before long the authorities became aware of what had happened with the consequence that the independent thinking of the Heir Presumptive did not amuse Queen Victoria, and Prime Minister Salisbury was incensed because the episode could lead to revolution among the proletariat. Events then reportedly took a sinister turn and a raid by the Special Branch on number 6 Cleveland Street in April 1888 resulted in the Prince being spirited away from his wife and child, and thence to India; to Annie Crook being incarcerated in a lunatic asylum for the rest of her life, possibly after brain surgery to ensure she had no recollection; and to Alice Margaret falling into the custody of Mary Kelly and then of Walter Sickert who by this time was married to Ellen Cobden. Knight then proposed that Mary Kelly realised that she had information that could be to her advantage and decided to blackmail the authorities, who in turn elected to kill her and the other four prostitutes with whom she had shared her knowledge. According to Knight, the royal physician Sir William Gull, the coachman John Netley, and Walter Sickert, committed the Ripper murders through a Freemasons plot at the behest of the Prime Minister Lord Salisbury. Gorman Sickert proposed that no lesser figure than Sir Robert Anderson was the third man in the plot instead of Walter Sickert but clearly Knight felt that this was unlikely. According to the Knight-Gorman Sickert account of events, after the raid in Cleveland Street in 1888 Annie Crook was removed to Guy's Hospital and confined for a period of 156 days while Mary Kelly fled to the East End with baby Alice. After her spell in Guy's Hospital, Annie Crook then spent the remainder of her life in workhouses and other hospitals before dying thirty-two years later, insane. Meanwhile, baby Alice somehow, by a 'tortuous route', found a way back to Walter Sickert and he placed her in the care of some poor relatives, but it was not long before misfortune brought her into the workhouse and a long period in institutions followed. Later, in about 1895, Sickert supposedly took Alice to Dieppe where she spent the rest of her childhood, after which time, aged eighteen, she left France and returned to England where she married William Gorman, but according to Knight the marriage ended up being one devoid of physical love on account of Gorman's impotence. So Alice returned to Sickert and became his mistress for twelve years, a move born of her loneliness and increasing deafness. By account, this relationship continued for more than twelve years during which she allegedly bore Walter Sickert a son, Joseph.

The Masonic conspiracy was largely hokum from the outset and it has not improved with age or embellishment. Although the story has been comprehensively discredited on many occasions since, it is worth considering some elements of the plot again, since they have relevance in other ways. It is documented in public records that Annie Crook was born in 1862 and that she did give birth to an illegitimate daughter, Alice Margaret, at St Marylebone Workhouse on 18 April 1885. Alice's father was not identified on her birth certificate, which obviously left the way clear for speculation that Annie's daughter had royal blood. Annie Crook was indeed a shop assistant and lived at 6 Cleveland Street, but in 1886 the building was demolished so the alleged raid on the premises could hardly have taken place in 1888! There is also no evidence that Walter Sickert had a studio in Cleveland Street, although that possibility is not conclusively checkable from Rate Books or census records. Rumbelow examined the same material that was available to Stephen Knight and objectively detailed the known whereabouts of the Crook family, including the movements of Annie's mother, Sarah Crook, of whom Knight makes no mention. Sarah Ann Crook was born in 1838 and died on 18 November 1916. She was an epileptic and spent much of her life in workhouses and infirmaries.[61] Annie Crook's whereabouts are traceable after 1888, thus she was not incarcerated against her will, nor incidentally was there any evidence that she was Roman Catholic. After the birth of Alice, Annie Crook spent much of her time in workhouses and infirmaries, with or without her daughter, and occasionally overlapping with her mother Sarah. Annie was also reportedly epileptic indicating, although not proof of, a congenital disposition towards the condition. In order to confirm the Knight-Gorman Sickert suggestion that Annie Crook was, from some time early in 1888, incarcerated for 156 days in Guy's Hospital under the supervision of Sir William Gull, Jean Overton Fuller inspected admission records for Guy's Hospital, but was unable to find any evidence that Annie Crook spent time there during the period stated or even that Gull was responsible for any admissions.[62] Prior to 22 January 1889 Annie Crook and Alice lived at 9 Pitt Street, Tottenham Court Road, not far from Cleveland Street; this was the last address recorded when they were destitute and spent a night at the St Giles Workhouse.[63] Annie Crook ended her days in the Lunacy Observation Ward of Fulham Road Workhouse, although there is no evidence that she was ever certified, or that she underwent brain surgery, and she died on 23 February 1920. Alice Margaret was also a frequent visitor to workhouses and infirmaries but apart from almost two months at Poland Street Infirmary spanning 1906 and 1907, she was never an inmate for more than a few days at a time. Her last recorded visit to the workhouse was at the end of April 1913. There are two references to Alice being deaf; the first relates to an application she made, when aged 17, to St Pancras parish for relief on 26 August 1902 at which time she reportedly had measles and was 'Stone deaf'; and the second involved a night at Poland Street Workhouse on account of her deafness and bad foot.[64] One unfortunate complication of measles is otitis media or infection of the middle ear. This painful condition when untreated, as was usually the case before the discovery of antibiotics, often led to compromised hearing and Alice's deafness could have been a consequence of this or some other infection.

The fact that she was still reportedly deaf three years after her measles infection suggests the condition to be permanent. Joseph Gorman Sickert confirms that his mother, Alice, was deaf and describes her as a nervous woman whose fears and unhappiness were born in the dreadful isolation of a workhouse childhood. Knight suggests that Alice Margaret's deafness was congenital and inherited from Prince Albert Victor; both he and his mother Princess Alexandria were deaf.[65] Clearly this would add weight to Knight's story but it has already been established that her deafness need not have been congenital. At the age of 33, Alice married William Gorman on 14 July 1918 at St Aloysius's Chapel, in St Pancras. Alice and William Gorman by account lived together until his death and had five children of which Joseph Gorman Sickert was one.[66] Gorman Sickert maintains that his father was Walter Sickert and in his account to Stephen Knight, he makes no mention of his siblings.

Because of the way she had been treated in childhood, it is suggested by Knight that Alice Margaret became over protective towards Joseph, and from his earliest days the boy was given the impression that some sinister memory haunted his mother's life. I suspect that Knight garnished this somewhat but even if such were the case, Gorman Sickert's version of his mother's youth is at variance with that given by Florence Pash, although this is more because of an absence of information rather than a conflict of information.[67] Florence Pash (1862-1951) was a friend and colleague of Walter Sickert and also a friend of Mary Kelly. Gorman Sickert was 25 when his mother died so he was certainly old enough to filter information, assess its accuracy and form impressions, but the source of what he believed about his mother's childhood may still have been a consequence of what Walter Sickert had told him thus we cannot regard his version as having priority over that of Florence Pash.

Walter Sickert almost certainly had charge of a young girl from time to time and there is a strong possibility that this was Alice Crook. In June 1885 Sickert married Ellen Melicent Cobden, the daughter of the Liberal MP Richard Cobden. Ellen was twelve years older than Sickert and of independent means. After their marriage, the couple visited the Netherlands and Munich before spending the summer in France.[68] Walter Sickert spent many summers in Dieppe both before and after his marriage.[69] On their return from France they moved to a house in South Hampstead where Sickert used the top floor as a studio. Clearly by the time he married, Sickert no longer had charge of any babies; there is no evidence that a child was integrated into his marriage and we can only assume that the infant was now either back in the charge of her mother or with friends. Even so, Sickert continued to see Alice and even employed friends to assist in her upbringing. Given Walter Sickert's increasing paranoia that a royal conspiracy wished Alice Margaret dead then it would be of no surprise that he took her off to Dieppe which he knew well and loved.

Far from being incarcerated for the remainder of her life after events in Cleveland Street, Annie Crook was free and her whereabouts generally traceable, so why did she not look after her child? Well, apart from brief periods, she probably did, and aided perhaps from time to time by Alice's grandmother –

although Sarah Ann was never a well woman. In 1902 when Alice was 17 there is documentation to suggest that Sarah, now aged 64, kept the three women in food when they then lived at 5 Pancras Street where they rented a single room.[70] If Sarah looked after her family at this time it is also likely that she assisted her daughter and granddaughter earlier, since Annie's capacity for earning would have been seriously limited after the birth of Alice. A woman who was not supported by a man in the late nineteenth century had very few options regarding her source of income. At least without the encumbrance of children women were able to work in legitimate trades proving they could find a job even though the pay was often derisory. But as soon as a woman had a baby her chances of finding employment were considerably reduced, and most women in that situation had no alterative other than to resort to prostitution and common lodging houses or a life in the workhouse, but even prostitution would have been difficult with a demanding infant.

With regard to the assertion by Joseph Gorman Sickert that Alice Margaret became Walter Sickert's mistress, there is a remarkable similarity between this account of what happened to Alice Crook and the circumstances of Walter Sickert's mother Eleanor. In 1830, Eleanor (also known as 'Nellie) was born the illegitimate daughter of an Irish dancer. Her mother neglected Eleanor and 'disappeared' to Australia leaving her 12 year old daughter in the custody of an anonymous bachelor who sent her abroad to be educated; first to school in Dieppe and later in Altona where she met Oswald Sickert. At the age of 18, Eleanor's benefactor revealed his identity as one Richard Sheepshanks, a former priest and secretary of the Royal Astronomical Society and fellow of Trinity College, Cambridge. Sheepshanks was in fact Eleanor's father and it has been suggested that an incestuous relationship may have followed but in any event Sheepshanks revealed to Eleanor at some point that he was her biological father.[71] When Eleanor announced that she was engaged to be married to Oswald Sickert, Sheepshanks was enraged, withdrew his assistance, and returned to England. Given the similarity of these two accounts, the inevitable corruption of tales told and retold, and the passage of time, it would not be the least bit surprising for the transposition of names to have occurred.

Jean Overton Fuller examines Knight's *Final Solution* against the background of what she had been told about Walter Sickert in 1948 by her mother who knew Florence Pash. By this account it is suggested for the first time that Walter Sickert is Jack the Ripper.[72] From the outset there is a problem in that the story may have evolved over the forty-two years before Overton Fuller eventually told it. Nonetheless, some elements of the Pash story are very similar to the Gorman Sickert story recounted by Knight. Florence Pash apparently knew that Walter Sickert had a relative named Joseph and she also knew the son's mother, Alice Margaret. Pash suggested that Sickert had a studio in a street a few doors away from a male brothel, and that Sickert employed a shop girl by the name of Mary Kelly to work for him as a nanny. Kelly left Sickert's employment because of irregular pay that depended upon the artist selling his pictures and, leaving Sickert to look after the child, she moved to the East End where she drifted into prostitution and became a victim of Jack the Ripper. Kelly supposedly started blackmailing Walter Sickert, possibly threatening to reveal details of his affairs with other women to his wife, and Sickert thus murdered Kelly and her friends. Overton Fuller investigates the detail of the story, and of that told by Gorman Sickert used in Knight's embellishment, but unfortunately I think that she has fallen into the trap of attempting to over interpret what may or may not be fact. An additional problem with the Florence Pash version of events is that of timing – there are scarcely any reference points, although Overton Fuller does give a chronology that charts Pash as first meeting Walter Sickert in December 1885, followed by involvement with his Cleveland Street neighbours, including Annie Crook and Mary Kelly, in 1886 and 1887. By this account Mary Kelly gave up her job as nanny to Alice Margaret and disappeared from the West End in 1887, subsequently to blackmail Sickert from the East End. The following table outlines the two versions of what Walter Sickert believed and there is an attempt to reconcile these with what else is known:

Walter Sickert's Story		The known facts
According to Pash/Overton Fuller	**According to Gorman Sickert/Knight**	
Raid in Cleveland Street took place – no dates	Raid in Cleveland Street took place in April 1888 and was witnessed by Walter Sickert – the raid was at 6 Cleveland Street	A raid at 19 Cleveland Street took place in June 1889. This need not have been the same raid seen by Sickert, but no evidence of a raid in 1888. 6 Cleveland Street was demolished in 1886
There was a male brothel in Cleveland Street	There was a male brothel in Cleveland Street	There was a male brothel at 19 Cleveland Street – there were probably also others
Sickert had a studio in Cleveland Street	Sickert had a studio at 15 Cleveland Street	No evidence that Sickert ever had a studio in Cleveland Street
There was a tobacconists shop at 22 Cleveland Street	There was a tobacconists shop at 22 Cleveland Street	There was a tobacconists/ confectioners shop at 22 Cleveland Street
Annie Crook lived at 6 Cleveland Street	Annie Crook lived at 6 Cleveland Street	Annie Crook gave her address as 6 Cleveland Street on her daughter's birth certificate

Walter Sickert's Story		The known facts
According to Pash/Overton Fuller	**According to Gorman Sickert/Knight**	
Annie Crook worked in the shop at 22 Cleveland Street	Annie Crook worked in the shop at 22 Cleveland Street	Annie Crook gave her occupation as shop assistant on her daughter's birth certificate and may well have worked in the shop at 22 Cleveland Street
Mary Kelly worked in the shop at 22 Cleveland Street	Mary Kelly worked in the shop at 22 Cleveland Street	No evidence that Mary Jane Kelly worked as a shop assistant
Annie Crook gave birth to Alice April 1885	Annie Crook gave birth to Alice April 1885	Annie Crook gave birth to Alice on 18 April 1885 in Marylebone Workhouse
	Annie Crook was incarcerated after the birth	Annie Crook lived free in society after the birth, but largely in workhouses
Mention of Sickert's wife	Brief mention of Sickert's wife	Sickert married Ellen Cobden 10 June 1885. They separated in 1896 and were divorced in 1899
Sickert looked after Alice	Sickert looked after Alice	Sickert probably helped to look after Alice initially then later moved her to Dieppe. Sickert was on honeymoon in Dieppe from June 1885. From 1891-1893 he spent summers in Dieppe then moved there permanently from 1898-1905 returning to London in 1905
Alice was Prince Albert Victor's daughter	Alice was Prince Albert Victor's daughter	No evidence. Alice most likely to have been Walter Sickert's daughter
	Alice married Gorman who was allegedly impotent	Alice married Gorman and they had five children, but Joseph Gorman Sickert makes no mention of his siblings
	Alice and Walter Sickert were lovers	No evidence - unlikely

Walter Sickert's Story		The known facts
According to Pash/Overton Fuller	**According to Gorman Sickert/Knight**	
Joseph was Sickert's son	Joseph was Alice Crook's son by Walter Sickert	No evidence but possible that Walter Sickert was Joseph Gorman Sickert's grandfather and not father
Alice and Florence Pash were involved in an accident	Alice and Florence Pash were involved in an accident in 1892 when Alice was 8 years old	No evidence
	Prince Albert Victor knew Sickert	No evidence
	Prince Albert Victor and Alice were 'married' in 1888. Mary Kelly witnessed the ceremony	No evidence – Mary Jane Kelly was in the East End during 1888
Mary Kelly moved to London from Cardiff		Mary Jane Kelly moved to London from Cardiff in 1884/1885
Mary Kelly left the West End for the East End in 1887	Mary Kelly left the West End for the East End – no dates	Mary Jane Kelly left the West End for the East End – autumn 1885 or early 1886 and probably lived in the East End from 1886 – 1888
Pash said that Sickert was blackmailed by Mary Kelly shortly after she left his employment.	Walter Sickert said that a blackmail note was received by someone in July or August 1888 but the victim of the demand was not named	No evidence
Sickert was Jack the Ripper	Walter Sickert was involved in the Whitechapel murders	No evidence that Walter Sickert was a murderer

There seem to be far more questions than are ever likely to be answered. The facts are sparse indeed and it would be very easy to weave any number of equally incredible stories around such a flimsy framework. The only proven facts are that a woman by the name of Annie Elizabeth Crook gave birth to a daughter named Alice Margaret Crook on 18 April 1885 and that a woman by the name of Mary Jane Kelly was murdered supposedly as part of a series in 1888. There was a male brothel at 19 Cleveland Street where a police raid did take place but that occurred in 1889 so if it was the same as the raid witnessed by Walter Sickert, then he got the timing wrong and misunderstood what took place. The male brothel was probably at this address in late 1885 but its existence earlier than that is uncertain. Walter Sickert's words do not constitute evidence, from either source, and while there are elements of the story that coincide from both secondary sources, this is hardly surprising since the stories of Florence Pash and Gorman Sickert both emanate from Walter Sickert as the shared source.

Thus if Sickert was correct in any or all of his story then it will not be proved by the versions coinciding because it is simply the case that Sickert told something approaching the same story to two different people. Florence Pash's version as related to Jean Overton Fuller by her mother is, by Overton Fuller's own admission, a story told in bits, disconnectedly, and in a way that made it difficult to understand. When considering the accounts given by Florence Pash and by Joseph Gorman Sickert it is necessary to bear in mind the routes of information and timing. If we take Walter Sickert as the origin then his account via Pash comes from Pash to Jean Overton Fuller's mother, to Overton Fuller and then to print in 1990; Overton Fuller was in possession of the information in 1948. The alternative version of the story comes from Walter Sickert to Gorman Sickert and then to print with some embellishments from Stephen Knight in 1976. Walter Sickert probably told Gorman Sickert the story in 1939 when he was about thirteen or fourteen and Sickert at this time would have been 79 – he died three years later. The opportunity for distortion of both versions is obvious but clearly more so for the version originating from Florence Pash. Also, Overton Fuller's account was prepared after reviewing the Knight-Gorman Sickert version so there is clearly the opportunity for unintentional bias.

If we accept that a woman by the name of Mary Kelly did work as a nanny to Sickert then it is fundamental to the story to demonstrate that the Mary Kelly mentioned by Pash and Sickert is in fact the Mary Jane Kelly murdered in Miller's Court – and we straight away run into difficulties. We have some information about the woman murdered in Miller's Court, but know little about the Mary Kelly allegedly working in Cleveland Street, other than her name and a description. What is known of Mary Kelly the nanny comes from the recollection of Florence Pash who described her as quite good looking with a good head of dark, bushy hair, suggesting that she would have been a good artist's model. Good looks are relative, although Elizabeth Phoenix, sister-in-law of Mrs Carthy, the woman in whose house the murdered Mary Jane Kelly lodged at Breezer's Hill off Pennington Street, described Mary Jane Kelly as being about '5ft 7in in height and of rather stout build, with blue eyes and a very fine head of hair, which reached nearly to her waist'.[73] Elizabeth Prater, who occupied the room above Mary Jane Kelly in Miller's Court described her to a newspaper as 'tall and pretty, and fair as a lily', a pleasant girl who 'seemed to be on good terms with everybody'.[74] And there are further reports that Mary Kelly the murder victim had blonde or red hair and not dark hair. One report suggests that Mary Jane Kelly's nickname was 'Ginger' and in another she was described as a blonde of medium height.[75] *The Daily Telegraph* described Kelly as 'tall, slim, fair, of fresh complexion, and of attractive appearance'.[76]

So, are there any other clues? Pash mentioned that the Cleveland Street Kelly had moved to London from Wales, where she had been employed in Cardiff Infirmary as a floor cleaner, hoping to get a better job. The Miller's Court murder victim had also lived in Cardiff before moving to London and Barnett confirmed that she had been 'in an infirmary there [Cardiff] for eight or nine months', but the suggestion here is that she was in Cardiff Infirmary because she was ill, and not as an employee. In spite of this minor discrepancy, this appears to give a much firmer indication that the two women are the same Mary Kelly, since two sources, Walter Sickert via Florence Pash and Kelly herself via Joseph Barnett, give the same details. But in fact, it does not, because Walter Sickert's recollections of Mary Kelly are seriously contaminated.

Although Walter Sickert is the source of both versions, the story is reinforced slightly by Florence Pash who was at least a contemporary of Sickert and may thus have witnessed or experienced some aspects of events, but she independently confirmed very little. The problem with the story as told to others by Walter Sickert is that his involvement with Annie Crook, her baby and Mary Kelly happened in 1885, and as such they were benign events. There was nothing untoward about the overlap of these individuals apart from allegations that Kelly blackmailed Sickert, if indeed this happened in 1885. It would not have been until the murder of Mary Jane Kelly on 9 November 1888 that Sickert would have had any reason to examine again the events of 1885 and this time he did so with prejudice. He immediately assumed that the woman murdered was the woman who had worked for him as a nanny, yet there was absolutely no evidence to substantiate such an assumption, apart from the fact that they had the same name. I have tabulated below the various points on which it is possible to draw comparisons between the two women.

It is immediately apparent from the table that the majority of what Walter Sickert knew about Mary Kelly could have been obtained from what he read in the newspapers and what remains generally shows variance between Mary Kelly the nanny and Mary Jane Kelly the murder victim. Essentially, there is nothing to reliably suggest that they are the same woman. A significant discrepancy relates to the Providence Row Night Refuge and Convent where Kelly is supposed to have stayed. By Gorman Sickert's account of events given in a statement to the BBC, Walter Sickert told him that Mary Kelly was known to nuns at a convent in Harewood Place, Close to Cleveland Street. Kelly apparently went first of all to their sister convent in the East End, which implies that she was in the East End before she arrived in environs of Cleveland Street. Overton Fuller suggests that this was not a factual recollection but a metaphor invented by Walter Sickert to save having to tell the sordid truth to the young Gorman Sickert; the interpretation being that 'nun' represented prostitute and 'convent' brothel. This would be reasonable enough had the story not been verified as probably having some basis in truth. There is an indication that the Mary Kelly known to Sickert was once resident in the Providence Row Refuge and Convent located in Crispin Street, close to Spitalfields Market. The Convent was opposite the eastern entrance to Dorset Street thus in close proximity to Miller's Court.

Mary the nanny known to Sickert - Mary Kelly	Mary the victim - Mary Jane Kelly	How reliable?
Irish	Irish	Not helpful
Pash via Overton Fuller; Quite good looking with good hair - dark and bushy – would have made a good artist's model but difficult and strong willed with ideas of her own.	Phoenix: 5' 7" and of rather stout build, with blue eyes and a very fine head of hair that reached nearly to her waist Prater: tall and pretty and as fair as a lily – a pleasant girl who seemed to be on good terms with everybody *The East London Observer*: A woman of about 25 years of age – a blonde of medium height. *The Daily Telegraph*: Of a fair complexion, with light hair, and possessing rather attractive features, dressed pretty well Maxwell and Lewis: a pleasant little woman; rather stout with fair complexion and rather pale (Both may have mistaken someone else for Mary Jane Kelly) Walter Dew: a pretty, buxom girl	Significant discrepancy – all reports suggest that Mary Jane Kelly was fair, blonde or even a redhead given that her nickname was 'Ginger' (*The Western Mail* 10 November 1888).
No mention of age	Aged 25	Not helpful
Known to have lived in the West End for a while	Once lived in the West End according to Barnett	Doubtful reliability - Cleveland Street is to the East of Marylebone and a considerable distance from Knightsbridge
Moved from Limerick to Wales	Moved from Limerick in Ireland to Wales according to Barnett	Unreliable - reported in the newspapers
Lived for a while in Cardiff	Moved from Cardiff to the West End in 1884 according to Barnett	Unreliable - reported in the newspapers

Mary the nanny known to Sickert - Mary Kelly	Mary the victim - Mary Jane Kelly	How reliable?
At some point moved from convent/refuge in the East End to Cleveland Street	No mention of this	Discrepancy - suggests they are not the same woman
Left Cleveland Street in 1887 and moved to the East End – Pash heard that she had moved	Left the West End and moved to the East End, according to Barnett, sometime in 1885 or 1886 – can not be narrowed down but probably no later than mid 1886	Discrepancy and otherwise unreliable – reported in the newspapers
Went with Walter Sickert to Dieppe at least twice in the summer of 1886 according to Knight/Gorman Sickert	Spent a short time in France according to Barnett. Partial corroboration from newspaper report (*The Star* 21 November 1888) suggesting Kelly worked for French lady living in Knightsbridge and occasionally visited Paris. After leaving the West End Kelly returned to collect dresses from a French woman	Discrepancy - suggests they are not the same woman
Cleaned floors in Cardiff Infirmary according to Pash	In an infirmary in Cardiff according to Barnett	Unreliable – reported in the newspapers, although no record that Kelly actually worked or was a patient in the Infirmary
Reportedly Kelly was an untrained governess – undertook domestic work and then employed as a shop assistant - seen working as a prostitute before drifting to the East End	No mention of working as a shop assistant but known to be a prostitute. Worked in a West End 'gay house' before moving to the East End according to Barnett. Supposedly drove around in a carriage while working in high class brothel	Discrepancy - suggests they are not the same woman
Alleged blackmailer according to Florence Pash – demand received by Sickert after she left his employment	Probably could not read or write – Barnett read newspaper reports of Ripper murders to her although she did receive letters from Ireland according to McCarthy (*The Daily Telegraph* 10 November 1888)	Not helpful - possible discrepancy

There is a tradition at the convent that there was indeed an association with a Mary Kelly and this belief was recounted by an elderly nun in an interview given to the BBC in 1973.[77] Knight suggested that Walter Sickert was instrumental in Kelly's relocation after being approached by the owner of the tobacconist's shop in Cleveland Street when he was in need of an assistant. Sickert allegedly mentioned this to Edmund Bellord, who was a Cleveland Street estate agent and member of the committee of the refuge, and the nuns recommended Kelly for the job. This was an improbable means by which to find a shop assistant, but the point of interest is that this evidence, anecdotal though it is, suggests that the Mary Kelly known to Sickert moved from the East End to Cleveland Street and then back to the East End – somewhat at variance with what is known anecdotally about the movements of Mary Jane Kelly. The fact that the Nuns of the Order of Sister's of Mercy thought it was the same Mary Jane Kelly murdered by the Ripper is based purely on assumption and they fell under exactly the same misapprehension as Sickert. Indeed, far from being proof that they are the same woman this story rather supports the suggestion that they are not.

Mary Kelly was a relatively common name among Irish immigrant women or descendents thereof in the late nineteenth century. Neither the full name nor the age of the Mary Kelly known to Sickert and Pash is recorded although even this may have been tainted by subsequent knowledge. Census data has proved to be unhelpful; there is no reference whatsoever to a Mary Kelly fitting age, location, or family circumstances in 1881 by which time Mary Jane Kelly should have been in Wales following her family's emigration from Ireland, and by the time of the 1891 census she was of course dead. Just by way of a snapshot in 1891, there were in excess of 80 women by the name of Mary Kelly resident in London at the time of the census and that was just the number aged between 20 and 40.[78] There were no photographs of Mary Jane Kelly prior to her murder and precious little left to photograph afterwards. Everything that Sickert told Florence Pash or Joseph Gorman Sickert about Mary Kelly was reported in the newspapers and because he assumed that the two women were the same, in Sickert's mind, the former assumed the identity and antecedents of the latter as reported in the media. Pash would also have read about the murders, so her account would have been independently tainted.

On balance therefore, it is more likely that the Mary Kelly known to Florence Pash and Walter Sickert was not the Mary Jane Kelly murdered in Miller's Court. Walter Sickert's story, regardless as to the source, is fatally flawed and it is unfortunate that so much has subsequently been written on the strength of it. There are probably two different women named Mary Kelly involved in this business and such is not as great a coincidence as it may at first appear. There is no way to demonstrate that the two Kellys were concurrent at the same location but they may have been in close proximity for a while during 1885 or early in 1886 with Mary Kelly in Marylebone and Mary Jane Kelly in Knightsbridge. If Walter Sickert was fooled into thinking that two Mary Kellys were the same woman, why should that not be the case for others, and perhaps for someone with malicious intent? This will be examined further when considering who murdered Mary Jane Kelly.

Having determined that Mary Kelly and Mary Jane Kelly were not the same woman the remainder of Sickert's story can be clarified to some extent, but as a consequence it all turns out to rather pedestrian. There are three factors for consideration before further examining the two versions and attempting to reconcile them with what few facts there are.

Firstly, one must ask why would Walter Sickert be so concerned as to the welfare of Annie Crook's child if she was fathered by another man – even if that man happened to be Prince Albert Victor? To do so makes no sense at all – what would Sickert's obligation be? Why would he make such a grand gesture at great personal inconvenience to himself when he had his own life and career to consider? By the Knight-Gorman Sickert account Annie Crook was not taken out of circulation until early 1888, when Alice Margaret would have been around three years old, and Overton Fuller suggests that Sickert looked after baby Alice in 1887. At this time Sickert was married to Ellen Cobden and they lived in South Hampstead where Sickert also had a studio and painted. It is extremely unlikely that Sickert's wife knew anything about Sickert's responsibilities to Alice so he would not have entertained the child at their home. So where would he have undertaken child minding?

Secondly, why would Walter Sickert have had any contact with Joseph Gorman Sickert unless they were related? By account of Overton Fuller, Pash also mentions Joseph Gorman Sickert as having some link with Walter Sickert, but there is no documented evidence that they were father and son.

The third point is of a more general nature. During the Victorian era there was no way of proving the identity of a child's father, and there was no reliable form of contraception, so if a woman had more than one sexual partner around the time of ovulation then she could attach responsibility to whomever she wished and there could be little argument assuming that the partners were not aware of each other. In effect, pregnancy was a matter of luck and fatherhood could be a matter of the mother's choice. Conversely, any man having sex with a woman known to be a prostitute could easily deny fatherhood and to such an extent that the woman probably would not even bother to suggest such.

So, with these points in mind what is the most plausible and likely course of events that caused Annie Crook, Mary Kelly, and Walter Sickert to overlap with each other? Gorman Sickert suggested that Walter Sickert had a studio at number 15 Cleveland Street, and although this has not been proved, it is possible that the artist did have a studio thereabouts, but only until his marriage in June 1885. Annie Crook and Walter Sickert probably knew each other when Crook was recorded as living and working in Cleveland Street. Their paths would have crossed and Sickert met Annie at some time during 1884. The couple had a sexual relationship and Annie Crook became pregnant in the summer of that year. There is no indication that Annie Crook worked as a prostitute at that time – she had a job and lodgings and maybe even earned a few extra shillings by modelling for her artist lover. However, Sickert was engaged to be married to a woman with social connections and independent financial means, so his relationship with Annie Crook was always destined to go nowhere, and her pregnancy would not affect that outcome. Nonetheless, Sickert still felt an obligation towards the child.

Sickert may well have visited local brothels, or at least kept an eye on the street girls in order to seek out new models, and it seems likely that the Mary Kelly known to Sickert worked as a prostitute, as well as being a shop assistant alongside Annie Crook. If there was a male brothel at 19 Cleveland Street in early 1885 then it was opposite the tobacconists shop at number 22. We know this from the trial of Earnest Parke in the course of the Cleveland Street Scandal in 1889 and the relevant history of the house is well recorded.[79]

On 18 April 1885 Annie Crook gave birth to Alice Margaret in Marylebone Workhouse and gave her address as 6 Cleveland Street and her occupation as shop assistant, but both of these situations would be affected by the birth of her daughter. It is likely that Annie Crook was given notice to quit her lodgings even before the birth of Alice, since with a child it would be impossible for her to work to earn money to pay for her lodgings. Sickert could not help her financially because he had no money and she was instantly destitute. Although Annie Crook only intended to enter the workhouse as a temporary measure while she gave birth, her descent was more permanent and her life sank to a low point from which she did not recover. Thus, Annie and Alice spent much of their time in workhouses and Gorman Sickert supports this when he suggests that his mother had a workhouse childhood.

By Jean Overton Fuller's account, Florence Pash knew Mary Kelly and witnessed Sickert looking after a baby girl. This could not have been other than after December 1885 because Pash had not met Sickert prior to that time. However, it does not mean that Sickert did not know Kelly before the end of 1885 or that she did not look after baby Alice before Pash met Sickert. Pash was in Dieppe in the summer of 1885 so she was definitely not in London during the immediate aftermath of the birth of Alice Margaret.

Sickert would not have had significant responsibility for looking after the child, even before he married and certainly not afterwards. He probably helped Annie Crook to survive on her own by occasionally looking after Alice while Annie tried to find work or, more likely, while she resorted to prostitution as a means to get herself out of the workhouse. But otherwise Sickert was unable to give significant help and after a couple of months he would have even less involvement because his marriage to Ellen Cobden was followed by a honeymoon on the Continent, and relocation later that year to South Hampstead. Annie and Alice were in Marylebone Workhouse for just over a couple of weeks after the birth and are not recorded as visiting again until early in 1989. After his marriage, Sickert perhaps continued to see his daughter occasionally and even employed friends, including Florence Pash, to assist in her upbringing, but Alice lived with her mother and grandmother for the remainder of the time. Sickert enlisted the help of Mary Kelly to act as nanny for which he had promised to pay her, although it remains something of a mystery as to where Mary Kelly could have looked after the child. By this time Sickert lived and worked in South Hampstead with his wife and there is no evidence that he rented any other studio or pied-à-terre. In any event, he could not meet his promise to pay Kelly who became fed up with looking after a child for no recompense and eventually left his employment. It seems likely that at this point Kelly threatened to tell Sickert's wife about his relationship with Annie unless he paid her what he owed. By Overton Fuller's account Mary Kelly left Cleveland Street in 1887 then blackmailed Sickert and according to Gorman Sickert, Walter Sickert received a blackmail letter from the East End in July or August 1888. It is plausible that the Mary Kelly known to Pash and Sickert may have tried her hand at blackmailing the artist but this was probably not on a great or protracted scale. Sickert may or may not have paid Kelly but in any event the two parted company when she left for the East End and Sickert pursued a new life. It is also possible that the blackmail threat did not directly involve Walter Sickert.

After Sickert separated from his wife in 1896 he would have been able to see Alice with greater frequency and when he moved to Dieppe in 1898 Alice possibly went with him for a while. Sickert's marriage was childless so he would have had special affection for Alice if she were indeed his daughter. At this time Alice would have been aged 13 and there is no record of her whereabouts from April 1894 until September 1904 when she visited St Pancras infirmary. Florence Pash looked after Alice for at least some of the time and was with her when an alleged attempt on her life took place in 1892 in London. Both Florence Pash and Joseph Gorman Sickert report this, but Pash's account, recounted by Overton Fuller, would be first hand. According to Pash, she and the little girl were returning from a walk and making for Charing Cross Station when a coach came straight at them just as they stepped into the road. Florence Pash jumped back onto the pavement but the coach mounted the kerb and the child was hit by the wheel and was taken to hospital. When Pash told Walter Sickert what had happened he told her not to blame herself and that the incident was almost certainly a case of attempted murder, after which Pash lived in fear of her own life. In Gorman Sickert's account the driver of the carriage was recognised as John Netley. This incident was almost certainly a genuine accident but it does illustrate the paranoia that embraced Walker Sickert at the time. So why did Sickert think that Alice Margaret's life was in danger? Assuming that Sickert knew the girl to be his daughter then where could a threat to her life possibly originate? Even if the Knight-Gorman Sickert version of the story were plausible and Alice was the daughter of Prince Albert Victor, there would still be absolutely no need whatsoever to kill Alice Margaret – her parentage could not be proved and she was not a liability; just another royal bastard. The reference to Netley sounds like Sickert's assumption rather than the result of a positive identification by any witness, and attempting to deliberately kill someone by horse and carriage on a public highway would be prone to failure and hardly a method of choice. There is no indication that any further attempts were made on the life of Alice Margaret, and it is difficult to see why Sickert should think that Alice's life was in danger unless this was a another consequence of misunderstanding. Sickert returned from Dieppe to live in London in 1905.

Alice subsequently married William Gorman and they had five children one of whom was Joseph. Although Joseph maintains that he is the illegitimate son of Walter Sickert it is rather difficult to see how this can be if the version of events outlined above is accurate. Joseph Gorman Sickert's cousin Ellen May Lackner confirmed that elements of Gorman Sickert's story had circulated within the family during his infancy, although her recollection was that Walter Sickert and not Prince Albert Victor was the father of Alice Margaret, and not the father of Joseph.[80] According to this version of events and in line with the belief of Ellen May Lackner, Walter Sickert would be Joseph's grandfather not father.

With regard to the substance of any royal or Masonic conspiracy story, such as there is any, several authors point to the fact that any secret royal marriage would have been illegal under the 1772 Royal Marriages Act which required that the sovereign give permission, thus there would have been no need to have instigated a complex and completely unnecessary means of negating the union. Given the fragile political climate of the day, however, there remained a realistic possibility of a political and public backlash ensuing had such a relationship, legitimate or otherwise, become public knowledge. In any event, if the objective was to silence several women by murdering them, then why carry out unnecessarily extravagant mutilations as part of the process? And why undertake brain surgery on Annie Crook when murdering her would, have achieved a much more reliable result? Much of the Stephen Knight-Gorman Sickert tale is erroneous or unsubstantiated speculation, although some of the input from Gorman Sickert probably represents a genuine contribution. Gorman Sickert further confused matters in 1978 when he claimed that the Masonic conspiracy element of his story was a hoax, although he later retracted the confession after Knight's death in 1985. But with Sickert now peripherally implicated, there was the opportunity to elevate him to the status of serial killer.

Stephen Knight, Jean Overton Fuller, and Patricia Cornwell have all suggested and tried to demonstrate that Walter Sickert painted representations of the Ripper murders or consciously or subconsciously placed clues relating to the murders within his paintings because he could not get the images of the women he had murdered and mutilated out of his mind. Speculation based upon such a highly subjective interpretation is not relevant to an analysis of murder evidence and should not be regarded as anything other than personal opinion. To some extent this is safe ground for speculation because interpretations are subjective and without evidence from the artist as to what he had in mind when he produced his paintings, they are impossible to disprove. Paintings are frequently open to multiple interpretations in much the same way that beauty is in the eye of the beholder. Vanderlinden examined Sickert's art and comprehensively dismissed the arguments of those who sought to implicate the artist by this shaky approach.[81] Specifically, it has been suggested that several of Sickert's paintings were a consequence of the painter having actually seen the murder scenes and that he could only have seen them because he was there when the women were killed and was thus Jack the Ripper. It can certainly be argued that there are similarities between some of Sickert's paintings and the images of the corpses of Catharine Eddowes and Mary Jane Kelly. For instance, *Le Journal* bears a likeness to the image of Catharine Eddowes as her body lay in a coffin, although the orientation is clearly different. The thrust of this argument is that photographic images of the murdered women were not published in this country until 1972 thus only the killer and a few others who witnessed the scenes could have known what the women looked like after they had been murdered. However, it has been pointed out that the mortuary and crime scene photographs of the Whitechapel murder victims were published as early as 1899 in France.[82] Sickert of course spent much of his time in France, was fluent in French, and had moved to Dieppe in 1898 so it is highly likely that such a sensational publication would have caught his attention. When one also considers that the only photographic images of mutilated corpses were those for Eddowes and Kelly, it looks increasingly to be the case that Sickert saw the very mortuary and crime scene images with which we are familiar today and that these could have been the basis for some of his paintings. In reality, the images of the victims that the murderer saw and remembered would have been appreciably different from those fixed by photographs taken at the mortuary and the crime scene, which further works against the argument. Sickert undoubtedly took advantage of an opportunity to work from such a unique source, which is why the perspectives tend to be similar.

In a broader context, Sickert's painting entitled *Amphitryon* has been used to suggest a hidden message from the painter. *Amphitryon* was painted around 1924 and also went by the alternative name of *X's Affiliation Order* – Sickert quite frequently, and in keeping with the practice of other artists, changed the name of his paintings and also produced several copies of essentially the same work. *Ennui* for instance exists in several sketched and painted versions. Knight suggests that Sickert's *Amphitryon* is 'the richest evidence of all that Sickert littered his art with clues'. Knight regards the painting as 'disturbing' and states that:

It [Amphitryon] depicts a gaunt Victorian room with a high ceiling. On the wall in the centre of a fireside alcove is some sort of ornament whose definition is indistinct, but can be nothing other than a death's head. This age-old harbinger of impending doom is gazing down upon a woman dressed poorly in blouse and long skirt. She is averting her face from its baleful gaze, her hand has been brought to her cheek in despair and a look of anguish is passing across her features. In suggesting that this woman is Marie Kelly with Death staring her in the face, I could justly be accused of allowing my imagination to run riot, except for one thing – the mysterious title of the picture. Like so many of Sickert's titles, it has never been explained. He gave it two names, X's Affiliation Order and Amphytrion [sic]. Remembering that an affiliation order fixes the paternity of an illegitimate child, can we escape the conclusion that Sickert was recalling the events of Cleveland Street? And who is X? Bearing in mind Sickert's story about the highest in the land disguising himself as a lesser being, and in that form seducing an ordinary girl and making her pregnant, consider the alternative title of this picture, Amphytrion. The legend of Amphytrion tells how Jupiter, King of the Gods, the highest in Olympus, disguised himself as a lesser being to seduce an ordinary woman, who became pregnant by him.[83]

Knight has taken the title and attempted to match it to his conspiracy theory in order to interpret the meaning, but unfortunately, he did not get his interpretation of the myth right.[84] But that is of lesser importance because there is an altogether different possible origin for the title of this painting and it does not lie in mythology. In his book about Edward and the Edwardians, Philippe Jullian wrote the following about London in the 1890s:

The wind of dissipation was blowing through London; a statue to Eros triumphant was raised in the centre of Piccadilly Circus on a modern-looking pedestal. All around this statue, in the theatres, in the Café Royal where artists and writers met, at the Amphitryon where millionaires gave fabulous dinner parties, and in the drawing rooms of Mayfair, London was in a state of singular effervescence, avid for rare pleasures and new crazes.[85]

The Amphitryon club is listed in Kelly's Postal Directory until 1897 and was located at 41 Albemarle Street, off Piccadilly. The objective of the club was to provide the attractions of a first rate French restaurant, while at the same time being exclusive. The subscription was three guineas, and no entrance fee was paid by the first 200 members who joined the club. No lesser persons that the then Prince of Wales, Prince Albert Edward, and the Duke of Connaught were inaugural members. Nevill recorded that:

The small clubhouse was comfortable enough, and the cuisine left little to grumble at. About 700 members were enrolled, and candidates kept flocking in. Members were only allowed to introduce three guests at a time, for the accommodation in the dining room was very limited.

An inaugural dinner was given by the Prince of Wales, and a highly successful evening was enjoyed by fourteen selected guests at a cost of £120. The chief faults of this club were its expense and its limited accommodation. A first-class dinner was absurdly expensive, costing £10 a head. In addition to this, the little tables were, on account of the smallness of the premises, so closely packed that intimate conversation was next to impossible. It must be observed, however, that there were private rooms upstairs which could be reserved for dinner-parties, and many were given.

After a short time the Amphitryon closed its doors and left behind it nothing but the memory of some excellent dinners and a certain number of heavy unpaid bills.[86]

There is every possibility that Sickert visited *The Amphitryon* club, but whether or not such was the case it was likely frequented by individuals with whom he was intellectually out of step. Sir Henry Irving the actor under whom Sickert started his career as an actor playing minor roles was almost certainly a member.[87] There is no evidence that Sickert a was member but well after the demise of the club he may have seen fit to depict a gaunt Victorian room with a lofty ceiling as a room at *The Amphitryon* club or maybe the painting was titled to convey a social message. Regardless as to what the artist wished to depict through the picture, this example illustrates that more than one interpretation can exist, each with equal validity, and such can never be used in the course of any objective evaluation.

The most recent author to examine Walter Sickert's role in the Ripper murders is Patricia Cornwell, who identifies Sickert as Jack the Ripper then constructs her case against him on three fronts; by characterising him as a sexually inadequate psychopath; by suggesting that he wrote the majority of the Jack the Ripper letters; and by attempting to demonstrate that his art contained clues to the murders.[88] This latter approach has already been dealt with and dismissed, although Cornwell does suggest additional evidence by way of sketches allegedly drawn by Sickert's hand when he was a youth, and others allegedly drawn by the artist in the guest book of the Lizard House in Cornwall where he is supposed to have stayed, possibly in 1889. In this latter case Cornwell suggests that the sketches in the guest book bear a striking resemblance to those on some of the Ripper letters. Cornwell gives further support to her suggestion that if Walter Sickert made these drawings, a disturbed, morbid and violent mind guided the hand, but this is unjustified over interpretation.[89] It is not known for sure who made the drawings, both are in the collection of Oswald Sickert, Walter's father, but it is certain that the artist lived in violent times and his art reflected no less that what went on around him.

There must also be significant reservations regarding assertions that Sickert had a pathological personality. Various clues to the nature of Sickert's character can be found in the literature, but most seem to have been misinterpreted. Jean Overton Fuller gives a small insight into Walter Sickert from the observations of Florence Pash.[90] Pash described Sickert as obsessive about cleanliness both in the studio and about his person and everything that touched it. The only evidence for this comes from the description of an incident whereby Sickert accidentally put on someone else's hat when at his mother's house. When he discovered the mistake he was horrified and immediately washed his hair. Overton Fuller also recounts that when in Dieppe, Sickert would hang all of his bed linen out of the window including the mattress every morning to air it. I'm not sure that either of these anecdotes is sufficient to label anyone with a compulsive disorder and they hardly demonstrate a propensity towards violence.

Delving into the childhood of offenders is always likely to prove fruitful and psychopaths commonly have a troubled youth, becoming involved in criminal activities at a very early age. There is no evidence whatsoever of such in Walter Sickert's background, even though Patricia Cornwell contrives to give him a psychopathic persona by selectively interpreting the opinions of others such as his sister Helena Swanwick (née Sickert) who may in any event have a somewhat distorted perspective of her brother. In fact, as Cornwell points out, almost everything that we know about the early life of Walter Sickert, from whatever source, can be traced back to Helena's memoirs, so any appreciation of his early life is inevitably skewed. And this is not helped by applying present day standards to interpret a Teutonic and Victorian upbringing. Helena describes her brother as a charming, energetic and quarrelsome little boy who made friends on command but was indifferent to them when they no longer amused him or served a useful purpose. She says that her brother was 'at once the most fickle and the most constant of creatures' and 'unreasonable, but always rationalising', being, 'Utterly neglectful of his friends and relations in normal times and capable of the utmost kindness, generosity and resourcefulness in crises – never bored except by people'.[91] That Walter got his way by 'manipulation, deception and charm' is frequently observed among children and demonstrates little more than the abilities to observe and to learn quickly! Helena Sickert's description of her brother reveals a man who is somewhat aloof, and an individual who did not need to rely upon other people. An intelligent man it seems, who tired easily of those who did not stimulate his mind.

Jean Overton Fuller points out that Sickert found misshapen models more interesting and one can certainly see from his work that he was less inclined to paint standard stereotypical beauties and by account, his favourite was a very fat model who had a squint and deformed feet. However, Sickert was full of compassion for a pretty model whom he found in tears and when he enquired as to the problem she told him that the dentist had told her that she would have to have all of her teeth removed. Sickert reassured the woman thinking that she would be able to have false teeth but she said that she did not have the money to buy false ones, which would mean that she could no longer be employed as an artist's model and no man would want to marry her. Sickert told Florence Pash and the two of them paid for artificial teeth and apparently two weeks later the model showed off her brand new teeth and also told them that she was engaged to be married.[92] Anecdotal though this may be it serves a useful indicator, since compassion is not a word that one would normally associate with a psychopath. Walter Sickert appears to be far from the malignant individual that some would have us believe and any assessment of the artist as a psychopath is flawed.

There are indications in the literature that Walter Sickert had a fistula – an abnormal opening from a normal passageway or duct. Fistulas can occur in many locations – rectal, urethral, vaginal, or oesophageal fistulas being the most common. In Victorian times correction would have to be out of necessity considering the relatively poor recovery rates for even minor surgical procedures, and Walter Sickert supposedly had three such operations before the age of five, the first two of which were undertaken in Munich. There is certainly no evidence to support any assertion that the corrective surgery undertaken on Sickert left him with a mutilated penis with which he was quite unable to enjoy sexual intercourse and was thus incapable of fathering children with 'devastating repercussions in Sickert's psyche'. But on this basis Cornwell's suggests that Walter Sickert was sexually inadequate, thus a misogynist, thus a killer of prostitutes.[93] All well and good if one accepts this rather fragile train of logic – except that none of the theory is substantiated by evidence. I doubt that such operations would have been conducted entirely without anaesthesia, which was commonplace by the 1860s, chloroform being the anaesthetic of choice, so suggestions that young Sickert was subjected to extreme physical pain and psychological trauma are speculative.

The only reference as to the anatomical location of Sickert's fistula comes from John Lessore, Sickert's nephew, who, according to Cornwell, suggested that Sickert had a urethral fistula.[94] Even if this were the case, such a condition, corrected or otherwise, would not have impotence as an inevitable consequence, and there is certainly no justification to suggest that he was hermaphroditic and that his gender at birth may even have been in doubt.[95] Even the site of the Sickert fistula is unconfirmed since the location given by John Lessore was based more upon 'family hearsay' than upon factual knowledge and the Honorary Surgeon under whom Sickert was treated at St Mark's Hospital in London, Dr Alfred Cooper, was a surgeon with experience in ano-recto and vaginal surgery. Indeed, St Marks Hospital is listed as specialising in the treatment of fistula and other diseases of the rectum.[96] Thus one can take it that the hospital was not experienced in uro-genital surgery and that the young Sickert would have been elsewhere if he suffered from a urethral fistula. The very fact that he was treated at St Marks strongly suggests that he had an ano-rectal lesion and not an abnormality of the penis. Whatever the circumstances of the fistula, there is no evidence that Walter Sickert did not have any children. In fact, there are indications that he did but once again proof is elusive.

Although psychopathic serial killers do occasionally voluntarily cease their activities, most do not and the fact that Walter Sickert lived until 1942 proved something of an anomaly in the case against him, since the Whitechapel serial killer ceased activities in 1891. A search by Patricia Cornwell for other murders for which Sickert, as Jack the Ripper, could also have been responsible led her to identify further murder victims after Frances Coles. The list of victims was countrywide and Cornwell suggested that his 'body count' could have been fifteen or many more before he died aged 81.[97] There is no support for this assertion, although the murder of Emily Dimmock, known as The Camden Town Murder, warrants close examination because of suggestions that she was a Ripper victim and that Sickert painted an image of her corpse being well placed by virtue of his studio in Mornington Crescent.[98]

On Thursday 12 September 1907, Emily Dimmock, a twenty-two year old prostitute, was found dead in bed at 29 St Paul's Road, Camden Town where she lodged with her common law husband, Bert Shaw. The room had been ransacked. Someone had washed their bloody hands in the sink and two of Bert's cutthroat razors were found in the room. Dimmock had been murdered some time between 12.30am and 3.30am, but her body was not discovered until Bert returned from work at between 11.30am and midday. Dimmock's throat had been cut and she bled to death from a deep wound to the left side of her neck, which was inflicted while she lay in bed.[99]

Sickert's painting *The Camden Town Murder* allegedly depicts Dimmock's body as she lay on the bed, so it is of interest to build up a picture of the room and circumstances in which Dimmock was murdered. If that differs significantly from the image painted by Sickert then we can say with some confidence that he was not there to witness the scene and he merely painted what he thought the scene must have looked like or that he titled a painting accordingly. In this respect, the orientation of Dimmock's body when she was murdered is important.

The Camden Town Murder painting, also entitled *What Shall We Do For The Rent,* depicts a forlorn looking man fully dressed sitting on the edge of and towards the foot of a bed on which, behind him, a woman lies naked on her back, with her head on the pillow and turned away displaying the left side of her neck. Her hand seems to rest against the man's leg and there is nothing in the picture that actually suggests the woman to be dead, or that she has wounds of any kind. The iron bedstead is orientated with the head end to the right of the picture and there is possibly a wall at the back of the picture against which the right side of the bed is situated. This orientation is much the same as that in which Mary Jane Kelly was found on her bed in the room at Miller's Court with the obvious exceptions that Kelly's body was extensively mutilated and her bed had a wooden headboard.

From court testimony it is evident that Dimmock's naked body lay in the middle of the bed when the police surgeon arrived.[100] She was found in a 'natural' position lying on her left side slightly on her stomach with left cheek on the pillow. Her right hand was extended on the pillow, her left hand was behind her back, the left knee was drawn up and the right knee was drawn up below the left knee, and both hands were clenched. The police surgeon suggested that her left hand had probably been close to her neck when the wound was inflicted and later moved for some reason so that it was in an unnatural position behind her – almost at right angles. The hand contained a blood clot. Her hair was in curling pins. Dimmock's left arm was clearly in a more natural position with her left hand in the vicinity of her neck when the wound was inflicted, yet the killer had moved her arm from this position to a point behind her back. The orientation of the bed is not known for certain but it seems likely from testimony that it was in much the same position as that for Mary Kelly, with the bed close to a wall on the right side. Furthermore, Dimmock's naked body was covered by the sheets when discovered. It is thus difficult to imagine a scene more dissimilar to that depicted in *The Camden Town Murder*. So unless Sickert suffered a catastrophic memory loss between seeing Dimmock's corpse in 1907 and painting *The Camden Town Murder* a few months later, it is safe to assume that he was not at the scene of the murder in any capacity. *L'Affaire de Camden Town*, painted by Sickert in 1909 similarly bears no resemblance to the manner in which Dimmock's body lay on her bed.

It is of interest at this point to briefly examine the circumstances of Emily Dimmock's death and suggestions that she was a victim of a serial killer. Apart from the wound to her neck there were no other injuries and no sign of a struggle. The configuration of her body was such that she was almost certainly asleep when attacked. The fatal cut was inflicted so decisively and accurately that she had little time to move from that position in the seconds that it took her to become unconscious. Her throat was cut almost from ear to ear with the deepest cut on the left side. The cut was almost down to the spine and severed major vessels on that side and cut through the windpipe so that she would have been unable to make a sound. The left side of her head was on the pillow so her killer needed to lift her head in order to get the knife under her neck and in doing so cut the bedding slightly.

Just for comparison I have detailed the circumstances of Emily Dimmock's murder in Table 2 and there are enough differences to clearly demonstrate that she was not a victim of Jack the Ripper and has never been seriously considered as such. There are similarities and differences between the murders of Mary Jane Kelly and Emily Dimmock that are useful to highlight and this I have done in the table below.

I should reiterate that I do not think either Mary Jane Kelly or Emily Dimmock were victims of Jack the Ripper, nor were they murdered by the same person, so any links in that respect can be ruled out. Importantly in this respect is the fact that Emily Dimmock's body showed no evidence of any mutilation and since her killer apparently had plenty of time it is certain that had he been Jack the Ripper, such an opportunity would not have been wasted.

Robert Wood, an acquaintance of Emily Dimmock, was accused of her murder and his trial commenced at the Old Bailey on 12 December 1907. On the 18 December the jury retired to consider their verdict but returned after just seventeen minutes. Wood was found to be innocent of Dimmock's murder and having reviewed the evidence it is difficult to see why he was accused in the first place.

Parameter	Mary Jane Kelly	Emily Dimmock
In bed when killed?	Yes	Yes
Side of the bed when wound inflicted?	Right	Centre
Bed against wall	Yes – right to wall – killer on victim's left	Yes - right to the wall – killer on victim's right?
Clothed or naked	Chemise only	Naked
Fatal would to neck	Yes	Yes
Side of fatal wound	Right	Left
Cut from	Right to left	Left to right
Defensive wounds	Possibly slight	None
Evidence of struggle	None	None
Blood spray from severed carotid artery	Yes – on wall to left of bed	No – victim bled into bedding, through and onto the floor
Mutilation	Extensive	None
Killer disturbed	No	No

As for Sickert's picture entitled *Jack the Ripper's Bedroom*, painted in 1908, there is an easy and obvious explanation for the origin of that title and no need whatsoever to seek out a more obscure interpretation. When Sickert rented rooms at Mornington Crescent in 1905, his landlady told him that, at the time of the Ripper murders, the rooms had been occupied by a consumptive and delicate looking veterinary student who, by her account, was out late on the nights of the murders, eager to see the newspapers the following day, and on occasion burned his clothes. Apparently, before the woman could inform the police of her suspicions the student's health deteriorated and he left London to live with his widowed mother in Bournemouth at which time the murders ceased. He supposedly died three months later.[101] Sickert no doubt believed what he had been told and even noted the name of the student in the margin of a copy of Casanova's *Memoirs*, which he subsequently gave away. The book was lost in the blitz before his notation could be deciphered and recorded. In spite of the best efforts of several researchers no part of this story has been substantiated. There has inevitably been speculation that the identity of the former occupant was no lesser person than Montague Druitt named in the report by Sir Melville Macnaghten, this being the 'private information' that convinced the then Chief Constable of Druitt's guilt. However, an Egyptian-born medical student by the name of Waller lodged at 6

Mornington Crescent in 1891 so there may be further confusion.[102] Sickert would have gained considerable satisfaction from the thought that he occupied Jack the Ripper's bedroom and knew the identity of the serial killer. This clearly inspired him and he painted the room, named the picture accordingly, and regularly related the tale.

A link between Walter Sickert and the Ripper letters is the central argument of Patricia Cornwell's assertion that the painter was Jack the Ripper.[103] Not all of the hundreds of letters received were actually signed Jack the Ripper or derivatives thereof, but for the sake of convenience I shall refer to them all as Ripper letters. Cornwell suggests that Sickert was the serial killer because he wrote the majority of the letters received by the police during and after the Whitechapel murders. There are two critical aspects to this argument that form the chain of logic and two questions must be answered beyond doubt before this could be used as anything like evidence. Firstly, how certain are we that any of the letters received by the police were actually from the killer of any of the Whitechapel murder victims, and secondly did Walter Sickert conclusively write any of those letters?

The simple answer to the first question is that there is no evidence whatsoever to confirm that the killer of any of the Whitechapel murder victims penned any of the letters. During the period spanned by the murders and in the months and years since, the police, newspapers, and even individuals associated with the matter received anonymous correspondence or semi-anonymous correspondence signed with obviously false names – thus was the origin of 'Jack the Ripper'.

The only way in which any of the letters could be reliably regarded as having been written by the murderer would be from the content. If the writer were to have mentioned events or details in correspondence that could only have been known to the murderer then there would be a pretty solid indication that the man who wrote the letter killed the victim. In fact had the killer of any of the Whitechapel murder victims written any of the letters then he would surely have done exactly that in order to ensure that the police knew of the authenticity; there would after all be little point in having your message lost among a host of pretenders and he could only have done this by giving details of his crime. The situation was to some extent complicated by the fact that the newspapers were keen to publish as much information as possible, including most of the post mortem details, in order to satisfy the frenzy of public interest. But even allowing for this the killer would surely know specific details of what he had undertaken and could easily have convinced the police as to the authenticity of his letters. After the initial spate of letters, it is fair to say that so much information about the murders was in the public domain that the correspondence quickly lost any significance that it may otherwise have had and there were only two letters that may have had relevance.

The *Dear Boss* letter was the first to be signed 'Jack the Ripper', and gave rise to the mythical identity of the serial killer, even though the authorities soon came to believe that it was the work of an enterprising journalist. The letter was received by the Central News Agency on 27 September and forwarded to the police two days later, the day before the murders of Elizabeth Stride and Catharine Eddowes. Four days later a postcard, also signed 'Jack the Ripper' and now known as the *saucy Jacky* postcard was postmarked in London on 1 October and also sent to the Central News Agency. Both the letter and the postcard are written in very similar handwriting and there is every possibility that the same person wrote both. The only relevance of the letter is the claim by the writer that he was about to start killing again and that this time he would 'clip the lady's ears off and send them to the police officers just for jolly'. Catharine Eddowes' right ear was indeed mutilated, a piece of the lobe fell from her clothing in the mortuary, but neither was missing and I think this was a matter of coincidence rather than giving authenticity to the letter.

The postcard makes reference to the 'double event' or the murder of two women the previous day. However, details of the double murder were published on the same day as the murders so there is little chance of proving that the writer of the letter had exclusive information. If a journalist had penned the *Dear Boss* letter then he surely also penned the *saucy Jacky* postcard and journalists would have been at the scene of the murders and able to gain information faster than most and certainly fast enough to scribble a postcard with specific reference to two murders on the same night and have it in the post within a matter of hours. If the serial killer wanted to write letters to the police then I am more inclined to think that it would have been to deny any involvement in the slaying of Mary Jane Kelly than to claim responsibility for the other murders.

The exact number of letters received is unknown but there were several hundred, many of which have since been lost. Some 210 survive in the National Archives and have also been published.[104] Patricia Cornwell examined these letters and concluded that the majority were written by the serial killer, dismissing the obvious differences in handwriting, style, grammar, spelling, content, paper, and ink by suggesting that such was less likely to have arisen because the letters were written by different people and rather more likely to have been a consequence of the murderer disguising his true style. Different regional postmarks were attributed to the Ripper travelling around the country by rail and posting them from different towns.[105] By establishing the collection of letters to be a homogeneous data pool it is obviously easier to draw conclusions, but the logic is seriously flawed and there is no evidence from paper type or watermark, handwriting, writing style, regional origin, or from any other parameter to suggest that the letters form a reliable data source from which useful information can be obtained. A search for links through so many letters is bound to throw up associations – it is almost unavoidable. But the associations are a product of coincidence and the supposed similarities, even taken collectively, do not come close to providing evidence that a significant number were written by the same hand, let alone that the Whitechapel killer was the author of any. The consensus of informed opinion, both at the time and following intense scrutiny since the murders, suggests that all of the letters supposedly sent by the killer were hoaxes.

Any argument to the contrary would require convincing evidence and currently one of the most irrefutable means by which individuals can be associated with crimes is the use of DNA profiling. Cornwell employed such a technique, but the thrust of the research was misdirected. Given the material that is currently available, it is impossible for forensic investigation to yield the identity of any of the letter writers with an acceptable degree of certainty, since there is no definitive and identifiable source of Sickert's DNA. Any scientific conclusion is only as good as the data upon which it is based and in this case the data pool is a heterogeneous collection of disparate correspondence that is close to useless from the perspective of objective evaluation. The theoretical approach by Cornwell was sound enough, the intention being to extract DNA samples from letters known to have been written by Sickert and compare the DNA profile with that obtained from Ripper letters. However, such an approach was never going to prove that Sickert was Jack the Ripper and the most that it could ever achieve would be to demonstrate that he wrote one or more of the Ripper letters, which is hardly the same thing. Unfortunately, it proved impossible to isolate nuclear-DNA from any of the samples of letters and documents examined, thus a highly individual-specific analysis could not be applied. Investigators did however isolate mitochondrial-DNA from some documents but the problem with this form of DNA found in cytoplasmic organelles of the cell is that it is far less specific and can not be used to identify individuals.[106] Although a valid forensic technique, mitochondrial-DNA analysis is relatively crude test and inappropriate in this instance considering that all of the correspondence under investigation had been handled very many times by many different people.

Walter Sickert has been referred to as a 'gentleman slummer' implying that he visited East End prostitutes for entertainment if not for sex. Sickert probably did visit prostitutes; indeed, they probably visited him even more frequently but primarily because they were a ready source of female models at a time when no respectable woman would remove her clothes for an artist. Prostitutes were imperfect beings; often unattractive, their anatomy and features personified the unglamorous street lives they led – but Sickert preferred this type of model.[107] Although there is no indication that he ever employed prostitutes for sexual gratification, in keeping with many other men of his time and status, he probably did. Sickert was undoubtedly fascinated with the seedier side of life and with the violence of street life. The Ripper murders attracted his attention and were a focal point for his interests.

So what is known about Walter Sickert's whereabouts at the time of the Whitechapel murders? There are indications that during the autumn of 1888 Sickert was staying with his mother and brother Bernhard in France.[108] Unfortunately, the exact dates of his stay 20 miles from Dieppe can not be fixed, but he probably left London in the middle of August because there is a drawing dated 4 August and after that there are no references to his being in town. On 6 September, six days after the murder of Mary Ann Nichols and two days before the murder of Annie Chapman, Sickert's mother wrote from St Valéry-en-Caux, to a friend about the 'happy time' they were having swimming and painting. It is suggested that Sickert probably remained in France until early October when he painted *The October Sun*, which was a picture of a local butcher's shop illuminated by the sunlight of late summer. Thus, he would also have been in France when Elizabeth Stride and Catharine Eddowes were murdered. Theoretically, Sickert could have travelled back and forth from Dieppe to London to commit he murders, slipping back unsuspected into an idyllic lifestyle in the French countryside, but when a hypothesis relies upon such improbabilities for support such is a pretty clear indication that it is weak on substance. However, by the time Mary Jane Kelly was murdered in Miller's Court on 9 November, Walter Sickert was in all probability back in London.

John Lessore thought suggestions that Walter Sickert was Jack the Ripper were "rubbish" and I cannot help but sympathise with his point of view. There is no evidence that Sickert was overtly or latently violent, he was not sadistic, nor disturbed, and he was certainly not a psychopath. He was an intelligent, talented, and disciplined artist who painted life as he saw it. He delighted in controversy but I doubt that he penned any of the Ripper letters, and even if he did then it proves nothing and suggests little more about the man than is already known. Sickert was a little eccentric and probably somewhat egocentric and in the course of his life he caused emotional hurt to the women in his life but such was more by carelessness and selfishness than by a desire to inflict pain. He was far from being a misogynist let alone a killer and to suggest that was Jack the Ripper is fantasy for its own sake.

Sickert's fascination with the Whitechapel murders was to some extent a consequence of an erroneous belief that he had once known the victim, Mary Jane Kelly, and a story grew around that belief, greatly embellished by supposition and rumour from other sources such that another self-perpetuating muddle is created to confuse and distract. But among the muddle there is a sinister element, a circumstance that may have led to Mary Jane Kelly being murdered in mistake for another woman with the same name. Of all the individuals proposed as suspects in the Jack the Ripper murders I believe that Walter Sickert is the least likely to have been the serial killer. Sickert killed no one, and although he may have been in possession of information relevant to the death of Mary Jane Kelly he was not instrumental in her demise or that of any other of the Whitechapel murder victims. The Ripper victims were killed because they were women and prostitutes, but I believe that Mary Jane Kelly may have been murdered because of her name.

5: Who killed Mary Jane Kelly?

It is impossible to fully appreciate the sight that must have shocked all who entered the room at 13 Miller's Court. Walter Dew, later to become Chief Inspector, was a young constable at the time and the first policeman on the scene and what he saw through the broken window 'was too harrowing to be described'. In his memoirs Dew stated that; 'It remained with me – and always will remain with me – as the most gruesome memory of the whole of my police career'.[1]

The manner in which the available information has been analysed in this evaluation strongly suggests that Mary Jane Kelly was not a victim of the same killer who murdered Mary Nichols, Annie Chapman, Elizabeth Stride, Catharine Eddowes, Alice McKenzie, and Frances Coles. This conclusion is valid because the circumstances of Kelly's death are significantly at variance with those for the victims of the serial killer. There is every possibility that Mary Jane Kelly was the unfortunate victim of an isolated random attacker who wanted to join in the slaughter and see his work immortalised but this is an unlikely scenario, so an alternative explanation must be found for her demise and the indications are that Kelly may have been killed by design. Her murder was a premeditated assassination that went precisely to plan – except that in all probability the wrong Mary Kelly was silenced. In order to explore this possibility we need to draw upon information from previous chapters and more especially from events surrounding Walter Sickert and establish a clear distinction between Mary Kelly the supposed nanny to Walter Sickert and Mary Jane Kelly the Miller's Court murder victim.

If Mary Jane Kelly was eliminated by design then there must have been a forceful reason why she had to be killed, so we are looking for someone with a need to permanently silence Kelly because of what she knew or because of what she threatened to do. This implies that she possessed information that she could use for personal gain. But if Mary Jane Kelly was a blackmailer then she certainly wasn't very successful. She, and presumably also Joseph Barnett, owed several weeks' rent amounting to 29 shillings when she was murdered; Kelly had absolutely no wealth and her existence was hand to mouth. She didn't seem to be under any immediate threat on the evening that she was killed. John McCarthy confirmed this, since 'The last thing he had heard of her was at one o'clock Friday morning, when she was singing in her room, and appeared to be very happy'.[2] Barnett suggested to the inquest that Kelly was afraid because of the recent murders, but not afraid of any specific individual and in that respect her fear was probably no greater than that of any other East End prostitute at the time. Maria Harvey, a fellow prostitute in whom Kelly would surely have confided made no mention of Kelly being in fear for her life and specifically told the coroner at Kelly's inquest that Kelly was not afraid of any man. Walter Dew thought that Kelly was afraid and recollected that; 'There was no woman in the whole of Whitechapel more frightened of Jack the Ripper than Marie Kelly'.[3] However, his comments were made in 1938, half a century after her murder. If Kelly was afraid then she certainly did not show it and walked the streets and took men back to her lodgings without caution. She had no concern that the man with whom she had until recently cohabited, her protector, had walked out and left her alone. This was not the behaviour of a woman who was desperately afraid for her safety. Kelly and other Whitechapel prostitutes continued working the streets because each thought that the next murderous attack would happen to someone else. Far from being concerned, Mary Jane Kelly appeared almost carefree, and there is ample suggestion that she did not feel that her life was specifically at risk. So was there something in her past that caught up with her? For this we can only rely upon what we know of Mary Jane Kelly as told by witnesses at her inquest, and from newspaper snippets. Because the Mary Kelly known to Walter Sickert and the Mary Jane Kelly murdered in Miller's Court are almost certainly different women, information relating to the two must be examined separately and not be merged.

Little is known about Mary Jane Kelly and even less can be substantiated. In fact, there are no independent sources or documentation to verify the heavily anecdotal history that we have. Different sources occasionally tell the same tale but the ultimate source was invariably Mary Jane Kelly herself, which hardly constitutes proof. There is no reason to assume that when Kelly related her background she did so with the deliberate intention to deceive, but because none of what she said can be verified there is every possibility that she may have concocted her own antecedents. Information about Mary Jane Kelly's history has already been covered when looking at the circumstances surrounding her death and from these scant details there are indications that she was born in Ireland, moved to Wales, then to the West End of London, briefly to France, then to the East End of London. Of this sequence, the only part that is known with some reliability is that Kelly moved to the East End of London and it was there that she met Joseph Barnett in April 1887. Kelly's whereabouts prior to that are unclear and the timing vague but according to what Barnett told the inquest, when Kelly moved from Ireland to Wales she lived in Cardiff where she married in 1879 aged sixteen. After the death of her husband Kelly allegedly moved to the West End where she found employment in a high-class brothel or 'gay house' as Barnett referred to it. Kelly's move from Wales seems to have been in 1884 and during her time in the West End she apparently travelled at least once to France, but, according to Barnett; 'she did not remain long. She said she did not like the part, but whether it was the part or purpose I cannot say'. According to Barnett, Kelly was not in France more than a fortnight and she returned to England and to Ratcliff Highway. A little more detail is provided by a newspaper report suggesting that Kelly entered the services of a French woman in Knightsbridge during which time she led a degraded life but drove about in a carriage and made several trips to Paris.[4] After returning to London Kelly moved to the East End where she first stayed with Mrs Buki in St George's Street, Ratcliff Highway which tallies with Barnett's account. There is no indication as to why such a huge change in location and fortune took place but it seems likely that Kelly fell out with her employers because she refused to work in Paris and thus could not repay their investment. The cross-channel trade in prostitutes was well established and William Stead, editor of the *Pall Mall Gazette* crusaded against the business with a series of articles entitled *A Maiden Tribute To Modern Babylon*.[5] It was alleged that women, and young girls were being forced against their will to work in brothels in Belgium and France often with the collusion of the foreign police. However, in reality, all women destined for foreign brothels had to make a formal declaration that they knew they were off to work in brothels and what was expected from them and in any event, the vast majority were not the coerced young innocents that the sensationalistic press would have wished their readers to believe.[6] Frequently however, promises did not match up to reality and the conditions under which the women lived and the payment they received fell well short of expectations. Those who quit the arrangement would inevitably incur the displeasure of their employers and be back on the streets without hesitation.

Some support for this as an explanation for Kelly's sudden fall from grace comes from reports that she returned to Knightsbridge in the company of Mrs Buki in order to attempt to recover 'numerous dresses of a costly description'.[7] These dresses would never have been Kelly's to recover. There were many French madams operating in the West End and the association of a brothel with a French element implied that the more relaxed continental attitudes to sex prevailed and it also suggested perhaps more exotic connotations in the midst of repressed Victorian England. It is possible that Mary Jane Kelly was employed as a 'dress lodger'. Among prostitutes in the West End there existed a subcategory of usually young and attractive girls who were unable to afford the kind of clothing that might show them to their best advantage, and thus attract a more discerning and wealthier clientele in up market areas. The women who employed these dress lodgers clothed them in fine and expensive dresses, and because of the value of the clothes, each dress lodger had a 'watcher' who kept a short distance from the girl when they were not on the premises, and who was paid a fixed wage to ensure that the girl did not abscond with the costly garments. Mary Jane Kelly appears to have been rather more attractive than the average street prostitute and the Ripper victims, who would not have been suitable as dress lodgers. It may be significant to note at this point that, had Mary Jane Kelly left her employers because she had threatened them or any clients with extortion, then she would have been warned that she would pay for such indiscretion with her life so it would be unlikely that she would have returned to attempt to collect the expensive dresses that she had to forfeit. Alternatively, had Kelly been unsuccessful in recovering the dresses, this could have been an opportunity for her to threaten to make trouble unless she received some recompense. There is no indication that her quest to collect the expensive dresses was successful.

From St George's Street Kelly went to lodge with Mrs Carthy at Breezer's Hill, Pennington Street and reportedly left there eighteen months to two years prior to her murder, which would be the autumn of 1886 or spring of 1887.[8] Kelly's move from the West End to the East End must thus have been during 1885 or 1886. After leaving Mrs Carthy, Kelly went to live with a man by the name of Morganstone opposite the Commercial Gasworks in Stepney, then, according to Barnett, with Joseph Fleming a mason's plasterer who lived in Bethnal Green Road.[9] Julia Vanturney, one of Kelly's neighbours in Miller's Court suggested that Kelly was fond of another man named Joe and this would have been Fleming.[10] By

1886 Mary Jane Kelly lived in Cooley's common lodging house in Thrawl Street, Spitalfields and while living there she met Joseph Barnett on 7 April 1887. Kelly's brief flirtation with France left its mark in that she adopted the French variant of her name and was occasionally known as Marie Jeannette instead of Mary Jane and Barnett knew her by this name.

Mary Jane Kelly had been a prostitute ever since her husband died earlier in the decade and in that respect she was not in a unique position. She had worked at both the upper end and the lower end of the oldest profession and in doing so she had lived in relative luxury in Knightsbridge and in the absolute degradation of the Whitechapel slums. In spite of such a marked decline in her fortunes she adapted and remained pleasant and good humoured except when over indulging in drink, which she was inclined to do. Her documented tendency to be 'quarrelsome and abusive' when drunk may not have endeared her to some, but there is no evidence in what is known of her life that would cause her to be in fear of an early and violent death and thus there is no obvious reason why she would be killed by design.[11]

Much of the information given by Walter Sickert and Florence Pash about the Mary Kelly known to them as a nanny is contaminated by what Sickert and Pash read in the newspapers following the death of Mary Jane Kelly. There is no independent information to reliably suggest that Mary Kelly and Mary Jane Kelly are the same woman and any points that apparently show similarities could have come from newspaper reports when Sickert and Pash *assumed* that the woman murdered was the Mary Kelly they knew a few years earlier. In fact when it comes down to physical descriptions, brief though they are for Mary Kelly the nanny and of limited reliability for Mary Jane Kelly, there is little to suggest that the two are the same. As we have already seen from what other general information is available, there are discrepancies between the two women and no reliable similarities to indicate that they are one and the same.

With regard to Walter Sickert's story, the only significant documented facts that exist are that a woman by the name of Annie Elizabeth Crook lived at 6 Cleveland Street, and that she worked as a shop assistant and gave birth to a daughter named Alice Margaret Crook on 18 April 1885. It is also known that there was a raid on a male brothel at 19 Cleveland Street that took place on 7 July 1889. This is a flimsy basis upon which to hang substance, especially when the remainder of the information is anecdotal and requires great care to interpret. However, if one ignores those details that could have been transposed then an interesting picture emerges.

Annie Crook worked in a tobacconists shop at 22 Cleveland Street, which was just across the road from number 19. There was certainly a brothel at 19 Cleveland Street in 1889 and activity was observed by a later occupant, Ann Elizabeth Morgan, who had seen as many as fifty or sixty persons, possibly more going into and coming out of the house on various occasions.[12] But what evidence is there to suggest that the same existed years earlier? At the trial of Ernest Parke in connection with the Cleveland Street Scandal, one John Saul, a male prostitute and pimp, gave evidence that he had known Charles Hammond, the proprietor of the brothel, since 1879 and that he remembered Hammond moving into 19 Cleveland Street just before Christmas 1885.[13] Hammond was in the prostitution trade thus it is certain that he wasted no time and was in business as soon as he moved in which can be assumed to be December 1885. This does not overlap with Annie Crook's employment at 22 Cleveland Street but it is reasonable to assume that Hammond took over rather than initiated a brothel at number 19 although there is no evidence for this. Anecdotal support for the presence of a male brothel in the vicinity of events involving Crook, Kelly and Sickert, comes from Florence Pash via the recollections of Jean Overton Fuller's mother who recalled that; 'There had been a house of prostitution only a couple of doors down the street', and that 'boys were available to men'.[14] This is seemingly supportive although there is no precise indication as to date or location. On balance the likelihood is that there was a brothel at 19 Cleveland Street before 1885, but the important date relates to the Mary Kelly known to Walter Sickert, who supposedly did not leave the area until 1887.[15] Thus there is plenty of overlap regarding Mary Kelly's presence in Cleveland Street, and according to Florence Pash, by account from Overton Fuller, when Mary Kelly departed she did so amid suggestions of dissatisfaction and blackmail.[16] Having already dismissed much of the information relating to the early history of Mary Kelly the nanny as being contaminated, when this is excluded very little else remains. However, it can be said that, based upon the accounts of Sickert and Pash, Mary Kelly was a reasonably attractive Irish girl with dark bushy hair who would have made a good artist's model. She was difficult and strong willed with ideas of her own and had previously worked as an untrained governess before undertaking domestic work while attached to the Providence Row Night Refuge and Convent before moving to Cleveland Street and employment as a shop assistant.[17] She had been seen working as a prostitute and in reality this was probably her trade and she clearly worked in and around Cleveland Street. There was no mention of Mary Kelly's age, and there is also a problem with timing in that there are no details from any account that provide fixed points around which the Sickert account can be built

Sickert knew Kelly and Crook and it is quite likely that he employed both women as models and both women probably worked as prostitutes in Cleveland Street. Tobacco shops in the proximity of brothels were often used as a 'reception' points so that clients could innocently make arrangements for services without having to enter the brothel.[18] It would be no surprise if such were the case in 1885 and that both Kelly and Crook were associated with the shop at number 22 and the brothel across the road. Sickert's constant search for models would have inevitably drawn him to prostitutes and he moved in higher class social circles thus West End bordellos would meet his needs. Whether he actually had a studio in Cleveland Street is uncertain but such need not necessarily have been the case and Mary Kelly or Annie Crook could have sat for him at other locations. It would be interesting to know whether either woman could be identified in any of Sickert's work from the period in question.

The birth of Alice Margaret caused upheaval for all concerned. Annie Crook would have been out of a job and home as soon as the baby was born and

Who killed Mary Jane Kelly?

afterwards Sickert probably felt some responsibility to help Crook either because he took pity on her or because Alice was actually his child. Clearly his paternity could not be proved but there was a good chance that Alice was his daughter although having a child by a prostitute would hardly be a reason to rejoice especially when he was due to be married a couple of months after the birth and reason enough why Sickert never admitted that he had a child. In fact such would be a very useful piece of information for anyone with blackmail in mind whether it could be proved or not. Whatever the precise circumstances, Sickert probably felt some obligation to help Annie Crook after the birth and since he had little money his assistance could not extended beyond looking after the child while Annie tried to survive after leaving the workhouse. The fact that Annie Crook gave birth in the workhouse does not mean that she was availing herself of the medical facilities, but that she had nowhere else to go.[19] Under any circumstances this would have been a devastating step, entering the workhouse was a last resort and a low point in Victorian society from which it was extraordinarily difficult to escape, and a child further limited Annie's prospects, thus she had little alternative other than to turn to prostitution. Annie was on the streets to earn what she could while others, including Sickert, occasionally looked after Alice. It is inconceivable that Sickert had full time responsibility for Alice and extremely doubtful that his wife knew about the child and even if she did she would never have been a party to bringing up her husband's illegitimate daughter.

Walter Sickert married Ellen Cobden at Marylebone Registry Office on 10 June 1885 and then went away on honeymoon to continental Europe, returning to live with his wife and work at 54 Broadhurst Gardens, South Hampstead where Sickert used the top floor as a studio. There were thus two months during which Sickert could have helped with no restriction other than his work but during that time baby Alice would have required almost constant attention from her mother thus I doubt that the two were separated for other than brief periods. Victorian Society paid little heed to the plight of pregnant women or working mothers as Engles pointed out and women with infants who worked in the mills had to leave work during their lunch break in order to feed their children.[20] But Annie Crook did not work in a mill, nor did she return to her job in the tobacconist's shop – she spent the rest of her life in poverty with frequent visits to the workhouse until her death in 1920. There is no reason why Sickert would need to have any involvement with Annie or Alice; there was no social pressure on him to do so and there was no external commitment through a royal connection, so it must be assumed that he obliged through guilt or genuine feelings of responsibility reinforcing the likelihood that Alice was indeed his daughter.

Florence Pash did not meet Sickert until December 1885 so she was not directly involved in events until after this time and the fact that she met and described Mary Kelly means that they overlapped from early in 1886 as baby Alice approached her first birthday. Pash met Kelly through Sickert but whether Kelly was employed as a part-time nanny or as a model to the artist at that time is unknown. Pash suggested that Kelly left Cleveland Street in 1887 so logically there is a time frame of up to a maximum of two years, but in reality probably much less

[240]

than that, during which Mary Kelly could have been called upon to take charge of baby Alice. Kelly became tired with the arrangement, especially since she was not being paid, so it is likely that she was only involved with baby Alice for a few months after which she allegedly made blackmail demands then left the area. Since Sickert lived and worked in South Hampstead, after his return from honeymoon, the location at which he and Kelly looked after Alice is a mystery. Even if Sickert had a studio in the vicinity prior to his marriage, and there is no evidence that he did, then he probably did not maintain such afterwards. Although this is a point to ponder, the absence of any identifiable location where Sickert could look after the child does not mean that he did not do so, and periodically he may have taken Alice to Dieppe to place her with friends. Although rather fragile by way of supporting evidence, the above provides a relatively simple and plausible explanation as to how the lives of Annie and Alice Crook, and Mary Kelly could have overlapped with that of Walter Sickert and indicates the likely relationships between them – but it does not provide a reason why Mary Jane Kelly was murdered in Miller's Court two years later.

To make progress from this point Sickert's mention of blackmail is important to consider, not because that particular event is necessarily of any intrinsic importance, but it introduces blackmail which was a very prevalent form of extortion in that era. Indeed, blackmail and robbery were both commonly associated with prostitutes at the end of the nineteenth century and the extent to which prostitutes and their bullies used both to supplement their incomes should not be underestimated. An interesting and frequently successful ploy was for a woman to approach a man and solicit him and while he stood listening to her, the bully, would emerge from the shadows, knock the man down with a blow and strip him of cash and any other valuables – this is intriguing in connection with the event that Israel Schwarz witnessed allegedly in Berner Street on the night of Elizabeth Strides murder.[21] It was also common for the woman and client to be 'discovered' together by her 'husband' who would then demand payment amounting to robbery in order that the story went no further.

A man engaging the services of a prostitute placed his vulnerability at her mercy and if the prostitute was a male then the risk was even greater. Blackmail did not recognise class distinctions and when Earl Russell, grandson of a prime minister and elder brother of Bertrand Russell, married in 1890 he was shortly thereafter the subject of attempts to extort payment from him by allegations of homosexuality and bestiality allegedly relating to premises in Cranbourn Street, Leicester Square, not an appreciable distance from Cleveland Street.[22]

In 1868 Rachel Leverson, otherwise known as 'Madame Rachel' and described as 'one of the most filthy and dangerous moral pests', was successfully prosecuted for fraud, a charge that understated her extensive activities in extortion and robbery. Leverson was another example of a blackmailer and extortionist who preyed upon those in Victorian society 'who would sooner submit to felony and fraud than that their names should be exposed to the public'.[23] In another contemporary example, one Charles Augustus Howell corresponded with the poet Algernon Charles Swinburne and by trickery elicited from him numerous letters concerned with Swinburne's sexual deviations which he pasted into an album and threatened to pawn unless he received an appreciable payment. The consequence of non payment being that the pawnbroker, who was in collusion with Howell, would sell the album to the highest bidder and a reputation would be ruined. There was nothing fundamentally illegal in this and Howell profited in the process. However, it was reported that he was found outside a Chelsea public house in 1890 with his throat cut and a half-sovereign wedged between his teeth as the reward of a slanderer.[24]

In addition to the suggestion by Florence Pash that Walter Sickert was blackmailed by Mary Kelly shortly after she left his employment as nanny, Gorman Sickert through Knight, stated that Walter Sickert told him that a blackmail attempt was made against a nameless victim in July or August 1888 for, according to Knight, 'a paltry sum' that in other circumstances would have been laughable. The letter originated from the East End but there is no indication to whom or from whom it was sent, although Knight implied that Mary Kelly was involved, or why Walter Sickert would have known anything about it.[25] There are thus suggestions that Mary Kelly attempted blackmail, but it is not entirely clear against whom this was targeted. If Kelly blackmailed Sickert then it was probably only for money that she was owed and I very much doubt that it was a continuing threat. Nonetheless Sickert thought that it was significant enough to mention to Florence Pash but whether or not Kelly was successful in her demand we shall never know. There is thus an inkling that Mary Kelly the nanny was not adverse to a little extortion should the opportunity arise and maybe she saw blackmail as an easier way to earn a living than prostitution.

Regardless as to whether or not she had any active involvement, Mary Kelly would have been aware that number 19 Cleveland Street was a brothel and both she and Annie Crook could identify some of those who availed themselves of the facilities, even if they only viewed from the tobacconist's shop across the road. This knowledge alone would have been insufficient reason to attempt blackmail, but if Kelly actually worked as prostitute at or in connection with the club then she would have far more information at her disposal. Apart from knowing the calibre of the clientele that frequented the club, she would also know their sexual proclivities and may even have personally entertained some of their number. The clientele was distinguished indeed, with no less than the Heir Presumptive, Prince Albert Victor, a regular visitor, and central to the issue.[26]

In order to examine the activities at 19 Cleveland Street it is necessary to leap forward a few years to 1889 when the police raided the club. By any association with the male brothel, Mary Kelly would certainly have acquired knowledge that implicated those in high places in homosexual liaisons, which would have taken a blackmailer of that era into highly productive, but potentially dangerous, territory. Although the police raid on 19 Cleveland Street occurred a year after the murder of Mary Jane Kelly and four or five years after the events linking Walter Sickert, Annie Crook, and Mary Kelly, it is of interest because it tells us three important facts; firstly that the police were previously unaware of the scale and nature of activities that took place in the brothel; secondly it tells us the status of some of the individuals who used the brothel; and thirdly we can see how the authorities reacted to avoid a scandal that involved the future king and other high-profile clients. These three factors were true in 1889 and they were also true earlier, so anyone who had convincing evidence that Prince Albert Victor visited a male brothel possessed powerful and dangerous information. When Charles Hammond moved into Cleveland Street, he had with him a wife, Madame Caroline, who was a French prostitute, and although suggestions are that the brothel at 19 Cleveland Street was a male brothel, it more likely served both homosexual and heterosexual tastes. It was evident from the scandal of 1889 what disastrous consequences would have ensued from revelations of such a nature. The involvement of members of the royal family in heterosexual pursuits, be they extramarital or otherwise and with prostitutes or otherwise, were generally of little or no concern if carried out with discretion. Such activities were tolerated and even royal bastards, be they of Catholic or protestant mothers, were of little consequence since paternity could never be proved and the bulky weight of the State would quickly suffocate any hint of a scandal. But, in spite of Knight's suggestions to the contrary homosexual engagements were a very different matter.[27] Indeed, the political dimensions associated with the 1889 raid were such that press reporting was stifled and there had clearly been manoeuvres to prevent the full facts being exposed in court and spilling into the public domain.[28] 'The problem posed by Cleveland Street was the gap between tolerance of heterosexual promiscuity, which the Prince of Wales [Prince Albert Edward] had taken about as far as it could be stretched, and the horror evoked by the spectre of homosexual prostitution, which was not supposed to exist at all'.[29] Prince Albert Victor was already in receipt of bad press and the newspapers would have loved nothing more than information regarding his presence in a male brothel, so a blackmail threat to give such a story to the press would have been far more likely to succeed than a threat to inform the police. And if the blackmailer could provide lurid details then so much the better. The political consequences could have been catastrophic; the succession would be under threat and the integrity of the monarchy would be permanently scarred. Thus we have a clear potential motive for blackmail and with serious consequences for both the target and the blackmailer, and to permanently silence anyone who threatened to ignite a scandal through salacious revelations would have been much the preferred course of action and would have been undertaken without hesitation.

The raid on 19 Cleveland Street and the events that followed have featured in books, and are otherwise well documented.[30] Significantly, Charles Hammond, fled to France just prior to the raid, but although the police wanted him to be extradited there was no such request on the instruction of the Prime Minister Lord Salisbury. Not surprisingly this inaction initiated rumours of a cover-up and there were suggestions that the pressure for concealment came not from Salisbury but from the Prince of Wales, father of Prince Albert Victor. Clearly the intention was not to bring back Hammond to face charges because to do so would then place his testimony in open court and thereby publicly implicate others in the business. The most serious outcome of this would be that Prince Albert Victor would be named as a frequent visitor to 19 Cleveland Street and a scandal would inevitably follow.

That Prince Albert Victor did visit the brothel is not in doubt even though his sexual orientation may have been.[31] Not that 19 Cleveland Street was the only establishment to cater for homosexual clients and there were others for peripheral sexual tastes. Indeed, it is suggested that Eddy was a member of the notorious *Hundred Guineas Club* off Portland Place which catered for transvestites, and was a frequent visitor.[32] The club is described as, 'by far the most extravagant homosexual club of the period, a much grander affair than Cleveland Street, which by comparison emerges as a *maison de passe*'.[33] At the club the members assumed the names of women, Eddy's assumed name being 'Victoria'.[34] The first trial of Oscar Wilde in 1895 revealed the existence of a male brothel at 13 Little College Street, Westminster, and several brothels in London where men were whipped by women or women by men for sexual gratification were listed by Henry Spencer Ashbee in 1877, with various addresses being in Soho.[35]

The owners of high-class brothels profited greatly from the proclivities of their wealthy and distinguished customers but confidentiality was the cornerstone of their business. A prostitute employed in an exclusive brothel would be required to exercise extreme confidentiality; but prostitutes were not the most conscientious members of Victorian society and their discretion was not gained by appeals to their better nature, but rather by threats of disfigurement and death should they step out of line. The stakes were high and blackmail threats would be met with a swift and uncompromising response. This was potentially a very lucrative opportunity for extortion, but one that carried an extreme penalty for failure. But would the word of a prostitute be enough to galvanise the press into action? Possibly not – the press probably already knew about such establishments and without substantial proof that men of political significance were availing themselves of the facilities, they would not risk being exposed to libel accusations. Any blackmail attempt would clearly stand a far better chance of success if the blackmailer had evidence of a more tangible nature; documents perhaps that would prove accusations.

A prostitute working at Cleveland Street, indeed, a prostitute working at any brothel frequented by London's elite, would have plenty of material for blackmail and the more extreme the activities of the brothel the greater the value of the information. I suspect that Mary Kelly saw an opportunity to use information for profit and she took a gamble; she had the potential to cause a huge amount of damage both to the lives of individuals and even to the credibility of the government and monarchy. But whom did she blackmail? There were generally only two choices; the clients of the brothel, or the owner. Since the Cleveland Street brothel entertained several Members of Parliament apart from Prince Albert Victor, there would have been no shortage of opportunities to threaten individual clients, but it is more likely that she threatened the proprietor of the establishment, and if her knowledge concerned 19 Cleveland Street, then Charles Hammond would have been the target. Even if a threat were made to a client, the matter would almost certainly be referred to the owner of the establishment whose responsibility it would be to ensure a permanent solution. In this regard Kelly seriously underestimated the consequences of her actions. After initiating a blackmail threat she would have little alternative but to leave Marylebone for the East End where she could hide among the noisome clamour, and at this stage she would assume a new identity. Regardless as to the target or success of her venture, arrangements were made for Mary Kelly the blackmailer and loose cannon to be found and eliminated, and the fact that it took two years to do so is of little surprise.

Arrangements for the assassination of Mary Kelly the blackmailer were in hand and the search would not end until she was dead. Unfortunately, there was no shortage of Mary Kellys in the East End, many of whom were also known by a nickname, and in all probability the woman pursued had long since changed her name. Anyone wishing to lose their identity and hide in Whitechapel would have little problem in the 1880s, and whoever was hired to find and kill Mary Kelly probably became a little weary of the quest after two years such that the criteria for establishing the correct identity were rather less stringent than was initially the case. Months of enquiries in public houses and on the streets eventually led the assassin to Mary Jane Kelly who lived in a court off Dorset Street. He discovered that she had moved to the East End at around the same time as her namesake and it was apparent that she once worked in a brothel operated by a French woman.[36] His enquires were discrete and may even have spoken to some of those who gave evidence at the inquest. Perhaps he spoke to Elizabeth Phoenix, to some of the other women in Miller's Court, or even to Joseph Barnett, without them having the slightest suspicion as to the reason for his casual questions. It matters not; the man employed to find and eliminate Mary Kelly had located the closest match yet. He watched her movements and waited for an opportunity. Good fortune was on his side. Kelly's paramour moved out and a serial killer was terrorising Whitechapel. This was a professional killer who planned his deed and probably did not work without an accomplice and in this respect I doubt that Mary Kelly's killer worked alone. He would almost certainly have employed someone to ensure that he was not disturbed while carrying out his work.

Much emphasis is placed on the importance of the statement given by George Hutchinson as he watched Mary Jane Kelly engage with a suspected killer.[37] His vantage point was perfectly positioned opposite Miller's Court. Hutchinson watched Mary Jane Kelly and the suspect when they met and when they went into Miller's court, and he loitered in Dorset Street for three quarters of an hour in case they should reappear. Hutchinson gave a remarkably detailed description of the suspect to the police and this description has come to be regarded by many as a reliable description of Mary Jane Kelly's killer if not of Jack the Ripper. I have already considered Hutchinson's statement to the police, but he also gave an interview to the newspapers in which he repeated pretty much the same story, with the addition of a couple of extra points of identification, most noteworthy being a 'massive gold watch chain, with large red stone attached'.[38] Both versions were otherwise similar and there were no major discrepancies between the two. Abberline believed Hutchinson, and the description of the suspect was widely circulated. However, the problem is not so much with Hutchinson's story, but with Hutchinson himself and there are two aspects of his statement that give reason to question his authenticity; why did he wait until after the inquest had concluded –

three days after the murder – to volunteer his statement to the police; and why did he apparently take such an extraordinary interest in what Kelly was up to?

Hutchinson was almost certainly where he said he was because another witness, Sarah Lewis, noticed a man resembling Hutchinson's description standing opposite the Court at 2.30am, 'as if waiting for someone to come out'. Lewis also saw a man and a woman further on along Dorset Street.[39] Lewis went along Miller's Court so she clearly saw Hutchinson but Hutchinson made no mention of seeing anyone other than Mary Jane Kelly and the suspect. Why Hutchinson waited for three days before coming forward was not explained or at least if there was an explanation it has not survived in print. As for Hutchinson's excessive interest in Kelly's activities he explained to Abberline that he was surprised to see Kelly with such a well-dressed man. This is a weak explanation that may suggest why he noticed the couple but it does not explain why he waited for three quarters of an hour for them to reappear from Miller's Court before he supposedly gave up and moved off. When one also considers the delay in informing the police, it seems on balance that Hutchinson was either lying or not telling the whole truth. He must have known that others had seen him standing in Dorset Street opposite Miller's Court and that alone would implicate him sufficiently to elevate him to suspect status. The fact that he waited until after the inquest may also be significant. Had he been to the proceedings at Shoreditch Town Hall earlier that day then he would have known that Sarah Lewis described his presence which may well have spurred him to talk to the police – after all, he did not know whether someone had actually recognised him as he watched events. Having said that, he undoubtedly placed himself at some risk, and by volunteering the information that he was at the scene he relied very much on the police believing his story. But what better way to improve his credibility than to distract attention with a detailed, and probably deliberately misleading, description of a striking suspect obtained in what was frankly the dimmest of street lighting? And there is only Hutchinson's word that he actually knew Mary Jane Kelly and had seen her before and that they had an exchange during which she asked him for a loan. Hutchinson may have been the observant bystander that he claimed to be, he may have seen absolutely nothing, he may have gone down the Court after Sarah Lewis disappeared and murdered Mary Jane Kelly, or he may have been an accomplice to whoever did cut Kelly to pieces. If he was anything other than the former then he was deceiving in a very dangerous arena and if such were the case then he was a good liar because he convinced the experienced Abberline that his account was the truth. I am very much inclined to suspect otherwise.

Mary Jane Kelly was no blackmailer. She worked as a prostitute, possibly with the collusion of John McCarthy from whom she rented the room. She drank to excess and could not even afford the rent. The excessive facial mutilation of Kelly effectively put her identification beyond certainly thus the assassin was sure to collect his fee.

I suspect that at some point during their association the Mary Kelly known to Walter Sickert mentioned to him what she had witnessed while working in Cleveland Street and what potentially damaging information she had at her disposal – she may have boasted about what she could do. Suggestions that royalty was implicated in events as reported by Sickert probably also emanated from Kelly. But Sickert would not need to know much – only that Mary Kelly had information that she was intent upon using for extortion – and he filled in the rest with speculation over the years and especially after learning of the death of Mary Jane Kelly in 1888. Walter Sickert made many assumptions after the murder of Mary Jane Kelly, probably fuelled by rumour from various sources, and although he had some pieces of a story, he largely came to the wrong conclusions. He related the tale to Florence Pash and also to Joseph Gorman Sickert along with other elements of his life and of his relatives. Pash retold the story to Jean Overton Fuller's mother and from there it passed to Jean Overton Fuller. Gorman Sickert was told the story when he was just thirteen or fourteen years of age by a seventy nine year old Walter Sickert – probably just before he and his wife, the painter Thérèse Lessore, moved to Bathampton and three years before he died. The chances of contamination, distortion and transformation in both cases were high. One cannot help but wonder that if Mary Jane Kelly had been the woman in Cleveland Street and nanny to Walter Sickert then surely she would have related far more about her life and the people she encountered to Joseph Barnett and he in turn would have told the inquest. But such was apparently not the case.

The announcement of the resignation of the Metropolitan Police Commissioner Sir Charles Warren on 9 November, which was also the day of the Lord Mayor's Parade, was a coincidence, and unrelated to the Ripper investigations or to the murder of Mary Jane Kelly. Warren had in fact tendered his resignation on the day before Kelly was murdered. But the offer of a pardon on the 10 November 'to any accomplice not being a person who contrived or actually committed the murder' who gave information leading to the murderer's apprehension and conviction, is of perhaps greater interest. This pardon was issued specifically in connection with the murder of Mary Jane Kelly and in the House of Commons on 23 November the then Home Secretary, Henry Matthews explained that; 'In the case of Kelly there were certain circumstances which were wanting in earlier cases, and which made it more probable that there were other persons, who, at any rate after the crime had assisted the murderer'.

After the murder of Alice McKenzie, Inspector Frederick Abberline was replaced as the officer in charge of the Whitechapel murders by Inspector Henry Moore. Abberline then investigated the Cleveland Street Scandal in 1889 before retiring early aged 49, soon after his promotion to Chief Inspector. Abberline's early retirement after investigating the death of Mary Jane Kelly and the Cleveland Street Scandal should not be regarded as indicative of anything. He merely took advantage of beneficial changes in retirement age and pension rights that came into force through the 1890 Police Bill.

The man who murdered Mary Ann Nichols, Annie Chapman, Elizabeth Stride, Catharine Eddowes, Alice McKenzie, and Frances Coles did not kill Mary Jane Kelly. They were all killed because they were women and probably because they were prostitutes; Mary Jane Kelly was killed by mistake. Jack the Ripper provided a very timely and convenient cloak under which the killer of Mary Jane Kelly could conceal the reason for her death and by and large he succeeded. Kelly's murder was, all things considered, an immaculate deception. The identity of the perpetrator is as illusive as that of Jack the Ripper and perhaps both are destined to remain so. But anyone hoping to find the identity of Mary Jane Kelly's killer will not be rewarded by looking for Jack the Ripper any more than a hunt for the serial killer will be illuminated by studying the details of Kelly's murder.

6: In conclusion

It is tantalising to speculate that the identity of Jack the Ripper, the Whitechapel serial killer who caused such terror among the population of the East End of London towards the final decade of Queen Victoria's reign, is already available and merely awaits discovery among the accumulation of testimony and reports that currently exists. Realistically I suspect that there is sufficient information to point researchers in the right direction and certainly enough against which the validity of suspects can be tested, but in all probability the name of the serial killer is not there for all to see nor in my opinion has it yet been mentioned. The true identity of Jack the Ripper remains a mystery as much today as it did well over a century ago. But even though it is not immediately possible to identify the killer, it is at least possible to characterise him, and by determining exactly how many victims he murdered, and the circumstances of each, there emerges a framework of personality, opportunity, and ability against which suspects can be assessed.

Few events in history have evoked such widespread and continuing interest or generated so much information as the Whitechapel murders and Jack the Ripper. But not all of the information is useful and some of it, a relatively large proportion in fact, is by accident or by design, downright misleading. As time passes, it seems less likely that any further useful information will surface, so the need to accurately assess what we already have, both to consolidate and to open up new directions of investigation, assumes a greater importance. Faced with such an overload of data researchers must be selective, set aside well-established but erroneous beliefs, revert wherever possible to first principles, and pursue an objective and dispassionate assessment. Such was the intention of this approach and whether I have been successful only the future will reveal. There is no doubt that the more familiar one becomes with events of 1888 and thereabouts, the more difficult it is to remain entirely neutral. Above all in this matter it is easy to lose sight of the victims and while I deliberately avoided complicating the evaluation with too many details of the victims' personal lives it makes it seem as though they were lifeless before they died. They were certainly victims before they encountered the Ripper; products of an elitist society that cared so little about those unable to pull themselves from the streets that it regarded them as a form of entertainment.

It is impossible for anyone examining these crimes to be totally dispassionate and the meagre personal possessions found on each woman is a sobering testimony to the quality of life that each had to endure. It is easy to forget that what each woman wore or carried with her was all she owned. The scrap of muslin and a comb that Chapman kept in her dress and a piece of broken mirror that Nichols owned were the last paraphernalia of womanhood that they clutched to, all aspirations long since evaporated into the noisome filth of Victorian London.

It was not the intention of this exercise to be sensationalistic, but no investigation into the Whitechapel murders would be complete without a certain amount of speculation. Theories by definition start as speculation and mature as emerging information migrates towards them, or wither if ultimately unsupported. I would hope that I have used the mass of information unearthed by diligent researchers over past decades to good effect and just because the true identity of Jack the Ripper remains elusive does not mean that progress can not be made. It is as important to exclude suspects as it is to identify them, and hopefully with this investigation there is a new set of criteria by which suspects can be assessed.

By showing that there were probably six victims and not five, and by demonstrating that Mary Jane Kelly was probably not a victim of a serial killer, the whole basis for examination has changed. And when identifying potential suspects it is also important to remember that not just anyone can be a serial killer. Moreover, such was the manner in which the Ripper executed his victims that he was unique even among his peers.

Table 1

Injuries sustained and the circumstances of death as detailed in post mortem reports or
inquest accounts for each of the five canonical Ripper murder victims
(see notes at end of table)

	NICHOLS	CHAPMAN	STRIDE	EDDOWES	KELLY	SIGNATURE
First names	Mary Ann	Annie	Elizabeth	Catharine	Mary Jane	
Occupation	Prostitute	Prostitute	Prostitute	Prostitute	Prostitute	Yes
Age at death	43	47	44	46	25	Possibly
Height	5ft 2in	5ft 0in	5ft 5in	5ft 0in	5ft 7in	Possibly
Date (d.m.y) and day of death	31.08.1888 Friday	08.09.1888 Saturday	30.09.1888 Sunday	30.09.1888 Sunday	09.11.1888 Friday	Possibly (Around weekends)
Time of death	3.30-3.40am	5.30-5.45am	12.40-1.00am	1.30-1.44am	2.30-4.15am	
Time body found	3.40am	6.00am	1.00am	1.44am	10.45am	
Victim intoxicated at death	Probably	Probably not	Probably not	Probably not	Probably	
Indoors/outdoors	Outdoors	Outdoors	Outdoors	Outdoors	Indoors	Yes (Outdoors)
Location	Street	Yard	Yard	Street	Lying on bed	Yes
Victim killed at scene	Yes	Yes	Yes	Yes	Yes	Yes
Light/dark outside	Dark	After dawn	Dark	Dark	Dark	Yes

Table 1 (Continued)

	NICHOLS	CHAPMAN	STRIDE	EDDOWES	KELLY	SIGNATURE
Lighting at time of death	None obvious	Daylight	None obvious	Limited from streetlamps	Low level and candle possibly	
Time taken with victim	<5 mins	<15 mins	<5 mins	5-10 mins	<30 mins	
Position when fatal wound inflicted (opinion of pathologist)	On ground suggested by coroner	On ground suggested by coroner	While falling to the ground	Lying on the ground	Lying on bed	
Death by	Haemorrhage from carotid	Haemorrhage from carotid	Haemorrhage from carotid	Haemorrhage from carotid	Haemorrhage from carotid	Yes
By wound to	Neck	Neck	Neck	Neck	Neck	Yes
Number cuts to neck	2	2	1	1	1 probably	Yes
Direction of cut of neck wound	Left to right by inference	Left to right	Left to right	Left to right by inference	Right to left by inference	Yes (left to right)
Fatal bleeding from which side	Both sides	Both sides	Left	Left	Right	Yes Left
Distribution of blood at crime scene	Minimal	Minimal	Minimal	Minimal	Considerable	Yes (Minimal)
Trachea severed	Yes	Yes by inference	Yes	Yes	Yes	Yes
Defensive wounds	None	Possibly (minor)	None	None	Possibly (minor)	

Tables

[252]

Table 1 (Continued)

	NICHOLS	CHAPMAN	STRIDE	EDDOWES	KELLY	SIGNATURE
Killer disturbed	Probably	Probably not	Probably	Probably not	Probably not	
Injuries from attempts to subdue victim	Bruising to jaws	Bruising to chin	None	None	None mentioned	
Fully clothed	Yes	Yes	Yes	Yes	Chemise	**Yes**
Clothing cut	No	No	No	No	Not mentioned	**Yes (Absence)**
Clothing torn	No	No	No	Bodice only	Not mentioned	**Yes (Absence)**
Clothing disturbed	Yes	Yes	No	Yes	Almost naked	**Yes**
Attempted suffocation or strangulation	None	Yes	**None**	**None**	None mentioned	**Yes (Absence)**
Screaming heard	No	No	No	No	Maybe	**Yes (Absence)**
Indication of struggle	None	**None**	**None**	**None**	**None**	**Yes (Absence)**
Stabbing injuries (external)	**None**	**None**	**None**	Incidental stab to groin	**None**	**Yes (Absence)**
Mutilation - facial	None	None	None	Considerable	Extensive	
Body cavities opened	Abdomen	Abdomen	None	Abdomen	Abdomen Thorax	**Yes (Abdomen)**

Tables

Table 1 (Continued)

	NICHOLS	CHAPMAN	STRIDE	EDDOWES	KELLY	SIGNATURE
Mutilation - organs removed from body	None	Yes	None	Yes	Yes	
Specific mutilation - other	None	None	None	None	Breasts	Yes (Absence)
Organs removed from crime scene	None	Uterus	None	Uterus Kidney (one)	Heart	Yes
Attempt to conceal body	None	None	None	None	None	Yes
Opinion of pathologist as to number of weapons	Single knife	Single knife	Single knife	Single knife	None given	
Opinion of pathologist as to type of weapon used	Long bladed knife – moderately sharp	Very sharp knife with thin narrow blade at least 5" long	Very sharp knife but not necessarily pointed	Sharp pointed knife 6" blade	Sharp by inference	Yes (Sharp or very sharp)
Opinion of pathologist as to skill of killer	Some	Considerable	Some	Considerable	Limited by inference	Yes (Skilled)
Opinion of pathologist as to handedness of killer	Right by inference	Right by inference	Right by inference	Right by inference	Left by inference	Yes (Right)
Probable approach of attack	From behind	From front	From behind	From behind	From left side	

Table 1 (Continued)

	NICHOLS	CHAPMAN	STRIDE	EDDOWES	KELLY	SIGNATURE
Legs drawn up – knees bent	Legs extended	Legs drawn up	Legs drawn up	Right leg bent left extended	N/A	
Other relevant points	Killer likely disturbed and progress halted		Killer likely disturbed and progress halted		So badly mutilated finer points of pathology lost	
Name of coroner	Baxter	Baxter	Baxter	Langham	MacDonald	
Date inquest opened and closed	01.09.1888 22.09.1888	10.09.1888 26.09.1888	01.10.1888 23.10.1888	04.10.1888 11.10.1888	12.11.1888 12.11.1888	
Names of pathologists or medical investigators	H Llewellyn	GB Phillips	FW Blackwell GB Phillips	FG Brown WS Saunders GW Sequeira GB Phillips	GB Phillips T Bond FG Brown	

Table 2

Injuries sustained and the circumstances of death as detailed in post mortem reports or inquest accounts for each of the remaining Whitechapel murder victims compared for serial killer signature components*
(see notes at end of table)

	SMITH	TABRAM	MYLETT	McKENZIE	COLES	DIMMOCK
First names	Emma Elizabeth	Martha	Rose	Alice	Frances	Emily
Occupation	**Prostitute**	**Prostitute**	**Prostitute**	**Prostitute**	**Prostitute**	**Prostitute**
Age at death	**45**	**39**	26	**40**	26	22
Height	**5ft 2in**	**5ft 3in**	**5ft 2in**	**5ft 4in**	**5ft 0in**	'Tall'
Date (d.m.y) and day of death/attack	03.04.1888 Tuesday	07.08.1888 Tuesday	20.12.1888 Thursday	17.07.1889 Wednesday	13.02.1891 **Friday**	12.09.1907 Thursday
Time of death	Attacked at 1.30am died following day from injuries	2.00-3.30am probably at around 2.30am	1.45-4.15am probably at around 3.30am	12.30-12.50am	2.13am	12.30-3.30am
Indoors/outdoors	**Outdoors**	**Outdoors**	**Outdoors**	**Outdoors**	**Outdoors**	Indoors
Location	**Street**	On landing	**Yard**	**Street**	**Street**	Lying on bed
Victim killed at scene	Died later	**Yes**	Probably	**Yes**	**Yes**	**Yes**
Light/dark outside	**Dark**	**Dark**	**Dark**	**Dark**	**Dark**	**Dark**

Table 2 (Continued)

	SMITH	TABRAM	MYLETT	McKENZIE	COLES	DIMMOCK
Death by	Peritonitis	Multiple stab wounds	Strangulation	Haemorrhage from carotid	Haemorrhage from carotid	Haemorrhage from carotid
By wound to	Trauma vagina	Chest and abdomen	N/A	Neck (2 cuts)	Neck (3 cuts)	Neck (1 cut)
Direction of cut of neck wound	N/A	N/A	N/A	Left to right inferred	Left to right (2) and right to left (1)	Left to right
Fatal bleeding from which side	N/A	N/A	N/A	Left	Left	Left
Distribution of blood at crime scene	N/A	N/A	N/A	Minimal	Minimal	Minimal
Trachea severed	N/A	N/A	N/A	No	Yes	Yes
Fully clothed	Yes	Yes	Yes	Yes	Yes	Naked
Clothing cut or torn	No	No	No	No	No	N/A
Clothing disturbed	No	Yes but in struggle	No	Yes	No	N/A
Attempted suffocation or strangulation	None	None	Cause of death	None	None	None
Screaming heard	N/A	No	No	No	No	No

Table 2 (Continued)

	SMITH	TABRAM	MYLETT	McKENZIE	COLES	DIMMOCK
Indication of struggle	N/A	Yes	**None**	**None**	**None**	**None**
Stabbing injuries (external)	**None**	Yes (39 wounds)	**None**	**None**	**None**	**None**
Body cavities opened	N/A	None apart from stab wounds	None	Superficial cuts to abdomen	None	None
Specific mutilation - other	None	None	None	None	None	None
Organs removed from crime scene	N/A	N/A	N/A	N/A	N/A	N/A
Attempt to conceal body	N/A	**None**	**None**	**None**	**None**	Covered by blanket
Opinion of pathologist as to type of weapon used	Blunt instrument	More than one knife used	Cord – no weapon	**Knife with short pointed blade**	**Knife – sharp not very sharp**	**Knife - sharp long blade**
Opinion of pathologist as to skill of killer	N/A	N/A	N/A	N/A beyond cut to throat	N/A beyond cut to throat	N/A beyond cut to throat
Opinion of pathologist as to handedness of killer	N/A	**Right**	N/A	**Evidence indicates right**	**Right inferred**	**Right inferred**

Table 2 (Continued)

	SMITH	TABRAM	MYLETT	McKENZIE	COLES	DIMMOCK
Other relevant points	Victim saw her three assailants	Possibly murdered by a soldier or more than one assailant	Doubt as to whether murder by client or accident	Killer likely disturbed and progress halted	Killer likely disturbed and progress halted	Killer would have had plenty of time to mutilate but did not do so

* Established in Table 1

Notes on tables:

Table 1

SIGNATURE – an entry in this column indicates that feature to be a possible component of the killer's 'signature'

N/A – not applicable

Entries in bold type are common to three or more murders and may be components of the serial killer's signature

Entries in normal type indicate characteristics that are neutral or are contrary to the features of the other murders and may indicate exclusion from the series.

NICHOLS: The pathologist suggested that cuts to the throat followed mutilation but the coroner effectively overruled that in his summary. The pathologist further suggested the assailant to be left-handed but such a conclusion doesn't really follow from the circumstances of the killing.

Table 2

Details for Emily Dimmock are also included because of suggestions that she was a victim of the Whitechapel serial killer

Entries in bold type are characteristics that may be identified as being components of the serial killer's signature

Entries in normal type indicate characteristics that are neutral or are contrary to the features of the other murders and may indicate exclusion from the series.

N/A – not applicable

Diagram 1 – Wounds to the neck and torso of Mary Ann Nichols

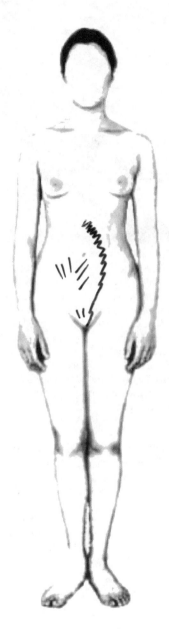

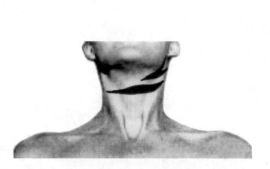

NECK: Two distinct cuts commencing on the left side. The first four inches in length and one inch below the jaw line from a point immediately below the left ear and the second cut starting just in front of the first and across the throat to eight inches in length. Vessels completely severed on both sides

TORSO: Primary wound towards the left side of the abdomen from base of sternum to pubis. Deep cut through musculature exposing abdominal organs. Multiple smaller and superficial cuts on the right side of the abdomen.

Diagram 2 – Wounds to the neck and torso of Annie Chapman

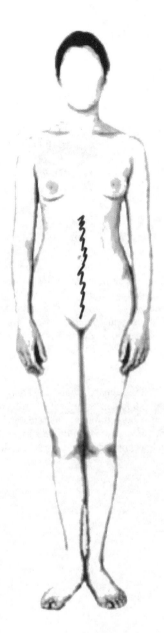

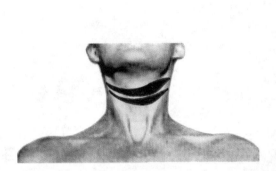

NECK: Almost certainly two distinct cuts reaching right around the neck, but medical testimony is not clear. There were two cut marks on the bone of the cervical vertebrae one-half inch apart strongly indicative of two separate cuts although at the surface they may have coincided. Philips referred to cuts in the plural and the coroner in his summary quite specifically states that Chapman's throat was cut in two places. Vessels completely severed on both sides.

TORSO: Vague reference only to the nature of the primary cut to the abdomen. Philips suggests that the abdominal cavity was entirely laid open suggesting a wound from the lower end of the sternum to the pubis. There were probably lateral cuts also to allow the skin to be reflected. Two portions of the abdominal skin were removed completely with some of the abdominal organs.

Diagram 3 – Wounds to the neck and torso of Elizabeth Stride

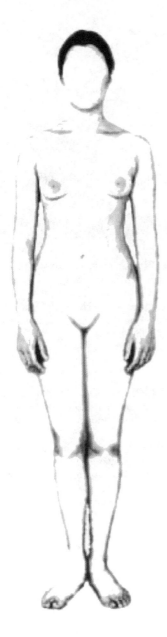

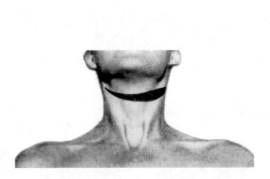

NECK: A single six inch long incision from left to right, being deeper on the left side and more superficial on the right side. Vessels almost completely severed on the left side but not injured on the right.

TORSO: There were no mutilations and no abdominal wounds to Elizabeth Stride.

Diagram 4 – Wounds to the neck and torso of Catharine Eddowes

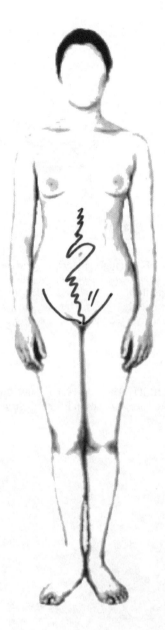

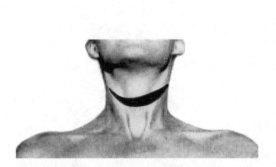

NECK: A single cut six to seven inches in length across and below the vocal cords and through to the bone on the left side. More superficial on the right side. Vessels completely severed on the right side and partially severed on the left side.

TORSO: Extensive abdominal mutilation - the primary incision into the abdominal cavity was depicted on a drawing by the City Surveyor and is clearly visible on the mortuary image of Eddowes' corpse after reconstruction. The primary wound did not extend beyond the abdomen – the thoracic wound apparent on the mortuary image was a consequence of the post mortem examination.

Diagram 5 – Wounds to the neck and torso of Alice McKenzie

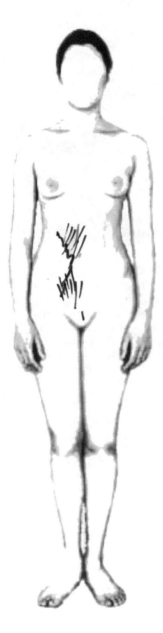

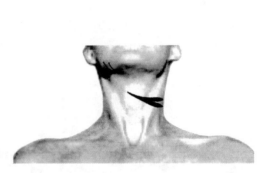

NECK: Deep clean wounds. Two cuts each three inches in length from the left side of the neck to just above the larynx. Cuts made slightly upwards with corresponding marks on the lower jaw. Cuts coincided leaving a triangle of skin, but testimony not altogether clear. Vessels completely severed on the left side but uninjured on the right side.

TORSO: According to rather vague testimony the principle wound was some seven inches in length and commenced seven inches beneath the right nipple, inclining inwards then outwards. Generally the wound cut into only the superficial skin layer apart from a three to four inch length that penetrated the subcutis at the lower aspect of the wound. In addition to the principle wound there were multiple superficial scorings, marks and scratches at the upper and lower ends of the principle wound. The abdominal musculature was not cut and the abdomen not penetrated

Diagram 6 – Wounds to the neck and torso of Frances Coles

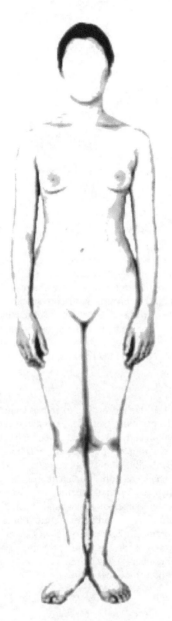

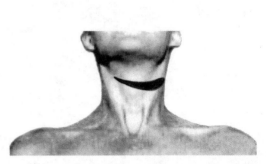

NECK: According to medical testimony there were three distinct wounds to Coles' throat, two passing from left to right and one in the opposite direction. All three cuts were made within the same wound and could only be distinguished internally. The composite wound was deepest on the left side. Vessels completely severed on the left side but uninjured on the right side.

TORSO: There were no mutilations and no abdominal wounds to Frances Coles

Diagram 7 – Wounds to the neck and torso of Mary Jane Kelly

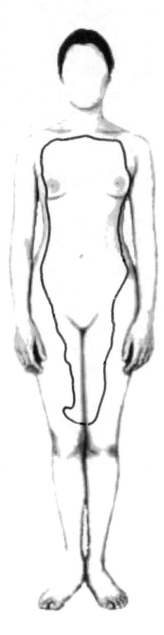

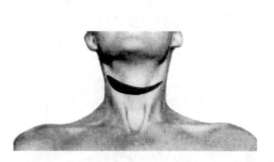

NECK: At least two cuts as evidenced by marks on the cervical vertebrae but these were possibly within the same wound. Cuts inflicted from right to left being deeper on the right side. Vessels completely severed on the right side but probably uninjured on the left side.

TORSO: Extensive mutilation with removal of skin from the whole of the abdomen, inner thighs, and thorax

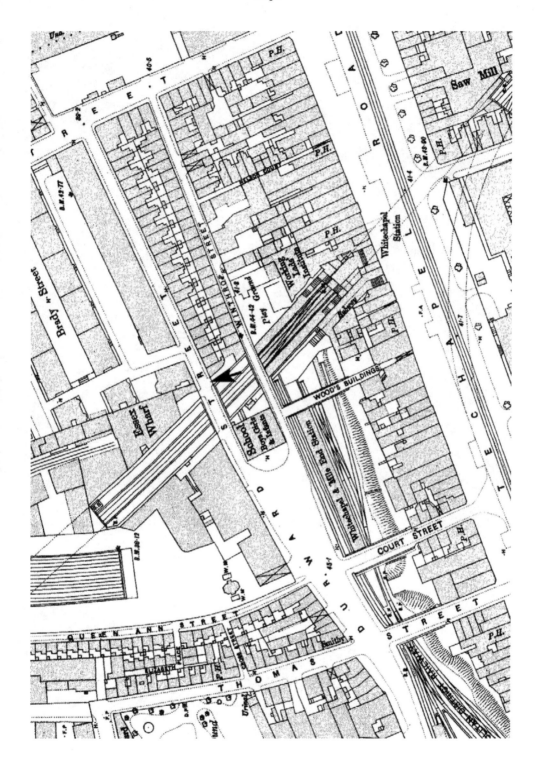

Map 1 – Site of the murder of Mary Ann Nichols at Bucks Row (Durward Street)

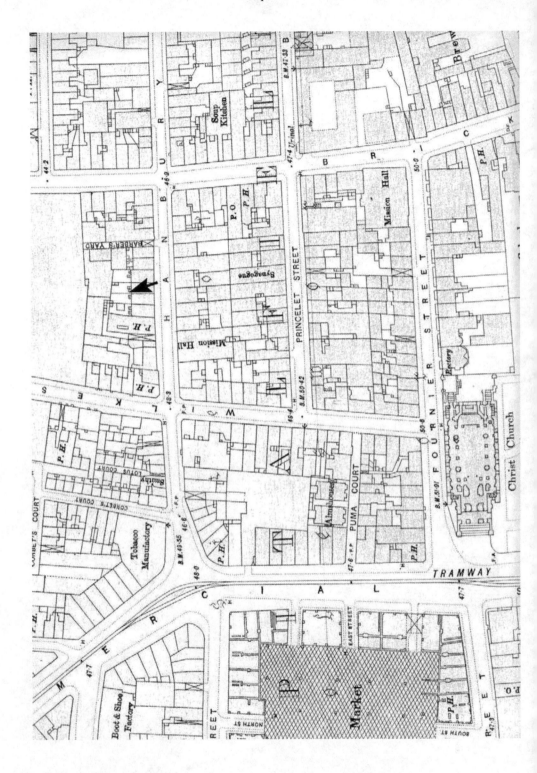

Map 2 – Site of the murder of Annie Chapman at 29 Hanbury Street

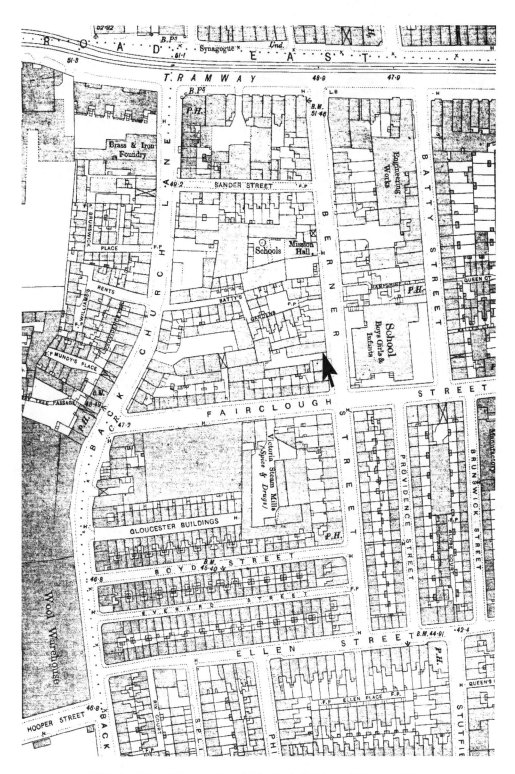

Map 3 – Site of the murder of Elizabeth Stride at 40 Berner Street

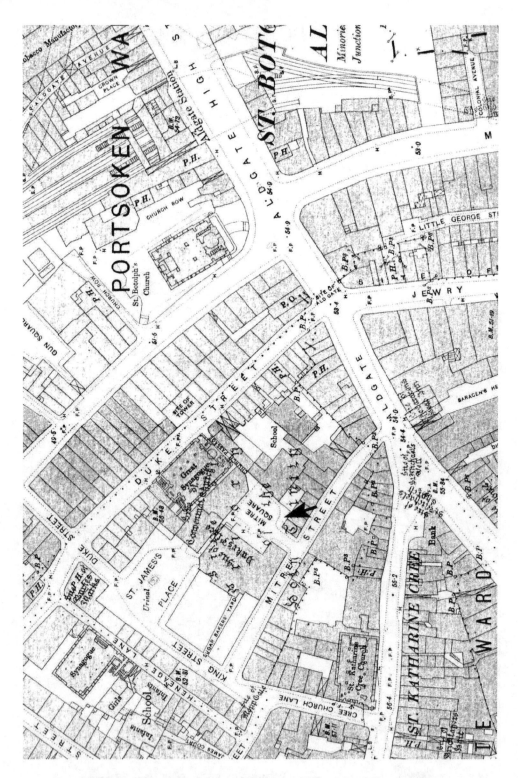

Map 4 – Site of the murder of Catharine Eddowes at Mitre Square

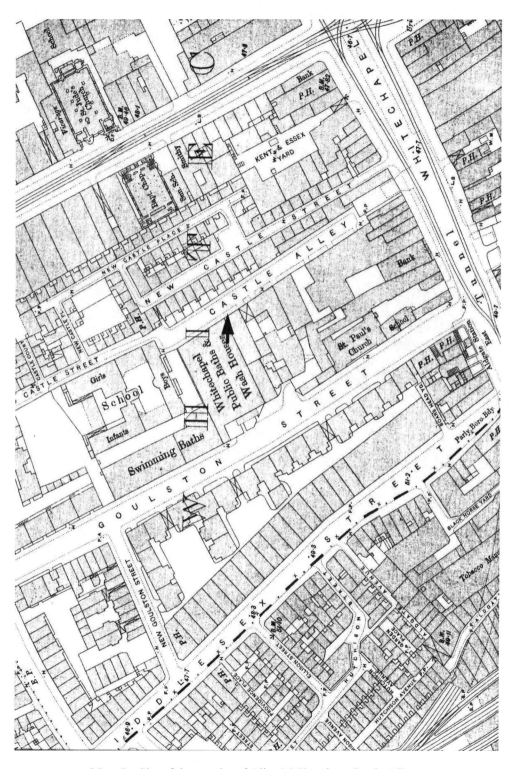

Map 5 – Site of the murder of Alice McKenzie at Castle Alley

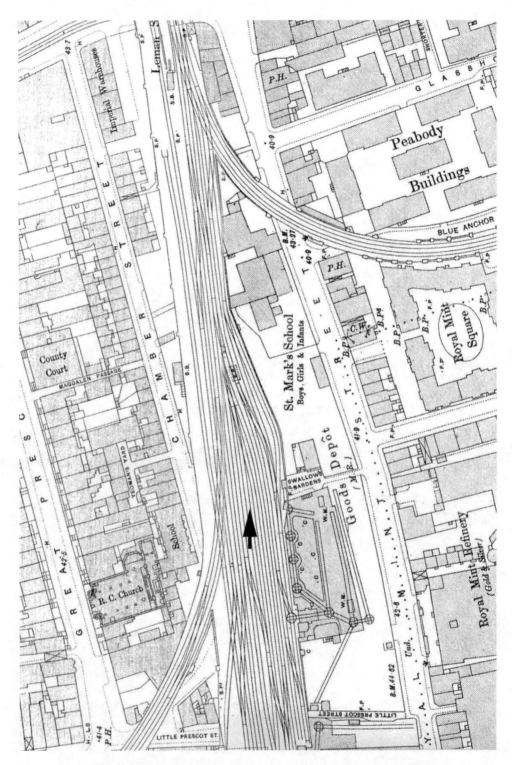

Map 6 – Site of the murder of Frances Coles at Swallow Gardens
(beneath elevated railway)

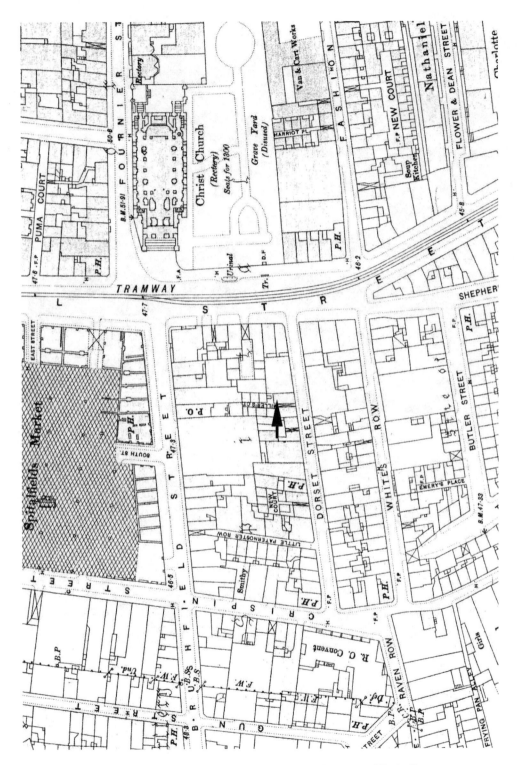

Map 7 – Site of the murder of Mary Jane Kelly at 13 Miller's Court

Illustration 1: The crime scene image of Mary Jane Kelly

Notes and Bibliography

Section 1: Conclusions are only as good as the data upon which they are based

1. MJ/SPC, NE1888, Box 3, Case Paper 19 (London Metropolitan Archives)

2. *The Daily Telegraph*, 13 November, 1888

3. *The Star*, 12 November, 1888

4. MEPO 3/3155

5. MEPO 3/3153, ff 10-18

6. MEPO 3/140, ff 177-83

Section 2: The Whitechapel Murders

1. MEPO 3/140, ff 177-83

2. Cornwell P (2002) *Portrait of a Killer – Jack the Ripper Case Closed*. London: Little Brown, p 300

3. St B.G./Wh/123/19 (London Metropolitan Archives)

4. Dew W (1938) *I Caught Crippen: Memoirs of Ex-Chief Inspector Walter Dew CID*. London: Blackie and Son, p 92

5. MEPO 3/140, ff 34; 36-59

6. Also reported as Catherine Millett or Lizzie Davis

7. MEPO 3/140, ff 1-2; MEPO 3/143; MEPO 3/143 ff B, E-Q; HO 144/221/A49301H, ff 2-14

8. MEPO 3/143, ff P-Q

9. Knight B (1997) *Simpson's Forensic Medicine* – Eleventh Edition. London: Arnold, p 90

10. HO 144/21/A49301H, ff 7-14

11. Anderson R (1910) *The Lighter Side of My Official Life*. London: Hodder and Stoughton, pp 137-9

12. *The Star*, 24 December 1888

13. MEPO 3/140, ff 123, 134-80; MEPO 2/227, f 9; MEPO 3/3153, f 20; HO 144/221/A49301K, ff 1-8

14. MEPO 3/140, ff 136-40

15. MEPO 3/140, ff141-7. Hibbert, Hibberd, Hebbert all reported for the anatomist from Westminster Hospital – Hibbert is used in this text

16. MEPO 3/140, ff 178-80

17. Maps examined were: Ordnance Survey 1894-6 Edition - 1:1056 scale, Ordnance Survey, Southampton. The following sheets collectively cover all of the Ripper murders: London Sheet VII; 57 (Chapman), 58 (Nichols), 66, (Eddowes), 67 (Stride, Eddowes, Coles and McKenzie), and 77 (Coles). London Sheet VII; 47 was also examined for the location of Church Row in connection with the murder of Chapman. In addition reference was made to the Ordnance Survey 1873-80 Edition – 1: 2500 scale, Ordnance Survey, Southampton. London Sheet XXXVI.

Mary Nichols

18. Sugden P (2002) *The Complete History of Jack the Ripper*. London: Robinson, p 42

19. MEPO 3/140, ff 235-41; HO 144/220/A49301, f 16; HO 144/220/A49301B, ff 177-9; HO 144/221 A49301C, ff 6-11; ff 128-34.

20. Nichols' body was found in the Bethnal Green police district, headquarters at Bethnal Green Road Police Station, but under the jurisdiction of the County of Middlesex (South Eastern District) coroner. The coroner's office was at 33 Spital Square, Whitechapel. Dr Rees Ralph Llewellyn was the Police Surgeon for 'J' or Bethnal Green Division whereas George Bagster Phillips was the surgeon for 'H' or Whitechapel Division.

21. Emma Holland was also reported as Emily Holland and Jane Oram

22. In fact, the warehouse was known as the Essex Wharf, and Buck's Row was a narrow street running off Brady Street in the east. Buck's Row ran parallel to Winthrop Street before both merged at the board school before running into White's Row, which then continued as far as Baker's Row. Buck's Row and Winthrop Street ran parallel to Whitechapel Road and were little distance from the main thoroughfare. Several streets and courts ran between Winthrop Street or White's Row and Whitechapel Road. Soon after the murder Buck's Row was renamed Durward Street

23. Ambulances were little more than handcarts

24. MEPO 3/140, ff 239-41

25. HO 144/221/A49301C, ff 129-34

Annie Chapman

26. Certain items were arranged close to the body – they may not of course have been Chapman's possessions

27. MEPO 3/140, ff 9-31, 242-56; HO 144/221/A49301C, ff 13-21, 136-45, pages 3f and 6e-f

28. *The Times,* 10 September 1888.

29. On the Ordnance Survey 1873-80 Edition map Hanbury Street is called Browns Lane. Public Houses are identified on both the 1873-80 and on the 1894-6 maps and correlate with census records for 1891 and 1901 as being at numbers 17 and 23 giving reference points to identify the location of number 29. Later photographs of 29 Hanbury Street show the frontage to have two doors from the street and a conventional shop front and window. There is no evidence to suggest that the 1888 building was like this and these are almost certainly later alterations.

30. Dimensions determined from OS scale 1/1056 1894-6 edition maps

31. Cooksley, Copsey, or Huxley, depending upon the reference source, but also reported as Mr and Mrs Copsey who were cigar makers

32. National Meteorological Library and Archives: The Meteorological Office Bracknell. Legal timing was first established by Act of Parliament in Great Britain in 1880 and Greenwich Mean Time (GMT) was the standard across the country. British Summer Time (BST) was originally introduced as a wartime measure in 1916 and continued. Thus, in 1888, and for all of the Whitechapel murders there was no daylight saving measure in operation and all times given are GMT.

33. There is some confusion as to the exact location of the man and woman; reporting in *The Times* suggests that they were 'close against the shutters of No 29'; whereas *The Daily Telegraph* reported Long as saying that they were standing between number 29 and Brick Lane. This discrepancy isn't crucial, but clearly if they were standing right outside number 29 then this increases the likelihood that they were Chapman and her killer moments before they made their way to the back yard.

34. Long reportedly referred to the man as being of foreign appearance and shabby genteel but she may have meant, or actually said and was misreported by accident or design, gentile. Genteel appears in both *The Times* and *The Daily Telegraph* and on other occasions of reporting. If Long intended to refer to the man as shabby gentile then this would suggest that he was foreign but not Jewish, and if shabby genteel then she thought him to be a foreigner who had seen better times.

35. *The Daily Telegraph,* 20 September 1888

36. There is some confusion as to the location of Long's place of residence not least because her address from her own testimony was reported as 198 Church Row in *The Times* and merely as Church Row in *The Daily Telegraph* but a police report of 19 October and the coroner's summing up of the case, as reported in both newspapers, detail Long's address respectively as Church Street, Whitechapel according to the coroner, and number 32 according to the police report. The only Church Street in Whitechapel that would give Long an easterly or northerly approach to Spitalfields market was actually the eastern end of Hanbury Road which, according to 1873-80 OS maps, was formerly known as Church Street. By 1896 Hanbury Street had replaced Browns Lane, Montague Street, Preston Street, and Church Street running from Commercial Street to Bakers Row. However, the most likely address for Elizabeth Long was Church Row, which was situated in Bethnal Green between Bethnal Green High Street and Hare Street. In 1888 St Matthew's Church, school, grounds, and mortuary, occupied most of the eastern side of Church Row with a few even-numbered residential properties. The western side of Church Row was almost entirely residential with house numbers running from 1 to 61. There was however not a number 32 in Church Row, and there certainly was not a 198. Long's address was reported as Church Row in inquest reports so there is no good reason to use any other address even though the number remains uncertain.

37. I have walked the distance comfortably in seven minutes

38. Chisholm A, DiGrazia C-M, Yost D (2002) *The News from Whitechapel: Jack the Ripper and The Daily Telegraph*. Jefferson: McFarland, pp 81-86

39. I have walked the distance comfortably in two and a half minutes

40. *The Daily Telegraph,* 10 September 1888

41. *The Daily Telegraph* referred to the resident nurse at the Whitechapel Infirmary as Sarah Simonds, but *The Times* reported her name as Mary Elizabeth Simonds

42. This is taken from *The Times* account on 14 September 1888 which differs factually from that reported in *The Daily Telegraph*, the latter stating that; 'The ordinary post-mortem case perhaps does not contain such a weapon', which is incorrect reporting

43. *The Lancet*, 29 September 1888 p 637

44. HO 144/221/A49301C, ff 137-45

45. Body temperature is currently employed as one of several indicators and even using internal measurement by rectal temperature or by a thermometer inserted into the liver through a cut in the skin, a calculation relative to ambient temperature is required

46. According to meteorological records for the Whitechapel area, the temperature on 8 September did not fall below 47° F (8°C) after a high on the previous day of 66°F (19°C) National Meteorological Library and Archives: The Meteorological Office Bracknell

47. Knight B (1997) *Simpson's Forensic Medicine* – Eleventh Edition. London: Arnold, pp 20-2

48. *Ibid*

49. *The Lancet*, 29 September 1888 p 637

50. *Ibid*

51. *Ibid*

52. Begg P (2003). *Jack the Ripper: The Definitive History*. London: Longman, p 165. Reporting in the *Alderley and Wilmslow Advertiser*, 5 October 1888, suggested that the *British Medical Journal* reported that 'the foreign physician who sought to purchase specimens [of uterus] was a gentleman of the highest respectability' and that 'he did not offer a large price and left London 18 months ago'.

Elizabeth Stride

53. MEPO 3/140/221/A49301C, ff204-16; HO 144/221/A49301C, ff 110-18, 147-59, 199-201

54. A report in *The Woodford Times* on 5 October 1888 described Berner Street (now named Henriques Street) as, 'a quiet thoroughfare running from Commercial Road down to the London, Tilbury, and Southend Railway'. In fact, it did not run that far or at least not directly so.

55. *The London Evening News,* 1 October 1888

56. *Ibid*

57. Marshall's assertion that he recognised her by her face and clothing more likely relates to his identification of her body at the mortuary rather than to the time he saw her in Berner Street

58. A few yards from where the body was found according to *The Daily Telegraph*, and a few yards up Berner Street according to *The Times* report of the same testimony.

59. 12.40am according to *The Daily Telegraph* and 12.35am in *The Times*

60. *The Times* on 1 October 1888 and *The Woodford Times* on 5 October 1888

61. Begg P, Fido M, Skinner K (1996) *The Jack the Ripper A-Z*. Third Edition. London: Headline, p 237

62. HO 144/221/A49301C, ff 148-59

63. According to the report in *The Times* he was of stoutish build, but *The Daily Telegraph* reported that Brown thought him to be of average build

64. *Daily News,* 1 October 1888

65. *Ibid* – this second reference in the same edition may have been a confused consequence of Fanny Mortimer's reported observation.

66. *The Daily Telegraph*, 6 October 1888. MEPO 3/140/221/A49301C, ff 211-16

67. Rumbelow D (1987) *The Complete Jack the Ripper.* London: Guild, p 75

68. Knight B (1997) *Simpson's Forensic Medicine* – Eleventh Edition. London: Arnold, pp 22-3

69. It has been suggested that Schwartz gave his evidence *in camera* since it was regarded so highly by the police who were anxious to protect a key witness but there is also the possibility that because he could not speak English his testimony was given only in writing.

70. MEPO 3/140 ff 204-6

71. HO 144/221/A49301C, ff 148-59. *The Star*, 1 October 1888

72. The shout of 'Lipski' was thus *to* the pipeman and not *at* the pipeman suggesting that it related to Schwartz.

73. Chisholm A, DiGrazia C-M, Yost D (2002) *The News from Whitechapel: Jack the Ripper and The Daily Telegraph*. Jefferson: McFarland, p 132; and Begg P (2003). *Jack the Ripper: The Definitive History*. London: Longman, p 188

74. It is suggested that Fanny Mortimer was Letchford's sister although her maiden name was Skipp. Begg P, Fido M, Skinner K (1996) *The Jack the Ripper A-Z*. Third Edition. London: Headline, p 247

75. Back Church Lane, Berner Street, Batty Street, or Christian Street all led from Commercial Road and all had passages and alleyways and public houses. Back Church Lane alone ran uninterrupted as far as Pinchen Street and the railway arches.

76. Ordinarily if one were to use an infamous name in order to insult another person then the inference is that the other person is committing a crime equal to that of the infamy. Israel Lipski was a Jew who was convicted of murdering Miriam Angel by pouring nitric acid down her throat fifteen months earlier. Lipski was hanged for the crime, and for a while thereafter 'Lipski' was used as a derogatory anti Semitic term. However, it could also have a more specific derogative use by suggesting 'woman killer'. With this in mind it is possible that the pipeman shouted 'Lipski' at the 'half-tipsy' man and came to the rescue of the woman who was being assaulted.

77. Letchford's and Mortimer's comments reported in the *Daily News,* 1 October 1888

Catharine Eddowes

78. MEPO 3/3153, ff1-4; 3/142, ff 2-3, ff 491-2; HO 144/221/A49301C, ff 162-81, ff 183-98

79. Inquest papers are filed in the Corporation of London Records Office – file refs Coroner's inquest (L), 1888, No. 135, Catharine Eddowes inquest, 1888 (Corporation of London Record Office)

80. This would be at a walking speed of 3.75 mph

81. *East London Observer*, 13 October 1888

82. The Imperial Club was unlikely to have been at 16 and 17 Duke Street since the even-numbered properties were on the north eastern side of Duke Street with odd numbers on the south western side. In the 1891 census number 17 was a private residence and 14–16 were uninhabited thus the more likely address placing the Club almost opposite the entrance to Church passage

83. In Lawende's inquest statement his distance from the club is given as 15 to 16ft; in *The Times* this distance is reported as 9 to 10yds or 27 to 30ft and in *The Daily Telegraph* he suggested that the couple were 9 or 10ft away from him. In fact, from scaled maps the distance from the entrance to Church Passage to the Imperial Club could have been no less that 25ft or so if directly across the road, so the suggestion that the Club was 9 to 10yds away as reported in *The Times* is reasonable. If Lawende passed within 9-10ft of the couple then he must have been walking past them and in the road

84. *Evening News,* 9 October 1888

85. Begg P, Fido M, Skinner K (1996) *The Jack the Ripper A-Z.* Third Edition. London: Headline, pp 247-8

86. *Evening News,* 9 October 1888

87. This is the Metropolitan Police and Home office version of the agreed wording – Constable Long misspelled 'Juwes' as 'Jews', and the City Police, as noted by Detective Constable Halse recorded the graffito as: 'The Juwes are not The men That will be Blamed for nothing'

88. Middlesex Street was formerly Petticoat Lane, but renamed in 1846 to avoid reference to women's underwear.

89. There are thus two references to Bright's disease, but this second recollection comes 22 years after the event. Richard Bright (1789-1858) is best known for his description of dropsy or oedema associated with kidney disease. Bright made the connection between dropsy and damage to the renal glomeruli, the filtration units of the kidney. The condition was known from the 1840s, as *Morbus Brightii*, or Bright's disease, but is now more commonly known as glomerulonephritis. The important feature of the disease as far as recognising signs in the intact organ is that the glomeruli are located in renal cortex or the outer portion of the kidney, and damage to the glomeruli would present as congestion or a darkening of the renal cortex in relation to the rest of the organ.

90. *The Sunday Times*, 21 October 1888

91. Present day preservatives or fixatives usually contain a solution of formaldehyde, which is very effective at killing bacteria and fixing the proteins thereby preventing autolysis. Alcohol is a popular preservative but little used as a tissue fixative today because it tends to dry out and harden the tissue

Alice McKenzie

92. MEPO 3/140, ff 259-93; 3/141, ff 9-14; HO 144/220/A49301, ff 17-18, 24-31; 144/221/A49301G, ff 23-31; 144/221/A49301I ff 5-10

93. Bond had been a Police Surgeon to Westminster Division following his return from service with the Prussian army in 1866 and at the commencement of the Whitechapel murders he was aged 47 with some 24 years of medical experience 21 of which were as a police surgeon. Phillips was aged 54 at the time of the murders with 27 years of medical experience, and 23 years as a police surgeon. Bond committed suicide in 1901, four years after Phillips died. Both medical men were thus pretty evenly matched in terms of education and experience and on that basis there is no reason to take the opinion of one above the other. However, it must be said that Phillips, by virtue of the location of his activities, would have been exposed to numerically rather more violent deaths than his Westminster counterpart and doubtless the nature of a significant number of those deaths would have been murderous attacks involving the use of a knife.

94. Actual name Margaret Cheeks, friend of Alice McKenzie and fellow prostitute

95. HO 144/221/A49301I, ff 7-10

96. MEPO 3/140, ff 259-62

97. MEPO 3/140, ff 263-71

98. MEPO 3/140, ff 259-62

99. Anderson R (1910) *The Lighter Side of my Official Life*. London: Hodder and Stoughton, pp 137-9

100. HO144/221/A49301I ff 5-6

101. HO144/221/A49301G ff 28-9

Frances Coles

102. MEPO 3/140, ff 64-118; 3/141, ff 31-2; HO 144/221/A49301G, ff 1-3

103. All newspaper reports and official documents record the location as Swallow Gardens, but the OS map of 1894-6 clearly labels the site as Swallow's Gardens. To avoid confusion Swallow Gardens will be used here

104. MEPO 3/140, ff 97-108

105. Sadler was confused as to the location of this shop and in his statement he said that it was in White's Row or Bakers Row but the shop was at 25 Nottingham Street and Coles was served by Peter Lorenzo Hawkes at between 7.00pm and 8.00pm. Inquest reporting in *The Times* on 21 February 1891

106. Sarah Treadway, the wife of the landlord, suggested that they were drinking for half an hour between 6.00pm and 7.00pm. Inquest reporting in *The Times* on 21 February 1891

107. MEPO 3/140 ff 75-8

108. There remains confusion as to the spelling of Callagher's name which could be Callana as reported in *The Times*, or maybe Calanna alias Calman as stated in a police report. Clearly the police were not in contact with her to any great extent otherwise one imagines they would have known her name.

109. MEPO 3/140 ff 86-8

110. I have walked the distance comfortably in seven minutes.

Mary Jane Kelly

111. Inquest testimony of Joseph Barnett reported in *The Daily Telegraph* and *The Times* and other newspapers on 13 November 1888.

112. Whether this is Limerick town or County Limerick is unknown. Much of Kelly's history came indirectly from Kelly herself and virtually none of it has been independently verified

113. Kelly's former common-law husband Joseph Barnett was not sure whether she moved to Caernarvonshire (now part of Gwynedd) or Carmarthenshire but the fact that she met and married a collier suggests that their location was more likely to be Carmarthenshire in the South Wales coalfields. The collier's name was possibly Davies although there is no confirmation of this

114. MEPO 3/3153, ff 10-18; MEPO 3/141, f 149; HO 144/220/A49301B, f 299; 144/221/A49301C, 42-6, 78-9, 224-6; 144/221/A49301D, ff 81-102; 144/221/A49301F; 144/221/A49301G, ff 4-7, 10-11; and CAB 41, 21/17

115. MEPO 3/3155

116. MJ/SPC, NE1888, Box 3, Case Paper 19 filed in the Corporation of London Records Office with additional witness statements filed as MEPO 3/140, ff 227-32

117. Post mortem notes MEPO 3/3155, ff 10-18; and correspondence HO 144/221/A49301C, ff 217-23

118. *Ibid*; Robinson cited in Chisholm A, DiGrazia C-M, Yost D (2002) *The News from Whitechapel: Jack the Ripper and The Daily Telegraph*. Jefferson: McFarland, p 213

119. Dew, Walter (1938) *I Caught Crippen: Memoirs of Ex-Chief Inspector Walter Dew CID*. London: Blackie & Son, pp 86, 146

120. MEPO 3/143, f B

121. MEPO 3/3153, ff 10-18

122. HO 144/221/A49301C, ff 220-3

123. Harrison S (1993) *The Diary of Jack the Ripper*. London: BCA, p 101

124. HO 144/221/A49301C, ff 220-3

125. MEPO 3/140 ff 227-9

126. *New York World*, 18 November 1888

127. MJ/SPC, NE1888, Box 3, Case Paper 19 filed in the Corporation of London Records Office

128. Knight B (1997) *Simpson's Forensic Medicine* – Eleventh Edition. London: Arnold, p 21

129. *Illustrated Police News*, 17 November 1888

130. MJ/SPC, NE1888, Box 3, Case Paper 19 filed in the Corporation of London Records Office

131. HO 144/221/A49301C, ff 220-3

132. MEPO 3/140, ff 230-2

Section 3: The characterisation of the Whitechapel serial killer

1. Knight B (1997) *Simpson's Forensic Medicine* – Eleventh Edition. London: Arnold, pp 100-1

2. *Ibid* p 91

3. Begg P, Fido M, Skinner K (1996) *The Jack the Ripper A-Z.* Third Edition. London: Headline, (under Jack the Ripper in Fact and Fiction) p 197

4. Hogarth, B (1936): *Trial of Robert Wood - Notable British Trials.* Toronto: Canada Law Book Company, p 255

5. 1320yds in 0.2hrs – 13200yds in 2.0hrs or 6600yds in 1hr or 3.75mph

6. Charles Booth's poverty map of 1889 – Life and labour of the people of London: The Charles Booth Collection, 1885-1905, from the British Library of Political and Economic Science

7. Hare R (1999) *Without Conscience.* New York: Guilford Press, *passim*

8. HO 144/221/A49301C, ff 220-3

9. *The People's Journal*, 27 September 1919

10. Howells M and Skinner K (1987) *The Ripper Legacy.* London: Warner, pp 98-104

11. *The Times,* 2 October 1888

12. *The Police Gazette,* 19 October 1888

13. Inquest testimony of Joseph Levy reported in *The Daily Telegraph,* 12 October 1888

Section 4: The suspects

The Macnaghten report

14. MEPO 3/140, ff 177-83

15. Begg P, Fido M, Skinner K (1996) *The Jack the Ripper A-Z.* Third Edition. London: Headline, pp 272-80

16. Begg P (2003). *Jack the Ripper: The Definitive History.* London: Longman, p 255

17. *Pall Mall Gazette,* 24 March 1903; *Pall Mall Gazette,* 31 March 1903

Montague John Druitt

18. Sugden P (2002) *The Complete History of Jack the Ripper.* London: Robinson, pp 380-96

19. The official records of the inquest into the death of Montague Druitt have not survived. Some testimony was reported in the *Acton, Chiswick and Turnham Green Gazette* on 5 January 1889 and mentions 30 December as Druitt's dismissal date but this is incorrect

20. *Acton, Chiswick and Turnham Green Gazette*, 5 January 1889

21. *Ibid*

22. *Richmond & Twickenham Times*, 5 January 1889

23. *Southern Guardian*, 5 January 1889

Aaron Kosminski

24. Anderson R (1901) *Punishing Crime, The Nineteenth Century,* February; Anderson (1907) *Criminals and Crime.* London, pp 3-4; Anderson (1910) *The Lighter Side of my Official Life.* London: Hodder and Stoughton, pp 137-9

25. Sugden P (2002) *The Complete History of Jack the Ripper.* London: Robinson, pp xiii-xvii, 397-423

26. Acton W 1857, *The Functions and Disorders of the Reproductive Organs in Youth, in Adult Age, and in Advanced Life.* London: Churchill. In his book, Acton specifically describes the appearance of someone who masturbates and is adamant that male masturbation led to insanity. According to Acton: 'The frame is stunted and weak, the muscles underdeveloped, the eye is sunken and heavy, the complexion is sallow, pasty, and covered with spots of acne, the hands are damp and cold and the skin moist. The boy shuns the society of others, creeps about alone, joins with repugnance in the amusements of his schoolfellows. He cannot look anyone in the face, and becomes careless in dress and uncleanly in person. His intellect has become sluggish and enfeebled, and if his evil habits are persisted in, he may end in becoming a drivelling idiot or a peevish valetudinarian. Such boys are to be seen in all stages of degeneration, but what we have described in but the result towards which *they all* are tending.' Acton was highly regarded in his day and although he undoubtedly made some positive contributions to Victorian beliefs he was also inclined mislead. His now famous assertion that women 'are not much troubled by sexual feeling of any kind', undoubtedly said rather more about Acton than about human female sexuality.

27. *The People's Journal*, 27 September 1919

28. Begg P, Fido M, Skinner K (1996) *The Jack the Ripper A-Z.* Third Edition. London: Headline, p 82. Martin Fido believes that Kosminski and Cohen may have become the subjects of confused identities in police reports

29. Begg P (2003). *Jack the Ripper: The Definitive History.* London: Longman. Note 11, p 285

Michael Ostrog

30. Sugden P (2002) *The Complete History of Jack the Ripper.* London: Robinson, pp xvii-xxi, 424-38

31. *Buckinghamshire Advertiser,* 10 January 1874

32. Sugden P (2002) *The Complete History of Jack the Ripper.* London: Robinson, pp 432

33. *Ibid,* p xviii

34. *Police Gazette,* 1 October 1883

35. Sugden P (2002) *The Complete History of Jack the Ripper.* London: Robinson, p xx

Francis Tumblety

36. Evans S Skinner K (2001) *The Ultimate Jack the Ripper Sourcebook.* London: Robinson, pp 674-6

37. *Rochester Democrat and Republican,* 3 December 1888

38. *Ibid*

39. CRIM 10/34; CRIM 4/1037

40. *Rochester Democrat and Republican,* 3 December 1888

Severin Klosowski (George Chapman)

41. Adam H (1930) *Trial of George Chapman - Notable British Trials Series*. Edinburgh: William Hodge

42. *Ibid,* p 201

43. *The Daily Chronicle,* 23 March 1903

44. Adam H (1930) *Trial of George Chapman - Notable British Trials Series*. Edinburgh: William Hodge. Testimony Annie Helsdown, third day of Central Criminal Court proceedings: 18 March 1903, p 124

45. *Ibid*, Testimony Dr James Maurice Stoker, third day of Central Criminal Court proceedings: 18 March 1903, pp 104-11

46. *Ibid*, Testimony Richard Bodmer, Public Analyst, third day of Central Criminal Court proceedings: 18 March 1903, pp 111-12

47. *Ibid*, Testimony William Henry Davidson, first day of Central Criminal Court proceedings: 16 March 1903, pp 68-71

48. *Ibid*, Sentencing of Severin Klosowski by Mr Justice Grantham, fourth day of Central Criminal Court proceedings: 19 March 1903, pp 164-5

49. A report in the *Stevens Point Daily Journal* of Wisconsin dated 2 May 1891 gives as much information as is available.

50. Neil A (1932) *Forty Years of Man-Hunting*. London: Jarrolds, p 27

51. Bleeding and purging, the latter employing tartar emetic, were popular practices in the armoury of the early physicians, but to be a surgeon or 'medical man' before the 1870s meant bloodletting, and a proper physician as opposed to a surgeon or an apothecary might distain such procedures. In the first half of the nineteenth century, a 'medical man' came to mean apothecary-surgeon or general practitioner, and 'doctor' meant a qualified member of the Royal College of Physicians in London, a tiny elite of physicians who supplied health care to the rich and consulted in difficult cases. The Medical Reform Act in 1858 created a single overseeing council for the entire UK, and stipulated that only the universities and the established corporations for Surgeons, Apothecaries, and Physicians of England and Wales, Scotland and Ireland could grant medical licences, and no longer the likes of the Archbishop of Canterbury. From that time onwards, only those registered by the General Medical Council, which the Act set up, would be considered 'qualified medical practitioners'. Bloodletting took the form of using a knife to open a vein, when it was referred to as venesection or phlebotomy, or by employing leeches to puncture the skin and feed from the blood until they were so distended that they fell off. Bloodletting was commonly practiced in England well into the nineteenth century and in 1861, Isabella Beeton, in *Beeton's Book of Household Management,* gave instructions for do-it-yourself bleeding 'in cases of great emergency'. Bloodletting generally fell from favour towards the end of the nineteenth century but the practice probably prevailed as a 'cure' for well after that time in less enlightened parts of the world.

52. *Pall Mall Gazette*, 31 March 1903

Walter Sickert

53. *Daily Express*, 5 June 1929

54. Overton Fuller J (2001) *Sickert & the Ripper Crimes*. Oxford: Mandrake; Knight S (1976) *Jack the Ripper: The Final Solution*. London: Harrap

55. Cornwell P (2002) *Portrait of a Killer – Jack the Ripper Case Closed*. London: Little Brown

56. Harrison M (1974) *Clarence: Was he Jack the Ripper?* New York: Drake, pp 68, 71-2, 90-2

57. Stowell T (1970) Jack the Ripper – A Solution? *Criminologist* 5 (18): 40-51

58. Jullian P (1962) *Edouard VII*. Paris: Librarie Hachette; Jullian P (1967) *Edward and the Edwardians*. London: Sidgwick & Jackson, p 144;

59. Court Circular Clears Clarence. *The Times,* 4 November 1970

60. Knight S (1976) *Jack the Ripper: The Final Solution*. London: Harrap, pp 21, 25-7

61. Rumbelow D (18970 *The Complete Jack the Ripper*. London: Guild Publishing pp 201-7

62. Overton Fuller J (2001) *Sickert & the Ripper Crimes*. Oxford: Mandrake, p 46

63. Rumbelow D (18970 *The Complete Jack the Ripper*. London: Guild Publishing p 204

64. *Ibid*, pp 205-6

65. Knight S (1976) *Jack the Ripper: The Final Solution*. London: Harrap pp 41-2, 263

66. Begg P, Fido M, Skinner K (1996) *The Jack the Ripper A-Z*. London: Headline, p 92

67. Overton Fuller J (2001) *Sickert & the Ripper Crimes*. Oxford: Mandrake, *passim*

68. Vanderlinden W (2002) The Art of Murder. *Ripper Notes* 39

69. *Ibid*

70. Rumbelow D (18970 *The Complete Jack the Ripper*. London: Guild Publishing p 205

71. Cornwell P (2002) *Portrait of a Killer – Jack the Ripper Case Closed*. London: Little Brown, p 46

72. Overton Fuller J (2001) *Sickert & the Ripper Crimes*. Oxford: Mandrake, pp 89

73. *The Star,* 12 November 1888. Possibly Mary McCarthy of 1 Breezer's Hill

74. *The Star,* 10 November 1888

75. *Western Mail,* 10 November 1888; *East London Observer*, 17 November 1888

76. *The Daily Telegraph*, 10 November 1888

77. Begg P, Fido M, Skinner K (1996) *The Jack the Ripper A-Z.* Third Edition. London: Headline, p 364

78. Data from the 1891 census; The National Archives

79. Montgomery Hyde H (1976) *The Cleveland Street Scandal.* London: Allen, pp 20-54; Chester L, Leitch D, and Simpson C (1976) *The Cleveland Street Affair.* London: Weidenfeld and Nicholson, pp 48-64

80. Begg P (2003). *Jack the Ripper: The Definitive History.* London: Longman, p 293

81. Vanderlinden W (2002) The Art of Murder. *Ripper Notes* 39

82. *Ibid*

83. Knight S (1976) *Jack the Ripper: The Final Solution.* London: Harrap, p 255

84. Vanderlinden W (2002) The Art of Murder. *Ripper Notes* 39

85. Jullian P (1967) *Edward and the Edwardians.* London: Sidgwick & Jackson, p 144

86. *The Amphitryon* is recorded in *London Clubs* as a "restaurant club" of the type that once seemed likely to become a popular feature of West End life, but soon ceased to exist. *The Amphitryon* did indeed have a short life and existed from around 1881 and the proprietor, Émile Aoust, was once maître d'hôtel at Bignon's in Paris. Nevill R (1911) *London Clubs*, pp 204-206

87. I have had sight of a document showing that Sir Henry Irving applied for membership to the Amphitryon Club. The application form was signed and he agreed to pay the annual subscription fee of three guineas.

88. Cornwell P (2002) *Portrait of a Killer – Jack the Ripper Case Closed.* London: Little Brown, *passim*

89. *Ibid*, pp 49-50

90. Overton Fuller J (2001) *Sickert & the Ripper Crimes.* Oxford: Mandrake, p 27

91. Swanwick H (1935) *I have been Young.* London: Gollancz *passim*

92. Overton Fuller J (2001) *Sickert & the Ripper Crimes.* Oxford: Mandrake, p 27

93. Cornwell P (2002) *Portrait of a Killer – Jack the Ripper Case Closed.* London: Little Brown pp 59-73

94. *Ibid*, p 62

95. *Ibid*, p 64

96. *Dickens Dictionary of London* (1888) Reprinted 2001 Moretonhampstead: Old House Books, p 120

97. Cornwell P (2002) *Portrait of a Killer – Jack the Ripper Case Closed.* London: Little Brown p 351

98. *Ibid*, pp 300-315

99. Testimony Dr John Thompson opening day of the trial of Robert Wood, Central Criminal Court 12 December 1907 as reported in Hogarth B (1936) *The Trial of Robert Wood - Notable British Trials*. Toronto: Canada Law Book Company Ltd, pp 81-84

100. *Ibid*

101. Sitwell O (1947) *A Free House, or The Artist as a Craftsman, being the Writings of Walter Richard Sickert*, London: Macmillan. P xxxix

102. Begg P, Fido M, Skinner K (1996) *The Jack the Ripper A-Z*. Third Edition. London: Headline, pp 411-12

103. Cornwell P (2002) *Portrait of a Killer – Jack the Ripper Case Closed*. London: Little Brown, pp 13-15

104. Evans S and Skinner K (2001) *Jack the Ripper Letters from Hell*. Stroud: Sutton, p 8

105. Cornwell P (2002) *Portrait of a Killer – Jack the Ripper Case Closed*. London: Little Brown pp 274-5

106. *Ibid*, pp 168-74

107. Overton Fuller J (2001) *Sickert & the Ripper Crimes*. Oxford: Mandrake, p 27

108. Sturgis M (2002) Making a Killing from the Ripper. *Sunday Times,* 3 November

Section 5: Who killed Mary Jane Kelly?

1. Dew W (1938) *I Caught Crippen: Memoirs of Ex-Chief Inspector Walter Dew CID*. London: Blackie & Son, p 86

2. *Illustrated Police News*, 17 November 1888

3. Dew W (1938) *I Caught Crippen: Memoirs of Ex-Chief Inspector Walter Dew CID*. London: Blackie & Son, p 150

4. *The Star,* 12 November 1888

5. Stead WT - The Maiden tribute of Modern Babylon. *Pall Mall Gazette* 6-10 July 1885

6. Pearson M (1972) *The Age of Consent*. Newton Abbot: David and Charles, p 41; Walkowitz JR (1980) *Prostitution and Victorian Society: Women Class and State*. Cambridge: Cambridge University Press, p 247

7. *The Star,* 12 November 1888

8. According to Elizabeth Phoenix as reported in *The Star,* 12 November 1888. Phoenix described Kelly as 'stout'

9. *The Daily Telegraph*, 13 November 1888 - Variously interpreted as Morganstone, Morgan Stone, or Morgestern but the original testimony came from Joseph Barnett at the inquest into Mary Jane Kelly's death

10. *The Daily Telegraph,* 13 November 1888 - Testimony of Julia Vanturney also reported as Venturney, Van Teurney and Van Turney, at the inquest into Mary Jane Kelly's death

11. *The Star*, 12 November 1888

12. Montgomery Hyde H (1976) *The Cleveland Street Scandal*. London: Allen, p 142

13. *Ibid*, p 144

14. Overton Fuller J (2001) *Sickert & the Ripper Crimes*. Oxford: Mandrake, p 21-2

15. *Ibid*, p vi

16. *Ibid,* p 20

17. *Ibid,* p 19

18. *Ibid*, p 55

19. Although each workhouse was allowed some flexibility in the style of clothing that it adopted they almost always ended up as uniforms of pauperism with, by law, the stamp of the workhouse somewhere on the garment. There was additional stigma for unmarried mothers who were further segregated and expected to wear either a distinctive yellow uniform on the 'canary wards' or an over dress or jacket from which the nickname 'jacket women' arose.

20. Pregnant women were obliged to work in factories 'up to the hour of delivery' otherwise they would lose wages and be in fear of being replaced if there were away too soon or for too long. It was not unusual for women to be at work one evening and delivered the next morning, 'and the case is none too rare of their being delivered in the factory among the machinery'. Engels observed: 'And if the gentlemen of the bourgeoisie find nothing particularly shocking in this, their wives will perhaps admit that it is a piece of cruelty, an infamous act of barbarism, indirectly to force a pregnant woman to work twelve or thirteen hours daily (formerly still longer), up to the day of her delivery, in a standing position, with frequent stoopings. But this is not all. If these women are not obliged to resume work within two weeks, they are thankful, and count themselves fortunate. Many come back to the factory after eight or even after three to four days, to resume full work. Engles F (1892) *The Condition of the Working Class in England* – First published in Germany in 1845. Reprinted in 1987 by Penguin Books. Engels remarked that the general mortality among young children must have been increased by the employment of the mothers and he was probably correct under the peculiar circumstances of the day. Having left the baby to return to work mothers were then obliged to leave work during their lunch break and 'hurry home to feed the child and eat something'. By account, one working mother went to the mill shortly before five o'clock in the morning and returned home at eight in the evening; 'all day the milk poured from her breasts, so that her clothing drips with it'. And in another case a woman was quoted as saying; 'My breasts have given me the most frightful pain, and I have been dripping wet with milk'. Astoundingly, narcotics were frequently used to subdue children while the mother was at work a practice 'fostered by this infamous system', and 'a chief source of many deaths from convulsions.'

21. Thomas D (1988) *The Victorian Underworld*. London: Murray, p 99

22. Russell JFS (1923) *My Life and Adventures*. London, p 157

23. Ballantine W (1882) *Some Experiences of a Barrister's Life*. London: Richard Bentley, pp 77-80

24. Wise TJ (1919) *A Bibliography of Writings in Prose and Verse of Algernon Charles Swinburne*. Privately published, p 220 (cited in 21).

25. Knight S (1976) *Jack the Ripper: The Final Solution*. London: Harrap, p 35

26. Harrison M (1974) *Clarence: Was he Jack the Ripper?* New York: Drake, p 191

27. Knight S (1976) *Jack the Ripper: The Final Solution*. London: Harrap, p 118; During the Victorian era homosexual activity was an insult to family values as well as constituting illegal practice. Buggery, or sodomy as it was called in Scotland, had been a capital offence from the time of Henry VIII in 1533 until 1861, when life imprisonment was substituted as the maximum penalty. In respect of homosexual acts not amounting to buggery, the only possible proceeding was by indictment for conspiracy to commit the graver offence, and this could only be proved by the evidence of an accessory, which was rarely possible to obtain. In 1885 the Criminal Law Amendment Bill was passing through parliament on route to becoming law when William Thomas Stead the editor of the *Pall Mall Gazette* sent a report on the prevalence of male homosexuality to the radical MP Henry du Pré Labouchere. Stead suggested to Labouchere that he should put down an amendment on the order paper designed to make homosexual acts between men not amounting to buggery or sodomy a criminal offence, whether in public or in private. Accordingly, Labouchere put down an amendment to insert a new clause in the Bill in the following terms: 'Any male person, who in public or in private, commits, or is a party to the commission of, any act of gross indecency with another male person, shall be guilty of a misdemeanour, and being convicted thereof, shall be liable, at the discretion of the court, to be imprisoned for any term not exceeding one year with or without hard labour.'

The amendment was accepted but the maximum penalty was changed from one year to two years with or without hard labour. The amendment was intended to clarify and improve the law but inadvertently changed it for the worse and it was soon dubbed 'The Blackmailer's Charter' because of the *private* element of the wording which would allow one partner in the 'crime' to blackmail the other under threat of testifying against him. The Bill became law on 1 January 1886 and one of the first prosecutions to be brought under the new Act was that relating to the male brothel at 19 Cleveland Street.

28. One consequences of the scandal was that Lord Henry Euston sued the North London Press for criminal libel after the editor, Ernest Parke, suggested that his Lordship was a visitor to 19 Cleveland Street, which in court they were unable to prove. The British libel laws effectively gagged the press although foreign newspapers were not so retrained in their coverage. In fact Lord Euston was thought to have visited 19 Cleveland Street as early as 1887.

29. Chester L, Leitch D, and Simpson C (1977) *The Cleveland Street Affair*. London: Weidenfeld and Nicholson, p 11

30. Chester L, Leitch D, and Simpson C (1977) *The Cleveland Street Affair*. London: Weidenfeld and Nicholson; Montgomery Hyde H (1976) *The Cleveland Street Scandal*. London: WH Allen

31. Harrison M (1974) *Clarence: Was he Jack the Ripper?* New York: Drake, p 110

32. *Ibid,* p 217

33. Chester L, Leitch D, and Simpson C (1977) *The Cleveland Street Affair*. London: Weidenfeld and Nicholson, p 56. *Une maison de passe* was in fact the French term for a brothel to which clients took their own partner and requested the use of a room. Certainly during a period of surveillance following the discovery of activities at 19 Cleveland Street the police witnessed men of 'superior bearing' arriving with boys in some instances and on two occasions with a soldier. After 'waiting about in a suspicious manner' they left without entering. 'Some of them arrived in separate cabs, and evidently met by appointment at the house for unnatural purposes.'

34. Harrison M (1974) *Clarence: Was he Jack the Ripper?* New York: Drake, p 217

35. Ashbee HS (1877) *Index Librorum Prohibitorum*. London, p 313 (cited in 21); Montgomery Hyde H (1948) *Trials of Oscar Wilde*. London: William Hodge, p 196

36. Cleveland Street is not in Knightsbridge and barely in the West End so the French woman to whom Mary Jane Kelly the murder victim returned in order to recover expensive dresses would not have been Madame Caroline

37. MEPO 3/140 ff 227-9

38. *The Daily Telegraph*, 15 November 1888

39. Inquest testimony Sarah Lewis reported in *The Daily Telegraph*, 13 November 1888.

Index